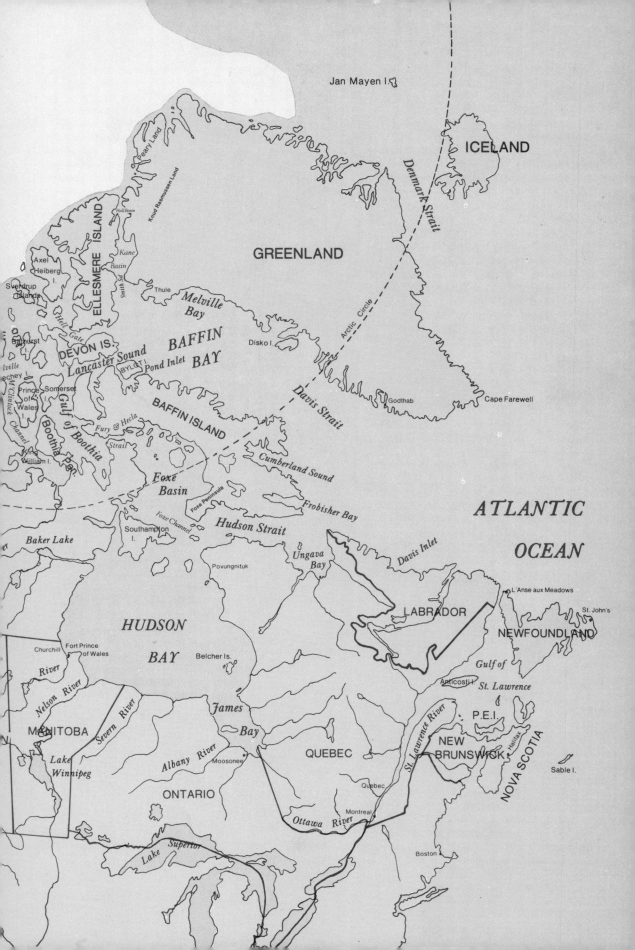

# The North Pole
## or Bust

To Bryce

Christmas 1980

Uncle George + Aunt Laura

# EXPLORERS OF THE NORTH

# *The* North Pole or Bust

## FRANK RASKY

**McGraw-Hill Ryerson Limited**

Toronto Montreal New York St. Louis San Francisco
Auckland Bogotá Düsseldorf Johannesburg London
Madrid Mexico New Delhi Panama Paris São Paulo
Singapore Sydney Tokyo

**The North Pole or Bust**

ISBN 0-07-082548-3

1  2  3  4  5  6  7  8  9  0  THB  5  4  3  2  1 - 9  8  7

Printed and bound in Canada



Canadian Cataloguing in Publication Data


Rasky, Frank, date
   North Pole or bust

At head of title: Explorers of the North.
Continues the author's The polar voyagers.

Includes index.
ISBN 0-07-082548-3

1. Explorers - Arctic regions. 2. North Pole.
3. Arctic regions. I. Title. II. Title: Explorers of the North.

G634.R36          910'.09'1632          C77-001385-6

# CONTENTS

# Chapter 1

# The Naval Gentlemen
# Cut the Ice

It would be easy to caricature the British Navy officers who at the beginning of the nineteenth century opened up what has rightly been termed the golden age of Arctic exploration. Those on centre stage sometimes seem like larger-than-life characters in a Gilbert and Sullivan comic operetta.

They appear to assume the pose of modest heroes. They are pious and proper early Victorians. And yet they are rollicking good chaps for all that. They suffer gallantly in the cause of Science. They are unflinchingly loyal to Monarch and Country. And they are eminently clubbable gentlemen. They all belong to the same royal geographical societies which have accorded them the status of "Arctic Worthies" and put the stamp of approval on their books of exploration so eagerly devoured by the British public.

It would likewise be easy to overplay the backstage drama, which, as in real life, was frequently more melodramatic than the theatrical show seen by the audience. The protagonists sometimes seem as vain and ambitious as any prima donna. They appear to have thirsted for promotion and titles. They feuded jealously for top program billing. They upstaged their rivals. And despite their pretensions, it was sometimes not pure science that they apparently cherished so much as the plaudits of posterity. To have one's name shine in lights forever in the history books—that was supreme stardom; and for that marquee billing some polar performers were willing literally to give up their lives.

But it would be glib to depict the British Navy explorers only in such simplistic terms. True, the captains and the admirals were not unblemished heroes. They tended to be flamboyant egotists with quirky eccentricities and a predilection for quarter-deck squabbles—especially the touchy Scots, of whom it was said that they were like hairy-legged

Highlanders with nary a clout to wrap themselves in except their pride and honor.

And yet there was a certain splendor about their naval strut and swagger. One must never forget that it took immense courage to steer a ship of straw-hatted, pigtailed, pathetically ill-equipped jack tars through a nightmarish maze of unknown straits and ice islands in the Canadian Archipelago. The officers in charge may have been snobs and blunderers on occasion, hard on their press-gang-recruited ragamuffin crew and fumblingly uncertain about how to adapt to the alien arctic environment. And yet they were wonderfully resourceful, a magnificent manifestation of man's unconquerable will.

Their imagination was captivated by the compelling beauty and cold indifference of the Arctic; its unknown perils and potential riches were a challenge to them. To the early Victorians, unruly nature was intolerable; it had to be subdued and scientifically codified and tidily mapped. If they failed to vanquish and tame it, at least they made a valiant effort. The showmen of the Royal Navy always did have a good sense of theatre, and the grandeur, the pathos, the scale, the sacrifice of their attempted Arctic conquest was in the finest naval tradition.

The curtain-raiser of the century's Arctic exploration was produced by a grim-visaged, beak-nosed impresario who also doubled as its most vinegary stage critic. This was Sir John Barrow, who rose from being a Liverpool iron foundry bookkeeper to *eminence grise* of polar expeditions. He was principal founder of the Royal Society of London, author of two acerbic histories of Arctic voyages, and for forty years Second Secretary of the British Admiralty. Except for the fact that as a youth he had made a summer cruise aboard a whaler to Spitsbergen, the arctic career of this self-acknowledged land sailor reminds one of W.S. Gilbert's admonition in *H.M.S. Pinafore:*

> *Stick close to your desks and never go to sea,*
> *And you all may be rulers of the Queen's Navee.*

One is tempted to thus characterize him. Yet, to be fair, Barrow was not quite that narrow. He was genuinely interested in geography, having served in civil service posts in China and South Africa. He had a certain sagacity and imperial vision, and earned himself a deserved place in history: he was the prime catalyst and propagandist responsible for the nineteenth-century renaissance in polar exploration. Still it must be said that Barrow could be a captious, sarcastic despot, who played favorites in his role as ruler of "the Queen's Navee."

By 1818, since Britannia had conquered Napoleon, Barrow felt it was time that her navy vanquished the polar regions. It would give work to unemployed officers. It would offer experience to would-be officers from the landed gentry class, who at that time either bought commissions or needed influence to win promotions in the navy. It would provide polar scientific lore for the savants of the royal societies. It would add ammunition to the personal prejudice held by Barrow that there was an open polar sea which the seventeenth-century explorer, William Baffin, whom he considered an inept stargazer, had failed to detect. Furthermore, national prestige demanded it. The Russians, who had laid claim to the Bering Strait, were becoming altogether too pushy, in Barrow's view.

"It would be somewhat mortifying," said Barrow to Viscount Melville, First Lord of the Admiralty, "if a naval power but of yesterday should complete a discovery in the nineteenth century, which was so happily commenced by Englishmen in the sixteenth, and another Vespusio run away with the honours due to a Columbus."

Exploration was to be an international sporting match with the top of the world as a playing field. Parliamentary prizes, ranging from five thousand to twenty thousand pounds, were offered to the first English teams to score the twin goals of the North Pole and the Northwest Passage.

The naval squadron that tackled the North Pole—and was beaten back by ice—was noteworthy only because one of its ships was commanded by a certain Lieutenant John Franklin. His name was later to become a household word, and we shall hear more of him later.

The second team directed to the Northwest Passage was notable because it contained no less than three champion Arctic Worthies. The most controversial star in this group was the commander of the contingent, a forty-four-year-old Scot named Captain John Ross. He certainly looked like no hero. Lady Franklin, who was later to join his many enemies and snub him most cruelly, drew this relatively balanced portrait after meeting Ross at a dinner party in which the married flirt genially offered to take her and eleven other young ladies with him on his next Arctic expedition:

"He is short, stout, sailor-looking, and not very gentlemanly in his person, but his manners and his language are perfectly so. His features are coarse and thick, his eyes grey, his complexion ruddy, and his hair of a reddish sandy hue. Yet notwithstanding his lack of beauty, he has a great deal of intelligence, benevolence and good humour in his countenance."

Other contemporaries were not quite so flattering. The Eskimos nicknamed him *Too-loo-ah,* "the Raven," because he was such a tough, irascible old bird. That he unquestionably was. The son of a poor Balsarroch minister, who taught him to hate whisky and preach piety, John Ross shipped aboard an East Indiaman at the age of nine. He was imprisoned by the French three times, and in three naval battles was wounded in thirteen different places—"both legs broken, a bayonet through my body, and five cuts in my head with a sabre." Yet at the age of seventy-three the old warhorse was still leading an expedition to the Arctic in search of his lost friend, John Franklin.

He had few real friends in the service. Most of his shipmates turned against him treacherously when he most needed friendship. His erstwhile supporters derided him as a dogmatic, hot-tempered windbag. At times he undoubtedly was. "Up-right, down-right and never-right," his arch-enemy, Sir John Barrow, lampooned him.

Yet for all his faults, John Ross was incontestably brave. He was a writer and a painter of considerable talent. He was an inventor who devised an ingenious "deep sea clam" for collecting marine specimens. He was an innovator who pioneered the steam-driven paddlewheeler for Arctic voyages. And ultimately he was the one explorer among the trio of determined prima donnas who perhaps most gains one's sympathy. He had the capacity to learn from his mistakes and, though a glory-grabber like the others, he was generous in handing out credit to his polar predecessors, including the Eskimos who taught him the art of survival.

His second in command, Lieutenant William Edward Parry, seemed on the surface far more suited to be cast in the heroic mold. "The beau ideal of an Arctic officer," secretary of the Royal Society of London, Sir Clements Markham, lauded him. Parry had all the romantic attributes. He was six feet tall, twenty-nine years old, a bachelor, and with his wavy chestnut hair and chiselled profile, inordinately handsome. Furthermore, he had a background that made him impeccably clubbable. He had acquired a strong religious bent from his grandfather, a Presbyterian minister; scientific curiosity from his father, a fashionable physician from Bath; and a good grounding in navigation, having gone to sea at the age of twelve and seen service aboard the whaling fleets off Spitsbergen. To add to this, he hungered for adventure—and promotion. He was tossing up whether to go on expeditions to the Arctic or the Congo ("ready for hot or cold," he confided to a friend). Then a treatise he wrote on *Nautical Astronomy by Night* won him

*Explorer John Ross.*

METROPOLITAN TORONTO LIBRARY BOARD

*Explorer James Clark Ross.*

NATIONAL MARITIME MUSEUM, GREENWICH

*Explorer William Edward Parry.*

NATIONAL MARITIME MUSEUM, GREENWICH

*Naval Secretary Sir John Barrow.*

NATIONAL PORTRAIT GALLERY, LONDON

the favor of Sir John Barrow and an eventual fellowship in the Royal Society.

Parry had many attractive traits. He wrote lucidly and with style. He set up a shipboard school for his illiterate sailors. He played the violin for the Eskimos. He loved to sing *Roland the Brave* to the two worshipful wives he eventually married. He was a theatre and sports enthusiast. On later expeditions he acted leading roles in comic operettas; he was the first Englishman to introduce masked balls and cricket to the Arctic. Indeed he sometimes seems an archetype of the privileged Englishman of his age: a rather precious, class-conscious squire to whom exploration was a gentleman's game. To Parry, ships were "charming"; criticizing the Navy was "infra dig"; and he was capable of writing archly of "those *darling* old fellows, Baffin and Davis." While hiking through the snow, rather than take snuff he would elegantly sniff eau de cologne.

Of course, his courage, enterprise and daring could not be faulted. Yet behind his mannered and well-bred air there was a hard streak of ruthlessness, quite common, one must say, among the early Victorian explorers. That perceptive diarist, Jane, Lady Franklin, gives us a hint of it: "He is a tall, large, fine-looking man of commanding appearance, but possessing nothing of the fine gentleman. His manner and appearance rather excite the idea of a slight degree of roughness and bluntness."

There was more than a slight degree of roughness in the way Parry administered thirty-six lashes each to two impressed seamen when the poor devils drank too much beer. There was even a cruder bluntness in the way Parry had a pilfering Eskimo tied up and flogged to set an example to his fellow delinquent aborigines. To Parry, the stern disciplinarian, all Eskimos and sailors were alike—"somewhat like children, and require constantly looking after." And there was more than a degree of ungentlemanly incivility in the way Parry savaged his superior behind his back. On first meeting Captain John Ross, Parry radiated camaraderie toward the "good-tempered, affable" veteran who was "clever in the surveying way and is a good seaman." But a year later, when his commander stood in the way of his own career, Parry was ready to knife "the blundering Ross" whose surveying was "wretchedly manufactured." It was a kind of rivalry, one must add in his favor, no less fierce than the jockeying for position then common in church, army or academic circles.

Midshipman James Clark Ross, the captain's seventeen-year-old

nephew, was a more subtle personality not so easily definable. We are not here concerned with the later global celebrity: the Sir James Clark Ross deservedly ornamented with medals from the geographical societies for having discovered the Ross Sea and Ross Ice Shelf in the Antarctic. At that time Sir Clements Markham described him as a short, squat, powerfully built Scot, remarkable for his flowery style of expression, his aquiline nose, and "very piercing black eyes."

When he enters our story in 1818, he was remarkable for being a very pretty youth with flaxen hair and a pink complexion that made him much in demand for playing female roles in Arctic pantomimes. His real-life role was a curiously feminine, malleable one, not unlike Iago's. His uncle had taken him to sea at the age of eleven, educated him and made a protégé of him. He had a natural aptitude for nature study (a gull and a seal were named after him). He was an expert marksman, whether in shooting polar bears or harpooning whales (some Eskimos nicknamed him *Angunasuktik*, "the Hunter"). He was a superb snow hiker (other Eskimos nicknamed him *Aglugkak*, meaning "He who takes the long strides," for he always seemed to be in a hurry and was impatient to advance quickly on his travels). And he had a keen scientific curiosity about terrestrial magnetism (thanks to his uncle, he was able to go as second in command on an 1831 expedition in which he won renown for locating the north magnetic pole).

Somehow he managed to win the trust of his uncle and Parry and Sir John Barrow, even as all three antagonists were feuding. Yet ultimately, when the chips were down and his personal glory was at stake, James turned against his uncle as cruelly as the others. Signing himself "Your affectionate nephew," he threatened to raise a scandal if "My dear Uncle," as commander of the expedition, dared to share credit for helping find the north magnetic pole. "I feel pledged to the world," wrote his nephew, to make it "distinctly understood" that "the merit of the discovery is due to me *alone*." Not content with this, he joined Barrow in maligning the seamanship of his uncle who had taught him all he knew.

The aging Sir John Ross (for all three of the explorers were to be knighted) responded sadly that his nephew was a clever but ungrateful whelp: "He strikes when he ought to protect; he calumniates when he ought to vindicate." And though it pained him to be ridiculed as "a cross-grained and sour-tempered cur," John Ross snapped back at the lot of them for playing "the humiliating game of a tin kettle tied to the dog's tail."

There was no wrangling apparent when Ross's squadron first set out from the river Thames in April of 1818. Rather there was a larking atmosphere, as though the crew of some ninety-five jack tars were going on a summer outing to Brighton. True, a couple of precautions had been taken. The two converted whaling ships under Captain Ross's command—the *Isabella* of three hundred and eighty-five tons and the *Alexander* of two hundred and fifty-two tons—had been strengthened with stout oak and their bows plated with thick armor. And among the supplies there were plenty of containers of Donkin & Gamble's lime juice; its vitamin C combated scurvy for at least six months, and the use of it as an antiscorbutic was henceforth to give the nickname "Limey" to every English sailor.

These sailors, however, were outfitted with such fanciful items as swanskin drawers, scarlet-cotton caps and forty umbrellas. For trading with the Eskimos there were thirty pairs of scissors, three hundred forks and knives, two hundred mirrors, one hundred and two pounds of snuff, fifty silk handkerchiefs, one hundred and fifty yards of red flannel, and a number of King James Version Bibles (written, of course in English).

Though Captain Ross was an ardent teetotaller, he allowed his business sense to overcome his temperance principles. He brought along two hundred and fifty-eight gallons of gin and brandy in case the Eskimo customers had a taste for liquor. A Scots fiddler was hired to play reels on the violin should the tars need musical encouragement when sawing canals through the ice floes.

The most picturesque sailor aboard (paid three pounds a month, like the other able seamen) was listed among the supernumeraries as "1 Esquimaux." This was a Christianized Danish Eskimo named John Sacheuse, hired as interpreter. He had apparently left South Greenland in a hurry aboard a British whaler, as a stowaway, in order to escape from an unfortunate love affair.

Sacheuse came in handy when the expedition reached a Danish-Eskimo whaling settlement near Disko Bay on the south-west coast of Greenland. The mixed-blood Eskimo women were invited aboard to have their portraits painted. (Ross says they were the color of mulattos.) Then they were treated to coffee and biscuits and a gay Arctic dance. While the fiddler scraped Scottish reels on his violin, the sailors twirled the Eskimo girls around the deck. Sacheuse presided as master of ceremonies, calling the tunes, it was said, as gallantly as Beau Nash himself.

Sacheuse appears to have been smitten romantically once again.

He became enamored of an eighteen-year-old girl who was the belle of the ball. An officer slipped Sacheuse a spangled lady's shawl to offer as a gift. "He presented it in a most respectful, and not ungraceful, manner to the damsel, who bashfully took a pewter ring from her finger and presented it to him in return," says Ross. "She rewarded him at the same time with an eloquent smile, which could leave no possible doubt on our Esquimaux's mind that he had made an impression on her heart."

Sacheuse was allowed to escort his new sweetheart to her village ashore. Since his journal was meant for publication, Ross remains discreetly silent about the love affairs doubtlessly struck up between his sex-starved crew and the some fifty other Greenland guests. One suspects that his press-gang sailors did more than dance reels with their female partners. In the nineteenth century, when the Royal Navy touched port, seamen commonly strung up hammocks from the ships' cannon in order to have a one-night liaison with the native women. Their mating gave rise to the expression, "son of a gun."

There were no mulatto-colored sons of guns to be seen a month later when the two ships dodged around the icebergs of the treacherous north Greenland harbor which Ross named after the First Lord of the Admiralty, Melville Bay. There, near modern Thule, Ross had his famous encounter with a band of polar Eskimos who had never before seen a white man.

His meeting with the Arctic Highlanders, as Ross called them, was preserved in a sketch drawn by Sacheuse. The painting reflects, with wry unconscious humor, differences between the two cultural groups. There are Captain Ross and Lieutenant Parry, elegant with their cocked hats and swords, braided blue uniforms and white gloves; they are posing on the ice field as full of pomp and circumstance as if reviewing the British fleet at Portsmouth. And there are the furclad Eskimos, prancing in front of their sled dogs and grimacing at their images in the *Kabloona* mirrors.

One wonders what the polar Eskimos really thought of these bizarre invaders, who appear to have flown to their icy land in winged sails from the sun or the moon. All we have to go by is Ross's journal, which treated their seven-day meeting with amused superiority. Although Ross was later to develop a profound respect for their culture, his initial glib response was to regard them as rather quaint primordial pets.

We are left with a picture of Stone Age children. They pull noses in greeting; are terrified by the grunting of a Shetland pig; laugh heartily

On his second expedition Ross befriended this one legged Eskimo and fitted him with a wooden one.
METROPOLITAN TORONTO LIBRARY BOARD

Captain John Ross astounded Eskimos with a mirror on his first Northwest Passage expedition of 1818.

at the sight of Ross and Parry being pulled in sledges by seamen rather than dogs; gaze in awe at a miniature painting of Ross's wife, which they think is a living being; shun proffered gifts of liquor and salt pork; and are apparently bribed with a snuff box containing a portrait of His Royal Highness, the Prince Regent.

Ross, pretty well following the trail of explorer William Baffin, was also quaint in his description of what he called the Arctic Highlands. One was amused to note that the icebergs seemed shaped like the lion and the unicorn of the royal arms. Swarms of white cigarlike dovekies fluttered over the beluga whales, and those sportive creatures, in the phrase of the ship's surgeon, emitted a shrill, ringing noise, like "musical glasses when badly played." One marvelled at crimson, claret-colored cliffs of snow (actually produced by a unicellular plant known as *Protococcus nivalis*); at fantastic peaks named the Devil's Thumb and Melville Monument and the Horse's Head, and at chalky precipices that reminded Ross of the white cliffs of Dover.

One cloud-cuckoo mountain range that he thought he saw was to haunt Ross for the rest of his life. On August 31, 1818 through a grey pall of fog, he sailed for about fifty miles westward into Lancaster Sound. This was the only feasible gateway leading to the Northwest Passage. Bad visibility and bad luck, however, barred Ross from making headway.

At three o'clock in the afternoon, while the other officers were at dinner, Ross was informed by the watch that the mist seemed to be lifting. The captain immediately went on deck, put on his spectacles, for he was short-sighted, and peered through his spy glass. "I distinctly saw the land, round the bottom of the bay, forming a connected chain of mountains," he noted.

It was a mirage, quite understandable in the Arctic. Abnormal refraction of the sun's rays sometimes creates the illusion that ice is land. Ross made the mistake of drawing a picture of his optical illusion. He named the phantom peaks the Croker Mountains, after another Secretary of the Admiralty. Convinced that Lancaster Sound was a land-locked inlet, he sailed for home—to become a laughingstock.

John Ross was justifiably proud of having verified the discoveries of William Baffin, which had heretofore been regarded as a figment of the imagination. But Sir John Barrow was infuriated, because *his* pride had been wounded. Espousing the theory of the open polar sea, Barrow had erased the very boundaries of Baffin Bay from the Admiralty maps. Now here was Captain Ross making a fool of his pet theories.

In turn, Barrow exercised his considerable talent for invective to make a fool of John Ross. In a malicious tirade Barrow mocked Ross for having devoted much time to pulling noses with Eskimos; he had spent six months on a pleasure cruise which could have been accomplished easily by the gentlemen of the London Yacht Club; out of a few bergs and rocks in Lancaster Sound the coward had confected "a pitiable excuse for running away home."

The officers on John Ross's ships were hungry for promotion on the new Arctic expedition that Barrow was expected to launch. They knew on which side their bread was buttered. Though they had been dining in the messroom at the time, they now had a sudden hindsight. They were ready to swear that Lancaster Sound was indeed ice-free and land-free, as Sir John Barrow had anticipated. In a pamphlet issued by one of the officers, Edward Sabine, Lieutenant Parry led other officers in turning against Captain Ross.

The captain's nephew, Midshipman James Clark Ross, was a bit more devious. On the one hand, he seemed to agree with his anti-uncle turncoats. On the other hand, his phraseology seemed rather ambivalent when he wrote an apologetic letter to his dear uncle to whom he was beholden.

"I feel it my duty to assure you," wrote Midshipman Ross, "that whatever I said was not intended to have been repeated out of the mess; and being uttered at the moment I had received a reprimand from you, anything I might have said to your prejustice was the impulse of passion; but as I was not upon deck at the time when you saw the land at the bottom of the bay in Lancaster Sound, what I said on that subject could not have been from my own observation. . . ."

The nephew went on to say to his uncle: "I also feel it my duty to acquaint you I was much misled, as well as other officers, by Captain Sabine, which I have already acknowledged, and which I hope you have forgiven."

His uncle graciously forgave him. For his nephew was among the officers selected to sail on the new assault upon Lancaster Sound commanded by Lieutenant Parry. Yet, though John Ross was smarting at being excluded from the expedition, he did not resent receiving the following begging letter from his nephew:

"My Dear Uncle, I was yesterday ordered on duty, and in consequence of not having a cocked hat and sword, I was reprimanded by the Lieutenant. . . . As I have not sufficient cash to furnish myself with both, I beg you will have the kindness to send me a sword and belt as soon as

possible. I have just enough money to get a cocked hat, and by wearing a great coat, I can get off for tonight without a sword.... Your affectionate nephew, James Clark Ross."

With cocked hats, swords, great coats and wolfskin blankets, Lieutenant Parry sailed from England in May of 1819 to launch the second naval attack upon Lancaster Sound. There was an air of gentlemen's jollity about it all. To celebrate the launching, Parry participated in "a charming party" in which "we sang the *Canadian Boat Song* as we rowed down the Thames.... I amused my party yesterday very much by putting my life preserver on Miss Browne, and making her blow it up, or inflate it, herself!"

The Miss Browne in question, to whom Parry was engaged, evidently jilted him while he was up in the Arctic. Parry was heartbroken ("I have always contrived to fancy myself in love with some virtuous woman") and was especially embarrassed by a jingle that went the rounds of the fashionable drawing rooms:

*Parry, why this dejected air?*
*Why are your looks so much cast down?*
*None but the Brave deserve the Fair,*
*Anyone may have the Browne!*

But Parry wore no dejected air at being assigned his first independent command. Sir John Barrow had provided a crew of ninety-four men and outfitted two ships square-rigged like whalers. One was the *Hecla*, a capacious bomb vessel of three hundred and seventy-five tons; Parry described her as "a charming ship." Her consort was a gun brig of one hundred and eighty tons, the *Griper*; Parry thought her charming, too, until she proved to be a "lubberly, shameful" disgrace to the Navy. As a good luck pet he took along Pincher, a black Newfoundland dog — much bigger and more adaptable to the north than his customary "pink and white doggie, Fido."

Pincher apparently brought good luck. The formidable middle ice pack of Baffin Bay proved unusually navigable that season. Consequently Parry reached the blue, ice-free waters of Lancaster Sound on August 3 — almost one month before John Ross had attained that controversial landmark. With "almost breathless anxiety," wrote Parry, officers and sailors crowded the mastheads to see if they could penetrate the Sound; and an unconcerned observer "would have been amused by the eagerness with which all the various reports from the crow's nest were received."

That evening, with many hip, hip, hoorahs, the two ships sailed triumphantly through the mythical Croker Mountains. Taking a facetious dig at John Ross, Parry named the first inlet he came to Croker Bay. An opening a little farther west he named Barrow Strait, after "my friend, Mr. Barrow, Secretary of the Admiralty." Not one to overlook the top provider of future promotions, Parry paid double tribute to the already over-publicized Viscount Melville, First Lord of the Admiralty. Near the western end of what is now known as the Parry Channel, where sandstone cliffs loom like "ruined towers and battlements," Viscount Melville Sound and Melville Island were duly enshrined.

Altogether, from Lancaster Sound to his farthest west at Melville Island, Parry explored some six hundred miles of the Parry Channel. It was a tremendous breakthrough. M'Clure Strait, that perpetually ice-choked bottleneck at the far end of Parry Channel, defeated him. Ice fields at least twelve feet thick prevented Parry, as they did the *S.S. Manhattan* in 1969, from sailing through to Alaska. Parry also deserves immense credit for having ventured about one hundred and twenty miles south down a detour waterway he called Prince Regent Inlet. Regrettably he turned back because of a warning "ice blink" — the luminous yellowish-white glare on low clouds that betokens ice. If he had continued southward, wriggling through the right openings in the Chinese puzzle of channels, he might have completed the Northwest Passage.

Parry scored another first. At Melville Island, in the shelter of Winter Harbour, the *Hecla* and the *Griper* became the first Royal Navy ships to winter in the Canadian Arctic.

The precautions that Parry took were singularly English and quite ingenious. For exercise the men ran around a cloth-roofed promenade on the topdeck in time to a ship's organ playing hymns. At a quarter to six each morning all hands warmed up a little, too, by scrubbing the decks with heated sand and stones. Determined athletes played cricket or skated on the ice. Daily doses of antiscorbutic limejuice became mandatory. Beer was brewed. Water cress was cultivated in hothouse frames. A stubborn sailor who preferred to eat meat drippings was sentenced by Parry to wear on his back a placard that made him an object of derision to his shipmates.

Parry was equally enterprising in the entertainments he devised to help while away the dragging hours of the arctic winter. He organized an amateur theatrical troupe and democratically acted comic roles in

the farces staged on the topdeck each fortnight. The first production of the Theatre Royal of North Georgia, *Miss in her Teens*, in which he played the part of Fribble, was proclaimed an uproarious hit. For Christmas Parry co-authored a comic operetta, *The Northwest Passage, or, The Voyage Finished*; the audience howled at the inevitable comic portrayal of a polar bear and an Eskimo. A weekly newspaper was published, *The North Georgia Gazette and Winter Chronicle*. A typical issue advertised for "a middle-aged woman, not above thirty, of good character, to assist in DRESSING the LADIES at the THEATRE. Her salary will be handsome and she will be allowed tea and small beer into the bargain."

Comedy of a grimmer sort occurred at the beginning of June. Parry decided to travel across Melville Island in the Navy's first overland Arctic trek. His eleven mariners were to navigate an unusual chariot. It was a huge cart, constructed of ship timber, with the red-painted wheels of a military field gun; and to make it more naval, two wolfskin blankets were strung up like sails.

Into this ship on wheels Parry stowed a cargo weighing eight hundred pounds. There were two tents made of blankets, piles of wood kindling to fuel a cooking stove, and provisions for three weeks. Each man was to be apportioned a daily ration of one pound of hardtack (biscuit), two thirds of a pound of "salt horse" bully beef, one ounce of saltpetre powder, one ounce of sugar, and half a pint of rum—plus a goblet with which to toast King George on His Majesty's birthday. In addition, each traveler carried a knapsack of up to twenty-four pounds—a backpack containing a spare pair of canvas shoes and stockings, a flannel shirt, a crepe veil to prevent snowblindness, a sleeping blanket, and a scarlet cotton nightcap to sleep in.

In a later overland expedition, Parry had his men awakened each morning with a brisk bugle blast of *Reveille*. On this trip, because of the dazzling glare of sun on ice, they slogged by night. They took time out to wash their shirts and put on clean ones, but they found it impossible to change their constantly soaked shoes and stockings; this mistake later caused Parry to suffer twinges of painful rheumatism.

Eventually the groaning axle-tree of the chariot collapsed under the load. They made a bonfire of the cart wood and cooked a "sumptuous supper" of ptarmigan.

The sportsmen pretty well restricted their hunting to birds—a Brent goose, eiderduck, ptarmigan and golden plover fell to their guns. The perky little snow buntings reminded Parry of the sparrows of England. He was charmed by the muskoxen, with their hatrack horns and

their shaggy hair so long as to make their feet appear "only two or three inches in length; they seem, indeed, to be treading upon it at every step." In his journal, Parry took pains to assure his fox-hunting readers that it was not unsporting when his gentlemen officers bagged a muskox bull in order to bring specimens of its meat back to England. It was a fair chase, Parry contended; "for though these animals run with a hobbling sort of canter that makes them appear as if every now and then about to fall, yet the slowest of them can far outstrip a man."

On his voyage home, Parry paused at an Eskimo village on the eastern coast of Baffin Island. Lording it a little over his discredited former commander, Parry felt that these aborigines *he* had discovered were infinitely superior to Captain John Ross's Arctic Highlanders. They were truly English Eskimos.

"There was a respectful decency in their general behaviour, which at once struck us as very different from that of the other untutored Esquimaux," wrote Parry, "and in their persons there was less of that intolerable filth by which these people are so generally distinguished."

The intelligent natives did not pull noses, but rather displayed deference by quickly picking up the English phrase, "Hurra, give way!" More than that, they were properly reverential toward the British Navy.

"They were extremely anxious to obtain our buttons," said Parry, "apparently more on account of the ornament of the crown and anchor which they observed upon them, than from any value they set upon their use; and several of these were cut off our jackets to please their fancy."

Parry arrived in England on October 30, 1820, to a deservedly triumphant welcome. He had pushed halfway through the Northwest Passage. He also brought back valuable specimens of arctic flora and fauna for the scientists to study. Parliament awarded him a prize of five thousand pounds to share with his crew. Rather touchingly, the humbled Captain John Ross instantly sent him a letter of congratulations: "I most sincerely assure you that had your good fortune been extended to Bering Strait. . . . I would have rejoiced still more, and without feeling any disappointment that the success was not reserved for me. . . . I trust my nephew will prove himself grateful to you and continue to deserve your friendship."

His nephew, James Clark Ross, seemed, as usual, ambiguously grateful. After Parry had sold the publishing rights to his journal for a thousand guineas, Midshipman Ross wrote the following my-dear-uncle letter:

"You will, of course, have seen that Captain Parry's book is published; he kindly sent me a copy 'with the author's regards.' He has paid me two or three compliments in the course of the narrative, rather colder, tho', than I expected; but one is always inclined to attach more consequence to themselves than other people do. This may now be my case, for I must confess I feel rather disappointed."

Sir John Barrow, of course, was jubilant. His theory of the open polar sea had been vindicated; and the Second Secretary of the Admiralty preened himself on having scuttled that fumbler, John Ross, and gambling on that splendid Arctic Worthy, Ted Parry.

"The ice is broken," crowed Barrow, "the door opened, the threshold passed, and the first stage of the journey accomplished."

Parry decided that the second stage of the Northwest Passage journey could be accomplished through Hudson Bay. Naturally, Barrow backed up his protégé. Two ships were outfitted for the 1821 expedition. The *Hecla* sailed once again; but another bomb vessel, the *Fury* replaced that poor sailer, the *Griper*.

This time Parry's luck began to run out. Thanks to maps drawn by Eskimos encountered, he was able to add still another geographic feature to the overly encumbered First Lord of the Admiralty. Melville Peninsula, a tongue of frozen land lapping into Foxe Basin northwest of Hudson Bay, was surveyed. But a narrow, two-mile-wide slit on the northerly tip of that tongue, which he hopefully christened Fury and Hecla Strait, proved ice-pestered and impassable. As Parry stylishly phrased it, his ships were gripped by the ice as vexatiously as Gulliver tied down by the Lilliputians.

The entire voyage, from 1821 to 1823, would have been a waste except for one joker in the pack dealt to Parry. He had the good fortune to bring along as his second in command a twenty-six-year-old Chichester Englishman named Captain George Francis Lyon.

A droll, puckish gentleman—"altogether very pleasing," he was eulogized by Lady Franklin. Lyon merited the praise. He was also witty, urbane, keenly observant, and, to use Parry's overworked adjective, truly charming. The young naval adventurer had already written and illustrated a delightful book on the mores of the natives he had met in North Africa. The same warmth and good humor illuminated "my private gossiping journal" about the Eskimos he observed for two winters on the coast of Melville Peninsula—at Winter Island, near modern Lyon Inlet, and at Igloolik, just south of Hecla and Fury Strait.

In a series of vignettes, both word pictures and pen-and-ink drawings, Lyon captured perhaps better than any other explorer some of the

enchantment and comedy arising from the meeting of the two cultures.

There was the scene when Lyon allowed himself to be tattooed by his adopted Eskimo mother, a jovial *amama* he nicknamed Mrs. Kettle. With forty stitches of deer sinew, tinted with lamp soot, she etched a variety of blue figures on Lyon's arm. She and her housemates all had a good laugh when Lyon squirmed at being so beautified. They were shocked to learn that English women had not the good taste to tattoo themselves, and were positively aghast when Lyon claimed that the ladies back home wore no breeches. *Kabloona* women, they clucked in sympathy, must be terribly cold.

There was the scene when Lyon introduced them to the wonders aboard the two ships which the Eskimos called *Paree-umiak* and *Lyon-umiak*. They were enraptured by his hand organ and loved to join in the chorus to ditties ending with "Tol de riddle loll." Quite naturally they assumed that the musical snuff box Lyon played was the child of the organ. They were repelled by the wine and cigars and snuff he offered them; but their stomachs were so well-oiled that they swallowed chewing tobacco and candles and soap with vast pleasure. They were properly awed by Lyon's black cat; by Parry's Newfoundland dog which fetched and carried sticks; and by the magic of lantern slides. But they couldn't understand why the *Kabloona* men should dress up in silly skirts for their theatrical pantomimes in freezing weather. They were baffled by the illustrations of horses which Lyon showed them in an encyclopedia. They were candid enough to remark that the pictures of crabs and frogs appeared to look exactly like white people.

There was the scene when they entertained Lyon with a drum dance. While the women sang with sweet voices and languishing glances, the men leaped around the igloo like Savoyard bears and engaged in the ritual of the *koonik* or nose rub. "The rubbee, if I may use the expression," says Lyon, "was led forward from the spectators by the rubber, who then rushed into the air outside to cool himself." Challenged to participate in the dance, Lyon distributed gift needles to the females present and then gracefully exacted *kooniks* "from all the prettiest in return."

There was the scene when the Kettle family invited Lyon to sleep overnight as their guest in the igloo. At midnight he was awakened by a feeling of warmth. "To my surprise, I found myself covered by a large deer skin, under which lay my host, his two wives, and their favorite puppy, all fast asleep and stark naked. Supposing this was all according to rule, I left them to repose in peace and resigned myself to sleep."

There was the scene in which Lyon introduced the game of

leapfrog to his Eskimo friends. Even the women with children at their backs would not be outdone by the men, and they formed a party of opposition leap froggers. Lyon tried to beg off from the exhausting fun, but new contestants would not let him rest in the igloo. "On going out, I found five men stationed at proper distances, with their heads down for me to go over them. Which I did amidst loud cries of *Koyenna!*—'Thank you!' "

And there were many affecting scenes with the children. Lyon adored them. With their sparkling eyes and jet black elf locks, he says, some were so rosy and pretty "that I longed to kiss them." He took one infant in his arms and gently rocked him asleep by crooning the nursery song, "Bye Baby Bunting."

Lyon was captivated by the Eskimos and tried to share some of his delight with his commander. Parry remained amusedly patronizing. He felt they were pickpockets and beggars; "selfishness is almost without exception their universal characteristic"; and the ingrates were forever yelling, *Pilletay!*-"Give me!" Parry did unbend sufficiently to play a violin concert for them, and joined Lyon in learning how to drive a dog team. "But I was completely fagged," Parry admitted, "and am now quite certain I should make a very bad Esquimaux."

Unfortunately Parry was not sufficiently open-minded to use Esquimaux travel methods on his later excursions. Like Antarctic explorer Robert Scott in the next century, the Englishman considered dog labor unsporting, and the prospect of eating the pets downright revolting. Lyon, however, took along a dog team of those "indispensable attendants"—as well as a pair of experimental Shetland ponies—on his next voyage.

In 1824, commanding the lubberly *Griper*, Captain Lyon brought with him the two Shetland ponies while making another bootless attempt to thrust through one of the blind alleys northwest of Hudson Bay. Terrific gales beat the *Griper* back; and Lyon was forced to shoot the troublesome ponies, "to the infinite regret of all hands, as they were very great favourites."

That same year Parry was compelled to abandon the ice-nipped *Fury* in an equally disastrous voyage; he left the wrecked ship and her supplies at a landmark called Fury Beach after bulldozing his way through Lancaster Sound and partly down Prince Regent Inlet. Then, in 1827, the returned *Hecla* took aboard eight reindeer—"charming animals," Parry termed them—and he set out for Spitsbergen determined to sledge to the North Pole.

*The Royal Navy cutting the ice, as depicted by the* Illustrated London News. *Jack tars used saws, picks and gun powder on the rocklike ice floes to create canals, then pulled ships through with capstan ropes.* METROPOLITAN TORONTO LIBRARY BOARD

*Determined to do everything in true naval fashion, the explorers hauled their cumbersome "sledge-boats" over the ice, aided by sails and kites.* NEW YORK PUBLIC LIBRARY PICTURE COLLECTION

This last of Parry's expeditions was a purgatory. The eight reindeer were abandoned. And the sailors literally had to crawl on hands and knees while pulling with horsehair dragropes two remarkable contraptions—each weighing three thousand and seven hundred and fifty-three pounds when loaded. Parry described them as "sledge-boats."

In the Royal Navy tradition, Parry named his vehicles the *Enterprise* and the *Endeavour*. Each was a hickory long-boat, twenty feet long, shod with steel runners. Awning-like duck sails flapped from a bamboo mast. And there were two big cartwheels, five feet in diameter, plus a small wheel in the back having a swivel for steering by, wrote Parry, "like that of a Bath chair."

At the awakening blast of a bugle, the jack tars heaved the sledge-cum-cart-cum-boat Bath chairs across jagged ice crystals sharp as penknives. They waded through knee-deep pools of icy water. They stumbled over southward-drifting ice floes that kept shoving them backwards over the distance they had traversed the day before. Finally, on July 26, 1827, even the indomitable Parry had to call it quits. While his exhausted men nursed their chilblains, he raised the Union Jack under a mackerel-colored sky and planted it at a point located at 82 degrees, 45 minutes north latitude, off Spitsbergen.

It was only four hundred and thirty-five miles short of the Pole, a fantastic record that was to stand for almost half a century; but this time Parry did not return home to gather laurels from his sponsor. The malignant Sir John Barrow did not approve of naval officers navigating overland in Bath chairs.

"This unusual kind of disgusting and unseamanlike labour," Barrow carped waspishly, "is not exactly fitted for a British man-of-war's man."

Captain John Ross, put on the shelf all these years, now stepped forward in a desperate attempt to redeem his tarnished reputation as an explorer. Barrow, his inveterate enemy, refused to supply him with an Admiralty ship. So Ross swallowed his temperance scruples and got backing for his private Northwest Passage expedition from a liquor distiller. The sheriff of London, Felix Booth, who had made a fortune from distilling Booth's Gin, put up seventeen thousand pounds. Ross scratched together three thousand pounds of his own money. Then he patched together a rickety eighty-five-ton, three masted, steam-driven sidewheeler, the *Victory*.

Ultimately she proved to be as wretched a sailer as Parry's Bath

chairs. But John Ross did not know this when his experimental *Victory*, engines clanking, boilers leaking, bellows pumping, and paddlewheels cranking, pushed down the Thames, mainly under sail, in May of 1829. Aboard her was a total complement of twenty-four officers and men. Second in command was James Clark Ross, who had sailed on his uncle's unlucky expedition of 1818 as well as on all four of Parry's voyages. John Ross had enlisted the services of his clever, ambitious nephew because of his arctic experience and interest in terrestrial magnetism. The plan was to pick up supplies that Parry had abandoned at Fury Beach in Prince Regent Inlet, explore that unknown alleyway southwest of Lancaster Sound, and, it was hoped, discover the ever-shifting north magnetic pole.

All three of these objectives were accomplished, and much more. Certainly Felix Booth had no reason to complain; the brand of his gin was plentifully advertised. His name was appended to the Gulf of Boothia, the broad waterway stretching south of Prince Regent Inlet; and it was attached to Boothia Peninsula, the northernmost chunk of mainland jutting from the modern Canadian Northwest Territories.

A high point of the expedition occurred on June 1, 1831. James Ross planted the British flag on the west coast of Boothia Peninsula, at 70 degrees, 5 minutes north latitude, and claimed discovery of the north magnetic pole. In his flowery fashion, young Ross regretted there were no fabled mountains of Sindbad on the flat granite beach to commemorate his achievement. "Had it been a pyramid as large as that of Cheops," he sighed, "I am not quite sure that it would have done more than satisfy our ambition." (An illustration exaggerates the scene somewhat: it shows James Ross peering through his telescope at the pole located on a gigantic ice pinnacle, while three celebrating Eskimos dance with their sealing harpoons under the arch of an appropriately flaming aurora.)

Fame of another sort escaped the grasp of young Ross. He crossed the ice to Cape Felix, built a six-foot cairn, and took possession of what he called King William Land. He made the mistake of not realizing that King William Island, as it is more accurately known today, is separated from Boothia Peninsula by Rae Strait—and that channel is a true path to the Northwest Passage.

His uncle made a similar error. While coasting southward down Prince Regent Inlet, John Ross had the bad luck to miss a mile-wide corridor, Bellot Strait, which cuts right across Boothia Peninsula—and that corridor is also one of the possible avenues leading to the Northwest Passage.

Although the Passage eluded them, the Rosses achieved something of greater significance. They successfully survived four winters in the high Arctic; and this was a record not equalled until the twentieth century. Three of those winters were spent imprisoned in the "thick-ribbed ice" of Felix Harbour on the east coast of Boothia Peninsula; and Captain John Ross deserves vast credit for recognizing that his men would have perished if it had not been for the Boothian Eskimos.

The seven hundred and forty pages of John Ross's journal make fascinating reading. They provide a character study of an arrogant sea captain who gradually, reluctantly, painfully learns humility under pressure of the remorseless Arctic. The supercilious gentleman, who once regarded the Eskimos as quaint organ grinder monkeys, is transformed into a cultural philosopher. As he becomes involved with them, he comes to appreciate their ingenious adaptability—and is the first naval explorer to make use of their survival skills.

At his very first meeting with a neighboring band of the natives, John Ross noticed that "their appearance was very superior to our own; being at least as well clothed and far better fed. . . ." So he persuaded his sailors, thinly clad in blue jackets and wadmal hose, Welsh wigs and carpet boots, to barter with the Eskimos for their fur tunics and gloves, sealskin boots and wolverine hoods. He observed that they rejected the white man's grog and salt pork, and realized that their experience "has shown that the large use of oil and fat meats is the true secret of life in these frozen countries." Consequently, although his crew insisted on having high tea at five o'clock and bitterly resented being deprived of Booth's Gin, the Scot made sure his seamen consumed the fresh fox meat, seal blubber and arctic hares supplied by the Eskimo hunters.

James Ross accepted Eskimo customs grudgingly. "Disgusting brutes!" he exclaimed of their table manners; according to him, the gluttons stuffed themselves like hyenas and boa constrictors. Nevertheless, he acknowledged that the fresh vegetation they gobbled from the stomachs of slain muskoxen was a much better antiscorbutic than lime-juice. Furthermore, he was glad to sleep in the snug igloos that his Eskimo guides built so swiftly when on excursions, and managed to cover some five hundred miles of unexplored territory traveling with their dog teams.

The elder Ross was constantly amazed by their ability to improvise. One of their sleighs consisted of frozen salmon packed together into a cylinder seven feet long. Another was constructed entirely of ice, runners and all. "No less beautiful than extraordinary, it had a delicate

appearance," he remarked. "Being transparent, it seemed indeed to be a sledge of crystal; while it was strong enough to bear the weight of all the stores which the owner had heaped on it. These carriages travelled much more lightly than our own, which were shod with iron."

He conceded that they were quicker to respond in the cultural interchange. "We discovered in them a strong propensity to imitation and to mimicry." They quickly became accustomed to English utensils, including forks for eating. "And they sometimes amused themselves in aping our gait and manners: above all, in the English custom of uselessly walking up and down under the notion of exercise. This principle extended to drawing, in which, even with our pencils, they were speedily proficient: while further rendering this talent very useful to us, in delineating the geography of the country."

Acting as a benevolent dominie, John Ross invited two intelligent Eskimo youths, Narlook and Ikmalik, to join the night school in which he taught his illiterate sailors reading, writing and arithmetic. The Eskimos were adept pupils, and seemed to be outstanding scholars at his Sunday Bible classes. "I took them into the cabin and read to them some portions of scripture from the Esquimaux Bible which I had received at Holsteinsborg in Greenland. This, which I scarcely expected, they seemed to comprehend: listening with great attention, and correcting my pronunciation; while making me repeat such words as seemed obscure, till they understood the meaning."

Whether the Eskimos genuinely grasped Christian principles, John Ross could not tell. But practical techniques they picked up immediately. In exchange for their lessons in spearing seals, he taught them how to make nets which brought in more than a thousand salmon in one haul. They were especially grateful when his ship carpenter served as surgeon to an Eskimo hunter named Tulluahiu whose leg had been chewed off by a polar bear. The carpenter fitted him up with an artificial leg, inscribed with the name of the *Victory*, and kept repairing it for the next several winters. Tulluahiu's wife sewed a sealskin boot for the wooden leg. She showered Ross with gifts of Eskimo parkas. And the overjoyed Tulluahiu did a merry clog dance on deck while the carpenter played on the fiddle, *The Army and Navy Forever.*

John Ross took a certain delight in comparing the Boothians with the "children of nature" of Igloolik whom Parry had found so selfish. "Such was not the character of the present tribe," declared the Scotsman. "They were not only kind, but as Falstaff says of wit, they were the cause of kindness in those around them, including ourselves."

They politely thanked the white men for dining in their igloos. According to Ross's steward, the husbands never failed, on request, to let the sailors borrow their wives for the night. They rarely lost their temper, and their laughter was infectious. Ross found himself longing for their social visits as he would the high society of London. One shriveled old invalid of seventy named Alictu was such amiable company that Ross pulled him on a sledge to the ship just to hear him chuckle.

He admired most of all their sunny temperament in the face of their icy winters. "I believe," Ross notes in his diary, "that it is the Esquimaux alone who here knows the true secret of happiness and rational art of living. . . . He smells at no flowers, for there are none to smell at; but he prefers the odour of seal oil. . . . If he never saw that utterly inconceivable thing called a tree, what matters it, when he can construct coaches of fish? . . . They could travel easier than we, could find delights where we experienced only suffering, could outdo us in killing the seal, could regale in abundant food where we should starve because we could not endure it. . . . The adaptation is perfect; his happiness is absolute. Had we been better educated, we should have done the same; but we were here out of our element, as much in the philosophy of life as in the geography of it."

The interminable winters became a nightmarish hell to Ross, and though he tried to cheer up his men with sing-songs and deck quadrilles, his diary entries keep lapsing into black moods of pessimism. His beset ship, dangling with icicles, seems like a bony skeleton, and the glowering blue ridges nearby assume the shapes of tombs. He curses the "chimera of the Northwest Passage" which has drawn him to this seaman's fate of a dead ship. And as one monotonous day drags into another, he wonders if he will ever reach his *padle-ak*—the Eskimo word for journey's end.

"The sameness of everything weighed on the spirits, and the mind itself flagged under the want of excitement," he broods. "In such a life as ours, even the capture of an arctic mouse was an event. . . . Everything was suffocated and paralyzed by the endless, wearisome, heartsinking, uniform, cold load of ice and snow."

He ruminates about the milkmaids of Holland who relish ice skating. "But to us, the sight of ice was a plague, a vexation, a torment, an evil, a matter of despair. It was ice which bound us and our ship in fetters of worse than iron. We hated its sight, because we hated its effects;

and everything that belonged to it, every idea associated with it, was hateful."

He dreams of schoolboys who take pleasure out of a rare winter's snowfall in Hyde Park. "But to us, during ten months of the year, all the elements above head is snow, the gale is a gale of snow, the fog a fog of snow, where our sofas are of snow, and our houses of snow: when snow was our decks, snow our awnings, snow our observatories, snow our larders, snow our salt; and, when all the other uses of snow should be at last of no more avail, our coffins and our graves were to be graves and coffins of snow."

In the spring of 1832, after three winters in this sterile desert, Captain Ross decided to abandon the ice-beset *Victory*. His plan was to haul his supplies and longboats some three hundred miles northward on sledges to Fury Beach and then hope to be picked up by a whaling ship in Lancaster Sound. It was an appalling, tortuous trek made at a tortoise pace over rock-like ice hummocks. One sailor was totally snowblinded, another crippled on crutches. Half the crew members were physically debilitated, and the other half mutinous. "I ordered the party to proceed," says Ross, "in a manner not easily misunderstood, and by an argument too peremptory to be disputed." He meant that he urged his crew forward at gunpoint.

Two months later they staggered onto Fury Beach. And there, after a futile boat trip to Parry Channel which was jammed solid with ice, Captain Ross resigned himself to spending a fourth arctic winter. Luckily there were enough provisions cached to keep them alive and enough wreckage from the *Fury* to enable them to build a house. Never had castaways had such a godsend of a shipwreck, Ross cheerfully noted, since Robinson Crusoe.

There was little enough cheer that dreadful fourth winter. Somerset House, as Ross named his so-called mansion on Somerset Island, was a timbered, canvas-roofed cabin divided into two rooms, one for the men and one for the officers. A four-foot-thick igloo wall of snow was built around it and two stoves were kept burning; but winds knifed through the canvas roof and snow blizzards froze them to their hemp mat beds.

In February, scurvy struck, taking the life of the carpenter, the third man to die on the expedition. When reading the burial services over his grave in below-zero chill, John Ross, himself then fifty-five, meditated pityingly: "His age was forty-eight; and at that time of life a seaman who has served much is an aged man, if he does not chance to be worn out."

Captain Ross's own ancient war wounds began bleeding due to scurvy, and he wondered whether he would be able to survive. His diary takes on a plaintive tone. "Do men write, on such occasions, what they think and what they feel?" he asks. "As to our course of life and feelings, these are things which poetry might tell once, but which neither poetry nor prose can repeat forever with the hope that anyone can listen, and understand, and feel."

He thinks back to his first glimpse of the polar bergs, which Eskimos call *peeka-loo-yung*. He reflects on how he once imagined they were such dramatic specimens of nature run wild, so gorgeously splendid, like castles and towers bejeweled, then splitting and cracking asunder in gales. "In all this there has been beauty, horror, danger, everything that would excite; they would have excited a poet even to the verge of madness." But now, after being jailed four years by those dazzling crystals, "Oh! for a fire to melt these refractory masses! . . . We were locked up by irruptable chains, and had ceased equally to hope or to fear. . . . The hopeful did not hope more, and the despondent continue to despair."

In July of 1833, though inwardly despairing, John Ross stirred up hope among his enfeebled men. They would attempt to row their boats up Prince Regent Inlet and pray that a whaler this time might rescue them. They bade adieu to their shack at Fury Beach with mixed feelings of relief and reluctance.

"We left nothing behind us but misery and the recollection of misery," Ross pondered. "Yet, in the comparison with what might have been, it was, heaven knows, a shelter from evils far greater, from death itself. And, such home as it was, it was a Home."

At four o'clock in the morning of August 26, 1833, Captain Ross reached his *pad-le-ak*—his journey's end. A ship was sighted near the entrance of Lancaster Sound. They burned wet powder to signal her. A rescue boat was lowered and came alongside.

"What is the name of your ship?" Ross asked.

"The *Isabella* of Hull," replied the mate, "once commanded by Captain Ross."

"I am that Captain Ross."

The mate was astonished. "With the usual blunderheadedness of men on such occasions, he assured me that I had been dead two years," wrote Captain Ross. Then, anticipating Mark Twain's celebrated witticism, he added, "I easily convinced him, however, that what ought to have been true, according to his estimate, was a somewhat premature conclusion."

*A fanciful sketch of dancing Eskimos after James Clark Ross located the north magnetic pole on June 1, 1831.* NEW YORK PUBLIC LIBRARY PICTURE COLLECTION

*Capt. Ross and his men, after wintering four years in the Arctic, were rescued with huzzas by the Isabella.* METROPOLITAN TORONTO LIBRARY BOARD

It was not the only ironic jest. By a prank of fate, Captain Ross was rescued by the same ship which he had commanded fifteen years before in his first jinxed effort to ram through Lancaster Sound.

With huzzas, his ragged, gaunt men were lifted aboard the *Isabella*, washed, fed, and put to bed. "Long accustomed, however, to a cold bed on the hard snow or the bare rock, few could sleep amid the comforts of our new accomodations," wrote Ross. "I was myself compelled to leave the bed which had been kindly assigned to me, and take my abode in a chair for the night."

They returned to London like heroes risen from the dead. John Ross was received by King William IV, shared a parliamentary reward of five thousand pounds with his crew, and was knighted. His patron, besides receiving all that publicity for Booth's Gin, was dubbed Sir Felix Booth. His nephew was promoted to captain and later, when knighted, too, had his accomplishments recognized in a ditty:

*Sir James Clark Ross, the first whose sole*
*Stood on the north magnetic pole!*

For Sir John Ross revenge was sweet. In his published writings, and in a theatrical panorama of his feats exhibited at Leicester Square, he was able to hit back at his enemies who had doubted his ability. His junior officer, Parry, had been derelict in his duty not to have advised him years ago that Lancaster Sound was navigable. ("That foolish man, Ross," retorted Sir William Edward Parry, "is determined *always* to get himself into a hobble.") That self-elected historian of Arctic voyages, Sir John Barrow, was a "babbling" ignoramus who ought to put down his poison pen and put a dunce cap on his blockhead. (Barrow retaliated with the wicked gossip that Ross had magnified the number of islets he had christened in the Clarence Islands in the Gulf of Boothia in order to accommodate all the bastard progeny of the Duke of Clarence who became King William IV.)

Ross paid little heed. Let donkeys bray, but others knew his true worth. The Lords of the Admiralty had recognized him as an Arctic Worthy by appointing him Rear Admiral. "And they," he declared, "have always been *gentlemen*."

Decorum of a sort soon was restored. The naval gentlemen closed ranks to begin the greatest search ever in the Arctic. Their brother officer, Sir John Franklin, was missing.

# Chapter 2

# Franklin and His Ladies

Gathering dust in the catacombs of the National Portrait Gallery in London today is a huge canvas by Stephen Pearce entitled *The Arctic Council*. It was not always hidden away and ignored. Back in the 1850s it was one of the most famous paintings of the early Victorian era. Queen Victoria herself first appraised it approvingly at Buckingham Palace. Then it was exhibited in London and sent on tour throughout Britain, attracting crowds wherever it was displayed.

The painting is no masterpiece. It is a stiff composite montage depicting a group of the most illustrious officers and explorers of the British Admiralty. Most of the ten are bemedaled and epauleted, and all of them wear grave expressions. They are gathered around a table heaped with maps of the polar regions as they plan their next strategic move. Old Arctic Worthies every one of them, the gentlemen are engaged in a humanitarian search unparalleled in the maritime history of the world. They are looking for their missing brother officer, Sir John Franklin.

Like the ghost of Caesar, Franklin's image looms over the august heads of the Arctic Council. His portrait hangs prominently on the left-hand side of the wall of the Council's conference chamber. The portrait, based on one previously executed by the artist J.N. Negelen, is disappointing to a modern observer. For all the glamour attached to his name—and he was unquestionably the most publicized Arctic explorer in the nineteenth century—Franklin looks superficially more prosaic than heroic.

We see a portly, bald-headed officer who was described as being below medium height and overweight at two hundred and ten pounds. He appears to be a bulldog of a man. He has heavy jowls, a domelike brow, and a thrusting chin. His pugnacity is offset by a benign countenance and brown bovine eyes that seem to convey bland kindliness. Altogether, a decent, dutiful seaman, one would imagine, but rather stolid and dull.

This impression is verified by his letters. His prose is turgid, his expression apt to be pompous, and his outlook narrow. He was so religiously puritanical that he frowned upon the reading of Sir Walter Scott's novels on Sunday. He was so tongue-tied emotionally that when he had to communicate how he felt about a dramatic experience his journal would stutter out an apologetic, "It is easier to be imagined than described." Officers under his command were so hidebound by tradition that sailors on his last Arctic expedition died in their tracks while lugging sledges uselessly loaded with his initialed silverware.

Sometimes obtuse and unimaginative he may have been, but he obviously had his sterling qualities. He must have had a rare gift for tact and diplomacy; for he was one of the few naval explorers able to win the friendship of almost all his prima donna rivals. He seems to have been extremely solicitous about the moral welfare of his sailors; they nicknamed him the "Bishop," not unkindly, because his daily shipboard sermons were so fervent. He was allegedly the beloved Great Chief to his Eskimo guides; one of them, Augustus, who also served as his valet, is said to have shed tears when his Great Chief left him. His mildness of manner was legendary. A nephew who served under him later recalled that Franklin trembled from head to foot whenever he had to flog a seaman. He was so soft-hearted, claimed a fellow arctic explorer, that he refused to swat the very mosquitoes stinging him; he would blow the blood-suckers off his fingers with the pious comment, "The world is wide enough for both."

The legends that haloed him are patently suspect. To gain a more intimate understanding of the man, one must go beyond the smokescreen of Victorian hero worship and consult the diaries and letters of his wives.

Franklin had two of them, and both were remarkable women in their own right. "One is even tempted to believe," says one of their biographers, Frances J. Woodward, "that the most interesting thing about Franklin is his choice of wives."

One is tempted indeed. His second wife particularly, Jane, Lady Franklin, might be said to have discovered the Northwest Passage. It

was she who commissioned the painting of the Arctic Council, and it was she who should have sat on it. More than any naval explorer it was she who was responsible for combing the Arctic solitudes until the last trace of her missing husband was found. It was driving Jane who goaded his ambition. And it was eloquent Jane who alternately flattered and badgered the Admiralty gentlemen into risking their lives on rescue expeditions. And it was beautiful, passionately dedicated Jane who sacrificed her private fortune to gain immortality as the widow of the Northwest Passage conqueror. An amazing woman was Jane, almost, one is tempted to believe, a Victorian combination of Cleopatra and Helen of Troy.

In her heyday, Jane was hailed by the press as the "English Penelope"—referring to the faithful wife of Odysseus in Greek mythology. Franklin's first wife, the former Eleanor Porden, won almost as much acclaim as the "Sappho of her time"—referring to the aristocratic lyric verse writer of the Greek island of Lesbos who committed suicide for the sake of love.

Poetess and lioness of London's literary salons, Eleanor was reputed to be Franklin's social mentor and the woman who most humanized him. She gave him his only child before she died stricken with tuberculosis. And before her death she sought mightily to infuse a little humor into her stuffy sobersides of a husband.

"Naughty boy!" she scolds him for his rigid Calvinistic strictures. "I should be inclined to say that my religion, like my character, was of a gayer nature than yours." She teases him for being a fusspot: "Remember that there is no nourishment in pepper." She berates him for his false humility, which is really the vanity of being thought superior to common praise: "I will venture to tell you that you have often reminded me of Coriolanus." Then she cites Shakespeare's rebuke of that inflexibly high-minded character:

*You would rather venture both your limbs for honour*
*Than one of your ears to hear it.*

Together Jane and Eleanor form a formidable team of personality molders. It is an extraordinary thing that both women were friends before Franklin married either of them, and that both women were so alike.

Both were liberated women of the Victorian age, each being free-spirited and independent-minded. Their freedom stemmed from their

*The Arctic Council: Standing as a pair at left are George Back holding up map to Edward Parry. Standing at right, pointing at map on the table, is John Richardson. Gray-haired Sir James Ross, fourth from left, stands directly under portrait of Franklin.*

wealth. Both were rich heiresses of the upper middle class. Jane's father was John Griffin, a London magnate in the silk-weaving industry, who took his lively, intelligent daughter on tours of the Continent. Eleanor, three years older than Jane, was the daughter of William Porden, a London architect of eminence. He doted on his precocious, verse-writing daughter, and began taking Eleanor before she was ten to lectures in science at the Royal Society. It was there that Jane and Eleanor and Franklin were later to meet.

Both were tiny, blue-eyed beauties, round-cheeked, complexioned like a rose, each with a heart-shaped face and pointed dimpled chin of a determined mold. Jane was the prettier of the two. Another woman once described her as "the most beautiful woman I have ever seen." Jane, who had a tart tongue at times, was not quite so flattering when describing the physical attributes of Eleanor: "She is a plain, stout, short young woman, having rather a vulgar though a very good-natured countenance . . . a very little person, and not very young, though she wishes to pass so."

Each had the energy of a tornado contained in that petite frame. Eleanor's strength was not quite so titanic. Her consumptive cough had caught up with her by the time she married Franklin at the age of twenty-eight, and her portrait shows her posed languidly on a divan, the invalid poetess with quill pen and paper, inspired by her Muse. Even so Jane wrote admiringly of the "learned Authoress": "She makes all her own clothes, preserves, pickles, dances quadrilles *con amore*, belongs to a poetical book club, pays morning visits, sees all the sights, never denies herself to anybody at any hour, and lies in bed or is not dressed till nine o'clock in the morning." On her part, driven by what she called her *furieuse curiosité*, Jane was the Aunty Mame of her day. Armed with a parasol and a notebook, she flew up in a balloon, voyaged down the Nile, visited a Tunisian harem, harpooned Australian sharks; she inspected the British Columbia gold fields in a canoe, the Russian steppes in a stage coach, Hawaiian craters on muleback, the Egyptian pyramids on camelback, and the temples of India on elephantback. Little wonder that Franklin said of her explorations: "You have completely eclipsed me, and almost every other traveller—females certainly."

Both were prodigious writers, and made Franklin aware of their superiority in the field of *belles lettres*. At the age of sixteen, Eleanor filled six books with a poem on scientific discovery entitled *The Veils*, which won her a membership in the esteemed French Institute. She

*Sir John Franklin, revered by his men, rather henpecked by his two wives, was responsible for mapping the roof of North America and inspiring the greatest manhunt in maritime history when he and 128 sailors vanished in the Arctic solitudes.* METROPOLITAN TORONTO LIBRARY BOARD.

followed it up with an epic poem in sixteen cantos entitled *Coeur de Lion*, which spilled over into eight volumes. Jane was an even more voluminous writer; she was a torrent of loquacity. Though none of her prose was published in her lifetime, she managed to crowd two hundred thick travel journals and some two thousand letters with her trenchant observations. A space saver, she would squeeze up to forty-two lines of handwriting to the page, sometimes scribbling around the margins, sideways, upside-down, and between the lines. If paper was unavailable, the compulsive diarist would jot down notes on her thumbnail. "I should like to have a copying machine," wrote Jane, "and dash off the sheets by the dozen."

Both, of course, were frustrated by their relatively inarticulate husband. Eleanor, who could toss off easily a poem of twenty stanzas celebrating Franklin's first Arctic expedition ("Sail, sail, adventurous Barks! go fearless forth/ Storm on his glacier-seat the misty North") was exasperated by the simple seaman's lack of talent for correspondence. "I had half a mind," she once gibed, "to pick up a second-hand copy of *The Complete Letter Writer* for your especial use."

Jane, irritated by the blandness of his prose, chided him: "You describe everybody alike as being so amiable and agreeable that I cannot tell one from the other, and by that means don't care for any of them. Suppose you try your hand next time in some spirited sketches and portrait painting. I know you *can* if you will. As it is, they all go in a bag together and tumble out all alike."

Poor Franklin, confronted with such voluble wives, could only stammer out: "I fear, as you perceive, my forte does not lie in epistolary composition. . . . Directly I am seated with my sheet of paper before me, all powers cease and I become quite stupid."

And both wives, despite their vehement protests, gained a reputation as inordinately ambitious women who manipulated their pliable husband according to their will. "I wish you would come home and do your own business," wrote Eleanor, when besieged by midshipmen applying to her for posts on Franklin's next Arctic expedition. "For I feel it very ridiculous to have all these gentlemen coming to me to try the effect of petticoat influence."

And Jane, who was once termed a meddlesome "man in petticoats," protested that she could not understand why people considered her a "strong-minded person, bold, masculine, independent. I am no doubt possessed of great energy and ardor, but I would rather hide than show it." Still the accusation kept being made, and it infuriated her.

"Why am I always to be conceived of as a tall, commanding-looking person, perhaps with a loud voice, too!" she cried. "I am not flattered by this visionary Lady Franklin."

Sir John Franklin, in short, appears to have been henpecked. (Significantly, perhaps, a favorite Shakespearean play that he read on his voyages was *The Taming of the Shrew*.) But then he seems to have long been accustomed to being swayed by domineering women.

In Spilsby, the little Lincolnshire market town where he was born on April 16, 1786, his grandmother was the dominating force. She was a widow, according to Franklin's Victorian biographer, Henry Duff Traill, "of masculine capacity and great resolution of character." She set up Franklin's father in a grocery-drapery shop. "Not content with acting as housekeeper for her son," we are told, the bustling woman "superintended the business in every department which admitted of female supervision with the utmost activity and success."

Franklin, the youngest son in a matriarchal family of twelve children, was a singularly weak and ailing infant. He was much petted as a consequence. But when he grew up to be a plump, overly inquisitive grammar-schoolboy, a whip which hung over the house landing was frequently taken down and used to curb his excessive curiosity. His religious zeal needed no curbing. On attaining manhood, we are told, the lad burned with an ambition to construct a ladder whereby to "climb up to heaven."

At the age of fourteen, he developed a second ambition. He wanted to run away and become a seaman. "I would rather follow my son to the grave than to the sea," exclaimed his father. So the youth was shipped off on a merchantman to Lisbon in the hope that it would cool his sea fever.

It did no such thing. Young Franklin, whose personal bravery has never been questioned, fought valiantly in two of Nelson's bloodiest naval engagements, at Trafalgar and Copenhagen. He was wounded while capturing a gunboat at the battle of New Orleans. He learned how to survive in intense heat when shipwrecked and marooned for six weeks while surveying the Great Barrier Reef off Australia. And he learned how to withstand intense cold while skippering, in 1818, the leaky naval brig *Trent*, which in a six-month expedition was beaten back by Spitsbergen ice, in a vain attempt to reach the North Pole.

Though a failure, this last voyage had given Franklin a taste of fame, and he secretly enjoyed it. "The bare circumstance of going to the North Pole is a sufficient passport anywhere," he confided in a letter.

He visited Leicester Square, where his portrait was displayed in a theatrical panorama of the polar assault. He didn't want to be recognized by the crowds, and yet in a way he did. "Have you seen my Phiz in the Exhibition?" he was to write to Eleanor Porden, whom he had started courting. "Do you consider the likeness good?"

In May of 1819, Lieutenant John Franklin, by now thirty-three years old, set off on his first overland Arctic expedition that was to bring him both celebrity and notoriety—a safari blighted by starvation, alleged cannibalism and murder. His plan was ambitious. He would canoe and snowshoe to the most northerly fur trade outpost in the Canadian Barren Lands, namely Fort Providence on the north shore of Great Slave Lake. Following the trail blazed almost half a century before by that tireless hiker, Samuel Hearne, he would trace the rapid-infested Coppermine River to its mouth. Then he would explore eastward along the unknown Arctic coastline as far as he could travel.

Before embarking on this audacious scheme, Franklin had an interview with the aging Sir Alexander Mackenzie, the only explorer alive who had attempted a feat of equivalent scope. He also extracted assurances from the Hudson's Bay and North West Companies, then in the last stages of their fur trade war, that they would supply guides, provisions and transportation.

The British Admiralty furnished Franklin with four naval men, each to be immortalized as a true Arctic Worthy.

The surgeon and naturalist of the party was a thirty-one-year-old Scot named Dr. John Richardson, later to be knighted for conducting his own Arctic expedition. Eleanor could barely tolerate him. She claimed that Franklin had become a fire-eating John Knox as a result of his comradeship with this religious zealot. Jane liked him. She described Richardson in her diary as "not well-dressed, and looks like a Scotchman as he is; a middle-sized man, he has broad, high cheekbones, a widish mouth, grey eyes and brown hair; upon the whole rather plain, but the countenance thoughtful, mild and pleasing."

Franklin loved him. One of twelve children, like Franklin himself, Richardson was always ready with an apt quotation from Scriptures or classical literature. His devout father was the provost of the town of Dumfries and an intimate of Robert Burns, who used to recite poetry to young Richardson. He was a sometimes tough, lion-hearted naval surgeon, who had served in the bombardment of Copenhagen. He danced the Highland fling for entranced Indians at Christmas balls

while the bagpiper skirled "There's Nae Luck Aboot the Hoose." And he was a talented wildlife writer who could rejoice in the whiteheaded finches of the subarctic with their cheery whistle of "O, dear, what can the matter be?"

Two gifted naval artists were brought along to draw sketches of the landscape and people. The liveliest was a twenty-two-year-old swashbuckler from Stockport in England, Midshipman George Back. He, too, won a knighthood later after exploring the Back River to its mouth in the Arctic. The fur traders nicknamed him "Bluebeak," because they considered Back a vain cockatoo of a fellow, with his long silky sideburns and his dandified French airs. The adventurer had been captured in battle by the French a year after he joined the Royal Navy at the age of twelve. So small that he could be carried in a basket slung across a mule, the young prisoner of war was taken across the Pyrenees to the fortress at Verdun. There he had studied French and art and reputedly had acquired a taste for "vice and roguery."

Though he helped save Franklin's life on several occasions with his hardihood, and was a vigorous prose writer and watercolor artist, Back was not altogether popular. Franklin was rather primly cool toward him. Back evidently liked tippling with too much camaraderie with the French Canadian voyageurs and, a womanizer, he had roving brown eyes which glittered at the sight of a pretty Indian maid. "He was a very pleasant fellow," a colleague said of him, "but if he was in love with himself, he had no right to suppose every lady he met was the same." Lady Jane Franklin disapproved of him, and her traveling companion and niece, Sophia Cracroft, expressed it in scalding language: "He is never the man to originate a handsome act but if he finds it popular; and that it will be successful, he steps in to take as much of the credit as he can secure. You must not think it harshness or severity when I describe him as intensely selfish, sly, and sycophantic."

Everybody seemed to appreciate the second naval artist, Midshipman Robert Hood. He was destined to die tragically on this expedition, leaving behind him some stark, sensitive, brooding portraits of Indians. Unlike most of the Arctic naval artists, he did not imitate the somewhat stiff style of the drawing master at the Royal Naval College at Portsmouth, John Christian Schetky. Hood was a frail, twenty-one-year-old mariner, the son of a minister from Bury, Lancashire. Like Back, he had an Arctic river named after him, and he evidently had a similar amorous weakness for Indian belles.

*Franklin's first wife, Eleanor (top left), was an invalid poetess and lioness of London's literary salons. His second wife, Jane (right), was a Victorian blend of Cleopatra, Mame and Helen of Troy.* METROPOLITAN TORONTO LIBRARY BOARD

*Explorer George Back was the controversial bon vivant, womanizer and artist on Franklin's expeditions.* NATIONAL PORTRAIT GALLERY, LONDON

The rivalry between the two artists was disclosed by the fifth member of the party. This was John Hepburn, a sturdy, twenty-eight-year-old able seaman from the Scottish Orkney Islands. Hepburn, who had been a prisoner of both French and American navies during the Napoleonic wars, was brought along by Franklin as a sort of handyman. He was handy indeed, proving to be the best outdoorsman and hunter among the British officers, and was extremely devoted to Franklin.

Years later, when at sixty-one he went in search of his missing commander, Hepburn revealed one of the scandals that marred the ill-fated 1819 expedition. It seemed that Back and Hood both sought the sexual favors of a Copper Indian maid named Green Stockings. Though under sixteen years of age, she had already served as the bed mate of two Indian braves, and her beauty was so beguiling that palefaces and Indians alike wooed her. Hood finally painted her portrait over the protests of her mother, who feared "that her daughter's likeness would induce the Great Chief who resided in England to send for the original."

Evidently King William IV, sufficiently satisfied by his various mistresses, was not so tempted; but Back and Hood were. After quarreling bitterly for the wench, they agreed to fight a duel at daybreak. Hepburn settled the brawl by privately drawing the charges from their pistols that night. "Poor Hood," Hepburn recalled, "had by the same woman a daughter, whom his family have sent for."

It was just one of the many crises that Franklin had to cope with on his three-year expedition. A collision with an iceberg almost sank the fur trade ship, *Prince of Wales*, taking his party to the initial jumping-off point, York Factory on the west coast of Hudson Bay. All five seamen suffered "galled feet and swelled ankles" as a result of trudging across the rugged terrain in alien snowshoes. Wintry winds froze the mercury in their thermometers and "the tea in our tea pots before we could drink it."

Franklin, a tender-hearted tenderfoot, was dismayed by the savagery of the people in *le pays sauvage*. The French Canadian voyageurs appeared to be a rambunctious, dissolute crew of merrymakers; when they weren't eating their sledge dogs they were beating them, "and habitually vent on them the most dreadful and disgusting imprecations." The Indian guides, bearing such outlandish names as Black Meat, Crooked Foot, Rabbit's Head, Long Legs, Humpy and Bald Head, were insatiable in their demands for grog; and it was shocking the way they settled an argument among their canoe-paddling wives

with a paddle blow on the head. Their leader was Akaitcho, otherwise known as Chief Big Foot. He was a dignified but demanding potentate with three wives and his private Dogrib Indian slave. The chief, according to Franklin's biased account, had to be placated with medals, rum, tobacco and laced uniforms before he would let his men hunt for the paleface strangers. (Akaitcho later proved most generous.)

The most cooperative people were two Eskimo interpreters dispatched from a fur trade fort in Hudson Bay. They were the Belly and the Ear, renamed Augustus and Junius by some wit to commemorate the months of their arrival in the Great Slave Lake region. Augustus particularly was a faithful servant who took goodnatured pride in serving Franklin his breakfast; as a reward Dr. Richardson named a northern butterfly after him, *Callophrys augustinus.*

The least helpful were the warring H.B.C. and Nor'Wester fur traders. They reneged on the promises made by their superiors in England. They demanded exorbitant prices for moldy pemmican. They were feuding so murderously that Franklin's party had to pitch tents midway between their rival encampments.

It took Franklin two years before he got down to the serious business of exploration. On June 14, 1821, he set out from his base camp to which he had given the bold name of Fort Enterprise. It was actually no more than a cluster of clay-chinked log cabins about one hundred and fifty miles north of the fur trade's northernmost outpost of Fort Providence. Rather naively, to prevent any Indians from breaking in during his absence, Franklin nailed on the barred door a sketch of a man's hand clutching a threatening dagger.

Franklin's cavalcade of white men, Indians and Eskimo interpreters presented a picturesque sight as they dragged canoes and sledges through rock and swamp from the River of the Toothless Fish (now known as the Yellowknife River) to the banks of the Coppermine. In Dr. Richardson's phrase, they looked like a motley procession out of Chaucer's *Canterbury Tales* with a touch of Hogarth's drunken Guards.

At Samuel Hearne's celebrated Bloody Fall they paused to examine the skulls of massacred Eskimos. The gruesome spectacle caused the Indians in the party to murmur at the prospect of perhaps meeting vengeful Eskimos ahead. When they sighted the dazzling blue, ice-choked Arctic Ocean (Franklin gave it the cumbersome name of King George IV's Coronation Gulf), it was the voyageurs who shuddered. "They were terrified," says Franklin, "at the idea of a voyage through an icy sea in bark canoes." However, that veteran seadog, Hepburn, calmed the fears of the Canadian rivermen.

Chief Akaitcho and his retinue of hunters departed southward, promising to cache meat at the Fort Enterprise base camp. Franklin's remaining party of twenty men sailed eastward, poling their two frail yellow birchbark boats around massive ice floes. It was a considerable feat Franklin achieved. Altogether he mapped and named five hundred and fifty miles of jagged Arctic coastline. One cluster of islets he proudly named the Porden Islands after Eleanor. By the end of August, though, raging gales and dwindling supplies forced Franklin to come to a halt. He planted the Union Jack on the highest sand hill of a cape he called Point Turnagain. Then he turned southward to return again to his base camp.

The trek back was a horror story. It was like one of those medieval tales in which a mad sorcerer strews one obstacle after another into the hero's path. Franklin's account of it is often moving because of his very inability to express emotion at the agonies endured. His intent was to take a short cut, which proved a bad mistake. He would push up the unknown Hood River. Then he would march more than four hundred miles across the cruel Barren Lands to Fort Enterprise.

He swiftly ran into trouble. In part, his woes evidently stemmed from the unequal distribution of labor and his incapacity to maintain naval discipline among the unruly Canadians. Besides carrying the two canoes, and doing all the hunting, the *engagés* were ordered to bear backpacks of at least ninety pounds each. "The officers," says Franklin, "carried such a portion of their own things as their strength would permit."

Their miseries began in September. Snow blizzards three feet deep imprisoned them shivering in their tents. Furious winds toppled over the men carrying canoes. Stabbing rocks lacerated their moccasined feet. Their pemmican supply ran out. They were reduced to eating the occasional shot partridge; the putrid bones of caribou whose flesh had long been devoured by wolves; and the bitter lichen, *tripe de roche*, which caused diarrhea among the officers. "There was no *tripe de roche*," Franklin was to note tersely, "so we drank swamp tea and ate some of our shoes for supper."

Because of exhaustion and hunger, Franklin was seized with a fainting spell. He generously paid tribute to his men who urged him to eat a remaining morsel of soup "with much kindness." He was also deeply touched when a canoeman presented each of the officers with a

small piece of meat saved from the last of his scanty allowance. "It was received with great thankfulness," said Franklin, "and such an act of self-denial and kindness being totally unexpected in a Canadian *voyageur*, filled our eyes with tears."

But soon he was cursing his mutinous voyageurs. They rebelled at carrying the heavy loads in their weakened state. They purloined scraps of food from the officers' mess. They secretly shot partridges and would not share the birds with the officers. They scrapped the fishing nets. Then, in an ultimate act of folly, they smashed the remaining canoe and floats, apparently so that they would not have to carry the burden. "The anguish this intelligence occasioned may be conceived," wrote Franklin, "but it is beyond my power to describe it."

When the band reached the unfordable Coppermine River, Dr. Richardson had an excruciating experience. He volunteered to swim across the rapids dragging a line attached to a willow raft. He first had the misfortune to step on a dagger, which cut his foot to the bone. Then, after plunging into the icy stream, his benumbed limbs became powerless. The others hauled him back with the rope, more dead than alive, and wrapped him in blankets before a fire.

"I cannot describe what everyone felt at beholding the skeleton which Dr. Richardson's debilitated frame exhibited," wrote Franklin. "When he stripped, the Canadians simultaneously exclaimed, 'Ah! *Que nous sommes maigres!*'"

It took them eight days to cross the rapids in an improvised canoe of canvas bedding, and on they staggered. Franklin tells us that he himself was reduced "almost to skin and bones." Back was so enfeebled he had to support himself with a stick while walking. Lamed Dr. Richardson was limping. Hood, the weakest, was wasted away to a shadow. Others could barely crawl on hands and knees through the snow drifts, and they began to drop off to their death by the wayside.

In desperation, Franklin sent Back and four of the most robust Canadians ahead to Fort Enterprise. He hoped they might find meat there cached by Chief Akaitcho's Indians; perhaps a rescue party could return with provisions before they all lost their strength.

But poor Hood's waning energy was already spent. The young artist pleaded to be left behind alone, so that he would not be a drag on his shipmates. Dr. Richardson and Able Seaman Hepburn would not hear of it. The two Scots nobly volunteered to stay and look after the invalid. Franklin reluctantly left them at a camping spot of willows and *tripe de roche*, and pressed on with his failing band toward the fort.

The next day there was another split in his diminishing group. Four of the voyageurs, including an Iroquois named Michel, wept that they could walk no farther. Franklin let them turn back to the invalid camp. Meanwhile he and the five remaining voyageurs struggled on through blustery winds and deep snow until they finally stumbled into Fort Enterprise. They were aghast. The place was empty: no food, no fire, no people.

"It would be impossible to describe our sensations after entering this miserable abode, and discovering how we had been neglected," wrote Franklin. "The whole party shed tears."

Franklin took a little solace from a note left by Back. The artist and his four Canadians hoped to bring relief from Akaitcho's Indian camp in the neighborhood of the fur trade's Fort Providence. That meant a herculean roundtrip hike of three hundred miles, and offered a slender chance of rescue.

Franklin and his comrades could only hope and wait. While they waited their vitality ebbed. They raked the ash heap for refuse bones, and Franklin found himself too weak to pound them for soup. They gnawed deerskin curtains torn from the windows. They ripped up floor boards for a meagre fire. They huddled close together for warmth in twenty-below-zero chill. They were so emaciated they could not lift a gun to shoot deer or rise from their blankets without a helping hand. "But even in this pitiable condition we conversed cheerfully," said Franklin, and he was pleased that his penitent companions "had entirely given up the practice of swearing, to which the Canadian voyageurs are so lamentably addicted."

After eighteen days, they heard footsteps crunching the snow outside. "*Ah! Le monde!*" exclaimed the Canadians expectantly. Surely it must be Back's Indian rescue party. But there at the door, haggard-faced, stood Dr. Richardson and Hepburn alone. They were the sole survivors from the invalid camp, and they had a hideous story to tell.

It seemed that Michel the Iroquois, who had left Franklin's hiking party with three other voyageurs, had arrived at the invalid camp alone. He told a credible tale of how the others had perished en route of starvation. He handed Hood, Richardson and Hepburn meat that was purportedly a hare and a partridge. As they ravenously devoured it, Hepburn rejoiced, "How I shall love this man if I find that he does not tell lies like the others!"

But soon Michel's suspicious behavior seemed ominously like that of a liar. When out hunting, he took a hatchet rather than the knife customary for cutting freshly killed game. It was as though, Richardson thought, he was using the hatchet to hack "something he knew to be frozen." A grisly suspicion grew when Michel returned with slices of meat which he maintained was part of a wolf he had slain with a deer's horn. It dawned on Richardson that perhaps they were eating the flesh of the voyageurs whom Michel had butchered and cached nearby.

This circumstantial evidence seemed confirmed a few days later. As though guilt-ridden, Michel muttered something surly about white people in the past having murdered and eaten three of his Iroquois relatives. And as the three present white men grew daily weaker on a diet of *tripe de roche*, Michel grew fatter and more overbearing in his strength. "It is no use hunting, there are no animals!" he taunted them. "You had better kill and eat me!"

There was a ghastly climax to his sulleness. One morning the two others left Michel arguing with Hood in front of the tent. A shot rang out. They rushed back to find Hood slumped over dead, a copy of *Bickersteth's Scripture Help* at his feet. Michel maintained that the artist had accidentally shot himself while cleaning a gun. But an examination of the body showed that the bullet had been fired through the back of his head. It seemed evident to Richardson and Hepburn that Michel had murdered him.

The two Scots made a meal of poor Hood's buffalo robe, and then had a private conference. Michel was growing increasingly arrogant, and from his vituperative language, it seemed clear that he intended to kill the two white men left in his power. Dr. Richardson concluded there was only one thing left to do. The surgeon hid behind a clump of willows, loaded his pistol, and waited. When Michel approached, he stepped out and shot him through the head.

Then Richardson and Hepburn hobbled from their invalid camp to Fort Enterprise and there they joined the others in a melancholy vigil of prayer and starvation. Two of the voyageurs slowly sank into a coma. "*Je suis faible! Je suis faible!*" they cried in sepulchral voices and then the death rattle was heard in their throat. The others were too weak to bury them and had strength only to move their bodies to the far side of the room. Another voyageur sobbed hysterically. Franklin read the Bible to him, and slept on a blanket on the floor beside him, and comforted him. And when Franklin and Dr. Richardson became too faint to

*Green Stockings, the seductive Indian maid wooed by Hood and Back.* METROPOLITAN TORONTO LIBRARY BOARD

*Chief Akaitcho (with son) aided Franklin's starving men at Fort Enterprise.*

*Richardson and Hepburn rejoin Franklin's haggard group after Hood's death.* TORONTO PUBLIC LIBRARIES, OSBORNE COLLECTION

hold a Bible, they recited aloud to each other a verse from the twenty-seventh psalm: "I had fainted, unless I had believed to see the goodness of the Lord in the land of the living."

As the shadow of death hovered over the cabin, they talked of religion by day, dreamed of feasting by night, and in between vainly tried to control their collective delirium. In the most affecting passage in his journal, Franklin wrote:

"I observed that, in proportion as our strength decayed, our minds exhibited symptoms of weakness, evinced by a kind of unreasonable pettishness with each other. Each of us thought the other weaker in intellect than himself, and more in need of advice and assistance. So trifling a circumstance as a change of place, recommended by one as being warmer and more comfortable, and refused by the other from a dread of motion, frequently called forth fretful expressions which were no sooner uttered than atoned for. . . .

"The same thing often occurred when we endeavoured to assist each other in carrying wood to the fire; none of us were willing to receive assistance, although the task was disproportioned to our strength. On one of these occasions, Hepburn was so convinced of this waywardness that he exclaimed, 'Dear me, if we are spared to return to England, I wonder if we shall recover our understandings.'"

On November 7, when Franklin was certain they would all be dead within days, he scrawled on the bottom of the page of his pocket diary: "Praise be unto the Lord! We were this day rejoiced by the appearance of Indians. . . ." Three of them sent by Back finally arrived loaded with deer meat, fat, and tongues. With utmost tenderness, Akaitcho's Indians washed them and fed them and nursed the survivors back to life. Soon they were well enough to snowshoe slowly toward Fort Providence, leaning on the Indians who deprived themselves of their own snowshoes to ease the walking pains of their patients. "Our feelings on quitting the fort," wrote Franklin, in a muted farewell to Enterprise, "may be more easily conceived than described."

Of his band of twenty men who explored the Arctic coastline only nine had survived. At Fort Providence he found the indefatigable Back and a hospitable Chief Akaitcho, who insisted on preparing a meal for the palefaces with his own hands, a function he never performed for himself. Bidding them farewell, the great chief explained that provisions had been delayed due to bad hunting and the warring of the fur traders.

"The world goes badly," he said. "All are poor. You are poor. The traders appear to be poor. I and my party are likewise poor. . . . I do not regret having supplied you with provisions, for a Copper Indian can never permit white men to suffer from want in his lands without flying to their aid." He laughed good-humoredly. "At all events, it is the first time that the white people have been indebted to the Copper Indians."

In October of 1822 Franklin arrived back in England to wide acclaim. He was promoted to post captain by the Admiralty and elected to a fellowship in the Royal Society. He was lionized at fashionable salons. People pointed him out as "the man who ate his boots." His weighty *Narrative of a Journey to the Shores of the Polar Sea*, though selling at four guineas for a lavish quarto edition, became an instant best-seller.

There were some shrewd critics, however, far from London's polite drawing rooms, who were far from impressed. These were the hard-bitten fur traders back in *le pays sauvage*. They read Franklin's journal and they were caustic about what it had glossed over. They thought it peculiar, to say the least, that all those who died in the wilderness, except Hood, had been veteran north country voyageurs. They felt that the retributory killing of Michel— without legal trial or investigation— was an unpardonable act for which Dr. Richardson "richly merited to be punished." They recalled how George Back had confessed frankly "to tell the truth . . . things have taken place which *must* not be known."

Franklin's genteelness was a special butt of their private jokes. "He must have three meals per diem," scoffed George Simpson, appointed head of the amalgamated fur trade companies. "Tea is indispensable, and with the utmost exertion, he cannot walk above *Eight* miles in one day."

Other traders passed around a parody of Franklin's ponderously written book. "Mr. Mildmay," as they sarcastically nicknamed him, was lampooned for naming the most inconsequential geographical features after consequential socialites. "This Island," the satire had Mildmay loftily proclaiming, "I have named Brown Bottom Island in honour of my friend and relative, Lord Brownbottom."

Eleanor Porden disagreed with these cynics. She was flattered to have her family name enshrined on the globe. She sent her fiancé a letter of thanks as well as a valentine poem. Unaware of the scandalous amour which Franklin discreetly hushed up in his journal, Eleanor signed herself "Green Stockings" and titled her love verses *The Esquimaux Girl's Lament*. One stanza read:

*Return! and the tempest shall pause in his wrath;*
*I will breathe out my spells on the land and the sea*
*Return! and the Ice shall be swept from thy path,*
*Nor the winds nor the waves dare be rebels to thee....*

The love letters that Franklin exchanged with Eleanor are in keeping with his strait-laced character. Her letters are lightly teasing. She wonders if he expects her to pull an Eskimo sledge. "After writing so long about Richard Coeur de Lion, I have contrived to catch hold of a Lion's heart, have I not?" And she playfully addresses him as "Most Faithless Saxon," "You very naughty boy" and "Mon très cher Capitaine." Franklin gravely replies that he has perused her "interesting communication." He discourses on the impropriety of writing letters on Sunday. And he addresses her—until she pleads to be called by her first name—as "My dear Miss Porden" or "My dearest Friend."

They were married on August 19, 1823. After that her letters make sad reading. They crackle with subtle undercurrents. Like any housewife, she worries about her husband's overweight and reprimands him for eating too many plums. She frets about his distaste for her coterie of bright literary lights and his protracted visits to relatives in Lincolnshire. "It seems that none of your family can do anything without you," she complains in semi-jocular vein, "and your self-love is flattered by it, you vain animal!" But there is nothing light-hearted about her reproaches for his morbid Sunday fanaticism.

"Last year you would have spent it like an anchorite," she rails. "Mild as you usually are, your looks and voice have actually terrified me, and the first time left an impression which I cannot recover.... I may well ask, 'Which is the counterfeit and which the true man?'"

On June 3, 1824, she gave birth to a daughter, christened Eleanor. Franklin enjoyed singing to the "little Puss" and the baby may have bolstered a little their eroding marriage. But the birth also accelerated the mother's worsening consumption, and we get a picture of Franklin staying away increasingly while his invalid wife was tied to her divan. In one letter to a relative, Eleanor writes with forced gaiety of "poor I, who was left at home," while Franklin was off gallivanting. "Such a flirt as he is! The like was never known. Only think of his being one of a party to gallant sixteen young ladies (ladies are always young, you know)."

One young lady he seemed to be seeing a lot of was Jane Griffin. He dined several times at her home, even on a Sunday while Eleanor

was pining away on her divan. At one dinner party we learn that Franklin was dancing attendance on Jane and her sister. "He gave us each an arm," says Jane, "and seemed to have us under his protection the greater part of the evening, which surely must have made us objects of envy." At another dinner engagement, less than a month before Eleanor's death, Jane tells us, "Captain Franklin kept me in constant talk."

He doubtless was talking about his forthcoming Arctic expedition. As a parting gift, Jane gave him a silver lead pencil, engraved with his crest, and a pair of fur gloves. Franklin thought the gloves the most useful present possible for his polar journey. Undeterred by past starvation, he, Richardson and Back intended to make a two-pronged exploration. The whole party would traverse the Mackenzie River to its mouth, after which they would divide. Franklin and Back would trace the unknown Arctic coast westward toward Bering Strait, while Richardson would trace it eastward to the Coppermine River.

Through the filter of time, it is difficult to tell exactly how Eleanor felt about her husband embarking on a polar expedition as she lay dying. She appears to have accepted it philosophically and almost with a sense of relief. With realistic insight into the explorer's psyche, she tells him that escaping to the Arctic was to him like the stimulus "of opium. . . . And when you returned to the sober routine of common life, you missed the excitement to which you had become habituated and seemed to fall, literally like Icarus, when his wings were thawed by the sun."

With the approach of February 16, 1825, when Franklin was scheduled to depart, Jane heard some idle gossip about the explorer's heartlessness in abandoning his sick wife. "My voice trembled with agitation, not unmixed with anger," wrote Jane, "while I replied to all this unfeeling nonsense." Yet Jane sounds rather laconic after a visit to her dying best friend, Eleanor. "Our tête-à-tête was rather a heavy one," the diarist noted. "Mrs. Franklin showed me a silk flag which she had borrowed as a pattern for one she is going to make for the expedition." Jane appears to have mustered more heartfelt sympathy for distraught Franklin, torn between his exploring commitment and his wife. "He was obliged to settle all his affairs," Jane observed, "as if his wife would certainly not recover and as if he himself would never return."

Franklin himself opted for naval duty first. He rationalized to himself that Eleanor had told him openly, "It would be better for me if you were gone." He consoled her by reading aloud with her the chapter

from Corinthians used for the funeral service: "O death, where is thy sting? O grave, where is thy victory?" And six days after his expedition left England, she was dead.

When Franklin first stepped onto an Arctic island at the mouth of the Mackenzie River, he remembered Eleanor with a certain poignancy. While whales and seals sported in the bluey-green polar sea and his men uttered three cheers and toasted the King with grog, the explorer planted the silk Union Jack which had been embroidered by his dying wife.

"I will not attempt to describe my emotions as it expanded to the breeze," wrote Franklin. "However natural and, for the moment, irresistible, I felt that it was my duty to suppress them, and that I had no right by an indulgence of my own sorrows to cloud the animated countenances of my companions."

Although he didn't mention it in his published journal, however, it must be said that a little west of the Mackenzie River, Franklin named an Arctic cape Point Griffin. It was named after the family name of Jane.

On this overland expedition, Franklin was far better prepared for emergencies. His party shared plenty of provisions from the now cooperative Hudson's Bay Company; four specially constructed mahogany longboats; and, in case Dr. Richardson had to ford icy rivers, a waterproof folding canvas canoe called the *Walnut Shell.* Instead of counting on a rabble of voyageurs, he had recruited nineteen tightly disciplined British seamen. Most of them were Highland Scots, and there was a bagpiper, George Wilson, whose screeching music impressed the Eskimos mightily.

The bagpiper was the life of the parties held at his base camp, Fort Franklin; this was a polyglot community of Indians, Eskimos, French Canadians and Gaels, which still flourishes today at the west end of Great Bear Lake not too far from the Mackenzie River. Here Franklin's mixed group played hockey, danced Highland flings, laughed at a comic cardboard puppet show staged by George Back, and evidently tippled heartily with what Back termed *l'eau de vie.*

"And many times we plied the flagons filled with odorous punch and rosy wine," wrote Richardson of a merry Christmas dance, "until the head growing heavier than the heels, we retired to needful repose." And Back, later reminiscing of his bouts over the peace pipe with neighboring tribes, coined a pleasant aphorism: "A social puff is to an Indian what a bottle of wine is to an Englishman—*aperit praecordia*—it unlocks the heart and dissipates reserve."

Franklin's most cordial ambassadors in helping win the friendship of the Arctic natives were his two Eskimo interpreters. Each was dressed up in a sky-blue uniform with silver medals almost as impressive as those worn by the naval officers. One was "our little friend," Augustus, who had served him so loyally on his last expedition. Junius having perished, the other was an equally devoted Hudson Bay compatriot named Ooligbuck. He was to act as Dr. Richardson's native diplomat, oarsman, caribou-hunter and aide-de-camp. Richardson remarks that the genial Ooligbuck was most obliging. Once, entreating Richardson to hop into the boat before being attacked by seemingly bad Eskimo people, Ooligbuck "took me on his back, and carried me aboard."

Augustus, though serving Franklin his breakfast, apparently gave him no pick-a-back; but the little fellow was clearly the lifesaver of Franklin's westward-traveling detachment. They almost lost their lives at the very outset of the exploration. Their two grounded boats were surrounded by a swarm of almost three hundred bartering kayakers from an Eskimo village in the shallow Mackenzie Delta. One of Franklin's oarsmen accidentally upset a kayak. The occupant was plunged into the water with his head in the mud. Augustus tried to placate the shivering Eskimo and wrapped him in his own greatcoat. But the indignant man would not be mollified. In reprisal he led the villagers in an attempt to plunder booty from the white intruders' boats. It was a good-humored rough-and-tumble at first. But it got ugly when Franklin's sailors began to belabor the natives with the butt ends of their muskets.

The villagers retaliated by pulling daggers, and clutched Franklin menacingly by the wrists. George Back in the other boat ordered his mariners to level their muskets and threatened to fire. A sketch drawn by Back depicts the mob of Eskimos scurrying in fearful retreat to the beach.

"I cannot sufficiently praise the fortitude and obedience of both the boats' crews in abstaining from the use of their arms," Franklin says. However, he had the good sense to add judiciously: "The first blood we had shed would have been instantly revenged by the sacrifice of all our lives."

The debacle ended with Augustus striding boldly alone on the beach. The peacemaker scolded the assembled villagers, and responding to his speech with "shouts of applause," they invited him to join them in a merry song and a drum dance. According to the lofty words

that Franklin puts in his mouth, Augustus harangued them as though he were delivering an address to the Royal Society:

"I regret that you should have treated in this violent manner the white people who came solely to do you kindness. My tribe were in the same unhappy state in which you now are, before the white people came to Churchill, but at present they are supplied with everything they need, and you see that I am well clothed; I get all that I want, and am very comfortable. You cannot expect, after the transactions of this day, that these people will ever bring goods to your country again, unless you show your contrition by returning the stolen goods. The white people love the Esquimaux, and wish to show them the same kindness that they bestow upon the Indians: do not deceive yourselves, and suppose that they are afraid of you; I tell you that they are not, and that it is entirely owing to their humanity that many of you were not killed today. . . ."

Franklin departed hastily from "Pillage Point," as he named it, ordering a gun to be fired across the bow of a kayak paddling in pursuit. Ironically, it turned out, the contrite villager was merely trailing them to return a tea kettle which had been filched.

Franklin took no chances with the other bands of Eskimos he encountered along the north shore of the present Yukon and Alaska. He drew a line on the beach some three hundred yards from his parked boats and had Augustus warn bartering Eskimos that they were not to step across that mark. The natives shook hands in agreement and were most amiable. They performed dances for the visitors, with the white men's bartered fish hooks dangling bizarrely from their noses. They kindly sewed sealskin patches on the soles of the *Kabloona* shoes worn threadbare after the sailors had hauled the boats along the shingly beaches. They drew maps on the sand, and expressed polite surprise that the explorers had not the foresight to bring dogs and sledges for travel when the ice would unite with the shore.

Franklin discovered the wisdom of what they had to say. He was held up for days by ice packed to the shoreline. His men pushed on, lashed by gales, whipped by sleet, bloodied by mosquitoes, and swallowed up by smothering fog. Franklin finally called a halt at a gravelly point he named Return Reef, one hundred and sixty miles from Alaska's Point Barrow, and returned to Fort Franklin. His men slogged back, their legs swollen and inflamed from wading through icy quagmires, but justifiably proud of having delineated three hundred and seventy-four miles of Arctic coastline.

Dr. Richardson's survey crew did much better. They charted nine hundred miles of new coast stretching from the mouth of the Mackenzie to the Coppermine. Richardson had a similar run-in with Mackenzie Delta Eskimos. But the Scotsman disarmed them with a canny expedient. He noted that their spruce-fir bows, strengthened by caribou sinews, were marvelous weapons, even more powerful than those of yew wood used by Robin Hood's archers of Sherwood Forest; he laid down the dictum that those were the only articles of trade he would accept in exchange for his combs and beads and other trinkets. Richardson had a high estimation of their intelligence. The Eskimos speedily comprehended the value of his pocket telescope, calling it *eetee-yawgah* (far eyes); and they were shrewd merchants in *noo-waerlook* (trade). "They are cautious not to glut the market by too great display of their stock in trade," he observed, "producing only one article at a time and not attempting to outbid each other."

Richardson had a somewhat lower estimation of their morality. Enticing Eskimo beauties sang and danced with ecstasy in their *umiaks*, and "bestowed on us some glances that could scarcely be misconstrued." More shocking still, these Circes had husbands who "offered to provide us with wives, if we would pass the night at their tents. For very obvious reasons," declared the Calvinist, "we declined all their invitations."

As a naturalist Dr. Richardson had a field day. Altogether he detected on the Arctic coastline one hundred and seventy species of flowering plants. The July air was perfumed, he says, by Lapland roses, yellow poppies and beautiful flaming red phlox, and in the moist valleys he gathered marigold-like cowslips. He was enchanted by the cheerful twittering of sand martins, the raucous laughing of the yellow-billed loon, and he marveled at the curves of limestone cliffs sculptured by pounding polar waves until they were as graceful as Gothic arches. At the end of his five-week sojourn, his two boats were flung between violent whirlpools and tongues of icebergs. The classics scholar thought of Jason and his Argonauts in Greek mythology, and he headed back being "reminded forcibly of the poet's description of Scylla and Charybdis."

When Richardson was reunited with Franklin, the good doctor expressed doubts about the practicality of what they had achieved. He wondered what use it would be when the remaining gaps in the Northwest Passage would be filled in. Richardson wrote a reflective letter to his wife (one of the three he was to marry, including Franklin's niece,

who was to bear him a child christened John Franklin Richardson).
"The discovery will, I suppose, be committed, like Juliet to the tomb of
all the Capulets," said Richardson, "unless something more powerful
than steam can render it available for the purpose of mercantile gain."

It was both a prophecy and an underestimation of a magnificent
feat. In Franklin's *Narrative of a Second Expedition to the Shores of the Polar
Sea*, the explorer mentioned casually that his two little sail boats attempted a landing at Prudhoe Bay. This was the fantastically oil-rich
Alaskan shore to be visited in the next century by the hundred-thou-
sand-ton tanker, *S.S. Manhattan*. Moreover, in the apt phrase of the
modern Arctic historian, Professor Leslie H. Neatby, Franklin's two
overland expeditions were not to be sniffed at: "He had put a roof on
the map of Canada, and given a definite shape to the North American
continent."

Franklin returned to England in the fall of 1827 to a blizzard of
tributes. The King knighted him. The Geographical Society of France
awarded him a gold medal. Oxford University conferred on him an
honorary degree and hymned his praises in verse:

*And on the proud memorials of his fame*
*Lives, linked with deathless glory, Franklin's name.*

One day Lady Franklin was to spur her husband's ambition by
recalling those lines. Jane Griffin became his wife not too long after the
returned hero came courting her with presents of arctic reindeer
tongues and three pair of Indian moccasins. A world-renowned suitor,
presenting such exotic gifts, was irresistible. They were married on
November 5, 1828. Franklin was then forty-two and Jane thirty-six.

On the whole, it seems to have been a happier marriage for
Franklin, though bearing some striking similarities with his previous
relationship with Eleanor. During their engagement, while Jane was on
one of her whirlwind travels to Russia, she sent her fiancé a revealing
letter. She addresses him playfully as "My dear Ivan" and signs herself
"Jane Ivanova." She reminds Franklin that she will never wear a con-
jugal ring as a "badge of slavery." And though "God forbid I should
ever be the wretched wife who obliged her husband from a sense of duty
alone," she will nevertheless make an effort to be a submissive helpmate.
"If you are a very prudent man, however," she warns him, "you will put
this letter by when I am in a rebellious mood; and, upon this consideration, I think you ought to feel infinitely obliged to me for furnishing you
with so valuable a document."

It turned out that an alliance with Jane was like being married to an untamable typhoon. While he was tied down to peacetime duties commanding the H.M.S. *Rainbow* in the Mediterranean, her insatiable curiosity "to see and know everything" led her to rove to the hot spots of the world. Whether she was experiencing an earthquake in the Grecian island of Zante, a revolution in Spain, Bedouin bandit gunfire in Arabia, or crossing the Nile on a date-tree raft in the teeth of a hurricane, it was all catnip to her spirit of adventure. "Don't think things *impossible* for me which are only a little *difficult*," the demon traveler wrote to her husband. "The amazing tonic power of great excitement; the danger is the being at rest again after it is over. . . ."

She was unremitting in her exhortations to get Franklin back into polar action. "The character and position you possess in society, and the interest—I may say celebrity—attached to your name, belong to the expeditions," she prodded him. "Your credit and reputation are dearer to me than the selfish enjoyment of your society. Nor indeed can I properly enjoy your society if you are living in inactivity when you might be in active employ." He had been thawing out far too long in the soporific Mediterranean. "A freezing climate seems to have a wonderful tonic in bracing your nerves and making you stronger." Then, citing the laudatory Oxford poem, she declares that "not I only but all the world" must again shout the deathless glory of Franklin's name and fame.

Franklin returned to England and tried to wheedle an explorer's posting from the First Lord of the Admiralty himself. "You will fancy, my dearest," he reports to her in obedient-boy fashion, "that your shy, timid husband must have gathered some brass on his way home, or you will be at a loss to account for his extraordinary courage."

Jane praises him for his diplomatic strategy. "Oh, what a coaxing, smooth-tongued rogue you are," she rallies him. "Who would think, my dear, that you had lived amongst the Polar bears."

But it was not to be. The Admiralty, after sending George Back out on two fruitless Northwest Passage expeditions, was in a cheese-paring economy wave and there was a hiatus in Arctic exploration. So Franklin marked time by accepting, in 1836, a job as Governor of Tasmania, the colonial island that is now part of the commonwealth of Australia.

It was a thankless job. Tasmania was then a dump for English convicts, dominated by intriguing colonists and a brawling yellow press. Franklin, the naive seaman, was not up to governing it. Jane quickly gained a reputation as the dowager queen who really ran the island, autocratically using four convicts as her palanquin bearers.

She doubtless was an interfering Governor's Lady, for her restless spirit chafed at docile domesticity. She was the first woman to climb Tasmania's four-thousand-foot-high Mount Wellington. The dauntless traveler then went over to Australia and became the first white woman to trek overland from Melbourne to Sydney. Then, as an outlet for her uncontainable energy, she assumed the role of Tasmania's Elizabeth Fry. She was determined to reform the penal colony's jailed prostitutes.

In a moment of introspection she confessed, "I am too apt to feel, 'I am holier than thou.'" She certainly felt that way about prostitutes. She believed the "female Helots" ought to be punished with the harshest form of hard labor, placed in solitary confinement and not permitted to see their illegitimate children. According to one irreverent account, she would drag Governor Franklin ("who would have preferred a yarn with some old sailor") along with her on prison visits. On one such reform mission, she urged the prison chaplain to preach moral homilies to the assembled harlots. In protest the hussies turned their backs, raised their petticoats, and smacked their bottoms resoundingly. "The Governor was shocked, the parson was horrorstruck," it was said, "and the ladies could not control their laughter."

It was with obvious relief that Governor Franklin turned to the more pleasant duty of welcoming fellow naval explorers bound for the Antarctic. In 1840, Captains James Clark Ross and Francis Rawdon Moira Crozier, en route to seeking the south magnetic pole, put into Tasmania to provision their two vessels, *Erebus* and *Terror*. "If you do not write regularly," Franklin bade them farewell with envious wistfulness, "we of this household will unite in condemning you as very lazy Discovery Chaps."

Three years later Franklin was fired from his Governor's job and, to clear his name, impelled once more to become a Discovery Chap. Jane, it seems, was the centre of the dispute responsible for his embarrassing recall to England. Franklin had peremptorily dismissed his administrative secretary on grounds that the man controlled the "despicable felon press" of Tasmania which had not shown sufficient respect for himself and Jane. Newspaper muckrakers had accused Franklin of being an "imbecile" administrator led around by the nose by his domineering busybody of a wife. "Vulgar twaddle!" Jane had dismissed the journalistic mud-slinging, but Franklin's sense of *amour propre* had been offended. The Colonial Secretary in London, Lord Stanley, sided with the dismissed civil servant. Governor Franklin was

humiliated to receive word of his recall on the same ship which brought his successor to Tasmania.

Franklin returned to England with a besmirched reputation. Jane roused him into going to the Admiralty with the hope of redeeming himself in a polar exploit. "Such an appointment," she said, "would do more than anything else to counteract the effect of Lord Stanley's tyranny and injustice."

The Admiralty was ready to listen to Franklin's proposal. A great Hudson's Bay Company fur trade explorer, Thomas Simpson, of whom we will read later, had closed up most of the gaps along the Arctic coastline. All that remained to do, apparently, was to thrust through the maze of channels southwest of Lancaster Sound and sail right through the Northwest Passage.

There were some rival Arctic Worthies who objected to Franklin's heading the expedition. They claimed he was too old, too overweight, too susceptible to cold, and the elderly fellow was bound to form the "nucleus of an iceberg."

Pulling strings in influential quarters, Jane pleaded, "I should wish Sir John to have it in his power to go and not to be put aside for his age." Lord Haddington, First Lord of the Admiralty, seems to have responded to the plea. He demanded no medical checkup, but in an interview with Franklin, the peer chaffed him a little about his age.

"You are not so young as you were, Sir John," Haddington is said to have remarked. "You are fifty-nine."

"No, no, my lord," Franklin is supposed to have made the rejoinder. "I am only fifty-eight!"

And so Franklin, two months short of fifty-nine, was given the command of the greatest Arctic expedition that any nation had yet mounted. A handpicked crew of one hundred and twenty-eight men, the cream of the navy, sailed with him to their doom.

Interestingly, the command was first offered to Sir James Clark Ross, newly knighted for his Antarctic exploits; but the forty-four-year-old Ross turned it down on grounds that his age unfitted him for the post. ("I think perhaps," Franklin told Jane, "that I have the tact of keeping the officers and men happily together in a greater degree than Ross, and for this reason: he is evidently ambitious and wishes to do everything himself.") As second in command Franklin was happy to accept Captain Francis Rawdon Moira Crozier, an experienced forty-nine-year-old Discovery Chap; the Irish seaman had accompanied James Ross to the Antarctic and had weathered three Arctic expeditions with Sir William Edward Parry.

Franklin's two ships were the ominously-named veterans of Antarctic ice: the three-hundred-and-twenty-six-ton *Terror* and the three-hundred-and-seventy-ton *Erebus* (Greek mythology's personification of Hades, son of Chaotic Darkness). Both were bluff-bowed, yellow-and-black, three-masted, iron-sheathed bomb vessels. By Victorian standards they were floating palaces. They were the first polar ships to be equipped with auxiliary screw-steam power for emergency use (converted railway engines of twenty horsepower each with screw propellers added). Each had central heating (the cabins were warmed by a hot water system).

Fortnum and Mason's and Goldner's had done them proud with provisions to last three years. There was a plenitude of tinned mutton, salt pork, chocolate, biscuits, raisins, mustard, pickles, lemon juice and a good supply of liquor: thirty-six hundred gallons of concentrated spirits and two hundred gallons of "wine for the sick."

Though devoid of items which the Eskimos would have considered necessities—such as fur parkas, blubber and dog teams—there were Victorian luxuries galore. For the officers' mess the cutlery was the costliest silverware, the glasses crystal, and the heavy silver platters initialled and crested. Barrel organs played fifty selections, ten of them religious hymns. There were mahogany writing desks for officers and seventy slates for teaching illiterate mariners their ABCs and a library of twenty-nine hundred volumes, ranging from *The Pickwick Papers* and *Nicholas Nickleby* by Charles Dickens to bound volumes of *Punch.*

Yet despite all this bounty, Franklin was feeling a little touchy. He had caught the flu and, for the sake of his health, he had given up his lifetime habit of taking snuff. A few days before his ships left England, on May 19 of 1845, Franklin was resting on the sofa and Jane was sitting beside him. She was putting the final stitches on the silk Union Jack which, in the tradition of explorers' wives, she had embroidered for planting on a high pinnacle in the Arctic. Concerned about his flu, Jane threw the flag over Franklin's feet. The touch of it startled her husband from his sleep.

"Why, there's a flag thrown over me!" cried Franklin. "Don't you know that they lay the Union Jack over a corpse?"

# Chapter 3

# Have You Seen Any Large Ships Lately?

In 1850 a strange scene was reenacted all along the northern rim of North America. Eskimos gaped at the sight. Hordes of white men stepped ashore from monstrous wooden *umiaks*. They opened up a magical little book bound in black leather. Then the *Kabloona* newcomers spoke a phrase in the *Inuit* tongue. They each asked the same question: "Have you seen any large ships lately?"

The search for Sir John Franklin had swung into full gear. The explorer and one hundred and twenty-eight men aboard the two discovery ships, *Erebus* and *Terror*, had vanished into the Arctic void in 1845. For the next two decades the mystery of those missing ships gripped the imagination of the public throughout Europe and North America.

Never before had there been such a concerted drive to unravel the unknown. Altogether some forty expeditions were sent out. Nearly four million dollars were spent. Countless lives were sacrificed. There was an epic sweep to the drama: intermingling acts of tragedy and comedy, scenes of courage and folly, and a large cast of heroes and jesters.

The search parties failed in their mission to recover Franklin's lost pair of three-masted vessels. Yet they achieved a bravura finale. They filled in geographical blanks on the map (decorating the Arctic with place names that sometimes read like a roll call of *Burke's Peerage* and the address book of the British Admiralty). They broadened *Kabloona* understanding of the Eskimo people. They developed the ability to cope with polar travel and survival.

That knowledge was won the hard way. So-called civilized white men were ludicrously slow to learn the common sense ways of Eskimo culture. In 1850, when all of fifteen search parties were combing the northern latitudes, the British Admiralty issued a quaint tourist guide. It was a hip-pocket-sized leather booklet entitled *Eskimaux and English Vocabulary*, and its one hundred and sixty pages are larded with unwitting humor.

Sailors were instructed to greet Eskimos with a salute of the arm held up at precisely forty-five degrees. At closer quarters, rubbing noses was designated the proper naval form of salutation. After asking if the pair of missing three-masted ships had been seen, the mariners were advised to scrutinize the aboriginal faces closely. This was to determine whether the primitives winked or nodded. A wink supposedly meant "No" and a nod meant "Yes."

During the search, the Eskimos doubtless had difficulty comprehending the *Kabloona* customs. To protect themselves from the cold, sailors, dressed in regulation white cotton jumpers, Welsh wigs and carpet shoes, were issued tin hot-water bags to tuck inside their regulation blue boxcloth pea jackets. The water bags froze. To help drag their boats mounted on iron sledges, some loads weighing as much as two thousand pounds, the sled-haulers flew large square kites. That didn't work either. To plow ships through rocklike ice floes, crew members blasted gun powder: up to six pounds inserted with a twelve-inch wick into wine bottles or empty mutton cans. When that failed, they sawed canals and pulled the ships through with capstan ropes like barge horses.

The entertainments devised to withstand the long winter nights were often ingenious. Some carved billiard tables out of blocks of ice. The billiard balls caromed off cushions made of walrus hide. Snow sculpturing rose to a high art. The prize statue was a stately Britannia, with Queen Victoria and the royal lion ranking as close seconds. Some ships carried their own wooden-block printing equipment. The puns and jests in their illustrated newspapers (a jack tar fetching a "pail of water"—namely a cord of ice slabs) were the source of much innocent merriment.

Some played quoits and some played ninepins on ice. Some played tennis and some played the English game of baseball known as rounders, and some ran pick-a-back races (with lesser ranks actually straddling the backs of captains). Aboard one ship a French magician mystified the local Eskimo *angekok* with his sophisticated bag of tricks. Aboard two other ships, separated by four hundred yards of ice fields, officers played chess via a connecting electromagnetic telegraph. It was perhaps the first time in the game's history where a chess match employed crude telegraph.

Shipboard theatres and masked balls achieved the ultimate in Arctic cruises *au grand luxe*. Her Majesty's playbills were printed on colored satin and silk. Pantomimes were staged in an eighty-foot by

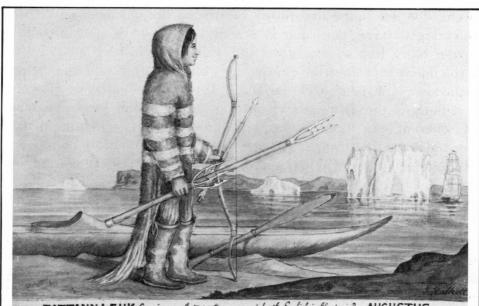

TATTANNAÆUK. *Esquimaux Interpreter, named, by the English in Hudson's Bay* AUGUSTUS, *the faithful follower of Captains S. John Franklin, & S. Geo. Back & D. Richardson, in their Arctic land Expeditions in N. America*

*"Have you seen any large ships lately?" was the question that 40 expeditions asked Eskimos after the disappearance of Franklin's Erebus and Terror in 1845.* HUDSON'S BAY COMPANY

*Amateur theatricals, initiated by Parry, were staged by many of the search expeditions.* NATIONAL MARITIME MUSEUM, GREENWICH

twenty-foot ice house decorously christened the Crystal Palace. After shivering onstage, petticoated "actresses" were obliged to arch their frozen hairy legs over a stove and swill hot whisky punch. In one resplendent *bal masqué* the quarter deck blazed with candle chandeliers. Drinks were dispensed at the Royal Intrepid Saloon. The crowning ceremony of the *Soirée Fantastique* was the arrival of the commodore. Masquerading in crimson robe and gilt chain as Sir Greasyhide Walrus, Lord Mayor of Kittiwake, he was driven aboard in a brougham sledge. His footpage was an Eskimo wearing livery with brass buttons and high hat.

Their devices for contacting lost Franklin were likewise fanciful. They shot off rockets. They flew balloons. They introduced "arctic postmen" whose mail, unfortunately, was never delivered. They let loose trapped blue foxes with messages contained in copper collars; but the sailors secretly recaught them and brought back the pelts for their sweethearts. They released carrier pigeons bearing maps; but the birds either froze to death, or, as in one extraordinary instance, flew three thousand miles — all the way back to the owner's pigeon loft in England.

Back in England, Lady Franklin was the heroine who dominated the arctic drama. Despite her denials that she shrank from publicity, Jane appears to have enjoyed playing her centre-stage role as the English Penelope. Wherever she went, as Jane phrased it, "my name procured me instant attention and civility."

She was quite aware that she embodied the element of romantic chivalry in the man-hunt, and she used every technique possible to focus public attention on what she called her "holy cause." She was a masterful manipulator of the newly emerging popular press (daguerreotypes of Franklin and his officers had appeared in the *Illustrated London News*) and she hectored every publication from *Blackwood's Edinburgh Magazine* to Charles Dickens's *Household Words* with anonymous articles and letters signed, ironically, "Impartiality."

She took up lodgings at 60 Park Mall in London and she assaulted the nearby Admiralty with such a barrage of demands that admirals quailed and called her strategic headquarters the Battery. She induced Parliament to post rewards of up to twenty thousand pounds for information relating to the lost ships and offered a private prize of three thousand pounds. She financed her own flotilla of three relief ships. She dispatched exhorting letters as well to Czar Nicholas I of Russia, Emperor Napoleon III of France, British Prime Minister Lord Palmerston and United States President Zachary Taylor.

There were a few cynics. "Is Franklin the only man lost," asked Thoreau in *Walden*, "that his wife should be so earnest to find him?" The Admiralty's sea parties, mocked Dr. Richard King, who had helped explore the Back River overland to the Arctic, would play theatricals "and other merryandrew tricks that the officers may make a book out of the sterility around them."

The books poured out. But people bought them and paid homage to Jane. At her suggestion, prayers for those serving in the Arctic were offered in sixty churches throughout England. Crowds gazed with awe at polar panoramas exhibited in Brighton and Vauxhall Gardens. Their sympathy was stirred by news reports of unanswered letters that she continually sent off on rescue ships: "I live in you, my own dearest—I pray for you at all hours. . . ."

The British public responded characteristically with subscriptions to her rescue funds, with crank suggestions, and with bad verse. A popular ballad hawked in the streets of London was entitled *Lady Franklin's Lament*:

*In Baffin's Land where the whale-fish blows,*
*Is the fate of Franklin—no one knows.*
*Ten thousand pounds would I freely give,*
*To learn that my husband still did live.*

*And to bring him back to a land of life,*
*Where once again I would be his wife. . .*
*I would give all the wealth I'ere shall have,*
*But I think, alas, he has found a grave.*

Some of the proposals made to her were freakish. One crackpot wanted to supply an invention for asphyxiating polar bears when in close embrace. Another eccentric suggested: "Why not employ picked men from convicted criminals?" Others told of having located the missing ships in a dream, and volunteered to pursue their vision. "My signal," wrote one channel skipper, who required twenty able-bodied seamen for his little rescue tug, would be, "Lady Franklin expects that every man will do his duty."

"You would be amused to read the varied communications she receives from almost all parts of the world," noted Sophia Cracroft, Jane's spinster niece, devoted confidante, and long-suffering traveling companion. "They embrace every form of insanity, delusion, spiritual agency, and even necromancy."

Jane did not dismiss occult science. She had once had the bumps

71

on her head read by a phrenologist, a swami named Deville. She thought his character analysis was fairly exact. He said she was combative, rarely at a loss for words, loved approbation, was inclined to destructiveness and self-esteem; and Deville had predicted, "Hope is large—that's good—that will be of use to you."

Now Jane consulted a clairvoyant, the celebrated Ellen Dawson of Grosvenor Square. The spiritualist peered into her crystal ball and saw a short, stout, elderly gentleman, with such a nice face, looking very happy and comfortable in a ship cabin containing portraits of Queen Victoria and Lady Franklin. Regrettably a cloud misted over his geographical location; but Jane was reassured by the medium, "Make your mind easy, all is well, all is quite right."

Jane evidently took to heart a more startling case of supernatural guidance. Captain William Coppin of Londonderry informed her of the ghostly revelation of his four-year-old daughter, Weasy. It seems that little Weasy, after dying of gastric fever, had appeared before the family in a blue wraith form. Asked about the whereabouts of Franklin, the ghost had projected on the living room floor a "complete arctic scene, showing two ships surrounded with ice and almost covered with snow, including a channel that led to the ships." Then, in round spectral letters three inches high, these words were scrawled on the wall, "*Erebus* and *Terror*. Sir John Franklin, Lancaster Sound, Prince Regent Inlet, Point Victory, Victoria Channel."

That vision proved to be an eerily accurate forecast, and Jane was inclined to put faith in it. She had always believed that her dutiful husband would follow naval orders. After entering Lancaster Sound, he would turn eventually southwestward either down Prince Regent Inlet or another south-trending alleyway. As it turned out, the two ships had indeed drifted southward as far as the ice-choked channel of Victoria Strait, due northwest of the Arctic mouth of the Back River. And survivors did, in fact, land near Victory Point—the spot on the west coast of King William Island where James Clark Ross had once erected a six-foot explorer's cairn.

Now, almost twenty years later, Sir James Clark Ross and the other old arctic hands of the Admiralty bullheadedly insisted on probing every possible spot but that one. Jane locked horns with them. She was bold enough to suggest that she personally accompany one of the early search parties in a supervisory capacity to make sure it headed in the right direction. The Admiralty's advisory Arctic Council advised her

against it—"without however," she was encouraged to note in her diary, "treating the matter as either ridiculous or absolutely impracticable."

When Sir James Clark Ross apparently failed to heed her advice on his 1848 search expedition, and instead seemed bent on making his own Northwest Passage discovery far northward, Jane's correspondence with him became somewhat cool. Her relations with his uncle, Sir John Ross, became glacial. In 1850 that seventy-three-year-old warhorse had sailed in the private yacht, *Felix,* and strayed up the northwest coast of Greenland. He returned with the fallacious rumor that Franklin's crews had been massacred there by Eskimos. Jane rapped him on the knuckles for bringing back such a horrible report. She wondered sarcastically if she ought to extend "a deep sense of gratitude to Sir John Ross for murdering her husband."

One sometimes has the impression that Jane ruled over the massive invasion of the polar regions like a Victorian schoolmistress. She instructed her favorite pupils to play a chilling game of snakes and ladders in the labyrinth of Canada's Arctic Archipelago. She dared them to climb from one puzzling strait to another. And she alternately flattered and scolded to keep them pressing on into the maze. It was a hazardous game, but she was absolutely determined to win recognition as the wife-widow of the hero who had vanquished the Northwest Passage.

There were four brilliant officers who made major contributions to Arctic exploration, and each helped produce vivid accounts of their expeditions. Jane's attitude to the four varied. One she loved, and one she revered. The remaining two delinquents, because they challenged her status, she publicly caned and expelled from the classroom.

The officer she loved was half her age. He was a twenty-five-year-old French naval lieutenant named Joseph René Bellot. It was understandable that she should have fallen in love with him, for the charmer seems to have endeared himself to everyone he met. He was a romantic who personified the essence of Gallic chivalry and gaiety. Though short of stature, he made many a British female heart flutter with his graceful dancing of the schottische. He had lively black eyes, a wisp of dark beard, full sensitive lips; and he boasted of a prominent nose and poetic eloquence to match the great Cyrano's.

"He talked, laughed, and passionately courted danger like a Frenchman," said a friend. Bellot agreed; but also said of his early military campaigns in East Africa's Madagascar and South America's Rio de la Plata jungles, "The mere sight of my face has been enough sometimes to put a stop to the cries or dry up the tears of a naughty or squalling brat."

*Naval Lieutenant Joseph René Bellot, not content with winning the French Legion of Honor, also won the heart of Jane Franklin. She wept for her beloved "French son" after he drowned seeking her husband in the Arctic. He discovered Bellot Strait.* METROPOLITAN TORONTO LIBRARY BOARD

The son of a poor Rochefort blacksmith, he had won a science scholarship at the French naval college. At eighteen, after being wounded in battle at Madagascar, he had won the knight's cross of the French Legion of Honor. Now, thirsting for what he called honorable fame in a hallowed crusade, the chevalier was eager to win his epaulettes in the Arctic.

In 1851 he brought with him to England a book of Byron's poetry, the two-volume narratives of Franklin's overland Arctic expeditions, and he offered his services free to Her Ladyship. "I will be for you a son, and have the inexhaustible devotedness of a son who is in search of his father," he said. "I bring, instead of polar experience, a boundless ardour. . . . Who would not feel himself filled with a holy ardour at the sight of the labours and mighty exertions of this devoted wife?"

Jane was captivated by the gallant's "charming and original" proposal, and accepted him as "my French son." Besides, she had need of an experienced naval officer to help command her private search ship soon to leave for Lancaster Sound and Prince Regent Inlet. She had acquired a Tom Thumb of a craft, a mere ninety-ton schooner from the Azores fruit trade, and renamed her the *Prince Albert*. The schooner was to have a total complement of eighteen men, largely Scottish Orkney Islanders and Shetland fishermen. A few had arctic experience, the most notable being that faithful able seaman, John Hepburn, now sixty-one, who had accompanied Franklin on his first overland Arctic trek.

Her greatest asset was her nominal captain, a Canadian Scot-Indian half-caste named William Kennedy. Though he knew little of the science of ocean navigation, Kennedy made up for it with his enlightened interest in northern native travel methods. Bellot romanticized him as a backwoods frontiersman, "one of those models from whom James Fenimore Cooper has taken his Pathfinder." Kennedy wasn't quite that, but close to it.

He was a gentle-faced, warm-hearted, ardently religious teetotaller of thirty-seven. As a boy at a Hudson's Bay Company post on the Saskatchewan River, he had been impressed by the piety of the visiting Franklin who in 1819 had taught the lad his ABCs. As an H.B.C. fur trader for eight years in Quebec and subarctic Ungava, the "far away" region of Labrador, he had been impressed still more by what he had learned from Eskimos on the shores of Hudson Strait. He had left the Company, disgusted by the way its fur traders liquored up and exploited aborigines like his Cree Indian mother, Aggathas.

Now Kennedy was prepared to be the first rescuer from an explor-

ing ship to experiment with Eskimo-Indian modes of survival. He intended to teach his crew how to make snowshoes and snowhouses; their clothes would be sealskin; they would try to rely on pemmican and caribou and ptarmigan; and they would travel via four light sledges pulled by a team of five Greenland sledge dogs. (Amusingly, in view of his mixed ancestry, Kennedy compromised by building the sledges in flat-bottomed Indian style and glazing the runners with Scottish oatmeal.)

Lieutenant Bellot got along harmoniously with Captain Kennedy. Both were enthusiasts. At Stromness in Scotland, where they were to embark, Bellot was enchanted to see that Kennedy obligingly flew the French tricolor as well as the Union Jack from the ship. Eager to learn, the Frenchman practiced along with his mentor the art of paddling Kennedy's twenty-foot-long imitation tin kayak.

They had a few minor tiffs. Bellot, a lover of French wine, felt a little dolorous to find that Captain Kennedy had banned all intoxicants from his "cold water" ship. "No spirits, save in the apothecary's shop," Bellot groaned in his diary. "O, Bacchus!... Turn away your eyes, ye vengeful divinities! Spare your faithless child!"

The religious zealot's firm belief in prayers rather than navigational instruments was also a trifle discomfiting. Bellot, who had given up attending Catholic Mass, was amused to note that Lady Franklin had interlarded Kennedy's sailing instructions with religious maxims; obviously "it was the only way of making the reading of the documents attractive for him." Still, Bellot respected Kennedy's sincere piety, though he respected his heart more than his head. The captain clearly relied on his second-in-command to provide the scientific brains of the expedition.

Lady Franklin and her niece, Sophia, came to Stromness in May of 1851 to see the ship off. It was a bitter-sweet farewell. The Scottish seamen sang *The Girls We Left Behind Us*. The *Prince Albert's* "brokenhearted little hand organ" (a gift from Prince Albert himself) ground out *The Garb of Old Gael* and, as a tribute to Bellot, the *Marseillaise*.

"Our parting with our dear little French friend was really painful," wrote Sophia. "He sobbed like a child as he took leave of my Aunt.... We are really *very* fond of him—his sweetness and simplicity and earnestness are most endearing."

In his journal Bellot wrote of Lady Franklin bidding him adieu: " 'Take care of yourself,' was all she could say to me, weeping. Poor

woman! If you could have seen how much the somewhat egotistical desire to make an extraordinary voyage has been succeeded in me by a real ardour and genuine passion for the end we aim at. 'I must supply your mother's place,' you said, as you inquired into the details of my equipment. Well, then, I shall be for you a son.... What human strength can do, I will do."

These tender sentiments were soon replaced by a less sweet sorrow. "Alas! I try in vain to conceal it — I am seasick. O shame! O despair! I look around to see who are the witnesses of my dishonour; fortunately I have none but accomplices.... Oh, the nothingness of human nature! ... A smell of whisky proves to me that not all my shipmates are sick only from the motion of the ship; some of them have been bidding a last farewell to the pleasures of this world before becoming real teetotallers."

With the aid of prayers read to him by Kennedy, he quickly regained his sea legs and *joie de vivre*. The agile-witted French Catholic began to appreciate the seemingly simple Scot Calvinists around him. "I am astonished to hear all the sailors talk to me of Shakespeare; one prefers *Macbeth*, another *Hamlet*. I doubt if Molière is so popular among French sailors."

Kennedy, despite his religious intolerance (this extremist maintained that Turks were doomed to hell) was a congenial shipmate. He hummed the boat chansons of the French Canadian voyageurs and Bellot loved to hear him spin yarns about life on the frontier. Kennedy said he dreamed one day of bringing the gospel to the Indians of *le pays sauvage* — a wish he ultimately fulfilled by becoming a missionary. Meanwhile, as they neared the ice pack off Greenland, Bellot reflected on Kennedy's daily sermons to his crew, "I know no spectacle more suggestive of thought than the sight of those few men singing the praises of the Lord amidst the solitude of the vast ocean."

Bellot asked to be awakened as soon as the first iceberg was sighted, and his "vagabond imagination" was immediately enraptured by what he saw. His journal glows with imagery. The bergs were like giant conch shells, like ripe pomegranates; they loomed like Kremlins and they cleaved through rushing waters like the Cascades of the Place de la Concorde. Their frail vessel glided around them in the moonlight "like the phantom through the windings of a marble labyrinth," and the ice under its shroud of snow was "the Arab in his white burnoos" or a virgin in a pale satin mantle.

"There is more poetry in this than in the burning lava crust of a

*Captain William Kennedy, the Canadian Scot-Cree Indian, experimented with snowshoes, dog sledges and tin kayaks.* COURTESY DR. EDWARD C. SHAW, RED RIVER HOUSE MUSEUM, ST. ANDREWS, MANITOBA

*Shoehorned into a crowded tent at night, the men cheerily sang "Oh! Susanna, Don't You Cry For Me."* METROPOLITAN TORONTO LIBRARY BOARD

volcano," writes Bellot. "What pencil could reproduce the thousand beauties of the sun gilding the mountains of ice that surround us and glisten like a cuirass?"

But the floes began to close upon them like the blades of scissors. Despite sawing and gunpowder blasts, they were cradled for weeks in the pack. Bellot comes to realize that the bergs, "for which I panted so long at the period of my feverish admiration, are an incessant menace suspended over our heads." After twelve hours of labor, they advanced just one mile. In his impotent rage he thinks of legendary Greek heroes.

"Never did I so well understand the defiance of Ajax, sublime in its exaggeration of human pride. It is like Sisyphus, seeing his stone roll down the mountain after he has succeeded with great toil in rolling it up. . . . Nature no longer feels her heart beat in the slumber of the north; she is like the pitiless machinery that cuts off the arm caught between the cogs of the wheels."

With a marvelous freshness of simile, Bellot comes to appreciate, too, the qualities of the Eskimos he met on both shores of Baffin Bay. In their fairy kayaks, they are like a new species of centaur, "half man, half boat"; their grisly-locked wives, sewing sealskins in snowhouses, appear at first sight like Macbethian witches. With their frightful teeth, they seem like a fish-eating race of lepers. But one man showed Bellot the marks of his own teeth on his arm. The Eskimo explained that his cherished son had died last winter, and the tooth bites were an expression of his grief.

"That poor savage, whom a moment before I looked on as a puppet, a thing little more amusing than a learned dog, at once became magnified in my eyes, and I was touched with the most profound respect at the aspect of a mourning father," reflects Bellot. "I ponder all the evening over this redemption of character by paternal love."

To make amends for his former condescending attitude, Bellot had the ship carpenter make a wooden leg for an unfortunate crippled Eskimo; and he acknowledged that, except for the uses of wood and iron, and for Christianity, the Eskimos were in many ways superior to the white men. "I could not, without emotion," he says, "see good Captain Kennedy praying to God to let the rays of His goodness fall on these poor heathens, who knew not what we were doing when we prayed for them, and came and sang at the hatchway during the evening hymn."

The technological superiority of the Eskimos became evident that winter when the travelling band left the ship berthed at Batty Bay on

east Somerset Island and tried adopting Eskimo devices on treks down Prince Regent Inlet. Bellot thought it a very cunning ruse to stalk seals by crawling over the ice on elbows as if on flippers; but, *ma foi!*, it was terrible, when you took a ducking in icy waters. Driving a dog team through pea-soup fogs and across snow-crusted crevasses was trickier than it first seemed. On one occasion, team and sledge tumbled into an abyss, and all "that could be seen was some six inches of Monsieur Bellot's heels above the surface of the snow." Slitted Eskimo goggles worked admirably; but an experiment with white man's gutta-percha rubber noses failed miserably. As Bellot remarked, with a *Dieu merci!*, "One man, gifted with perhaps too prominent a nose, complains of frostbite."

It took him up to three hours to construct a crumbly snowhouse. "An Esquimau would smile, perhaps, at the sight of our *chefs-d' oeuvre*; but, as they shelter us sufficiently, that is all we can desire." He became a more proficient igloo snow mason after undergoing a hilarious "Black hole of Calcutta" experience in which thirteen snowshoers tried to shoe-horn themselves for the night into a tent intended for six campers. Kennedy described their dilemma with much levity:

"A London omnibus, on a racing day after five o'clock, was the only parallel I could think of.... It was arranged that we should sit down six in a row, on each side, which would leave us about three feet clear to stretch our legs. Mr. Bellot, who formed the thirteenth, being the most compact and *stowable* of the party, agreed to squeeze in underneath them. He stipulated only for a clear foot square for his head alongside the tea kettle.

"Being unprovided with a candlestick, it was arranged that each of us should hold the candle in his hand for a quarter of an hour and then pass it to his neighbour. Thus by the aid of our flickering taper, through the thick steam of the boiling kettle, we had just enough light to prevent us putting our tea into our neighbour's mouth instead of our own."

They passed the hours singing "Oh! Susanna, Don't You Cry for Me" and whaling ditties ending with a chorus of "Cheerilie, ah!" and "Cheeri-lie!" The choruses were interrupted, says Kennedy, with Bellot, smothering under the weight of twenty-four legs, crying out to the six-foot-tall carpenter, "Kenneth, you monster! Take that clumsy foot of yours off my stomach, will you?" Whereupon the carpenter, in his eagerness to comply, apparently drove his foot into poor Bellot's eye. "And so, passing the song and joke around, Mr. Bellot occasionally making a sudden desperate effort to get up, and settling down again in

despair—with a long 'blow' like a grampus—we make a night of it."

It was not, of course, all horseplay. Bellot helped lead a tortuous dog sled expedition from Batty Bay to Fury Beach. This was the shipwreck beach on the west side of Prince Regent Inlet where Sir John Ross's castaways had spent such a melancholy winter almost two decades before. Bellot's seemingly rough travel companions were most considerate on the journey.

"The first night, when I was half asleep," he says, "I saw them, one after another, come and wrap me up and make sure that my feet were not frozen. A buffalo robe stretched on the snow, another over our wet clothes, and our boots for pillows, enabled me to enjoy the soundest sleep."

But soon their eyelashes were glued together in the thirty-below-zero chill, and the sharp spicula of drifting snow left their faces puffed and scarred as if by blows of the fist, and their frostbitten skin peeled off in flakes as large as halfpence. Sometimes they had to axe steps out of icy mountain slopes polished as hard as the whitest marble. Sometimes they got lost, and groping their way through semitransparent mists and dazzling snow mirages, they were so despairing that they repeated prayers as they stumbled along. Sometimes they tried to dry their frozen boots under their armpits as they slept beneath iron-hard blankets in amateurishly constructed igloos.

"A little hole, no bigger in diameter than the barrel of a quill," Bellot marveled, "often becomes a funnel for the admission of a bushel of snow when it blows or drifts."

Their incessant thirst was the worst hardship. "It is impossible to get water otherwise than by melting snow," the scientific-minded Frenchman observed. "This is a fact of which people unacquainted with these barbarous regions have no notion. They imagine that the snow is as easy to swallow as in our comparatively mild winters. The enormous difference of temperature between the stomach intestines and the snow, or the outer air, causes a sort of suffocation cramps, or rather a sensation of intolerable burning."

All of them were stricken with little blackish spots on their legs which signified scurvy. Kennedy was crippled worst of all, and his arthritic pains were agonizing. Yet it was wonderful, remarked Bellot, to watch his rheumatic captain persist in stalking caribou in Indian fashion: gun fixed to his head to give the impression of antlers, crawling on all fours across the snow crust. But the treeless high Arctic was not

Kennedy's customary bush country, and yapping sled dogs kept scaring off the prey, and the hunting was poor.

Their rations grew scanty, and despite their best intentions, the seamen had difficulty digesting Eskimo fare. Bellot personally found frozen uncooked ptarmigan and arctic fox pies a gustatory delight, almost the equal of *perdrix rôti*; but the others of his caravan grimaced and thought the bill of fare as unpalatable as dead alley cats.

On their last march the semi-starved travelers were reduced to a daily meal of half a pound of pemmican and a pint of tea. Bellot found himself dreaming of ham and wine and freshly baked bread; and a food cache near Fury Beach began to loom in his imagination as a Parisian hotel signboard bearing the inscription: "*Table d' hôte and board.*" They reached the cache in mid-May, and tossing aside the rules of prudence and sobriety, Bellot notes: "We spend three days in eating, drinking, and sleeping; drinking, sleeping, and eating; sleeping, eating, and drinking."

Rarely did Bellot lose his Gallic insouciance. "Inwardly I was afraid, on two several occasions, that my courage would fail," he confided to his diary. "But I kept these momentary conflicts to my own breast, and no one can say that a French officer gave way when others stood firm." He roused his men with three hurrahs in John Bull fashion, and thus always maintained esprit de corps. In his loyalty to the absent Kennedy on one trek, he even took to leading his caravan in Calvinist hymns and worship.

"I could not forbear smiling at the numerous contrasts which distinguish my present life," he mused. "I am many thousand miles distant from my country, commanding men of a foreign nation. An officer of a military marine service, I am among men bound solely by a civil engagement. A Catholic, I endeavour to keep alive in their minds a different religion in which they have been educated, and the precepts of which I deliver to them in a tongue which is not my own. Nevertheless, I cannot complain . . . for there is not one of them who does not regard me as a countryman, and obey me as if I were really so."

The French chevalier justly felt that he had won his arctic epaulettes. After an absence of sixteen months, their gallant little crew returned intact to England. They had covered some eleven hundred miles with Eskimo dog team—which they had left behind for another Arctic search party that might follow their precept of using these "camels of the northern deserts." The high point of their expedition had

been the discovery of Bellot Strait. This was the mile-wide corridor that separates Somerset Island from Boothia Peninsula. It links Prince Regent Inlet with Peel Sound—the southward alleyway down which Franklin's expedition doubtless sailed en route to the Northwest Passage.

Lady Franklin sent Bellot many tender letters while he was temporarily recuperating in France. "Come quickly and see if we shall not again welcome you as a hero and a most beloved friend—to me you are more," wrote Jane. "Mr. Kennedy was moved almost to tears at your letter to him. His heart is in his mouth whenever he speaks of you. Come to me again, my dear, and come often. Your very affectionate Jane Franklin."

Jane wanted him to take command of a fresh expedition by way of Bering Strait. Captain Kennedy had been so impressed by Bellot's scientific attainments that he was willing to serve as the French explorer's second-in-command. Bellot gracefully declined. He felt that Jane might thus be reproached by her countrymen for giving command to a foreigner. "I dare say you have read in my very heart," he wrote to Jane, "and however wrong my notions of things may be, they are sure to be redeemed by a boundless feeling of respectful affection for your Ladyship."

Bellot enlisted instead as an ordinary lieutenant aboard another British rescue ship seeking Franklin near the entrance of Lancaster Sound. In August of 1853 he volunteered to carry dispatches to the incompetent commander of the naval relief armada, Sir Edward Belcher.

With two other sailors, Bellot found himself marooned on a drifting ice floe. With the skill of an experienced arctic mason, he taught his companions how to build an Eskimo snowhouse. Then he tied up his books of poetry in a bundle and picked up his walking stick, and blithely ignoring a gusting gale, he said, "If God protects us, not a hair of our heads will fall to the ground." The last his shipmates saw of him was his walking stick floating near the ice floe, and they knew that Lieutenant Joseph René Bellot, at the age of twenty-seven, had drowned in the polar sea.

Jane Franklin helped raise funds for his red granite monument on the right bank of the Thames at Greenwich, and she grieved, "Who in this country could love him as I did, or owe him half so much?" And in the high Arctic, it is recorded, the Eskimos cried, "Poor Bellot! Poor Bellot!" and they wept.

*Bellot's death by drowning, while marooned on an ice floe with two sailors, was sketched melodramatically.*

*Robert McClure, ambitious and hard as narwhal horn, delineated an impassable, ice-blocked Northwest Passage.* NATIONAL PORTRAIT GALLERY, LONDON

*McClure, looking bizarre in arctic attire.* METROPOLITAN TORONTO LIBRARY BOARD

Before his death Bellot had remarked in his journal that British sea-men seemed a curious race: "They call want of judgment the admirable temerity of the man who perseveres in risking his life in a manner almost certain." Such a man was a daring Irish officer, Lieutenant Robert John Le Mesurier McClure—one of the two explorers with whom Jane clashed.

McClure (sometimes spelled M'Clure) was the sort of man who sparks controversy. His published journal, *The Discovery of the Northwest Passage*, was discreetly edited for him (laundered might be a better word) by a brother officer and fellow Irishman named Sherard Osborn. According to Osborn, McClure was a Victorian paragon who upheld the Royal Navy verities. "With a granite-like view of duty," Osborn lauded him, the hero was "stern, cool, bold in all perils, severe as a dis-ciplinarian, self-reliant, yet modest as became an officer."

This panegyric is open to question. Osborn, a prolific polar jour-nalist, confessed elsewhere that he himself was prone to pile on Irish blarney or "ginger" to make his popularized books sell. Other contem-poraries held a more critical view of McClure's personality. They felt he was driven by an almost ungovernable ambition. He was iron-nerved, yes, but the glory-seeker was more ruthlessly steeled in his resolve to find the Northwest Passage than to discover the fate of Franklin.

When he enters our story in 1850, McClure's ambitious drive for independent fame had long been thwarted by a slow rise in the ranks. His father had been an Irish army captain who had died before Mc-Clure was half a year old; his mother was the devout daughter of the rector at Wexford, Ireland. He had been educated at Eton and Sandhurst and had entered the Royal Navy at seventeen. But he had served in a subordinate rank on two previous Arctic voyages.

Now, aged forty-three, he was given the subsidiary captaincy of the four-hundred-ton, copper-bottomed H.M.S. *Investigator*. She was one of two ships under the leadership of Commander Richard Collinson or-dered to find Franklin via the circuitous route of Cape Horn and Bering Strait. Collinson, like so many polar explorers a clergyman's son, seems to have been a Captain Bligh of a martinet; he was described by his lieutenant as "a lean, spare, withered-looking man with a vinegar coun-tenance."

McClure was more complex than that. His portrait painted about that time suggests a character in conflict. We see an erect, ramrod-straight figure in arctic explorer's jacket, gun strung over his back and

telescope under arm. He has set lips, thinning red hair, and an eaglelike countenance. One feels he is hard as narwhal horn. Two elements in the portrait, however, seem in striking contradiction. His ungloved left fist may be clenched in grim determination; but his blue eyes appear to convey a surprising softness, almost the bathos of Irish sentimentality.

That personality split was revealed in the private memoirs of McClure's hired interpreter and sole confidant on the four-year expedition. The friendship between Johann August Miertsching and McClure was an odd one, for no two men could be more unlike. Miertsching was a thirty-three-year-old German pietist from Saxony, a burning-eyed, black-haired Moravian missionary, who had spent his early manhood among the Eskimos at Okak in Labrador. Though he had a rugged constitution and was a skilled caribou hunter, he was a gentle man. He played religious hymns on the guitar, enjoyed collecting arctic butterflies, and, like Captain William Kennedy, was a zealous saver of Eskimo souls. Miertsching's memoirs present a deeply moving picture of the austerely religious evangelist wrestling with the devil to save the soul of his fanatically ambitious skipper.

The devil obviously won the first round. McClure gave the slip to Commander Collinson's ship in the Pacific; he took a dangerous shortcut via the foggy Aleutian Islands; and he arrived at the prearranged rendezvous point off Alaska a fortnight in advance of his lagging senior officer. There the splendid prospect of possibly winning the Passage prize alone proved overly tempting to McClure. But before he could make his solitary dash up Bering Strait, the impetuous junior officer encountered opposition. He had an embarrassing meeting with *another* Admiralty vessel—the search supply ship H.M.S. *Herald.* Her captain was Henry Kellett, an Irish sea dog from Tipperary, who was an old friend of Captain Collinson. Captain Kellett would not swallow Lieutenant McClure's bluff that Collinson's flagship had gone on ahead, and so he gave chase to the *Investigator.*

"Had you not better wait forty-eight hours?" Captain Kellett had the *Herald's* sublieutenant, Bedford Clapperton Pim, hoist the signal.

"Important duty," McClure signaled back, speeding ahead. "Cannot, on my own responsibility."

Miertsching had a sneaking admiration of his "impatient" captain's audacity. He was like Nelson of old, who raised a telescope to his blind eye at an admiral's signal to retire from action. Yet the missionary grieved sorely over the Irishman's harsh treatment of his crew of sixty-four men. In his haste to steal a march on Collinson, McClure had

flayed the bare backs of his mariners with as many as four dozen lashes of the cat-o'-nine tails and kept putting his quarrelsome officers under arrest.

"Ach!" sorrowed the evangelist. "The fury of the captain was terrible, positively inhuman."

Not that the rabble of a crew was much better, in the missionary's view. They were drunken, profane sinners. "I feel," he lamented, "as if my lot had been cast among half a hundred devils." Five rowdy sailors had contracted venereal disease at Honolulu. And with the Eskimo women of Alaska, says Miertsching, the highest-ranking officers behaved so shamelessly "that here one will soon have an Anglo-Eskimo colony."

Miertsching had a constant struggle trying to win McClure back to the charitable ways of his devout Irish mother. The relationship between the two men was a tenuous one. Miertsching seems to have been regarded as a sour, narrow bigot by most of the sailors. And for some reason, perhaps because he felt aloof and lonely among his officers, or perhaps because he felt the need of a moral conscience, McClure took a fancy to the company of the missionary. He often invited Miertsching into his cabin to discuss religion and seemed to enjoy hearing him play on the guitar the hymn, *How Great a Bliss to Be a Sheep of Jesus.*

"The captain shows me unvarying kindness," the evangelist rejoiced in his diary. "Daily our friendship grows warmer."

But the captain was a moody man and his friendship blew hot and blew cold. One day Miertsching began distributing Moravian Brotherhood religious tracts to the crew. "The captain laughed heartily and gave it as his opinion that his people were not such simple folk as my Eskimos," Miertsching recorded. "He asserted that on a ship at sea no one could hold that form of Christianity which is observed on land. At sea a man must have spirit and not hang his head."

The evangelist replied fervently. "I told him I would gladly call myself and really *be* a Christian, and yet I held my head every whit as high as he."

McClure shrugged. "You are not yet a true seaman or you would have other views," he said. "You should have given the leaflets to lost women, who would have given you more thanks than my sailors."

The sedate Moravian soon had to ward off lost Jezebels himself. At the Arctic mouth of the Mackenzie River, near the present Eskimo settlement of Tuktoyaktuk, apparently McClure's mariners indulged in more than nose rubs. "Charming young ladies, with brightest of eyes

and whitest of teeth" greeted them. The Eskimo sirens, according to McClure's journal, proved that "Byron's theory concerning cold climates and chastity is not always supported by fact."

At first McClure held the conventional patronizing attitude toward the Eskimos. He was loftily amused by what he called their thievish and knavish propensities. With one hand they asked for gifts and with the other hand they picked your pocket. But Miertsching's genuine love for the natives seems to have influenced the impulsive Irishman for, at another Eskimo village later, the missionary was able to describe a delightful scene.

"Captain McClure, his heart moved at the thought of quitting these simple folk," writes Miertsching, "turned back, and, noticing a young mother poorly dressed with her child inside her jacket, took off his downy scarf of red wool and ran to throw it over her shoulders. Perplexed and troubled, the young woman looked around as if seeking something, then took her child, kissed it repeatedly, and offered it to Captain McClure. When I had made her understand that the captain was making her a gift—a wholly gratuitous gift—she began to kiss her child anew with a rapturous expression which seemed to say, 'Then I may keep you too!' "

Along the Arctic coastline, the most hostile of Eskimos threw down their arms and embraced Miertsching as a brother as soon as they saw him running toward them in his Eskimo tunic and crying out Labrador words of friendship. One village patriarch begged the missionary to live with them. As an inducement, he offered a sledge and dogs, and when that bribe didn't work, he presented his sixteen-year-old daughter with the words, *Takka unna!*—"Take her!" Though Miertsching found her "a girl of very lovely appearance," he regretted that he had to turn down the alluring offer. His *angajuga*, or "leader," was ordering him back to their floating island of a ship.

Angajuga McClure was more interested in learning from the natives' scrawled maps what he would find if he tried to penetrate the main ice pack to the north-east. They replied with dread it was the "Land of the White Bear" and they urged him to stay away from that deathtrap of eternal ice.

Undeterred, McClure set sail into unknown waters. His crew blasted a path through "coachwheeling" fifty-ton floes. Everywhere in front of them were those "hedgerows of Arctic landscape"—stupendous

*Johann August Miertsching, the Moravian missionary from Labrador, wrestled for McClure's soul aboard the Investigator.* COURTESY NIELS JANNASCH

*Sunday prayers and hymns helped solace ice-wracked and scurvy-sick seamen.* NATIONAL MARITIME MUSEUM, GREENWICH

pileups of emerald green and pearly blue ice hummocks.

At length the *Investigator* groped part way up newly discovered Prince of Wales Strait. This was the berg-studded neck of water that separates vast Banks Island to the north and even vaster Victoria Island to the south. Balked by the unyielding ice of Prince of Wales Strait (which was not penetrated by a vessel until the next century) McClure pushed on overland by man-hauled sledge. In the early dawn of October 27, 1850, McClure climbed a limestone cliff on Banks Island. He peered through his telescope across the "great hills and dales of blue crystalline sea ice" of the strait that was to bear his name. Less than thirty nautical miles away he could detect the nearest point of Melville Island. Less than two hundred miles away was the Winter Harbour of Melville Island—the place where Sir William Edward Parry had wintered three decades ago in 1819/20.

"Can it be that this water," wrote McClure in his private log, "shall prove to be the long-sought Northwest Passage? Can it be that so humble a creature as I am will be permitted to perform what has baffled the talented and wise for hundreds of years?"

It was a Pyrrhic victory. The *Investigator* was immobilized for three awful winters pinned close to the shores of Banks Island. The second and third winters were spent locked in a providential Bay of God's Mercy (since shortened to Mercy Bay) on the northwest end of Banks Island. Melville Island was so heartbreakingly near. Yet all the gunpowder blasting in the world would not enable the ship to navigate the hellish floes that perpetually jam what is now called M'Clure Strait. Even the *Manhattan* in the next century could not ram through those blockbusters of ice.

"Ice, captain," reported McClure's mate from the crow's nest. "Nothing but ice. As far as the eye can reach, I do not see a spoonful of water."

The captain responded with alternate rages and tears of frustration. In April of 1852, he harnessed six men to a sledge and they tramped the some one hundred and sixty miles across M'Clure Strait to Parry's Winter Harbour. They hoped to find a rescue ship at Melville Island sent from nearby Dealy Islet. But nobody was there. After leaving a note in a sandstone cairn , they trudged mournfully back to the beset ship, and Miertsching tells us his captain "wept like a child."

The missionary attempted to cheer him up with Easter meditations, by cobbling cork-soled boots for him, and presenting him with gift bunches of white violets, golden anemones and purple-blossomed sax-

ifrage. "I spend hours and hours with my dear captain," the evangelist wrote. "We read; we talk; every day strengthens our mutual understanding. Oh! How friendship adds charm to life! God be thanked for this pleasant relationship."

But the captain's moods of despondency deepened. One day he summoned Miertsching to his cabin and pointed to two verses in the Bible.

"See how Holy Writ mocks me?" cried McClure bitterly. "In this crisis and extremity, when all our lives are trembling in the balance, I opened the Bible to find words of comfort. And thus it answered me in Psalm 34 — in flat contradiction to our present situation: 'O magnify the Lord with me and let us exalt His name together. I sought the Lord and He heard me and delivered me from all my fears.' "

The winter of 1852/53 was beyond his worst fears, and McClure seems to have verged close on madness. He cut down the fuel for the ship's stoves, and the crew's cabins were heated with glowing-hot cannonballs. He reduced to two-thirds the daily rations of the sailors — though not of the officers — and watched his men rake through the previous winter's garbage heap for refuse. Miertsching says that his dear captain was sorely grieved to see his emaciated mariners eat uncooked lemmings and wolves and caribou hides; yet one wonders at McClure's needlessly brutal naval discipline. When three starved sailors were caught stealing the food of the ship's mascot dog, Mongo, McClure punished the trio of poor wretches with a cat-o'-nine-tails lashing.

When McClure ordered the daily rations of the mariners cut down to half the usual portions, it was too much for the ship surgeon, Dr. Alexander Armstrong. Along with a delegation of crew members, the physician urged the captain not to take that stern measure. Twenty-one men were hospitalized with scurvy, one with blackened teeth falling out. Two men had gone insane, one berserk lunatic raving that he intended to kill the captain. Others, with frostbitten toes amputated as a result of hauling sledges, were in such a weakened state that when they tried to hunt on the ice for game their arms broke "like glass." McClure refused to accede to their pleadings. In his journal Dr. Armstrong, who seems to have hated McClure's guts, made a notation about the captain's heartlessness. Bay of God's Mercy ought to have been so named, he wrote, from the "fact that it would have been *a mercy had we never entered it.*"

But the cruellest blow was yet to come. Navigating the Northwest Passage with his yet-to-be liberated ship had become a mania for Mc-

Clure. So he issued orders in the spring of 1853 that he and the thirty healthiest men would remain in the *Navigator* for another winter and then try to bash through the ice of M'Clure Strait. The other "weakly hands" would have to run the risk of escaping via two sledge-hauling parties. One group of cripples would travel east toward Lancaster Sound; the other group would attempt reaching the Hudson's Bay Company posts hundreds of miles southward of the mouth of the Mackenzie River.

Dr. Armstrong demurred vehemently that the cripples would die en route. "It had no result," he said of McClure's stubborn rebuff.

Miertsching, picked to go with the Mackenzie River party, had gloomy visions of his doomed companions and himself perishing as corpse prey for wolves. Yet he felt sympathetic toward McClure; for in his own quirky way, the captain was no longer a fallen Christian, but had returned to the fold of the Lord. The evangelist wrote:

"After dinner today the captain and I took a walk together and spoke with regret of our coming separation. 'If you get to England,' said he, taking me affectionately by the hand, 'and if you hear no more of Captain McClure and his men, you may imagine that his body lies somewhere wrapped in the good fur coat which you were kind enough to give him, enjoying a long and tranquil sleep until awakened on the day of Resurrection by the Redeemer in Whom is all my hope and trust.' "

On April 6, 1853, while the two parties of cripples were preparing to set out, the Redeemer played a merciful trick in His Bay of Mercy. One of the scurvy-sick seamen had died the day before; and McClure was pacing the beach, wondering where the poor fellow might be buried in the frozen tundra. Suddenly McClure saw a stranger approach in advance of a rescue sledge party. The man's face was tanned raven-black by the sun and his voice screamed a greeting in the wind like one of those rapacious birds.

"In God's name," stammered McClure. "Who are you?"

"I'm Lieutenant Pim, late of the *Herald*, now of the *Resolute*," said the beaming rescuer. "Captain Kellett is in her at Dealy Island."

By miraculous coincidence, the two sea dogs, who had tried to halt McClure at the Bering Strait gateway three years previously, had gone almost around the world to relieve him. While his rescue party fed the near-starved crew with bacon and cocoa, Lieutenant Bedford Clapperton Pim recounted the chain of circumstances. He told how Captain Henry Kellett was aboard one of five newly dispatched search ships

scouring the Parry Channel; how McClure's forlorn note had been accidentally found in the sandstone cairn at Winter Harbour; and how Kellett was now anxiously awaiting word in the good ship *Resolute* anchored off Melville Island at the little islet of Dealy.

McClure sledged back with Pim the some one hundred and eighty miles to the *Resolute*. "You can imagine," said Captain Kellett, "my delight in shaking hands with him."

But Kellett was a little taken aback at his fellow Irishman's new line of blarney. The inexorable McClure still would not surrender his obsession. No matter what the risk or sacrifice, he clung tenaciously to his *idée fixe* of sailing his salvaged ship through the Northwest Passage to Lancaster Sound.

Kellett reluctantly agreed on two conditions: if the *Resolute*'s impartial physician and McClure's Dr. Armstrong found the physical condition of the "Investigators" satisfactory; and if twenty of his crew members volunteered to stick by McClure and not abandon his ship.

The medical survey verified the wisdom of Kellett's caution. *None* of the crew was free from the taint of debilitating scurvy, and *two* more had died of the disease. Yet in the face of these stark facts, McClure insisted on asking for volunteers. Only *four* seamen, together with the five officers, stepped forward.

Dr. Armstrong informs us of the unpleasant detail that McClure spitefully continued to keep his mariners aboard ship deprived on short rations until the end of May. And on June 2, as the cripples prepared to abandon the *Investigator*, the captain ill-humoredly mustered all hands on deck for the last time. "A few words—*not complimentary*—were addressed to the men, and all were piped to take their respective places on the ice."

Miertsching tells us that the march across M'Clure Strait to Melville Island was more like a totter of halt and lame scarecrows out of a painting by Hieronymus Bosch. Snow-blind, often holding onto each other for support, "we had to draw the sledges while crawling on our hands and knees."

Yet the trek was not without its elements of gallows-humor. Miertsching painted this somewhat macabre scene:

"It often happens that the beard of a sleeper freezes to his woollen sleeping bag because in the bitter cold his breath congeals into ice; and, because he cannot set out on the march with a sleeping bag hanging from his chin, he must submit to a process of liberation. . . . The process is this: The man's tent mates sit close around him with their short tobac-

co pipes well ignited, and by this means finally succeed in separating the man from his bed. This is a genuine vapour cure; for the smoke from the six to eight pipes under his nose brings him to the verge of suffocation."

A second element of comedy was introduced by the self-styled Commander-in-Chief of the Arctic Squadron searching the Parry Channel. The commodore of the five rescue ships was Sir Edward Belcher, a sort of Admiral Blimp of the Royal Navy. His brother officers pithily described him as an "old tartar," a "self-trumpeter" and a "ninny." His two-volume polar book, extravagantly titled *The Last of the Arctic Voyages*, indicates that they were not far off the mark.

Belcher, a stout, Halifax-born naval surveyor, had delusions of being a fiction writer. He was the author of an unsuccessful three-volume tome, *Horatio Howard Brenton: A Novel of Navy Life*. Now the inexperienced arctic navigator saw visions and claimed that he had witnessed a polar bear's nest. He maintained that he was an infallible weather prophet. He boasted that he had the faculty of predicting impending accidents—though he somehow did not anticipate blundering his ships into the heaviest ice. His excuse was that "too many cooks spoil the broth," meaning he refused to pay heed to his skilled ice pilots.

Sir Edward made himself thoroughly unpopular. He arrested several of his officers; and he had himself pulled on a so-called Queen's Coach sled by twelve of Her Majesty's footmen. His footmen, by apparent accident, immersed him in an ice puddle. "It might have been an intentional interpretation of my title, Commander of the Bath," fumed Sir Edward, "but it was beyond joke."

The principal accomplishment of his armada's disastrous blitz of the Parry Channel was the rescue of McClure's crew. That rescue was botched up, too. The luckless crew of the abandoned *Investigator* had to spend a fourth winter squeezed into one of Belcher's ships. Then, in the spring of 1854, Belcher inexplicably decided to abandon four of his ships and march everyone across the ice and squash them into the overcrowded *North Star*. If McClure was an extremist about salvaging a ship, Belcher was clearly an extremist about scrapping them.

Even the gentle-mannered Miertsching was provoked into sniping at the fatuous Belcher. Among Belcher's belongings being stowed on the cramped *North Star* was a big chest marked "nautical instruments." The chest was broken while being hoisted aboard, Miertsching remarks indignantly; it had to be opened and the "instruments" which it contained were found to be three dozen bottles of *Franzbrandwein*.

Two transport ships managed to arrive in time to relieve the nearly

three hundred seamen crowded into the *North Star*. "We greeted them with great unspeakable joy," wrote Miertsching. "Our worthy Captain McClure, with whom I stood on the ship's poop, could not restrain his tears; gratitude overwhelmed him at being thus set free after years of imprisonment in the ice."

And so, despite the death of a total of five crew members from the *Investigator*, the missionary gave forgiveness to his sometimes erratic and ruthless captain. They had, after all, both shared in glory. Miertsching recalled how he felt when he had trudged across the ice of M'Clure Strait: "There I stood on Melville Island, and, all starved and wretched as I was, I could not suppress the proud thought that here in this polar region, I was the only Wend from Germany, and that I had a share in the Northwest Passage, sought for three hundred years, and now discovered by us."

On their return to England, Miertsching suffered an ignominious fate. The leaders of the Moravian Society rewarded the missionary by dispatching him, not to his beloved flock of Eskimos in Labrador, but to South Africa, there to practice his hard-earned polar knowledge among the Hottentots.

McClure, for his part, grasped most of the kudos he so ambitiously sought. He won a parliamentary prize of ten thousand pounds, a knighthood, and gold medals from the British and French geographical societies. The one thing he did not win was the indisputable glory of having girdled the two oceans by ship.

Lady Franklin denied him that honor. "It would ill become me," she wrote icily to the Admiralty, "to question the claims of Captain McClure." But that enterprising officer had discovered *a* northwest passage, and he had ignored the fate and contributions of the missing Franklin expedition.

"What I presume to claim, for those who can urge nothing for themselves, is the first discovery of *the* navigable Passage," asserted Jane. "My Lords, I cannot but feel there will be a stain on the page of the Naval Annals of England when these two events—the discovery of the Northwest Passage and the abandonment of Franklin and his companions—are recorded in indissoluble association."

The invincible woman would simply not give up. Two sledge-explorers, Dr. John Rae and Francis Leopold McClintock, then stepped into the limelight and contributed a touch of greatness to the unfolding drama of the Arctic man-hunt.

# Chapter 4

# The Sledge Supermen

*Whither sail you, Sir John Franklin?*
*Cried an Esquimaux in Baffin's Bay;*
*To know if between the land and the Pole,*
*I may find a broad sea-way.*

*Come down, if you would journey there,*
*The little Esquimaux said;*
*And change your cloth for fur clothing,*
*Your vessels for a sled.*

*But lightly laughed the stout Sir John,*
*And the crew laughed with him too;*
*A sailor to change from ship to sled,*
*I ween, were something new!*
Ballad of Sir John Franklin (1850s)

During the Great Search for Franklin and the missing *Erebus* and *Terror*, no spectacle stirred the British public quite so much as the man-hauled sledge crew. Artists of the *Illustrated London News*, the *Graphic*, and the *Penny Illustrated Times* vied to embellish the exploits of this new breed of supermen. They were the gladiators of the Victorian era. They were the symbols of British naval might conquering the brute force of the Arctic. A whole folklore grew up around them.

In the bolder-than-life engravings of the illustrated weeklies they

*A quaint sketch from* Illustrated London News *of an explorer showing the front page of the magazine to Eskimos. Press publicity built sledge-haulers into mythical heroes.* METROPOLITAN TORONTO LIBRARY BOARD

were presented as almost mythical matadors. You marveled at their strength. Crews of six bearded jack tars, in blue pea jackets, canvas boots and flannel mufflers, harnessed themselves to horsehair dragropes and hauled sledge loads of up to two thousand pounds. You were awed by the hostile arena they braved. With an officer walking alongside to urge them on, they were ready to overcome the protean sea ice, the yawning crevasses, the horrors of the long polar nights. And you were thrilled by the parade-like pageantry of it all. Fifteen sledges manned by more than one hundred mariners might march in single-file procession, kites flying, canvas sails bellying in the wind from tent poles, sometimes a fife and drum band playing.

For sheer showmanship you couldn't match naval rituals transferred to the polar sledge crew. As though it were a man-of-war, each iron-runnered oaken sledge bore a swaggering name: *Hotspur, Resolute, Succour, True Blue, Adventure*, or simply *Hero*. An identifying silk pennant fluttered from every sledge: the cross of St. George, the star of the North, the emblem of a lighthouse, a shield, a lance thrusting forward. And each banner carried its own sledge platoon motto: "Nothing adventure, nothing win," "Faithful & Intrepid," "By faith & courage," and sometimes an entire verse, "Gaze where some distant speck a sail implies/ With all the thirsting gaze of enterprise."

Just as there were sea chanties, so did sledge-hauling songs become part of the naval tradition. The most popular chanty had a rousing chorus:

> *One, two, three, haul!*
> *Push on, my lads, push on!*
> *There's nothing will discourage us,*
> *Seeking where the lost have been,*
> *A gallant band may yet be seen;*
> *So push on, my lads, push on!*
> *One, two, three, haul!*

There was a strict adherence to naval discipline and spit-and-polish. Decks couldn't be swabbed, but the arctic tundra could. After a stop was made for a chunk of salt pork and tea, whiskbrooms were mustered to sweep out the holland tents. The officer in charge of each sledge platoon conducted an inspection to make sure that all pebbles were removed—a drill known as "picking the feathers."

Despite the class distinctions between naval ranks, every sledge

unit was fraternally bound by the Royal Navy's famous sense of duty and cocky *esprit de corps*. Rivals laid bets on their sledges as if they were racing for a Newmarket cup, and some tried to increase their speed — an average rate of one to two miles covered per hour — by improvising for their boat-sledges crude velocipedes. A genre of sledge humor arose, and the stiff-upper-lip comments of these folk figures became part of naval legendry. Sergeant Jefferies of the Royal Marines, after his sledge platoon had plodded over scalloped peaks and around cliff paths that wound like a corkscrew, reported to his commander with a military salute, "Just like the Khyber Pass, sir, in 1841." Asked if he were equal to dragging his two-hundred-pound share of the load, another man said, "Oh, yes, sir, and Sir John Franklin, too, when we find him."

The average daily march was about ten miles trekked across treacherous terrain in eight hours, and it was a mark of pluck to take it with a grin and a shrug. "We have every variety of traveling — ice, water, sludge," remarked one naval rating. "If you stick to the land, there you are, you know," ran another celebrated witticism, "but if you get out into the open pack, why, where are you?" In the below-zero chill, your very breath formed into a snow wreath known as a "barber," and your numbed limbs were left lifeless except for the ache of your straining muscles; but it was proper form to dismiss these trifles with a jest. "How are your feet?" an officer might ask. The common jaunty rejoinder was, "Oh! I hope they are all right, but I've not felt them since I pulled my boots on."

In his *Stray Leaves from an Arctic Journal*, Lieutenant Sherard Osborn, the Irish journalist-officer, gives us an almost cozy picture of the camaraderie that knit his sledge crew together.

"Gallant fellows!" Osborn applauded them. "They met our commiseration with a smile and a vow that they could do far more. They spoke of cold as 'Jack Frost,' a real tangible foe, with whom they could combat and would master. Hunger was met with a laugh and a chuckle at some future feast or jolly recollections told, in rough terms, of bygone good cheer. And often, standing on some neighbouring pile of ice and scanning the horizon for those we sought, have I heard a rough voice encouraging the sledge crew by saying, 'Keep step, boys! Keep step! She (the sledge) is coming along almost by herself. There's the *Erebus's* masts showing over the point ahead! Keep step, boys! Keep step!' "

What Osborn glossed over was the cruel toll exacted by the sledge hauls. Snowblind Point and Torture Cove were not named in jest. A good many frostbitten toes and fingers were amputated. (One sailmaker

later said he could always predict weather changes in the West Indies from the pain he felt in his old arctic stumps.) Some sledge-haulers were crippled for life. Others fainted in their harnesses and died in their tracks.

The Parry Channel became a kind of battlefield. Its official cemetery was a rocky pinprick among the icebergs some two hundred and fifty miles west of the entrance at Lancaster Sound. Though named Beechey Island, it was really a triangular-shaped peninsula, three miles long and eight miles in circumference, jutting out of one of the land masses on the north side of the Parry Channel off Barrow Strait.

Beechey Island was the one site of Franklin's lost expedition that the early search parties stumbled upon. Franklin and his crew of one hundred and twenty-eight had wintered there in 1845/46. The searchers knew that because they came upon the graves of three mariners belonging to the missing vessels. Oaken headboards with their dated inscriptions bore pious testimonials to the trio who had died in 1846: "Thus saith the Lord of Hosts, consider your ways—Haggai, 1,7."

The relic searchers did not consider their ways. They continued to sacrifice lives in the man-killing drudgery of the man-hauled sledge party.

Two exceptional explorers found other relics, and, at the same time, revolutionized the archaic naval concepts of how to navigate overland in the Arctic.

One, whom Lady Franklin came to detest, was a Hudson's Bay Company officer named Dr. John Rae. An Orkney Island Scot, with incisive originality and contempt for orthodoxy, he was the genius of Eskimo-style polar travel. He was more than that. Rae once described himself as a Jack-of-all-trades. It was a good definition, for he was so multi-talented.

He was a giant of a man, a sort of Hemingway among polar explorers, who reveled in his muscle and brain power. Virility came first. He actually enjoyed the rigors of living in his homemade snowhuts; he took pleasure out of quaffing caribou blood—"with as much relish as a London alderman supping on turtle soup." He was a champion snowshoer; his record hike was one hundred miles in one sleepless day and night. He beat the Eskimos in indefatigable dog sledding; altogether he journeyed an estimated six thousand five hundred miles by foot or dog sled. He was an inventive designer of his own umiak-like sailboats; he once figured he had boated six thousand seven hundred miles as an explorer. He derided the cumbersome and costly baggage

that freighted down Admiralty expeditions; the Scotsman carefully calculated that he had explored one thousand seven hundred and sixty-five miles of new Arctic land at an average cost of two pounds and five shillings per mile.

Above all, Rae prided himself on being the foremost sportsman among polar explorers and, a crackshot, he gloried in his marksmanship. With a single bullet he once shot two caribou bucks one hundred and ninety yards away. It was his contention that the leader of every Arctic expedition should be able to "live off the land." He proved his point on his four expeditions by bagging with his musket at least one-third of the game needed to feed his entire party.

As if all this were not enough, the surgeon was a first-class naturalist. He established a record of three letters to the editor of *Nature* on the same page; he filled that erudite science journal with articles on such arcane subjects as "Sounds of the Aurora," "Intelligence in animals" and "Do flying fish fly?" He was an esthete who loved classical music; he was the first explorer to name an Arctic island after an opera singer—the "Swedish Nightingale," Jenny Lind.

He was a strutting egotist, supremely self-confident, as he had reason to be; but perhaps his most engaging personality trait was his tendency to conceal that healthy ego under a mask of self-deprecating humor. "You appear to think that I have got a head stuffed with all sorts of knowledge," he once wrote to his superior in the fur trade. "The head is big enough certainly outside, but whether there is a large quantity of bone in it, I have not yet tested."

His fur trade colleagues had a high opinion of that leonine, imperial-bearded head of his. It was set on brawny shoulders; coal-black eyes smoldered between two thickets of chestnut-colored sideburns; and it featured moustachios curled upwards theatrically. "Remarkable for manly beauty in form and feature," a contemporary described him, "combined with a temper that was quick and somewhat fiery."

His temper was quickest to blaze up at the British Admiralty clique. Rae maintained a running feud with its official hydrographer as well as Sir Clements Markham, secretary of the Royal Society. They represented the naval establishment, and Rae wielded his switchblade wit to poke fun at their advocacy of man-hauled sledge travel. Besides, they had the gall to filch credit due to Rae for his Arctic discoveries and bestow them upon the Royal Navy.

"The Hydrographer seemed astounded at my audacity," Rae was to note disparagingly, "in venturing to question his right coolly to hand

*Dr. John Rae of the Hudson's Bay Company was the genius of Eskimo-style polar travel who reveled in his muscle and brain power. The discoverer of Rae Strait, he was first to find Franklin relics. He was snubbed by Lady Franklin for his ungentlemanly revelation that the dying Englishmen had resorted to cannibalism.* NATIONAL PORTRAIT GALLERY, LONDON

over about 700 miles of Arctic coast surveyed by the Hudson's Bay Company's expeditions to a naval officer who visited the place a year later and made a survey far less minute."

Rae had a particularly high standing among Eskimos. They nicknamed him *Meeteelik*, meaning "Place of the duck." The nickname was meant respectfully, because the great *Kabloona* hunter gave the appearance of a waddling eider duck when swathed in his sealskin and caribou robes.

R.M. Ballantyne, the H.B.C. clerk and author of such boys' adventure books as *Hudson's Bay*, met Rae in 1845, when the thirty-two-year-old explorer was preparing to embark on his first Arctic expedition. The novelist's impressions are revealing. Ballantyne said that Rae's "pushing, energetic character" made him ideal to lead the expedition. "He was considered by those who knew him well to be one of the best snowshoe walkers in the service, was also an expert rifleshot, and could stand an immense amount of fatigue. . . . He was very muscular and active, full of animal spirits, and had a fine intellectual countenance."

Rae ascribed his intellectual curiosity to his father, an H.B.C. fur factor agent at Stromness in the Orkneys, who was an intimate of Sir Walter Scott's. Young Rae picked up his ability to "rough it" in the Orkney moors with his five brothers. "I learned to shoot as soon as I was old enough to lift a gun to my shoulder," he later said. "By the time I was fifteen, I had become so seasoned as to care little about cold or wet, had acquired a fair knowledge of boating, was a moderately good climber among rocks, and not a bad walker for my age."

The Edinburgh University graduate acquired snowshoeing skill during his decade of service as an H.B.C. surgeon at Moose Factory at the subarctic bottom of James Bay. There he developed his keen competitive spirit as well as a touch of arrogance toward namby-pambies who could not match his herculean endurance. He tells of toughening himself up for his first Arctic expedition by making a snowshoe hike of twelve hundred miles. At the end of two months of constant traveling "the only man who had accompanied me the whole distance was found to have lost 26 pounds in weight (he was certainly rather fat when he started) whilst I had gained two pounds."

Rae lost any excess poundage on his gruelling excursion of 1846/47. His aim was to sail two little twenty-two-foot-long dorries, the *North Pole* and *Magnet*, up the west coast of Hudson Bay as far north as Repulse Bay. This was the site of the present Eskimo settlement tucked

under the base of Melville Peninsula. Rae and his self-sufficient comrades would winter there in a tiny stone house, heated with an Eskimo oil lamp and provisioned by their own guns. Then his overland snowshoe and sledge treks westward would fill in gaps on the eastern Arctic coastline left untraced by his great H.B.C. predecessor, Thomas Simpson, of whom we shall read in another chapter.

Rae achieved more than that on his journey. He delineated the southeastern coast of Boothia Peninsula, that northernmost chunk of icy land joined to North America (named after Sir John Ross's gin tycoon) and proved conclusively that it was no island. The trip was further notable because on it Rae was persuaded to give us his most detailed account of how he adapted to the Eskimo style of living.

It was truly said of Rae that he was "a man of action with a constitutional shrinking from multiplying words." He scorned the florid tomes turned out by polar dabblers from the Navy. A superb nonexaggerator, he wrote in a lucid, painstakingly factual style, and was alert to note everything of interest about the flora and fauna and native customs.

In his slim volume, *Narrative of an Expedition to the Shores of the Arctic Sea*, Rae paid generous tribute to the four intelligent aborigines who aided his band of nine French and Orkney boatmen. There was a resourceful Cree Indian, Nibitabo, conceded by Rae to be "one of the keenest sportsmen I have ever met with"—the supreme accolade. There was Ooligbuck, the Fort Churchill Eskimo interpreter on Franklin's second overland expedition; Rae was intrigued by his dexterity in swinging a wolf around by the tail—although Rae topped him by giving the wolf a *coup de grâce* blow on the head with his gun butt. There was Ooligbuck's son, William; the lad was something of a scamp, who purloined his father's tobacco—but a good sealer and whaler for all that. Then there was that merry little Eskimo fellow, Ivitchuk (meaning Walrus); he taught them to appreciate the gourmet qualities of blubber and caribou blood—and in turn acquired a taste for *Kabloona* tea and chocolate.

Indeed all four taught the white man the skills of survival on the fringes of *Akkoolee*—the Eskimo word for the Arctic Sea. Rae learned how to decoy snow owls by dragging along by a rope a bit of fur shaped like a lemming. He quickly discovered that his McIntosh coat was no means of combating forty-seven-below-zero temperatures and bartered it for Eskimo garments. He became a "tolerably good" snow igloo

mason. Comparing his seven-foot-long, steel-runnered oaken sledges with those of the Eskimos, "I soon saw the advantages of iced runners over the iron ones, and determined to have ours done in the same way." He observed the wisdom of traveling lightly, and he was swiftly able to cover a minimum of sixteen miles a day with a travel party of five picked men, eight dogs and two small sleds loaded with minimal provisions: three bags of pemmican, seventy caribou tongues, flour, tea, chocolate, sugar, and a little alcohol and oil for fuel. When his seal oil lamp ran out of fuel, he learned to grub under the snow for the native substitute—the *Andromeda tetragona*—"an interesting and beautiful herb in the eye of a botanist, but giving no promise to the ordinary observer that it could supply warmth to a large party during a long arctic winter."

Rae did not deny that there were hardships aplenty. Frost glued the pages of his science books together and made his watch stop ticking. Scanty rations compelled him to pull in his belt by six inches and sometimes the proud *pedestrian*, as he called himself in underlined fashion, couldn't perambulate too well. "Walking became most difficult," he admitted. "At one moment we sank nearly waist-deep in snow; at another we were up to our knees in salt water; and then again on a piece of ice so slippery that, with our wet and frozen shoes, it was impossible to keep from falling. And sometimes we had to crawl out of a hole on all fours like some strange-looking quadrupeds."

There was no doubt that Rae belonged to the hairy-chested he-man school of polar literature. He had to keep proving himself the victor in a test of strength and cunning against the wiles of the north country. His comic sense of the ridiculous was the one thing that saved him from being a boaster. One bitter night he had no fuel available to dry his soggy clothes or heat his whale blubber. "I therefore adopted the plan that a celebrated miser took to warm his food," he jested, "by taking them under the blanket with me at night, and drying them by the heat of the body." When his best sled dog was attacked by a wolf, he comforted the poor wounded creature with Scottish verse. She was like Tam O'Shanter's mare in Robert Burns' ballad of Cutty Sark:

*The wolf had caught her by the rump*
*And left poor Surie scarce a stump.*

His pawky humor in making light of hardships seems to have been contagious. "Our few discomforts, instead of causing discontentment,

furnished us with subjects of merriment," says Rae. The butt of their jokes was one particular Orkney boatman. "He had his knee frozen in bed," Rae goes on to say, "and I believe the poor fellow (who by the bye was the softest of the party) was afterwards very sorry for letting it be known, as he got so heartily laughed at for his effeminacy."

One is relieved to learn that the super-masculine Rae did suffer one discomfort. The athlete was no teetotaller (for he enjoyed a wee drap of the best Scotch whisky, although never when hiking on what he called an Arctic "tour"). But the snuff-taker was a nonsmoker and he could not abide the smell of his comrades' pipe tobacco. So Rae eventually was forced to build a separate snowhouse. He preferred to sleep in frigid but nicotineless solitude, while his companions filled up their warmer bed chamber with their pipe smoke.

Apart from that petty annoyance, Rae felt there was nothing more exhilarating than a long polar "pedestrian tour," the crisp snow squealing underfoot, the clean tangy air biting his nostrils, a limitless unexplored domain stretching before his eyes. He felt godlike. One passage in his journal captures something of his buoyance:

"The night was beautiful, and, as all my men had gone to sleep, nothing interrupted the stillness around but the occasional blowing of a white whale, the rather musical note of the *caca wee* (long-tailed duck), or the harsh scream of the great northern diver. Yet I could not close my eyes.

"Nor was this wakefulness caused by the want of comfort in my bed, which I own was none of the most inviting, as it consisted of a number of hard-packed bags of flour, over which a blanket was spread.... To a man who had slept soundly in all sorts of places—on the top of a round log, in the middle of a swamp, as well as on the wet shingle beach—such a bed was no hardship.... Yet the novelty of our route, and of our intended mode of operation, had a strong charm for me, and gave me an excitement which I could not otherwise have felt."

After tramping over six hundred and fifty miles of newly discovered Arctic coastline, Rae concluded with a heartfelt salute to his band of companions, "By George, I never saw such a set of men."

Rae's next expedition, of 1848/49, was not accomplished with hikers as hardy. Sir John Richardson had asked him to serve as second in command of a search mission to locate Franklin on the Arctic coast between the Mackenzie and Coppermine Rivers. Although he would have preferred to have been leader of the expedition, Rae finally con-

sented. He was disappointed in the four lubberly sailboats which the British Admiralty had built for Richardson. But he was absolutely disgusted by the twenty Royal Navy sappers, miners and marines hired by Richardson to man them. Rae had difficulty bridling his temper, for they were a bunch of lazy softies, not a "pedestrian" or a sportsman among the lot. It was obvious that Rae and his Eskimo interpreter, a brave lad named Albert One-Eye, would have to hunt fresh game for the whole troupe.

On the whole, Dr. Rae got along amicably with Dr. Richardson. The sixty-one-year-old veteran of Arctic overland excursions was getting a little rusty in the joints. But Rae respected the spunky old Scot for at least striving to keep up with his own walking pace.

"When fully equipped and ready to start, he read prayers in a most impressive manner outside the tent," Rae recounted. "And our appearance, with gun on shoulder and loads on our backs, reminded me much of what I had read of the Covenanters of old, when they worshipped in the glens and on the hillsides, prepared at a moment's notice either to fight with or flee from their persecutors."

We have a delightful picture of the two surgeon-naturalists, both graduates of Edinburgh University, competing as Great Medicine Chiefs with native *shamans* and strolling on long nature rambles. They paused occasionally to admire the flesh-colored limestone cliffs and to botanize among the saxifrage that brightened the bleak landscape like peach blossoms. Both had a good laugh at the slippery swamp lichen which made the footing of hikers precarious and which the Chipewyans had named "women's heads." "You may kick them," explained the ungallant Indians, "but they cause you to stumble and never get out of the way."

When they rafted supplies across a turbulent stream, Richardson had disturbing memories evoked of his hapless swim across the Coppermine on the Franklin expedition thirty years before. However, to Rae it was "mere child's play." He had come equipped with an ingenious inflatable Halkett boat devised by a Hudson's Bay man. It was a lightweight india-rubber contrivance that could be strung on your shoulder, and after air had been blown into the nozzle, it could carry as many as four men. Rae and Albert One-Eye propelled it easily across one hundred and forty yards of icy rapids, using two dinner plates as paddles.

Rae tells us in his private memoirs that, although Richardson was

pleasant enough to name the Rae River after him, they had a few amusing clashes of temperament. Dr. Richardson was a Bible-thumping Calvinist; Dr. Rae was an irreverent freethinker who liked to "bother the parson and keep all the godly in hot water." Richardson, the moralist, was shocked by Eskimo seductresses hospitable enough to offer their sexual favors for the night. Rae, who was more easygoing, noted that their H.B.C. host at a fur trade post seemed to have hidden away his lovely daughter. "Perhaps he feared," Rae quipped, "that either Sir John or his second in command might prove a gallant gay deceiver."

Joking further on that amorous theme, the thirty-five-year-old Rae (actually to remain a bachelor for twelve more years) confided, "I am becoming quite a grey-headed old fellow, and it is high time for me to be thinking of looking out for a *better half.* However pleasant, charming, and useful the native ladies are in some respects, I do not at all fancy buckling myself for life to one of them. The *womankind* of the family have done their part in supplying Her Majesty with subjects, and I do not wish the male portion to be so far *distanced* in this respect." His brother in the fur trade, Rae says, "has got only one *legitimate* little Rae," then he adds the droll sally, "and myself not one either on the right or wrong side of the blanket—that I am *aware* of."

With a certain amount of relief, one senses, Rae left the exhausted Dr. Richardson to winter at an H.B.C. post on Great Bear Lake. Meanwhile Rae prepared to continue the Franklin search on his own. Tragic and comic events, however, were to hamper the explorer.

The tragedy occurred in 1849. Rae, with a boatload of five men, was beaten back by ice after descending the Coppermine River. He was heartbroken when his Eskimo guide, Albert One-Eye, was drowned at Bloody Fall in a mishap caused by the incompetence and cowardice of the steersman. Brave Albert was the only man who ever lost his life on a Rae expedition, and the explorer was extremely distressed. "Albert was liked by everyone for his good temper, lively disposition and great activity in doing anything that was required of him," mourned Rae. "I had become much attached to the poor fellow."

The farce was provided by Royal Navy explorers competing with Rae to discover traces of Franklin in the Mackenzie River Arctic region. Rae was being maliciously unfair, for the British Navy contained many brave men who understandably were out of their depth when coping with an alien environment in which Rae was so thoroughly grounded.

Nevertheless, on the basis of gossip picked up from crew members of H.M.S. *Plover*, Rae could not resist the temptation of honing his barbed wit on a brass hat named Commander (later Rear-Admiral) Thomas Edward Laws Moore.

According to Rae, Moore and his officers were proponents of the mobile hotel school of arctic travel. When they wintered at Fort Franklin on Great Bear Lake, they did nothing but complain. "These self-sufficient donkeys," he wrote, "come into this country, see the Indians sometimes miserably clad and half-starved, the causes of which they never think of inquiring into, but place it all to the credit of the Company...."

Evidently Moore considered it *"awful work"* if he had to walk a few steps off a floating deck. Rae had deprived himself of stores from the H.B.C. fort and provided Moore's party with forty-five hundred pounds of pemmican, Rae's own best nautical instruments, a forty-foot-long boat, and the Company's most trusted Indian guides. Moore regarded the pemmican distastefully as dried goat's meat and was rumored to have thrown the "offal" overboard. The grumbler complained he had no valet to wash his clothes or prepare "a proper meal on our *'country fare'* "; moreover he reportedly indulged in indecorous sexual charades.

Commander Moore, according to Rae, played the role of a grand nabob. The captain kept an Eskimo girl in the cabin of H.M.S. *Plover* "for purposes that were but too evident." And when Moore took his fair lady out for an airing, the pasha did it in style. He had one officer running before and one officer running behind his opulent cariole.

In contrast, when Rae set out from Fort Confidence at Great Bear Lake for his epic expedition of 1851, he remarked dryly that his trappings were somewhat less "luxurious." The Scotsman was proud to say that his mobile boudoir consisted of a deerskin sleeping bag, a pocket comb, a toothbrush, and a bar of coarse yellow soap. The pride of the light traveler was well justified. His journey of more than two thousand five hundred miles, by foot, dog team and boat, was one of the most remarkable on record. He mapped seven hundred miles of new coastline. He introduced the system of using an advance dog team "fatigue party" to cache extra supplies for the return trip home. And he personally journeyed over the most rugged part of the overland route with just five dogs, two one-hundred-pound sledges, and two picked men on a ration of two pounds per man per day. Yet he managed to cover eleven hundred miles in thirty-nine days, achieving a speedy

average rate of almost twenty-eight statute miles traveled per day. "This is, I believe," Rae truly boasted, "the most quickly performed Arctic journey on record."

His feat won Rae the Founder's Gold Medal of the Royal Geographical Society. He had surveyed the southeast coast of Victoria Island and pinned the monarch's name on newly discovered Victoria Strait. This was the perpetually ice-clogged channel immediately west of King William Island. Tragically, if he had been able to cross the same fifty miles of Victoria Strait to King William Island, he might have found traces of the missing Franklin expedition. It was not for lack of trying. The ice stream was too treacherous. Sleet squalls blew up an ugly chopping sea. And, as Rae pointed out, his dogs were thin as laths, his buffalo skin moccasins were lacerated to shreds by limestone rocks, so that with each step he left a trail of blood in the snow. And the arduous trip "added not a few grey hairs to my scanty wig."

He deeply regretted that he had not been able to accommodate Lady Franklin. She had been bombarding him with letters to search southeast of King William Island. Rae's relationship with Jane was most cordial then, for she had recently visited "my Dear Old Mother" in the Orkney Islands. "She made herself a great favorite with everyone by her kindness of manner and affability," Rae noted, "and speaks in *raptures* (!!!) of our bleak rocks."

Lady Franklin was far from rapturous about the results of Rae's final Arctic trek of 1853/54. After wintering in snow igloos at his old Hudson Bay haunt of Repulse Bay, Rae made a magnificent sledge and snowshoe safari of eleven hundred miles. He traveled with a small party of four men, including William Ooligbuck, the young Eskimo interpreter. This time his expedition approached King William Island from the east side, though not landing on it. They fought their way up the west coast of Boothia Peninsula and discovered the twenty-mile-wide water highway that now bears the name of Rae Strait.

In effect, Rae had tracked down the missing link in a navigable Northwest Passage, although it wasn't appreciated at the time. He proved conclusively that King William Land, as geographers had heretofore mistakenly called it, was not a land mass joined to Boothia Peninsula. Rather the illusory peninsula was an island.

On his 1851 expedition Rae had already stumbled upon another piece in the jigsaw puzzle. He had discovered Victoria Strait on the *west side* of King William Island and he had found that it was a roadblock in

the Passage. It was a dead-end street, an ice-blocked cul de sac, which had trapped Franklin. So if Franklin's two vessels had detoured instead to the relatively ice-free *east side* of King William Island and jogged around Rae's newly discovered Rae Strait, the *Erebus* and *Terror* might well have sailed clear through the Northwest Passage.

Unfortunately Rae's fine detective work did not then receive the recognition it warranted. It was overshadowed by a second revelation infinitely more melodramatic. At Pelly Bay off the Gulf of Boothia Rae met a particularly intelligent Eskimo named In-nook-poo-zhee-jook who was wearing a gold cap band around his head.

"I asked him where he obtained it," Rae reported, "and he said it had been got where the dead white men were."

It was the first solid clue to indicate the whereabouts of the lost Franklin expedition.

From this Eskimo, and others at Repulse Bay, Rae pieced together a horror story. According to his informants, the *Erebus* and *Terror* had been crushed by the ice in Victoria Strait. In the spring of 1848 a party of more than thirty white men were seen faltering southward on the northwest coast of King William Island. All except the officer were hauling sledge dragropes and all except the officer looked thin. The stout, middle-aged officer (so presumed because he had a telescope strapped over his shoulder and carried a double-barreled gun) bought a seal from the Eskimos. He indicated by sign language that he hoped his famished men would be able to shoot deer upon reaching the south-eastern *noo-nah* (mainland) near the Great River, meaning apparently the Arctic mouth of the Back River.

Later in the season, said the Eskimos, a terrible fate had befallen the *Kabloona.* All thirty-odd of them had perished. At least five of their corpses were seen scattered about on an island a day's journey from the Back River, at a place eventually to gain the gruesome name of Starvation Cove.

None of the Eskimos claimed to have seen the white men. They had heard the story from others. But it was clearly more than hearsay testimony, for Rae bought from them clearly identifiable evidence: a round silver platter bearing Sir John Franklin's name; Franklin's star-shaped Guelphic Order of Hanover; twenty-four silver teaspoons, dessert spoons and forks engraved with crests or initials of Franklin's officers; two pages of a Naval Student's Manual; an initialled flannel undervest; and a surgeon's knife and scalpel.

No scalpel could have slashed at nerve ends as sharply as the shocking report which Rae hurried to bring back to England: "From the mutilated state of many of the corpses, and the contents of the kettles, it is evident that our wretched countrymen had been driven to the last resource—cannibalism—as a means of prolonging existence."

That unsavory news electrified the British public, and Rae became the victim of Victorian indignation. Everybody knew that Englishmen never ate one another, and if they did, it wasn't proper to talk about it. It was charged that William Ooligbuck had misinterpreted the "wild tales of a herd of savages" who had probably butchered defenseless Englishmen themselves. And Rae was viciously attacked for not having visited King William Island to verify their secondhand rumors. Instead the mercenary had shown unseemly haste in hurrying to England to collect the prize of ten thousand pounds offered to the solver of the Franklin mystery.

Rae protested in vain. He believed in the truthfulness of his peaceful Eskimos. He was unaware of the reward. He had rushed back to forestall any further naval blundering. He issued a statement not designed to make him popular with officialdom. "Four ships of Her Majesty's Navy were in the Arctic Sea," he said, "searching for the lost expedition in every direction but the right one."

The Admiralty hemmed and hawed and finally asked the Hudson's Bay Company to dispatch in 1855 a three-canoe search party to the mouth of the Back River. Since the canoe investigators had neglected to bring an Eskimo interpreter, they could pick up no fresh news. But they did return with a few more telling relics: a letter clip; a plank bearing the name *Terror*; a backgammon game board presented to the *Erebus* by Lady Franklin.

By now the Admiralty wanted to wash its hands of the whole affair. It was involved in the Crimean War, and it would not squander any more money on helping Lady Franklin to find her lost husband. It even balked at paying Rae's justly earned prize money. Rae threatened to take legal action, and reminded the bewigged admirals that since 1854, "I have lost much of my time (which, although not worthy the consideration of their Lordships, is of great value to me)." Only then, in 1856, did Whitehall post notice that he was entitled to the reward.

Lady Franklin was furious at both the Admiralty and the presumptuous Rae. When all officers and men of the lost expedition were deemed dead and their names struck off the Navy list, Jane refused her widow's pension. "She changed the deep mourning she had been

wearing for years," we are told, "for bright colours of green and pink as soon as the Admiralty notice was gazetted."

She cannoned the Admiralty with impassioned letters. "It is with great reluctance that I find myself obliged to contest Dr. Rae's claims," she protested. "But he did not go out of his way to test the startling facts communicated to him . . . at second or third hand." She deplored the niggardly dispatching of "no more than a birch bark canoe expedition on a flying visit of a few days. . . . The tranquil presence of a vessel is necessary to extract the whole truth from the natives."

She entreated their Lordships not to "place an extinguisher upon the light which has arisen in that dark corner of the earth, whither we have been directed as by the finger of God." And she implored their Lordships not to "leave it to a weak and helpless woman" to "bring back some journal, or some precious document, otherwise lost to us forever from voices hushed in the grave."

Their Lordships turned deaf ears to her pleas. Jane then showed them she was no weak and helpless woman. She initiated a fund-raising campaign to finance a private expedition. Subscriptions totaling some three thousand pounds poured in from subscribers and she bought a "consecrated ship," a one-hundred-and-seventy-seven-ton screw steam yacht, the *Fox*. Rae was the first volunteer to offer his services. Like Shakespeare's raging Cleopatra, who would kill a messenger bringing bad news about her Antony, Jane cut Rae dead.

"Dr. Rae has cut off his odious beard," she wrote of the snubbing, "but looks still very hairy and disagreeable."

The officer she chose instead to command her featherweight yacht was the heavyweight champion among all naval sledge explorers. He was Francis Leopold (Paddy) McClintock, a handsome, blue-eyed, dimple-chinned level-headed Irishman of thirty-eight. It was a sagacious choice, for McClintock (sometimes spelled M'Clintock) acknowledged that he had learned considerably from the experience of his sledging rival. Praising that "distinguished Arctic traveler, Dr. Rae," McClintock wrote, "I believe he and his party were the first white men who maintained themselves in the arctic regions by their own unaided exertions."

In some ways the Irishman and the Scot seemed superficially alike. Like Rae, McClintock was an avid walker and coined his own quaint phrase for his record hikes; he found nothing more bracing than a polar "*pediluvium* ramble." In the spring of 1853 he completed one of the

greatest sledge-hauling journeys of all time—more than fourteen hundred miles in one hundred and five days, during which the Irish traveler mapped nearly eight hundred miles of undiscovered Arctic coastline and appended to his discoveries such Irish names as Prince Patrick Island, Ireland's Eye and Emerald Island. Like Rae, he was an ardent sportsman. He once stalked two polar bears by approaching them from behind a flying kite; and to McClintock's eternal credit, the hunter debunked the alleged perils involved in polar bear shooting.

"It is only when wounded or pressed by extreme hunger that the polar bear becomes fierce," wrote McClintock. "In all our adventures with bears . . . we found them to be inquisitive, timid except when hungry, and somewhat stupid."

Like Rae, he was a keen naturalist. One of the many rare fossils the geologist collected was named after him, *Loxionema McClintocki*. He almost broke his neck bringing back arctic specimens of an ivory gull's egg, black spiders, caterpillars, and the *Cerastium alpinum* (vulgarly known as the mouse-ear chickweed) to the Dublin University Zoological and Botanical Society.

Like Rae, he took an interest in the arts and sciences. He named an Arctic cape after the novelist, Charles Dickens. He took pains to write his meticulously accurate journal in a spare, athletic prose. Occasionally it was graced with fanciful humor or a poetic allusion. To McClintock the moon hung in the polar sky like a frosted silver melon; seals came out of their ice caves to bask voluptuously in the sun and—

*Flounce and tremble in unwieldy joy*

Finally, like Rae, McClintock had a resilient and inquiring mind. He was slower to break from tradition than Rae. But ultimately the innovator learned that Eskimo travel and survival tactics excelled anything contrived by Her Majesty's Navy.

Yet, of course, there were dissimilarities. Physically and temperamentally the Hudson's Bay man and the Royal Navy man were quite unlike. If Rae was the Hemingway of sledge exploration, McClintock was its F. Scott Fitzgerald. The Scot was an exhibitionist, bearded and barrel-chested; the Irishman was introspective, clean-shaven and surprisingly slight of stature. His contemporary biographer and brother sledge-hauling messmate, Sir Clements Markham, described him as reserved and somewhat indisposed to talk. "Short, slender, but wiry,"

*Lieutenant Francis Leopold (Paddy) McClintock was the champion among naval sledge explorers. He unraveled the mystery of Franklin's fate. Of more vital importance, by delineating King Edward Island, he helped unscramble the jigsaw puzzle of the Northwest Passage.* NATIONAL PORTRAIT GALLERY, LONDON

Markham pictured him. "Quick in his movements, as in his decisions, he was always quiet and perfectly calm, seeing everything done himself without noise or fuss."

The chief difference between the two explorers was a matter of ego. Rae, the rugged individualist, was a compulsive showoff of his muscular superiority and, with his abrasive wit, was inclined to rub weaklings the wrong way. McClintock, conditioned by the teamwork tradition of the Navy, disciplined his own vanity, held his temper coolly in check, and was more interested in maintaining the respect of his crew. "Under the most aggravating circumstances," another naval messmate said, "his face would not alter a muscle ... except occasionally a little quiet chuckle and a rub of the hands." His crews were said to revere him for his sense of fair play, and Lady Franklin once commended him for "your sunny good temper, which is worth a thousand a year to you."

Paddy McClintock worked his way up to the naval topdeck from grinding poverty. He was one of a poor family of fourteen children born at Seatown Place, Dundalk, Ireland. His long-lived mother, Elizabeth, was a minister's daughter, and he worshipped her to the point that he did not marry until he was fifty-one years old. His father, in charge of the customs house at Dundalk, used to take little Paddy out quail-shooting, riding and fishing in the nearby mountain glens until the boy became a thorough sportsman.

At the age of twelve McClintock thrilled to the boys' sea adventure tales written by Frederick Marryat, and joined the Royal Navy as a cadet. He had his fill of adventures. He helped capture a piratical slaving ship off Cuba, shot wildcats off the Spanish Main, became a powerful swimmer off the coast of Brazil, and hunted big game on the coast of Labrador. At the age of twenty-nine, after winning certificates in steam engineering and mathematics at the Royal Naval College in Portsmouth, Lieutenant McClintock was ready to apply his toughened muscles and acute intelligence to the logistics of arctic sledge-hauling.

He served on three Franklin search expeditions in the Parry Channel polar regions, from 1848 until 1854, and what he saw of naval travel techniques distressed him. "One gradually becomes more of an *animal*," he reflected, "under this system of constant exposure and unremitting labour."

He looked at his sledge-hauling crew and he pitied them. "Thoughtless, of course," he thought, "as true sailors are." Yet his heart went out to them. Ten of the bluejackets on his sledge detachment suffered terribly from blistered feet, frostbite, and the spitting of blood.

Yet they pleaded to continue the march. They were keyed up by the rah-rah spirit of McClintock's heavy sledge, titled *Perseverance*, and its blue cross flag and its brave motto, "Persevere to the end."

"I shall never forget the anxious entreaties of some of these men to be allowed to continue the journey," McClintock later pondered in a scientific paper he wrote on his sledge-hauling experiences. "When they found they could not conceal from me their wounds, they shed tears like children."

McClintock decided to experiment and improve their lot. He made many bad mistakes. Among other blunders, he tried imitating Sir William Edward Parry by having sixteen men drag two carts across Melville Island. The heavy iron wheels, three feet in diameter, sank into the snow up to the axles. The men looked like weaving shuttlecocks trying to yank the caravans out of muck and mire. After six weeks of intense labor, their snow wagons had inched a mere fifty miles from the ship. "My good rifle sank to rise no more," wrote McClintock dolefully, and he admitted carts were hopeless.

Persevering, following his sledge motto, the experimenter gradually perfected new travel methods. He invented a portable alcohol stove: it enabled his sledge-haulers to melt snow quickly for drinking water and boiling pemmican—the fat, pounded meat which McClintock shrewdly assessed to be "the most nutritious description of food that we know of" for polar travelers. He designed lighter one-hundred-and-fifteen-pound sleds made of Canadian elm. He adopted Rae's "fatigue party" system of sending out auxiliary sledge crews to cache food along the intended line of march; that ensured the main sledge party of reserve supplies on the homeward journey.

But all this was done with jack tars harnessed to still overburdened sledges. Not until 1854, after two of his men had virtually died in harness, did McClintock gain an insight into the value of sled dogs. Twelve of them had been left aboard ship from a previous expedition by a Danish ice pilot named Carl Petersen, who was thoroughly experienced in driving dog teams in Greenland. McClintock lacked that experience, but he attempted to drive the team of twelve with the aid of one sailor. He accomplished an amazing four hundred and seventy miles in fifteen days, or an average of thirty-one miles per day. In comparison, a man-hauled sledge crew was lucky to achieve thirteen miles in one day. Neither could the men subsist on dog rations of bear meat once every two days. It was a lesson McClintock did not forget.

In 1857, when Lady Franklin entrusted command of the *Fox* to McClintock, Carl Petersen was one of the first recruited. "McClintock I know," said the grey-bearded Dane. "With him will I serve." Two young Greenland Eskimos, Anton Christian and Samuel Emanuel, were to be hired as well to help drive the Greenland sleighs and twenty-two dogs. The pair of "Esquimaux auxiliaries," as McClintock termed them, proved to be wonderful seal hunters; and though a mite uncomfortable at being washed, having their hair cut, and being garbed in sailors' uniforms, ended the voyage beaming—saying they had been treated well—"all the same as brothers."

Of the total crew of twenty-five men, seventeen had previous arctic experience. One of the exceptions was the civilian physician-geologist, Dr. David (Dockie) Walker. He was noteworthy because of his long ropelike moustaches of vaudevillean proportions and because he was the first photographer to go on a polar expedition. Captain McClintock's second in command was a veteran Arctic hand, Lieutenant William Hobson. "Strong and vigorous," Hobson was described, "with the merriest face in the world, and ready for anything."

The little three-masted steam yacht was a merry ship. She was equipped with plentiful Allsopp's strong ale and three tons of pemmican; a silk banner embroidered by Lady Franklin for the dog sledge and a bottle of champagne to celebrate the successful completion of their mission. In June of 1857 Lady Franklin waved goodbye to her "sincere and attached friend," Captain McClintock, as his "little band of heroes" aboard the *Fox* slipped out of Aberdeen with instructions to head for King William Island.

It took them almost three years before they set foot on it. The *Fox*, as the sailors phrased it, was soldered, as if by a tinker, in ice for two winters. The first winter, 1857, was spent locked for eight months in the brutal middle pack off Greenland. Trapped as if in a floating cage, the *Fox* drifted in the heart of a stout old floe more than thirteen hundred miles, almost to the entrance of Cumberland Sound.

The winter of 1858/59 found the *Fox* hemmed in at the east end of Bellot Strait. This was the twenty-mile-long alleyway linking Prince Regent Inlet with Peel Sound. Five times the *Fox* tried to slither through the whirlpools and boiling eddies that boobytrapped the mile-wide Bellot Strait. "With cunning and activity worthy of her name," says McClintock, "our little craft warily avoided a tilting match with the stout blue masses which whirled about." But halfway through the

Strait she had to retire defeated to her lair, which was christened by the crew, "Fox's Hole."

The captain was at his descriptive best when writing about his attempts to extricate his ship from the pack. "We have been coquetting with huge rampant ice-masses," McClintock noted during one nerve-wracking session; and the terrific thumping against his lightweight yacht made him understand "how men's hair has turned grey in a few hours." The "ice artillery" of the sheeny floe bergs, colliding and grinding around him, induced the scientist to catalogue the noises produced. Sometimes it sounded like the incessant roar of distant surf; sometimes like the low moaning of a sobbing wind. And sometimes it was a harsh screeching, "as if trains of heavy wagons with ungreased axles were slowly labouring along."

McClintock put on a good face, in true Navy style, each time his ship was cradled in ice. "Under the circumstances I did the best to insure our safety," he wrote; and to reassure his crew, "looked as stoical as possible."

The crew accepted both winters of ice imprisonment with relatively good cheer. Guy Fawkes Day was celebrated with a night parade around the decks, with beating drums and clanging gongs, and an effigy of the dastardly Fawkes was burned amid appropriate fireworks. Plum pudding donated by Lady Franklin was consumed on Christmas Day and on New Year's Eve Captain McClintock was serenaded by an orchestra of flutes and concertinas, banging tea kettles and howling sled dogs.

On more sober occasions the jack tars studied native survival techniques under the tutelage of Carl Petersen and the two Eskimo interpreters. They were given lessons in seal-hunting, igloo-building and the art of handling sled dogs. It was hard going. Few could stand the taste of blubber, it took them hours to construct a snowhouse, and McClintock admits he was repelled by Petersen's assertion that puppy dog flesh was as flavorsome as mutton. McClintock conceded, moreover, that breaking in his team of six sled dogs, consisting of Omar Pasha, Rose, Darky, Missy, Foxey and Dolly, was such a terrible trial that it caused him to lose his temper.

"The amount of cunning and perversity they displayed to avoid both the whip and the work was astonishing," he observed. "They bit through their traces and hid away under the sledge. Or they leaped over one another's back, so as to get into the middle of the team out of the

way of my whip, until the traces became plaited up, and the dogs were almost knotted together. The consequence was I had to halt every few minutes, pull off my mitts, and, at the risk of frozen fingers, disentangle the lines."

Despite his sternest intentions, he could not resist treating them as gently as English pets. "Poor dogs!" he commiserated as they coiled under the snow. "They have a hard life of it in these regions. Even Petersen, who is generally kind and humane, seems to fancy they must have little or no feeling. One of his theories is that you may knock an Es-quimaux dog about the head with any article, however heavy, with perfect impunity to the brute. One of us upbraided him the other day because he broke his whip handle over the head of a dog. '*That was nothing at all!*' he assured us. Some friend of his in Greenland found he could beat his dogs over the head with a heavy hammer—it stunned them certainly—but by laying them with their mouths open to the wind, they soon revived, got up, and ran about '*all right.*'"

By the end of the second winter his crew members were a little more hardened but not so high-spirited. "We know all each other's stories by rote," McClintock noted. "In fact, we take a malicious pleasure in *correcting* each other when telling them."

Their sole visitor was a lugubrious raven croaking overhead, and the symbolic bird of doom seemed to fascinate McClintock. "The gloomy bird sails slowly past," he recorded, "and even the clear starlight is sufficient to render visible to you an ice ring round his throat."

The crew members were depressed because the two ship engineers had died: one had taken a fatal tumble down the hatchway and the other's death was attributed to a combination of apoplexy and winter melancholy. In each instance McClintock read funeral services over the victim by flickering lantern light, and then joined the crew in dragging the body by sledge to a hole in the ice where it was committed to the deep.

"What a scene it was!" the captain mourned. "I shall never forget it. The lonely *Fox*, almost buried in snow, completely isolated from the habitable world, her colours half-mast high, and bell mournfully tolling; our little procession slowly marching over the rough surface of the frozen sea guided by lanterns and direction posts, amid the dark and dreary depth of arctic winter, the death-like stillness, the intense cold, and the threatening aspect of a murky, overcast sky; and all this

heightened by one of those strange lunar phenomena, a complete halo encircling the moon as well as six mock moons. Scarcely had the burial service been completed when our poor dogs, discovering that the ship was deserted, set up a most dismal unearthly moaning."

It seemed like a spooky foreboding. As he prepared his sledge crews and dog teams to lay finally the ghost of Franklin's lost men, missing now for fourteen years, dark questions kept intruding on McClintock's thoughts. "Can white men find subsistence wherever Esquimaux do?" he wondered. "Can white men adopt the habits of wild Esquimaux insofar as to become domesticated amongst them?"

The spring of 1859 would decide the answers. In bitter February weather McClintock made a preliminary excursion, planting supply depots along the coast of Boothia Peninsula strung out about one hundred and eighty miles south of where the *Fox* was berthed at Bellot Strait. Then he made his April arrangements. He and Lieutenant Hobson would lead separate search detachments. Each party would consist of a sledge drawn by four men and a sledge pulled by six dogs. The plan was to make a complete circuit of the diamond-shaped, five-thousand-square-mile King William Island. McClintock himself would patrol the eastern and southern areas of the diamond, comb the estuary of the Back River, and then circle up the west coast of King William Island. With characteristic kindness, he would give Hobson the first chance to explore the northwestern part of the island near Victory Point. That point offered the most promise of being the locale where Franklin's lost crews might have landed and left documents and it would mean a promotion for McClintock's junior officer.

There Hobson did indeed unearth the sole written record of the ill-fated expedition that was ever brought to light. Inside a rock cairn, stained by the rust of its tin cylinder case, one corner rotted away, was a sheet of stiff blue paper. It was the official printed form of the British Admiralty exploring ships designed to be cast into bottles in the sea. Around the margin of the document was scrawled a grim story dated eleven years before:

Sir John Franklin had died on Friday, June 11, 1847, at the age of sixty-one. A total of twenty-four officers and men had perished. The ice-wracked *Erebus* and *Terror* had been beset in Victoria Strait some fifteen miles northwest of King William Island since September 12, 1846. The one hundred and five souls remaining had deserted the ships on April 22, 1848, and had landed at Victory Point under the command of Cap-

*Slow to learn the value of Eskimo dog teams, British seamen died pulling senselessly overburdened sledges.*

tain Francis Rawdon Moira Crozier. And tomorrow, meaning April 26, 1848, he intended starting out with the survivors on a march of more than two hundred miles to the mouth of the Back River.

"So sad a tale," said McClintock, "was never told in fewer words."

But human remnants of the survivors had yet to be found, and when McClintock and other searchers found them, they bore a mute testimony to a sadder tale still. McClintock tried to soften the blow by calling it noble devotion to naval duty. But the truth remained inescapably that the tragic march down King William Island was a rank-conscious military bungle as appalling and as pathetic as the Death March of the Six Hundred at Balaclava.

From evidence ascertained from Eskimos, and from the bleached bones of apparently sawn-up skeletons later collected, King William Island was an open-air graveyard stretching from Victory Point to Starvation Cove off the Back River. It was a cemetery of unburied sledge-haulers who had died in their tracks while senselessly hauling useless cargo of the officers. Among the bric-a-brac picked up there were such things as monogramed silver plate and blue delftware china, a hollow brass curtain rod and the ornaments of a marine's plumed military dresshat, sword belts and bands of gold lace, the silver prize medals of officers won at college for mathematics and medicine, even a mahogany writing desk.

On a windswept limestone ridge McClintock was startled to discover the dissevered skeleton of what appeared to have been an officer's servant or batman. Among his belongings were a clothes brush, a horn comb still containing a few strands of light brown hair, scraps of a copy of *Lloyd's Weekly Newspaper*, a parody of a sea chanty, and spelled backwards a mock version of the biblical litany, "O, Death, where is thy sting?"

Nearby were remnants of a wind-tattered military uniform. At one time it may have been meticulously brushed and polished, but it was pitifully inadequate for arctic travel. The trousers had been of fine blue cloth; the shirt colored cotton; and the double-breasted blue cloth jacket had been edged with silk braid, with each sleeve slashed and bearing five silkcovered buttons. For warmth the dead man had worn a blue cloth greatcoat and an elegant black silk neckerchief, as though he were going on a military parade, a wedding, or a funeral.

McClintock conjectured that the steward, exhausted, hungry and cold, had sat down on the stony ridge to rest, and then slumped for-

ward—never to awaken from his funereal sleep. It brought to McClintock's mind the graphic description given to him by an old Eskimo woman. "They fell down," she said, "and died as they walked along."

On a limestone shingle beach, sixty-five miles from where the *Erebus* and *Terror* had been beset, McClintock was transfixed by the ghastly spectacle of two other skeletons. The pair of former sledge-haulers were lying like limp rag dolls in the bow and afterpart of an awning-roofed firwood boat, twenty-eight feet long and weighing about seven hundred and fifty pounds. Supporting the boat was an enormous iron-runnered oaken sledge, weighing six hundred and fifty pounds. Two double-barreled guns leaned against the boat, loaded as though ready for hunting, and it seemed remarkable that the pair had apparently starved, although they were still provisioned with a supply of tea and nearly forty pounds of chocolate. Even more remarkable was the superfluous load of baggage they had to haul apart from the combined fourteen-hundred-pound-weight of boat and sledge. It was an incredible array of stuff to drag on a life-or-death stagger.

Strewn about were: red, white and yellow slippers of calfskin bound with a bow of scarlet silk ribbon; towels and sponges and scented soap; red sealing wax and a glass seal with the symbol of Freemasonry; silver forceps and a silver pencil case and five silver watches; kid gloves and blue serge frock coats and colored silk handkerchiefs; a copy of *The Vicar of Wakefield;* six religious books, including *Christian Melodies* and *Family Prayers* and a New Testament in the French language; purgative pills; a raincoat; bayonet scabbards; four feet of a copper lightning rod; and twenty-six pieces of monogramed officers' silver plate, of which eight bore the crest of Sir John Franklin.

McClintock was shocked. The variety of articles was "truly astonishing," he wrote with understatement, "and such as, for the most part, modern travelers in these regions would consider a mere accumulation of dead weight, of little use, and very likely to break down the strength of the sledge crews."

McClintock sledged back to the *Fox* with mixed feelings about his accomplishments. His expedition had discovered eight hundred miles of new coastline. He had unraveled with unequivocal evidence the mystery of Franklin's fate. Yet certain nagging questions plagued him.

Had he and the other sledge supermen blazed the path of a Northwest Passage that was navigable? "Perhaps some future voyager," McClintock reflected wistfully, "profiting from the experience so fearfully

and fatally acquired by the Franklin expedition, and the observations of Rae . . . and myself, will succeed in carrying his ship through from sea to sea."

Fifty years later the Norwegian explorer, Roald Amundsen, aboard the forty-seven-ton herring fishery boat, *Gjoa*, was destined to make that wistful dream come true.

But could white men truly adapt themselves to the Arctic? McClintock wasn't so sure. A third crew member of the *Fox* had died, this time of scurvy. Hobson and two other officers were so scurvy-riddled that they could neither walk nor stand. And white members of the sledge parties, including McClintock himself, had proven unable to spear seals, build snowhouses, survive on raw meat, or travel exclusively by dog sledge as self-sufficiently as the Eskimos. The notion of the naval supermen was therefore demonstrably a myth.

"It is," he told the Royal Dublin Society on his return home, "evidently an error to suppose that where an Esquimaux can live, a civilized man can live there also."

McClintock's return was much heralded. Queen Victoria invested him with a knighthood. The Admiralty promoted Lieutenant Hobson to the rank of Commander. Parliament rewarded the crew of the *Fox* with a prize of five thousand pounds. The Royal Geographical Society awarded its Patron's Gold Medal to Sir Leopold McClintock and its Founder's Gold Medal—never before conferred on a woman—to Lady Franklin.

Jane felt vindicated. She regarded Sir Leopold as "one of the bravest and ablest" of her polar knights. In his popular published journal, *Voyage of the Fox in Arctic Seas in Search of Franklin and His Companions,* he had acknowledged: "They forged the last link of the Northwest Passage with their lives."

Lady Franklin, Sir Francis Leopold McClintock and Dr. John Rae were made of the same tough fiber. All three lived on to be very aged and active late Victorians.

Although the recommendation was proposed in high circles by the Hudson's Bay Company, Dr. Rae never did win the knighthood he so richly deserved. He was not a member of the British Admiralty establishment, and he had stepped on too many toes. After retiring from the H.B.C. service at the age of forty-three, the rugged "pedestrian" kept stepping out on his tireless "tours." Two years later the walker snowshoed the some forty miles from Hamilton to Toronto in Ontario in

seven hours, dined out the same evening, and showed no signs of fatigue. At forty-seven the explorer was probing away at the inland glacier ice on the west coast of Greenland. At fifty-one the boater participated in a telegraph survey across the Rocky Mountains to the Pacific coast and traveled hundreds of miles along the Fraser River in a small dugout canoe without a guide. In his old age the sportsman was still reckoned a crackshot at grouse-shooting in his native Orkney moors; and at the age of seventy, on behalf of the Orkney Artillery Volunteers, "Private J. Rae, M.D." won the prize at Wimbledon for rifle-shooting.

When he died of the flu at the age of eighty in 1893, his obituary in the *Times* said, "Until his last illness, no more vigorous looking or active man walked the streets of London." He was buried, according to his wish, under the shadow of St. Magnus Cathedral at Kirkwall in the Orkneys. He lies there in the yard of the cathedral, his memorial in the nave inscribed, "Arctic Explorer, Intrepid Discoverer of the fate of Sir John Franklin's last Expedition." His life-size figure, carved out of stone, would have pleased him. He is shown recumbent, wrapped in a buffalo sleeping bag, wearing his moccasins and arctic traveling clothes, with a book and his gun by his side.

Captain Francis Leopold McClintock continued to rise in the Royal Navy, and adventured far and wide. Eight months after the return of the *Fox*, he was commissioned to apply his scientific mind to the possible laying of a transatlantic cable and was surveying the coasts of Greenland, Iceland and Labrador aboard H.M.S. *Bulldog*. As Naval Aide De Camp to Queen Victoria, he accompanied the Prince of Wales up the Nile and visited Cairo and the Pyramids. Appointed commander-in-chief of the West Indies and North American station, he retired a much-bemedaled admiral.

At the age of sixty-nine he had not lost his interest in polar travel. "I am glad to know that you are poking up the embers so as to keep the arctic pot boiling," he wrote to a naval messmate. "I wish I were now preparing for a trip to the North Pole, for I regard it as being within the reach of this generation." He lived not quite long enough to see the Pole attained. After catching a chill, he died smiling at the age of eighty-eight in 1907. At the foot of the Franklin monument in Westminster Abbey an alabaster tablet reads: "Here also is commemorated Admiral Sir Leopold McClintock. . . . Discoverer of the Fate of Franklin in 1859."

Before his death McClintock served as pall bearer at the funeral of Lady Franklin. Jane, perhaps the most passionate traveler of them all,

*Graves of Franklin's men on Beechey Island—a sad testimony to mythical
naval supermen who wouldn't adapt to Eskimo ways.* METROPOLITAN TORONTO
LIBRARY BOARD

*McClintock was shocked to find two skeletons and Franklin's silverware
in a boat which the poor wretches had to haul.*

devoted herself to perpetuating her husband's name on whirlwind tours of the world. In Brazil, Japan, Hawaii and Alaska she was acclaimed as though she were dowager queen equal in rank to Victoria. In Rome it was *she* who granted an audience to Pope Pius IX, insisting, "There would be no nonsense about it—no kneeling I mean—but the ceremony observed as with any Sovereign." In Salt Lake City, where she stopped off to disapprove of the Mormons, she regally allowed the much-married Brigham Young to call on her, and it was said to be the first time that the Mormon President had ever "paid a visit of ceremony or respect to any woman." In San Francisco a race horse was named after her. In the Cariboo gold-rush region of British Columbia, she was paddled up the Fraser River by twelve Indian voyageurs and was greeted by a white banner hanging over the canyon at Yale proclaiming that the gold miners had named it "Lady Franklin Pass." In Spain she climbed the highest mountain, and in India, at the age of seventy-seven, she rode an elephant out of Delhi to visit the two-hundred-and-thirty-eight-foot-high red sandstone column of Kutb-Minar. "I need not say," wrote Sophia Cracroft, her niece and long-suffering traveling companion, "that she went to the top."

At the very end, in 1875, she was spending her last remaining energy arranging for a Carrara marble statue to be erected in Westminster Abbey which would declare that her husband had given his life "completing the discovery of the Northwest Passage." A fortnight before the unveiling, the indomitable woman died at the age of eighty-three.

The base of the statue bears a bas-relief of a ship frozen in ice and above it the phrase, "O ye frost and cold, O ye ice and snow. . . ." The main epitaph was composed by the Poet Laureate, Lord Tennyson, who was Sir John Franklin's nephew by marriage. It reads:

*Not here: the white North has thy bones, and thou*
*Heroic Sailor Soul*
*Art passing on thy happier voyage now*
*Toward no Earthly Pole.*

Fittingly, a second inscription was added to the cenotaph:
*This monument was erected by Jane, his widow, who after long waiting and sending many in search of him, herself departed to seek and to find him in the Realms of Light.*

# Chapter 5

# The Mystery of Thomas Simpson

Of all polar explorers perhaps none was so paradoxical, so theatrical, so prickly and so enigmatic as Thomas Simpson. He was a Master of Arts and a literary scholar from King's College, Aberdeen. Yet he cut a romantic figure as a Hudson's Bay Company frontiersman on the prairies and polar floes. His mysterious death, like his life, was fraught with melodrama. He conducted three spectacular Arctic expeditions by boat, dog sled and snowshoe. But the haunted and obsessed glory-seeker was doomed to die on horseback on the hot plains of Red River Valley, believing his feats were not appreciated. There, after killing two traveling companions, he was either killed by his own hand or murdered by assassins who thought he held the secret to the Northwest Passage.

Historians today differ strongly about the man and his murder. They do agree upon the scope of his achievements. Almost single-handedly, in 1837, 1838 and 1839, he blazed most of the path to be followed by later seekers of the Northwest Passage. He filled in the major geographical gaps on the Arctic coastline left untraced by Sir John Franklin's two overland expeditions in the 1820s. He was the first white man in the Victorian era to make effective use of pemmican as his prime Arctic ration. He taught Dr. John Rae and other travelers who came after him the imperative of living off the land like the Eskimos, of hiking on snowshoes like the Indians.

It is the character of this mercurial, high-strung Scot that has most baffled the historians, for he was so full of contradictions. One minute

he would rejoice in being the brawniest and brainiest frontiersman who had ever mastered the north country. The next minute he would be brooding self-pityingly, "What are we but poor worms when the force of the elements is arrayed against us?" In one breath he would admire the glorious freedom found in the wilderness by Indians and Eskimos. In the next breath he would be damning the "brutes" and "barbarians" for leading such licentious lives.

One feels that he was constantly warring within himself: the pedant battling the man of action, the intellectual in conflict with the romantic, the Calvinist prude striving to overcome the would-be libertine. He keeps wanting to escape to the compelling beauty and idyllic innocence of *le pays sauvage*—to the tinkling bells of his dogteam, his pawing steed on the Indian buffalo hunt. But he keeps recoiling from his savage impulses and struggles back to Victorian respectability. Ultimately the split became too great and he seems to have cracked under the strain.

Physically Thomas Simpson did not look like the "young Lochinvar come out of the West" he imagined himself to be. His doting young brother, a fur trader named Alexander Simpson, described him as being a short, squat, broad-shouldered man, only five feet five and a half inches in height. "His face was round and full, and its expression was open and engaging," said Alexander, who was a very biased witness. "Brown hair clustered in thick curls over a brow of massive breadth. The eyes were small and had a merry twinkle, giving an air of laughing cheerfulness to the upper part of his countenance; while, in striking contrast, the expression of the mouth was that of stern decision." A portrait painted of Thomas does depict the powerful shoulders, but otherwise he appears rather dour: fuzzy-whiskered, baggy-eyed, the mouth not so much decisive as purse-lipped with sanctimonious disapproval.

Superficially his personality does not at first appear very prepossessing either. He was evidently a prig; he abhorred swearing, smoking and drinking. He was apparently a puritanical mama's boy; he scolded hospitable Eskimo girls for being "w- - - -s" (his nice-Nellyism for whores). He was a naive idealist about white women; it pained him when these "ethereal beings" condescended "to the sublunary enjoyment of eating and drinking, still worse of gossiping." He was a snob; he took as his credo a Latin quotation from the poet Horace, "*Odi profanum vulgus et arceo*," which Thomas interpreted to mean, "Contempt for the low pursuits, sordid desires and grovelling habits of the vulgar herd."

Easily his most unattractive trait was his overbearing arrogance. He was certain that he towered over his colleagues. He hungered for

status and fame. His consuming ambition was to win recognition as the sole discoverer of the Northwest Passage, and few explorers have betrayed their obsession so nakedly. "Our principle," he once said, "was 'Risk all for glory'."

He also coveted the title of his all-powerful cousin, George Simpson, resident Governor-in-Chief of the Hudson's Bay Company. This was obviously a delusion of grandeur that Thomas Simpson nursed. His cousin, twenty-one years older than himself, was a short, dynamic, Machiavellian figure, reputed to be as ruthless as he was devious. He was an illegitimate orphan from the Scottish moors of Lochbroom who had risen by sometimes unscrupulous tactics to become the Little Emperor of the Canadian fur trade. He had no intention of letting his young kinsman challenge him as pretender to the throne.

Yet Thomas felt he was entitled to usurp George Simpson's position as though it were his natural due. At the age of twenty-five, when he was still a lowly clerk-bookkeeper in the H.B.C.'s Red River Colony (the present Winnipeg, Manitoba) Thomas clung to the belief that it was his destiny to "step into the Governor's shoes." With characteristic cocksureness, he boasted, "I wish I were five years older; in every other respect, without vanity, I feel myself perfectly competent to the situation; and, with one or two exceptions, hold the abilities of our *bigwigs* here in utter contempt."

When the Little Emperor thwarted his ambitions, Thomas released his frustrations in a venomous tirade directed against his cousin. "He has been to me a severe and most repulsive master," wrote Thomas. "By assuming a harsh manner towards me, he should have known . . . that the necessary effect on a young and generous mind would be a reciprocal repulsiveness, perhaps hatred. . . . He has become wavering, capricious, and changeable; he has grown painfully nervous and crabbed. He is guilty of many little meannesses at table that are quite beneath a gentleman, and, I might add, are indicative of his birth."

And yet it would be wrong to leave the impression that young Thomas was no more than a pedantic, querulous braggart. With all his faults, he was a sensitive, extraordinarily gifted Scot. Governor George Simpson, not one to hand out compliments easily, acknowledged a few of his cousin's attributes in his private character reference book on the fur trade: "Considered one of the most finished scholars . . . perfectly correct in regard to private conduct and character . . . is handy and active . . . one of the most complete men of business in the country."

Young Thomas had many more talents than that. He was an accomplished astronomer and botanist; he enjoyed studying what he called the "party-coloured sky" of the north country and collecting specimens of the *Chrysanthemum arcticum* and *Aster alpinus* which enameled its summertime meadows.

He matched Dr. John Rae as an outdoorsman. He prided himself on being a "good leg" on snowshoes. He thought nothing of racing his sled dogs on foot to achieve a record "promenade" of seventy miles in one day; then he relaxed at a midnight supper and dance in which he showed a pair of cool heels while the bagpiper skirled "Red River Jig."

He was quick to adopt Eskimo skills in boating, whether in an umiak or four kayaks lashed together. His third expedition, of 1839, in which he covered more than fourteen hundred miles in "our sweet little craft," was reckoned to be the longest small-boat exploratory voyage ever negotiated in the high Arctic seas.

He was one of the few H.B.C. officers who rejoiced in joining the Indians in a Red River Valley buffalo hunt, "my trusty double-barrel slung at my back," his nimble pony galloping across the prairie free as the wind. "I highly relished the animation of the chase," he wrote buoyantly, "and the absolute independence of an Indian life."

Camping out at night in forty-below-zero chill merely added zest to what he called the carnival time. "With your chamber dug into the snow," he rhapsodized, "your bed a litter of pine branches spread on the frozen soil; your bedding a blanket and (sometimes) a skin; the starry heavens your canopy . . . more refreshing sleep is enjoyed than awaits many a one sunk in cushions of down and curtained with silk."

It is true that Thomas jeered with malicious wit at the stilted style of the narratives written by his rival naval explorers. The literary critic dismissed Sir John Franklin's two published journals as a "dry, prosing concern." Sir George Back, who in 1834 had canoed up to little Montreal Island at the Arctic mouth of the Back River, was not deemed a much better writer. He was an exquisite artist, Thomas conceded; but "his book is a painted bauble, all ornament and conceit, and no substance."

Yet Thomas, who admittedly had a soaring ego, was not entirely expressing professional jealousy. He *knew* that he was superior, as a writer, and he was right. His own journal, *Narrative of Discoveries on the North Coast of America*, far surpassed theirs. It is one of the neglected masterpieces of polar literature. Few explorers have described with such

*"Risk all for glory" was the motto of Thomas Simpson, who died theatrically after filling in links in the Northwest Passage.*

*Governor George Simpson, the Little Emperor of the Hudson's Bay Company, both aided and thwarted his glory-hungry cousin.* HUDSON'S BAY COMPANY

literary flair the colors, the smells, the cutting cold and the luminous beauty of the north country. One understands why he named Byron Bay in the Arctic after what he called the "immortal bard," for Thomas Simpson had a sympathetic rapport with Lord Byron and was himself the first poet of the Arctic.

It was this Byronic side of his nature that Thomas exposed so freely in letters to his brother, Alexander. In his private letters he could swashbuckle boyishly, expressing how it felt to be a north rover with "the sextant as my wife, the gun & snowshoes my mistress." To "my dearest Alic" he could reveal himself as a fun-loving, non-ascetic fellow who secretly yearned for an amorous roll in the snow with an Eskimo beauty: "Hurrah for a *Husky* wife! Our worthy mother favoured me with some lengthy strictures respecting Indian connections. What would she say to see me figuring by-and-by with a young Esquimaux wife and a pair of urchins in her boots?" (Evidently he did have connections with an Indian or Esquimau belle; for in a later letter he asks that a woman at a fur trade post be paid three pounds to take care of "my little chaps," and regrets he cannot afford more money to "give the boys only absolute necessaries.")

Finally to "my dear, my only brother" the sometimes cranky and difficult Scot was able to communicate a genuine tenderness: "After the cool and reserved demeanour I must assume in public, it is inexpressibly delightful to unbosom myself to you. My naturally warm feelings have been sufficiently chilled and tutored to distrust the friendship of the world; for what is it all compared with the love we bear each other?"

Young Alexander responded with an equivalent out-pouring of fraternal affection. "I loved him as David loved Jonathan," he said simply. After Thomas died his adoring brother wrote a biography, *The Life and Travels of Thomas Simpson, the Arctic Discoverer.* Mainly it was a piece of blind hero worship, as uncritical of Thomas Simpson as it was scathing toward that "frozen martinet with a heart of ice," George Simpson. Nevertheless, Alexander in one intuitive sentence put his finger on the mainspring of his brother's character. "Even from childhood," he wrote, "there was a strong feeling of enthusiasm, almost amounting to romance, governing him."

The romantic enthusiast came from a rigid Kirk of Scotland home in Dingwall in the Ross-shire Highlands. His mother was a clergyman's daughter and evidently a very Christian woman. Despite her meagre resources, she had earlier taken in and raised her deserted bastard

nephew, George Simpson. Thomas's father was likewise extremely devout. After studying for the ministry, he settled down in the little town of Dingwall to become an impecunious parochial schoolmaster. He died when Thomas was thirteen and young Alexander but ten. He left his widow and two sons scantily provided with a schoolmaster's pension of twenty-five pounds a year.

The poverty left its mark on Thomas. "O God!" he later bewailed his fate to dear Alic. "Why were we born poor and friendless when many a dolt inherits a fair estate?"

Thomas was a frail consumptive as a child and that also left its imprint. The boy was said to be a sickly, timid weakling, lacking in self-confidence. He shunned sports and rough games and lived vicariously through the poetry of Lord Byron and the novels of Scottish derring-do written by "dear Sir Walter."

A bursary helped him study for the ministry at King's College in Aberdeen. He became proficient in Greek and Latin literature, the natural sciences and mathematics. He was a leader in the college debating society; he developed into a muscular exercise enthusiast on the moors of Lochbroom; he began lusting for travel and adventure; and, according to his brother, Alic, became a debonair Lothario with "a strong *penchant* for ladies' society."

When he graduated at the age of twenty, having won his M.A. degree and the university's top Huttonian literary prize, he decided to give up further divinity studies. He was all afire to make a name for himself in the frontiers of the New World. His cousin, George Simpson, who had risen to Governor of the Hudson's Bay Company, had made him an offer too tempting to resist. He would become George's secretary, at a beginning salary of forty pounds a year, and the possibility was held out that he would make a swift ascent to the top in the fur trade service.

The wilderness apprentice quickly learned how to Indianize, as he phrased it, whether in a birchbark canoe, on horseback, or with snowshoes. He reveled in the rugged life with all the vigor of one who had been a delicate near-invalid as a boy. He was an extremist about it, just as he was about most things. In February's piercing cold he was assigned to travel by dog sled with Indian companions from the H. B. C.'s York Factory on Hudson Bay to its prairie outpost at Red River Colony. With characteristic zeal and competitive spirit he insisted on racing the entire seven hundred miles on snowshoes.

"I never felt fatigued," he boasted, "though I left two of my men completely knocked up on the way." Then he quoted a Latin verse from the poet Ovid—"who must have been a traveller in a hyperborean region"—and spoke of the delights of building a winter campfire and wolfing down fresh game from the hunt.

Unhappily Red River Colony proved to be a stifling place for a high-spirited young man with his vaulting ambition. It was a settlement of about five thousand Scots and French Canadians and Indian mixed-bloods; and Governor Simpson set his cousin to the plodding task of doing the bookkeeping for its fur trade voyageurs. Thomas resented the lowly job. He took out his resentment on the native buffalo hunters whose wild freedom he secretly yearned for and envied.

It was almost a love-hate he felt for the Indian half-castes. He admired their *Métis* skills of hunting and following trails on the prairies. But it was tragic the way these magnificent frontier rovers became enslaved addicts to H. B. C. rum. The "uncontrollable passions of the Indian blood" then inflamed them to terrible violence. "While they lose the haughty independence of savage life," thought Thomas, "they acquire at once all the bad qualities of the white man."

Thomas became luridly embroiled in these racial tensions. A drunken Métis lurched into his office one night and demanded money on his overdrawn H. B. C. account. Thomas told him to get out. The man refused and insulted him. In the scuffle that followed, Thomas, known for his "firey" temper, gave him a black eye and a bloody nose.

The incident developed into a racial *cause célebre*. The Métis of the Colony staged an Indian ancestral war dance outside the gates of the fort and demanded that Governor Simpson publicly flog his cousin. Otherwise, they swore, Thomas might be assassinated and "the plains of Red River will be red with the blood of white men."

The Governor pacified the rebels with a keg of rum. He further intimated his intention of expelling his cousin from the Colony. Thomas was furious. Rather than lose face in that fashion he would hand in his resignation. The Governor shrank from that alternative and Thomas stayed on.

Young Alic Simpson, who had also entered the fur trade, describes an aftermath of high melodrama. Apparently the Governor refused to provide a night guard in case the Métis decided to attack and kidnap or kill Thomas. So the two brothers slept in the same room for ten days, door securely barricaded, guns cocked, and "determined to sell our lives dearly."

The Métis revolt soon blew over. But it was not forgotten. Thomas never forgave the Little Emperor for not supporting him in a crisis. Alic never forgot the threat of assassination; it was remembered with painful remorse six years later when his brother clashed in mortal conflict with the mixed-bloods of Red River.

In the interim Thomas Simpson left Red River Valley for the great adventure of his lifetime. He could thank the Old Lady of Fenchurch Street, the collective nickname for the ruling H.B.C. Committee at London headquarters. The Company's grant of monopoly trading rights in the Canadian wilds was scheduled to come up before Parliament for renewal. It would therefore be good public relations if the Gentlemen Adventurers bestirred themselves from their forts and began playing an active role in the search for the Northwest Passage.

Resident Governor Simpson was ordered to send out an exploration party forthwith. It would fill in the two major blanks on the Arctic coastline left untraced by Franklin's overland expeditions in the 1820s. One was a one-hundred-and-sixty-mile gap west of the Mackenzie River; it would link Franklin's Return Reef with Point Barrow on the cap of Alaska. The other was a stretch of some three hundred miles far east of the Arctic mouth of the Coppermine River; it would connect Franklin's Point Turnagain with the hazily undefined waterway believed to exist in the vicinity of the estuary of Back River and partly explored King William Island.

The Little Emperor had no real interest in Arctic exploration. He couldn't understand, as he later confided to Dr. John Rae, why fools would "trouble themselves with this useless passage, which for all purposes of commerce, exists in vain." Nevertheless, orders were orders and the foolishness of the Old Lady of Fenchurch Street had to be tolerated with suave cynicism.

Almost out of necessity the Little Emperor fixed his cool blue eyes on his cousin. Aware that Thomas was the most accomplished surveyor and mathematician in the service—and perhaps anxious to get him out of the way of the hotheads of Red River Colony for a cold spell—the Governor chose him to head the first expedition to Point Barrow. But aware also of his youthful impetuosity—Thomas was only twenty-eight—the Governor decided that the command would have to be shared with an older, restraining hand.

The nominal leader was to be Chief Trader Peter Warren Dease.

He was a steady, veteran Bay man approaching fifty, and the headstrong Thomas was bound to clash with him. Dease's one recommendation was that he had been a pemmican purveyor for one of Franklin's expeditions. Otherwise he was best known for his fiddle-playing, his "fair rib" Indian wife, his many "bits of brown" half-caste offspring, and his easygoing disposition. "A most amiable, warm-hearted, sociable man," Dease was described by a fellow fur trader, "quite free from that haughtiness and reserve which often characterize those who have little else to recommend them."

Haughty Thomas was bitterly disappointed that he would have to share leadership. He considered himself handcuffed to a stick-in-the-mud who was "a worthy, indolent, illiterate soul." His brother, Alic, regarded the appointment as a case of outright jealousy, and that the Little Emperor had deliberately downgraded his rising young cousin "to cast my brother into the shade."

Still, half a command was better than none and Thomas grabbed at it. He brushed up on his astronomy; he studied books devoted to the Eskimo vocabulary and customs. And to prepare himself for the vivid journal he intended to write, he reread his Shakespeare, Plutarch, Gibbon and beloved Sir Walter Scott.

There was an element of the theatrical posturer about Thomas, and that hammy streak was displayed right at the outset of his three grandstand exhibitions of arctic traveling. On December 1st of 1836 he was scheduled to start out with four dog teams from Red River Colony on a thirteen-hundred-mile trek through the deep snows of present Manitoba and Saskatchewan up to Lake Athabasca's Fort Chipewyan on the north tip of Alberta, where Dease awaited him. To prove his hardihood to the world, Thomas virtually ran the whole distance on snowshoes, sometimes racing the dogs down steep hillsides, sometimes urging them on when they left blood tracks on ice hummocks which pierced their white cloth dog booties. He thus managed to cover up to thirty-seven miles a day, and he gloried in leading the pack.

"The dogs, in fact, were so accustomed to follow me," said Thomas, "that when, at any time, I quitted my usual station in front, they stopped. They kept looking wistfully back. And the whips of their drivers failed to inspire them with the same ardour till I assumed the lead. Then they testified their satisfaction by straining to keep at my heels, the leader often thrusting forward his black muzzle to be caressed."

Neither would he permit the blizzards in forty-below-zero chill to

hamper his unrelenting pace. They braved the blast, all muffled up save their eyes. "Each eyelash was speedily bedizened with a heavy crop of icicles," he said, "and we were obliged, every now and then, to turn our backs to the wind and thaw off these obstructions with our half-frozen fingers."

The record promenade was worthwhile just to watch the expression on Dease's face when he arrived at his destination in forty-six days—a month before he was expected. With barely concealed bravado the hiker wrote back to Red River Colony, "How light and exhilarating is the free air of the North contrasted to the penthouses of York Factory and Red River! It shall go very hard on me if I ever turn *copyist* again. Seven years of that work well nigh made a fool of me; but now I feel the mind expanding again with elasticity. . . . In short, my dear friend, I am happy, most happy."

Thomas spent the next four months happily preparing for his voyage down the Mackenzie River to the Arctic Sea, more than fifteen hundred miles north. Being astronomy-minded, he named their two twenty-four-foot sail boats after the twin stars of Gemini, *Castor* and *Pollux*. They were gaily decorated with paint made from colored earth; each carried a collapsible canvas canoe; and evidently because of the British fetish for cleanliness, each carried a washboard.

Apart from that luxury, Thomas was determined that the expedition should try to live off the land, as much as possible, "like the natives." There was, however, another concession to their civilized tastes. In addition to thirty bags of pemmican, weighing ninety pounds each, the boats were loaded with more than eleven hundred pounds of Red River flour. He felt that pemmican alone as a daily ration became cloying; mixed with flour and water it made a delicious soup known as a "bergoo." Sprinkled with wild strawberries and saskatoon berries, it became a most regal dessert that the Indians called a "rubaboo."

The crew of twelve coast rovers, as Thomas grandly named them, was to consist of a polyglot mixture of Scots Highlanders, Orkney Islanders, French Canadian voyageurs, and Indian half-castes. Two of them, James McKay who was a Highlander, and George Sinclair who was a mixed-blood, had served as steersmen on Sir George Back's previous expedition down the rapid-strewn, iron-ribbed Back River up to Montreal Island on the river's Arctic estuary. Thomas, a crotchety perfectionist of a critic, rightly complimented the two as "consummate" canoemen and hunters; to this very day their Métis descendants continue that tradition in the Canadian north country.

An auxiliary sailboat, the *Goliah*, carried twenty-one yapping sled dogs. The H.B.C. men in charge were to be dropped off with their canine cargo at the north-east end of Great Bear Lake in the present Canadian Northwest Territories and erect log-cabin wintering quarters there. Names of the wilderness forts then being carved out by frontiersmen have a wonderful resounding ring to them—Fort Defiance, Fort Resolution, Fort Good Hope. With typical panache, Thomas decided to name his brave little speck of civilization "Fort Confidence."

"Soon we hope to be on our ocean theatre," he wrote with a flourish in June of 1837. "But whether to enact a comedy or a tragedy, the fates must determine."

It may have been the theatrical streak in him, but on his summer descent of the Mackenzie River Thomas proved himself a scene-painter nonpareil. He saw drama in everything, and he pictured each vignette with marvelously fresh images, sometimes with a sophisticated twist of wit, more often with a glow of childlike wonder.

"The majestic river and its high banks were steeped in a flood of light," he wrote, when his chanson-singing voyageurs paddled past the Arctic Circle in a blaze of golden sunshine at seventy-seven degrees Fahrenheit. "The day was lovely, and I fed my eyes with gazing on scenery so novel and romantic that forcibly recalled to mind my native highlands."

It was like a pastoral Arcadia teeming with beauty and life. Swallows and swans nested in the Mackenzie's cliff Ramparts, which glistened as if encrusted with pure white salt. Briar roses and blue lupins and purple-pink fireweed perfumed the spruce woods and he collected garlands of them. "Two large buck deer galloped past us, looking in the twilight, with their huge antlers, like goblin huntsmen on horseback." At the burning banks of Norman Wells his party breakfasted on freshly shot black bear, with wild onions as sauce, "and lighted our fire with coals of nature's kindling."

Sometimes they exchanged greetings with families of Loucheux Indians, floating down the river on A-shaped log rafts and picnicking on wild raspberries and strawberries. Sometimes they stopped to Indianize with encampments of Chipewyans and Dogribs and Slaves, who "squatted, like so many beavers, in their lodges on the muddy banks." The women, having "an affectionate and pleasing address, whined and simpered after their most attractive fashion," and the naked children

crowded around the gaily painted boats for their bazaar gifts of buttons and rings and bright beads. "Wherever we landed," Thomas said of these inoffensive, good-natured people, "logs were instantly carried to the water's edge, to enable us to step ashore dry-shod."

He had rather harsh things to say, however, about the Eskimos he met in the vicinity of the Mackenzie River Delta. They were "a stout, well-looking people, with complexions considerably fairer than the Indian tribes." They were thievish and aggressive predators, though, jeering at the newcomers with raven-like calls of "Caw-caw!" Like Sir John Franklin before him, Thomas was forced to fire a volley of blank shots over their heads. Thomas confided in a somewhat dyspeptic and prissy letter to his brother, Alic:

"The women danced around us, and were indefatigable in their blandishments. They are w- - - -s without an exception. The men are a set of lousy, good-humoured, thievish, pimping rogues. Without firearms I should be sorry to trust to their tender mercies, notwithstanding their smiling physiogs."

Happily the Eskimos he met along the Arctic coastline west of the Mackenzie turned out to be far more congenial hosts. At four o'clock in the afternoon of July 9, "the Arctic Ocean burst into view," he recorded. "We saluted it with joyous cheers," and soon after, "we enjoyed a very cold bath in the sea."

His boat journey along the mountain-and-ice-girdled sea on the roof of Yukon and Alaska was arduous. Yet Thomas makes it seem enchanting, like a sight-seeing trip through the crystal palace at a carnival of wonders. The sun burned through a misty opaque veil, which eventually revealed a party-colored sky; the carmine and purple shafts of the arching aurora seemed to rustle like silk; and seals and whales cavorted in a silver, undulating sea, which appeared transformed by the magic wand of mirages into the burning sands of Egypt. And the icebergs were spectacular palaces in a fairyland.

"We twisted and poled our way through them," wrote Thomas, "the transparent masses exhibiting every variety of fantastic shapes — altars, caverns, turrets, ships, crystal fabrics — which changed as we gazed upon them. Often rolling over or breaking down with a thundering noise, they tossed our little boats on the swell caused by their fall."

Eventually, near a point he called "Boat Extreme," the narrow sea lanes became clogged with massive floe bergs. "Our sweet little boats," said Thomas, threatened to be squeezed as if by a nutcracker. "By

*Thomas Simpson sometimes traveled in kayaks lashed together. On his 1839 expedition, he covered 1,400 miles — the longest journey by small boat ever negotiated in the high Arctic.* METROPOLITAN TORONTO LIBRARY BOARD

means of portages made from one fragment to another—the oars forming the perilous bridges—we at last got boats and ladings secured on a
large floe where we passed a horrible night."

Like Eliza on the ice floes in *Uncle Tom's Cabin*, Thomas managed
to leap ashore. But it appeared that his expedition had reached an im-
passe. The ice seemed impenetrable; the men were racked by a knifing
wind and clinging fog; and Peter Warren Dease was beginning to feel
his years. But Point Barrow was a mere fifty miles away, and Thomas
Simpson would not give up.

He was determined to push on, alone if necessary, by foot. The men
unanimously volunteered to accompany him, and he chose five, leaving
the others with the fatigued Dease at Boat Extreme.

His foot party slogged on in an epic of endurance. They forded salt
creeks, soaked to the waist. They camped overnight on splintery granite
beaches, their clothes crusted with hoar frost and ice. At a place appropriately christened Fatigue Bay they shivered like shadow men in a
slicing wind.

They were rescued from their misery there by a band of friendly
Eskimos, who "almost overpowered us with caresses." In exchange for
trinkets the natives plied them with bags of whale oil and blubber,
sealskin boots and caribou robes, and helped them make a tiny fire out
of the roots of dwarf willow between three upright chunks of turf. An intelligent female geographer drew a map of the route they were to follow;
others provided them with four slender oars and an agile skin umiak
which could float in six inches of water. "And we arranged our strange
vessel so well," says Thomas proudly, "that the ladies were in raptures,
declaring us to be genuine Esquimaux, and not poor white men, or
*Kabloonan.*"

A few days later, on August 4, 1837, "I saw, with indescribable
emotions, *Point Barrow*, stretching out to the northward." It was a long
low spit, composed of gravel and coarse sand, this northernmost tip of
Alaska, and with three joyous huzzas, Thomas unfurled the Union Jack
and took possession in the name of Britain.

The cheers of the celebrants aroused from their slumbers a village
of Eskimos who had been sleeping in their tent encampment nearby.
They poured out of their tents and there followed much trading and
jollification.

The village patriarch was an amiable host, with a monk-like
tonsure, a labret dangling from his lips, and wearing a caribou tunic

shaped like a headwaiter's swallowtail dress jacket. The voyageurs nicknamed him *Mallette*, meaning "suitcase," because the obliging fellow headed a procession of Eskimos and whites, serving as flag-bearer, with the Union Jack being carried on his fish spear. Like a good maître d'hôtel, Mallette also wielded a long sausage-like roll of raw whalemeat; he sliced off chunks and liberally shared the delicacy with all diners.

Each party was vastly entertained by the sharing of goods and customs. Thomas was most impressed by the Eskimos' cunningly contrived utensils: their sledges shod with whale-bone; their lasso-like ivory bola balls for capturing flying geese on the wing; their waterproof raincoats fashioned of seal bladders for kayaking. The Eskimos, in turn, were amazed when he lit a piece of touchwood with a magnifying glass, and they were terror-stricken when he applied his gold watch to their ears. "They certainly took it for a *tornga*, or familiar spirit," observed Thomas, "holding some sort of mysterious communication with my 'speaking book.'"

Both groups found highly diverting an exhibition of the other's cultural dances. The Eskimo women were delighted when the *Kabloona* Highlanders staged a very spirited Scottish reel. On their part, the Highlanders were entranced when the girls danced around in a circle, sang their musical airs and, when it became too hot, doffed their upper garments to sway like seminude land-mermaids.

Thomas watched their exotic dancing for a while and then took a solitary walk along the beach to the farthest reaches of Point Barrow. He seemed intoxicated by the mystic feeling which grips so many polar explorers once they have accomplished the first leg of their mission—a blend of heady elation and of letdown. He gazed at the blue expanse of open ocean beckoning to the west.

"So inviting was the prospect in that direction that I would not have hesitated a moment to prosecute the voyage to Bering Strait in my skin canoe," he reflected. "I could scarcely, in fact, suppress an indefinite feeling of regret that all was already done."

He comforted himself with the thought that the riddle of the passage from the east had yet to be unraveled. He would be the man to do it, vowed Thomas, if only he would not have to share the glory with that burdensome drag, Peter Warren Dease.

Merrily chanting Highland boat songs in the umiak, he and his men paddled back to pick up Dease and the others at Boat Extreme and

then prepared to make the ascent of the Mackenzie. Utterly bewitched by balmy August in the north country, Thomas was in a lyrical mood. His men paused to have another sea bath among the burnished icebergs, to play leapfrog with the Eskimos on the flanks of snow-capped mountains, and to gambol through the flower-studded valleys.

"I watched while the men slept," he wrote. "The night was serene, and not a sound broke upon the solemn stillness, save the occasional notes of swans and geese calling to their mates, and the early crowing of the willow ptarmigan, as the soft twilight melted into the blush of dawn.... Bands of reindeer, browsing on the rich pastures along the brooks, imparted life and animation to the picture.... Two fine does were shot; and I almost envied the Indians and Esquimaux, who, dispersed along the rivers and the valleys, were now enjoying the brief season with that zest which perfect freedom alone can give."

But by the time they reached their Fort Confidence wintering camp on September 25, Thomas was forced to change his tune. A bitter snowstorm was raging. Inch-thick ice coated their kettles. A solitary Canada goose, the very last straggler of the rear guard, took melancholy flight southward. And their log-cabin fort was besieged by sick and starving Indians. Thomas took pity on them and went out hunting in a desperate effort to feed them.

Meanwhile the letters he dispatched to the fur traders down south took on an edged and strident tone. "I, and I *alone*," he wrote to Alic, "have the well-earned honour of uniting the Arctic to the great Western Ocean."

He beseeched Governor Simpson to give him sole command of next summer's expedition. "Do not reject my just claims, although I am one of your own relatives," he half-begged, half-threatened. "I cannot help feeling sore that you should have considered it necessary to entrust another with the command."

His pleading was to no avail. June 6, 1838, found Thomas setting out for his descent of the Coppermine River shackled in joint command with Dease. Though it chafed, Thomas tried to make the best of it.

He had prepared this second expedition most thoroughly. During the long dark arctic winter at Fort Confidence, he had made three exploratory trips by dog sled and snowshoe across the Barren Grounds stretching between Great Bear Lake and the Coppermine River. Two of his best dogs had frozen to death in the sixty-below-zero cold; swirling snow drifts three feet high had almost buried him; one of his voyageurs

had died of a heart attack. Yet Thomas had resolutely surveyed more than one thousand miles. He was absolutely determined to find the best path east by which his expedition could drag and sail the *Castor* and *Pollux* to the head of the Coppermine River. The route he had located was a newly discovered tributary river, the Kendall, and a series of swampy lakes which he appropriately named the "Dismal Lakes."

Now, with the willow catkins budding and the first dandelions popping their yellow heads out of the tundra, everything seemed most auspicious. His party of ten men piled the two sailboats, baggage, snowshoes and caterwauling sled dogs on top of iron-shod sledges, and off they skimmed across the crusted waterways.

"We hoisted the sails to a fair wind, and, placing the crews at the drag ropes, set out at the rate of two knots an hour over the ice, colours flying," Thomas wrote jubilantly. "This extraordinary spectacle will long be a subject of tradition among the natives."

On the banks of a Dismal Lake he initiated another tradition. "I chanced to find a white wolf's den, containing four fine brindled pups. I took possession of the prize, and carried them on my back across the portage, intending to send them to Fort Confidence, and to train them to the sledge."

That night a snow squall blew up from the north-east, and Thomas displayed tenderness for the wolf cubs which he intended to h sled dogs. "My young pets were peculiarly sensitive to the noted. "Though I carefully wrapped them up in my cloa would serve them than to crawl under the blankets and hud me. They were coaxing little creatures, and, having prod petites, I found no difficulty in inducing them to change the

He added to his retinue two Hare Indians, Little Keg and noted for their skill in hunting Barren Ground muskoxen. " standing their dread of the Esquimaux, and of the unknown per sea," says Thomas, "they proved in the sequel no contemptibl aries. We made them clip their shaggy locks; and all hands clubbed to equip them in thorough voyageur costume."

They proved to be thoroughgoing voyageurs indeed. They helped those consummate steersmen, Sinclair and McKay, to man the two boats down what Thomas called the very jaws of death—the brawling green rapids and flying ice fragments of the semithawed Coppermine River. When they reached the Arctic Ocean on July 1, it was amusing how the two Indian hunters wondered at the frisking seals (which they

termed sea beavers) and promptly set out to catch the new prey.

It was not so amusing to Simpson, though, when he found the ocean almost totally blocked with floes of white, unbroken ice. "The islands lying off the coast reposed amidst the glittering field as if they were gigantic stones set in enamel," and zigzagging round the floe bergs in their tiny boats reminded him of the evolutions of an expert ice skater. Day after day they struggled eastward against their obdurate foe. They hacked and hauled, lunged and shoved with their iron-shod poles. By August 20 the planks of their boats were ice-jagged and torn; the sultry summer high temperature of eighty-eight degrees Fahrenheit in the flower-blooming sunshine had changed sharply into a torment of frost, fog, snow and storm. But they had reached Franklin's farthest— Point Turnagain.

Dease was all for calling it quits and turning back. Simpson would have none of it. The explorer was as obdurate as the solid ice that blocked further passage of their boats. He was resolved to achieve "at least a *portion* of the discoveries which we had fondly hoped to complete. . . . I argued that our honour was pledged in the cause."

He proposed setting out on foot for a journey of ten days. As at Boat Extreme the year before, the crews at this newly named Boathaven unanimously volunteered to accompany him. He chose five voyageurs as well as those two fine Hare Indian hunters, Little Keg and Anglice, and they set out in high spirits each bearing fifty-pound backpacks.

Simpson pushed his band of hikers to the uttermost limits of human endurance. They sloshed through icy swamps; they pierced their feet on red sandstone rocks the size of a man's fist. Two of his men were so painfully lame that they had to hang onto each other to get up on their swollen and inflamed legs again.

After covering one hundred miles of newly discovered coastline, Simpson reluctantly called a halt. He trudged up a sandstone cliff on a rocky cape and peered through his telescope northward and eastward across the channel that had been named Dease Strait. "A vast and splendid prospect burst suddenly upon me," he said. A bold and lofty height of land loomed through the blue mists northward, and he named it after England's girl queen, "Victoria Land," now known as Victoria Island. More splendid still, he rejoiced: "The sea, as if transformed by enchantment, rolled its free waves at my feet, and beyond the reach of vision to the eastward."

The sight of that open sea lane beckoning eastward tantalized him.

If only he had an Eskimo umiak, he thought regretfully, he would have continued his exploratory voyage, alone if need be. "I cast many a wistful look towards the open water," and resolved to return next summer and navigate it "through thick and thin." On August 25, 1838, he built a rock cairn on the red sandstone cape where he was standing and named it Cape Alexander, "after an only brother who would give his right hand to be the sharer of my journeys" and "whom I love with an affection that the world, as it goes, knows little of."

On his return to his winter camp at Fort Confidence, Thomas minced no words in the official dispatches sent to Governor George Simpson. "All that has been done is the fruit of my own personal exertions," he wrote bitingly. "My worthy senior, like Franklin and Back, was alarmed by the storms, the snow and frost." Dease had been as useless as the Old Man of the Sea who burdened the back of Sindbad the Sailor in *The Arabian Nights*. If Thomas had been alone in command, he would have pushed on boldly as far east as Boothia Peninsula.

"But my excellent senior," Thomas lashed out, "is so much engrossed with family affairs that he is disposed to risk nothing; and is, therefore, the last man in the world for a discoverer."

But the Little Emperor would not yield to his cousin. Thomas was further frustrated because he thought the Old Lady of Fenchurch Street was depriving him of the world acclaim he felt his exploits already warranted. Little knowing that his expeditions had been hailed in the London *Times* and that the Royal Geographical Society had awarded him its gold medal, Thomas expressed his mounting exasperation in a letter to Alic.

"I confess I apprehend some slippery trick on the part of the concern on which my discoveries throw lustre," he said. "They cannot, however, bar the foot of the throne against me."

In mid-June of 1839 Thomas set off for his descent of the Coppermine River determined to carve out a kingdom of discovery so spectacular that nobody could gainsay his achievement. He had twelve coast rovers on this, his most magnificent expedition. Besides Sinclair and McKay, Little Keg and Anglice, he had acquired a superb Eskimo guide. This was the redoubtable Ooligbuck, who had served as valet and interpreter for Sir John Franklin; he was later to swing wolves around by the tail for the H.B.C. sportsman-explorer, Dr. John Rae.

Peter Warren Dease, of course, was nominal leader. But by now the aging fur trader was ready to acknowledge he was a mere supernumer-

ary to young Simpson. One senses that Thomas maintained a characteristic love-hate relationship with Dease. He liked the old fellow because of his bonhomie; yet he resented him because Dease stood in the way of his single-minded ambition. In his journal Thomas speaks pleasantly of Dease enlivening the long, languorous winters at Fort Confidence with violin sonatas for Indian dances. He goes on to say, "Mr. Dease and I live together on the happiest footing; his old wife, a little grandchild, and a strapping wench, a daughter of his brother, joining our mess." Yet at the same time Thomas tolerated his worthy senior only because Dease "moves just as I give the impulse."

On this third boat excursion Thomas kept Dease and the others hopping. He was in an exuberant, self-confident mood, more sensitively in tune with the north country than ever before. Beautiful weather favored them; the men plied their paddles gaily down the Coppermine with just a single portage; mosquitoes began swarming in the warm June sunshine; and Thomas smelled the fragrant white blossoms of the Labrador tea plant and wild sorrel.

Solid sea ice stalled them for a few days at the mouth of the Coppermine near Bloody Fall, but Thomas took it with good grace. Skulls of Eskimos massacred by Samuel Hearne's Indians were still strewn near Bloody Fall, and Thomas thought it would be nice to promote interracial harmony in that gruesome locale. On a tributary stream nearby which he had discovered and named the Richardson River, he came upon encampments of frightened Eskimos.

"Have mercy on us," they cried. "We are afraid."

Ooligbuck brought the trembling Eskimos to the *Kabloona* tents and Thomas staged a picnic party in their honor. The guests were much entertained when the white men tried their hand at paddling kayaks. Anglice gave a demonstration of a Hare Indian dance and a jovial old Eskimo nicknamed the Dancer was prevailed upon to return the courtesy. Little Keg, says Thomas, was never so proud in his life as when the Eskimos consented to sleep side by side with him in the tent. Thomas himself patted their fine dogs, cut off some bright buttons from his clothes to give to the ladies, and admired their long-tailed caribou skin garments shaped like an English dress coat. The Dancer responded by measuring Dease for a pair of sealskin boots and promised to have them waiting at Bloody Fall when the *Kabloona* coast rovers returned from their eastward journey along the *Akkoolee*—the Arctic sea.

Ice in the *Akkoolee* parted as though it were the Red Sea, says

Thomas, leaving a glorious expanse of foaming water. By July 26 they were camping at the red sandstone Cape Alexander, almost a month before they had reached that farthest hiking point the previous summer. It was a moderate fifty-six degrees in the afternoon sunshine; white-backed ducks were skimming over the cerulean blue lane of open water between the ice and the green mossy shore. Ahead of them beckoned "ground never yet trodden by civilized man."

Thomas pushed his boatmen on excitedly through intermittent thunderstorms, showers of hail, and a fog-mantled sea. On August 16, 1839, with flags flying, they landed on Montreal Island in the Arctic mouth of the Back River. Five years previously to the very day the artist-explorer, Sir George Back, had camped on that spot, a few miles from his northernmost point of discovery.

Thomas, after having traversed the vast coastline stretching from Point Barrow, Alaska, to this tiny island in the eastern Arctic, could not resist gloating a little over his rival explorer. His voyageurs uncovered a cache made by Back's campers—two pounds or so of chocolate, two bags of pemmican, two cannisters of gunpowder, a box of percussion caps, and an old japanned tin containing three large fishhooks. The pemmican was literally alive with maggots, which the voyageurs called *taureaux* or "bulls"; and Thomas laughed at the witticism of their French phrase, "The Isle of Montreal will soon be populated with a colony of young bullocks." The chocolate, though wrapped in oilskin, was so rotten that Thomas could hardly boil a kettleful of it. Nevertheless, he savored the hot chocolate, for he could then say he had breakfasted on the identical camping spot of "our gallant, though less successful, precursor."

One might have thought Thomas was satisfied. He had completed his main task of linking the Pacific Ocean with Back's farthest. He had also passed through the ten-mile-wide Simpson Strait—the significant water highway separating the continent from King William Island and forming a vital link in the Northwest Passage. Yet the tenacious Thomas Simpson could not rest content. There were still four days left before the date set for his expedition's return journey. Why not *complete* the Northwest Passage?

It was an audacious gamble. He wanted to sail on to the farthest limits of Sir John and James Ross's explorations of 1829 to 33. He would determine whether Boothia and King William were islands or peninsulas joined to each other and the mainland.

He summoned his band of coast rovers and explained to them the importance of continuing on eastward. "To their honour," he wrote, "they all assented without a murmur."

At nine o'clock that evening, without even a day's rest on Montreal Island, his voyageurs bent at their oars and struck out for the farthest visible land to the northeast. In astronomer fashion, Thomas gazed through his telescope at the bell-jar sky and felt exalted.

"It was a lovely night," he wrote. "The fury of the north lay chained in repose. The Harp, the Eagle, the Charioteer, and many other bright constellations gemmed the sky and sparkled on the waters, while the high Polar star seemed to crown the glorious vault above us."

But their luck turned. A cruel northeast wind set their cockleshell boats creaking and pitching in buffeting waves. After four days of strenuous rowing, they were forced to put into a bay in the horsehead-shaped land mass at the base of Boothia Peninsula. On August 20, 1839, Simpson had his weary men erect a limestone rock cairn. He was heartbreakingly near his goal—some forty miles south of yet-undiscovered Rae Strait and about sixty miles south of where Sir James Ross had crossed the ice from Boothia Peninsula to King William Island. But flocks of Canada geese were bugling southward in long triangular flights; the smell of winter was in the air.

Thomas Simpson acknowledged surrender—until next year. The rivulet winding into the bay of his farthest point east of discovery he named the "Castor and Pollux," after "our gallant boats, old and worn-out as they were, which acquitted themselves beyond our most sanguine hopes."

On the return boat trip westward the explorer relentlessly squeezed the last ounce out of his discovery rovers. In the face of searing winds, choppy seas and snowsqualls, he ignited his men into rowing along the north side of Simpson Strait while he traced sixty miles of the southern shore of King William Island. At a cape which he reckoned to be fifty-seven miles south of Sir James Ross's Victory Point, he had his men build another limestone cairn, which was saluted with the usual volley of gun fire and appropriate flag-planting. Nine years later Sir John Franklin's ill-fated expedition was destined to perish in that region from starvation. It is therefore interesting that Thomas reported the place was abounding in muskoxen, caribou and vast numbers of snow geese.

The inexorable Simpson was not yet finished. "The men declared that the chill of the salt water 'cut them to the heart' as they waded

ashore with the baggage," he noted. Yet he persisted in surveying more than one hundred and fifty miles of the south coast of Victoria Island, meanwhile ecstatic about the wonders he saw.

"I have seldom seen," he wrote, "anything more brilliant than the phosphoric gleaming of the waves when darkness set in. The boats seemed to cleave a flood of molten silver; and the spray, dashed from their bows before a fresh breeze, fell back like a shower of diamonds into the deep. It was a cold night; and, when we at last made the land, cliffs faced with everlasting ice, obliged us to run on for a couple of leagues before we could take the shore with safety. . . ."

Icicles were hanging in banana-like clusters when they finally reached the Coppermine River's Bloody Fall. The first thing they saw there was a long pole to which was attached the custom-tailored sealskin boots delivered as promised by the Eskimo Dancer at the commencement of their voyage. As a reward they cached fishing nets and their surplus pemmican. Then, though most of his voyageurs were suffering from acute pains and swellings in the limbs, the inexhaustible Simpson led them in giving chase to a huge bear. Across the Barren Grounds they trekked, up to the knees in snow; and on September 24, 1839, "in the teeth of a strong northwest gale, with blinding snow and a temperature of 14 degrees, we reached at dusk the friendly shelter of Fort Confidence."

Thomas could look back triumphantly to having accomplished a boat journey of more than fourteen hundred geographical miles—the longest heretofore recorded in the annals of Arctic travel. After generously paying off Little Keg and Anglice, who "appeared affected as we shook hands with them," he staged a grandstand finish to his north country promenades. In what he boasted was "an unrivalled winter journey of two months," he axed paths through piling snow drifts for his dog team, and snowshoed almost two thousand miles back to Red River Colony.

He had been away from so-called civilization for more than three years, and his arrival at the fur trade settlement on February 2, 1840, was a curious letdown. The first thing he saw was a domesticated Saulteaux Indian named Land Grass, "returning comfortably drunk from the settlement, with his wife and party, whose appearance struck me as squalid and inferior to that of the tribes more remote from civilization."

The frontiersman had another letdown in store for him. All afire with the flag-planting fever, he proposed that Governor George Simpson equip him with a single boat, and that summer he would complete the last link in the Northwest Passage, sailing right through to Hudson Bay. The Little Emperor threw cold water on his dreams of glory. In a chilly letter the Governor offered not a word of praise for his cousin's feats, nor permission to continue with his discoveries: only a suggestion to take a year's leave of absence.

Thomas burned with resentment. He would not be brushed aside, as his brother Alic said, by a "relative whose jealousy of his cousin's rising name was now but ill-disguised."

Thomas sent the Little Emperor a spleenish note. "So far from wishing to avail myself of the leave of absence which you have so kindly offered *unasked*," he declared sarcastically, "it gives me great uneasiness." If the Governor were such a skinflint that he flinched at risking the Company's money, then Thomas would pledge for the expedition every penny he possessed—all of five hundred pounds plus his future salary.

"Fame I will have, but it must be *alone*," wrote Thomas with unabashed ambition. "My whole soul is set upon it. . . ." Then he added a denigrating aside reflecting his prejudice, "My worthy colleague on the late expedition frankly acknowledges his having been a perfect supernumerary; and to the extravagant and profligate habits of half-breed families I have an insuperable aversion."

Receiving no answer from the Governor, Thomas dispatched a letter outlining the same proposal to the Bay Company Committee in London. Waiting to hear from the Old Lady of Fenchurch Street, Thomas tried to busy himself, while eating his heart out with impatience. He wrote his brilliant narrative account of his expeditions as well as brooding letters to Alic and a few intimates in the fur trade.

One feels that his years of Arctic striving, his consuming ambitions, his smoldering frustrations, were straining tautly an already unstable mind. An almost manic-depressive split was reflected in his journal and his letters. The frontiersman who reveled in the prairie chase after wolves and buffalo now thought, "There are few sounds more melancholy than the nightly howling of the troops of wolves that attend the motions of the buffalo. The mind is oppressed, as it were, with a feeling of intense loneliness." The polar traveler who gloried in his strength now reflected, "What are we but poor worms when the force of the elements is arrayed against us?"

*Simpson was slain after leaving the Colony with a wagon train of Métis buffalo hunters.*

*Simpson's "firey" temper provoked a native war dance at Red River Colony.*

And with supreme megalomania the boating explorer, who had collected about him such a brave band of native voyageurs for his last great voyage, now cast white man's slurs upon them: "It must not be supposed that our crews, though good and true men in their way, were all good sailors. Besides the steersmen, we had, in fact, but two Europeans in each boat entitled to the name. The remaining six, comprising a *Canadien*, an Iroquois, a Cree, two Hare Indians, and an Esquimaux, knew about as much of handling a sail as they did of geography or geology."

Weeks slipped by, and the Old Lady of Fenchurch Street remained silent. His hopes soared when London dispatches arrived at Red River Colony in March, only to be dashed when they failed to contain any instructions.

"Last night the long looked-for packet from England arrived," he wrote despondently, "but it brought me no word of remembrance from any one. . . . I never remember being so thoroughly in the blues in my life before."

With the desperation of the obsessed, he tried to solicit funds for his polar voyage from local H.B.C. officers. But, according to Alic, Governor Simpson then "effectually prevented the immediate organization of a renewed expedition." Consequently, Thomas felt he had no recourse but to bypass the Governor and go directly to London headquarters via the United States and negotiate sponsorship in person.

He came to that decision on June 3, 1840, after the canoe brigade arrived with again no word from the Old Lady of Fenchurch Street. Ironically, on that very day, the H.B.C. Directors in London were signing a document giving him sole command of the new expedition he so burningly craved.

Two days later, on June 5, Thomas scrawled a hasty note to his dear Alic before departing on the last journey of his life. His spirits had been "low for a great part of the spring"; he was traveling with companions on horseback, all well armed in case they should meet a war party of Sioux Indians on the plains; and he expressed a loving "farewell, my dearest brother."

What happened nine days later on the Dakota plains of Red River Valley was as bizarre as any melodrama ever written by Thomas Simpson's beloved Sir Walter Scott. Some said it was murder; some said it was suicide; and some said it was Indian mixed-blood vengeance inspired by Governor Simpson. Whatever it was, it remained a

mystery—a tale told not by "dear Sir Walter" but by a pair of illiterate Métis who swore to the truth of their conflicting stories in depositions taken by prairie justices of the peace.

The most plausible evidence was recited by a Canadian half-caste named James Bruce. The testimony which he signed with an "X" before a United States territorial lawman, went this way: Simpson had been traveling with a wagon train of Red River Colony buffalo hunters who were carting game southward. Thomas had impatiently galloped ahead with four Métis. He appeared to be restless, sick and uneasy. While two of the party were putting up the tent, Thomas shot and killed them. He said they had been plotting to murder him that night for his papers, possibly believing that the valuable documents contained the secret to the Northwest Passage.

Thomas then offered James Bruce five hundred pounds to keep quiet about the double killing and to take him back to Red River Colony. Bruce refused. Instead he and the other Métis rode off to find the wagon train. They left Thomas with his double-barreled shotgun all alone with the two dead mixed-bloods.

At sunrise Bruce returned with other buffalo hunters. "Mr. Simpson!" they called out as they closed in on horseback. "Mr. Simpson!"

They got no answer except the report of a gun, and saw smoke, and heard a shotgun ball whistling over their heads. Bruce cried out, "He is firing at us."

"I think," said one of the others, "he has fired at himself."

They found Thomas Simpson dead, holding the muzzle of his gun on his breast, and with the top of his head blown off. He was just thirty-one years old.

The Métis dug a hole in the ground. Then they cut the tent into a makeshift shroud and wrapped all three bodies together in it and buried Thomas Simpson and the two Métis in the red-stained earth of Red River Valley. It was a humbling end for one of the most vainglorious of Arctic explorers. As he once said in an unwitting epitaph, they were all but poor worms when arrayed against the force of the elements.

What really motivated the seemingly senseless bloodshed on those lonely plains will never be known. Alic Simpson, half-crazed with grief, resigned from the fur trade and devoted himself to vindicating his brother and hurling accusations against Governor George Simpson.

Was the Governor implicated in the murder in an attempt to block the Northwest Passage which might hamstring the fur trade? Were the

*Métis* avenging what Alic called their "long-treasured animosity" against Thomas and had they concocted the suicide story to cover up their assassination? Had Thomas shot two of the conspirators in self-defense and then killed himself because he had cracked up mentally? Those unanswered questions remain in the realm of controversy to this very day.

There was a richly ironic sequel to the tragedy. The Little Emperor, who scorned the hunt for the Northwest Passage and thwarted his cousin's grasp at glory, gained the most benefit from all the striving. A carpet bag containing Thomas Simpson's brilliant narrative of his three expeditions was found at the death scene. The Governor took possession of the journal. He claimed that he wanted to embody it in an Arctic book of his own, which, "if I can command a little leisure time, I have it in contemplation to publish." Alic managed to pry it loose and had it published in 1843, after charging hotly that the Governor had tampered with his brother's papers.

The missing papers, according to Alic, would have let him document a court case against the Governor for the more than two thousand pounds owed by the H.B.C. to Thomas Simpson's estate. The Little Emperor blocked payment of that financial reward, though the money would have gone to Thomas's widowed, seventy-two-year-old mother in Dingwall, who had served as George Simpson's own foster mother. Instead, we are told, the Governor callously withheld both documents and financial reward and granted the widow the "merest pittance."

Yet in the end the Little Emperor, who shared little love for his heroic cousin or heroic polar expeditions, emerged the victor from all this behind-the-scenes melodrama. In January of 1841, a little more than six months after the death of Thomas Simpson, Queen Victoria summoned George Simpson to Buckingham Palace. There, amid appropriate fanfare, he was knighted Sir George Simpson—as a reward for his alleged encouragement of Arctic exploration.

The theatrical Thomas Simpson had set out for his polar stage in June of 1837, declaring with a flourish that the fates would have to determine whether a tragedy or a comedy would be enacted. And so it ended with a bitter touch of both.

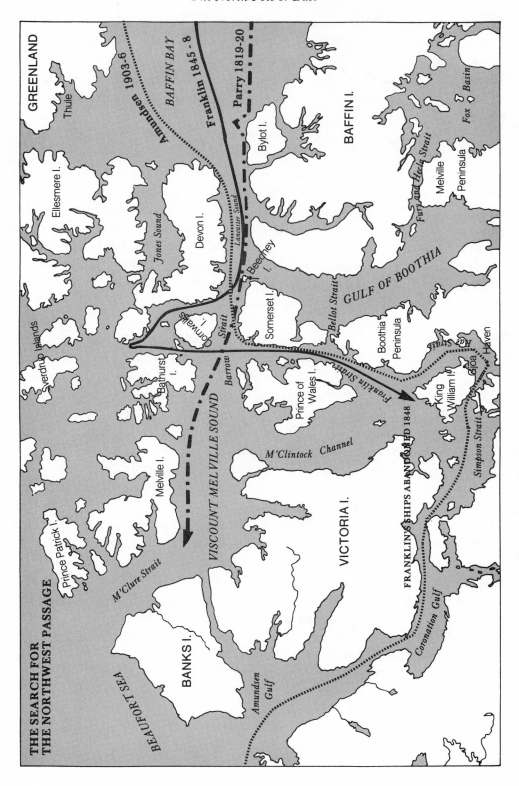

THE SEARCH FOR
THE NORTHWEST PASSAGE

GREENLAND

Thule

Ellesmere I.

Sverdrup Islands

Prince Patrick I.

BEAUFORT SEA

M'Clure Strait

BANKS I.

Amundsen Gulf

Melville I.

Bathurst I.

Jones Sound

Devon I.

Cornwallis I.

VISCOUNT MELVILLE SOUND

Barrow Strait

M'Clintock Channel

VICTORIA I.

Coronation Gulf

Amundsen 1903-6

BAFFIN BAY

Franklin 1845-8

Parry 1819-20

Bylot I.

Lancaster Sound

Beechey I.

Somerset I.

Prince of Wales I.

Bellot Strait

Franklin Strait

FRANKLIN'S SHIPS ABANDONED 1848

Boothia Peninsula

King William I.

Gjoa Haven

Rae Strait

Simpson Strait

BAFFIN I.

Fury and Hecla Strait

Melville Peninsula

Fox Basin

GULF OF BOOTHIA

158

# Chapter 6

# The Eskimo
# from Philadelphia

Nothing is worth living for but to have one's name inscribed on the Arctic map, said Alfred, Lord Tennyson. The Poet Laureate of Britain made the remark long before composing his celebrated epitaph for his missing uncle, the "heroic sailor soul," Sir John Franklin. During the mid-1800s Tennyson's declaration resounded like a clarion call in the ears of adventurers throughout the English-speaking world.

It was immensely appealing to the intrepid and the rootless in the burgeoning cities of the United States. The frontiers of the Far West were fast being peopled by the restless in covered wagons, and here was the opportunity to pioneer in the untenanted Far North. There was the chivalric appeal of aiding that lady in distress, Jane Franklin, to find lingering traces of her lost husband. There was the sportsman's appeal of beating the British at their game of charting the Northwest Passage.

And now, with characteristic enterprise, the Americans added another appealing element to the polar quest: a combination of the practical and the patriotic. Edgar Allan Poe of Baltimore had written a piece of science fiction to outdo Jules Verne. It was titled *The Narrative Of Arthur Gordon Pym*. It dealt with a mythical explorer who had discovered a mythical tropical sea beyond the circumpolar ice belt inhabited by mythical South Sea Islanders. In the imagination of some American dreamers, fact became mixed with fantasy, just as it had in the days of Henry Hudson and William Baffin. There was the tantalizing prospect of locating untapped whaling grounds in an open polar sea

north of Baffin Bay. And, equally tempting, why not plant the Stars and Stripes on the North Pole itself?

The American thrust toward what he was to call the Iceless Polar Sea was initiated by an improbable gentleman from Philadelphia named Dr. Elisha Kent Kane, the first American to play the role of Eskimo. It was Kane who answered Tennyson's plea to put the poet's name on the Arctic map. A Greenland crag was duly christened by the explorer "Tennyson's Monument."

Kane's own monument was a saucer of icy water, one hundred and ten miles long and about eighty miles at its widest, known today as the Kane Basin. On the east side of it are the sugarloaf mountains and glacial clamshells of north Greenland. On the west side, shaped like a dragon's head, lies Canada's Ellesmere Island, seventy-seven thousand square miles of ice and rock and snow, the tenth largest island in the world.

To the south of the basin is Smith Sound, the gateway to the Pole discovered by William Baffin more than two centuries previously. Guarding the gateway, like two granitic gargoyles, stand the crimson cliffs of Cape Alexander and Cape Isabella. Kane called them the Arctic Pillars of Hercules.

Between those pillars and the Arctic Ocean there is a channel of water stretching some three hundred and fifty miles. In its day it was popularly known as the American Highway to the geographic North Pole.

Kane's push nearly halfway up the liquid avenue made him a national hero. He was acclaimed "the outstanding American polar idol of the midcentury." His two-volume book, *Arctic Explorations*, describing his adaptation to Eskimo life, was said to be found along with the Bible on every parlor table in the nation. At his death in Havana at the age of thirty-seven, a scant sixteen months after the return of his expedition, the flags in the United States Capital were lowered to half-mast. His body was conveyed across the nation for burial in Philadelphia with obsequies paralleled only by the homage paid to Abraham Lincoln's funeral train.

Kane was nonetheless an unlikely man to be the United States Navy's representative responsible for planting the Stars and Stripes five hundred and seventy miles short of the Pole. Physically and temperamentally he was not cut out to be a seaman or a semi-Eskimo. He could not navigate a ship. He was constantly seasick. He was afflicted for most of his life with rheumatism and a chronic heart murmur.

By all accounts he was a frail, fine-boned, elegant man, just five feet six inches in height. There was a romantic aura about him. His beard was brown and silky. His moustaches were long and curling. His forehead was domelike, his nose aquiline, his voice melodious. But it was his eyes—those "dark gray eyes with a wild-bird light in them"—that everyone remembered. "When they were in the torrent tide of enraptured action, the light beamed from them like the flashing of scimitars," wrote his Victorian biographer, Dr. William Elder, "and in impassioned movement they glared frightfully."

His personality was quixotic and quicksilver, hard to pin down because he was so contradictory. He was a pragmatic idealist, a sentimental scientist, an aristocratic egalitarian. According to Dr. Elder, he detested naval discipline: "the distinctions of rank outraged his frank democracy of feeling." Yet at the same time he could not tolerate insubordination; it sometimes triggered off in him explosive violence. "Nervous excitability was a marked character of his temperament," said Dr. Elder. "He would take no sauce from anybody," and when thwarted was "tense as a steel spring under pressure."

His very intensity—what he called his "life force"—seemed to magnetize people. Sir Clements Markham, secretary of the British Royal Society, which awarded him a gold medal, wrote: "His was certainly a charming personality, talented, cheerful and enthusiastic." Undoubtedly true, for Kane was plentifully endowed with the gentlemanly graces. He was among the most colorful of Arctic scene-painters, whether in words or on canvas. He had a well-rounded knowledge of the natural sciences. Despite his frail constitution, he was physically courageous. He was a horseman of note; a connoisseur of fine wines and Havana cigars; a *boulevardier* who attracted women; and he had a wonderful flair for extravagant, cockeyed, American humor.

Like a good many other explorers, he was strongly histrionic. In the Yankee slang of his day he was a "puffer," an exaggerator who liked to color drab reality with a high yaller varnish. One suspects that he would have made a good Mississippi steamboat gambler and, indeed, perhaps he imagined himself to be one. He was an incurable romantic, of course, always assuming studied poses, always taking flight from his wealthy Philadelphia home to the most outlandish places and seeking out bizarre adventures. It was as though he was turning his back on the constricting Victorian code of conventions. Whatever it was that drove

him—perhaps it was a yearning for Rousseauesque simplicity, perhaps it was the need to prove masculinity in that fragile body of his—he did everything with operatic dash. Wherever he toured around the world he felt impelled to dress and playact a role. "My Thebes life is a very wild one," he wrote to his parents on an Egyptian jaunt down the Nile. "I am in native dress, with a beard so long that I have to tuck it in."

He prepared himself to face the Arctic almost as though he were going on some garish masquerade party. He took along a Kentucky rifle; a cashmere gown which he had received as a gift from a Hindu priest; a Mormon wolfskin; and what he called "a somewhat ostentatious Astrakhan fur cloak." At home, while writing his Arctic narrative, Dr. Elder tells us, Kane would work at a frenzy until three in the morning. Then he would go into his yard for a couple of hours and crack his thirty-three-foot-long Eskimo dog team whips. "He would crack them," says his admiring biographer, "like a pistol."

One gains another insight into Kane's eccentric character from a more intimate source. This was his sweetheart, Margaret Fox, who published after his death a book entitled *The Love-life of Dr. Kane.* Despite its spicy title, the collection of love letters is highly revealing.

Margaret Fox was a thirteen-year-old Canadian spiritualist who had moved from a farm in Bath, Ontario, to Rochester, New York. There she and her two sisters created a sensation with their floor-rapping apparent communications with the spirit world. The sisters toured the United States and impressed such respectable personages as James Fenimore Cooper, Horace Greeley and William Cullen Bryant. A conclave of doubting medical men declared the so-called rappings were fraudulent—the result of the sisters cracking their own knee and ankle joints under the table. Dr. Kane was sceptical, too, when they staged a seance in Philadelphia. Nevertheless, though he was sixteen years older than Margaret, he became wildly infatuated with the nymphet, much like Humbert Humbert with Lolita.

There is no reason to question the authenticity of the love letters he sent her. Newspapers of the day, including the New York *Times* and the *Tribune*, hinted at the lurid affair. Eventually it gained so much notoriety that Kane's family issued a statement to the Associated Press. It was claimed that Kane was merely putting the little girl through a private school in Philadelphia.

The letters suggest that he was more deeply involved with Margaret than that. He addresses her as "That dark-eyed little Maggie

*Dr. Elisha Kent Kane, Byronic boulevardier, pushed nearly halfway up the 350-mile American Highway to the Pole.*

*"Sugar Plum," "Pet Lamb" and "Toots" were Kane's endearments for his clairvoyant sweetheart, Margaret Fox.* METROPOLITAN TORONTO LIBRARY BOARD

of mine," "Sugar Plum," "Dear Pet Lamb" and sometimes "Toots." Maggie, much cooler in her ardor, knew him as "Dear Dr. Kane," "Lish," "Ly," and because he frequently lectured her on morality, "the Preacher."

One gathers that Maggie, despite her dark Madonna eyes and sweet pouting lips, was a hardboiled little gold digger. Kane was aware of this, but he could not resist her charms—"that strange mixture of child and woman, of simplicity and cunning, of passionate impulse and extreme self-control." He confesses that he is easily deceived. "I am a weak man and a fool; weak, that I should be caught in the midst of my grave purposes by the gilded dust of a butterfly's wing; and a fool because, while thus caught, I smear my fingers with the perishable color."

He keeps plying her with gifts: a diamond bracelet, a Newfoundland dog, dinners at Delmonico's fashionable restaurant in New York City. Yet the minx remains standoffish. He pleads with darling Maggie to love him, "not the sort of *half-affected* milk and water love which you now profess, but a genuine, confiding affection." He teases her with a rueful poem:

> *Purely though I love her, and worship none above her*
> *Madly as I adore her, and sadly as I bore her.*

He wishes that she were "a pure, simple-hearted, *trusting* girl" and tries to persuade her that his intentions with her are quite serious. "Now to you I am nothing but a cute, cunning dissembler; a sort of smart gentleman hypocrite, never really sincere, and merely amusing himself with a pretty face...."

Maggie holds out for nothing less than a marriage engagement. When she was sixteen, we are told, Kane performed a private ceremony in front of Maggie's mother. He took some bunches of grapes, wove them into a garland, placed it on Maggie's head, and solemnly pledged that she was his wife in the sight of heaven.

Maggie then appears to have succumbed to his amorous advances. Evidently they had secret trysts in the third-storey bedroom of her mother's home on Twenty-second Street in New York. He arranges to have her portrait painted. "Don't be afraid of your neck and shoulders. I want you to look like a Circe, for you have already changed me into a wild Boar."

He sends her impassioned *billets doux*. He longs to gaze "at your dark eyes and pouting lips. How much more a pleasure it is to do more than gaze!" And he urges her to "read this letter over as you go to bed, and imagine dear Elish' patting your hands, or pressing his rough beard against your glowing cheeks. Don't think of me as the wicked person I have learned to be. . . . You know I am a queer mixture of good and bad."

The bad part of him appears to have taken over, for Kane ultimately was forced to break off their secret engagement. Polar duty called. More important, evidently, what he termed his Royal Family was threatening to cut the playboy off if he continued his love affair with a common farm girl so far below his social station. Kane bade her a fond farewell full of romantic affectation:

"In a few weeks I will be away from you. Thick-ribbed ice, sterner than warriors' steel, will separate me from you. . . . Maggie, dear, you have many traits which lift you above your calling. You are refined and loveable; and, with a different education, would have been innocent and artless; but you are not worthy of a permanent regard from me. You could never lift yourself up to my thoughts and my objects; *I* could never bring myself *down* to yours.

"This is speaking very plainly to my dear confiding little friend, Maggie Fox, who sometimes thinks she loves me more than a friend. But Maggie, darling, don't care for me any more. I love you too well to wish it, and you know now that I really am *sold* to different destinies; for just as you have your wearisome round of daily moneymaking, I have my own sad vanities to pursue. I am as devoted to my calling as you, poor child, can be to yours.

"Remember then, as a sort of dream, that Doctor Kane of the Arctic Seas loved Maggie Fox of the Spirit Rappings."

Elisha Kent Kane was the eldest son of what was indeed the Royal Family of Philadelphia. His parents were rich and socially prominent Presbyterians. His father, a graduate of Yale Law School, was a federal court judge and a man of patrician and scholarly tastes; he headed the American Philosophical Society. Kane's mother, of the wealthy Dutch Van Rensselaer family, was a great beauty in her day; she was said to be endowed with the "energy, nerve, elasticity, and warm-heartedness which became famous in her son."

Young Kane was a sickly, pampered boy. He rebelled against his many private tutors and seemed bent on escaping from the confining orthodoxy of his family. He appears to have been a scientifically minded

dreamer; his favorite reading as a youth consisted of chemistry books, *Robinson Crusoe* and *Pilgrim's Progress*. Despite a near-fatal bout of rheumatic fever, he graduated from the University of Pennsylvania medical college at the age of twenty-two, standing at the head of his class.

After that he was governed by an overmastering desire for reckless adventure. It was as though he was racing with the clock against his feeble constitution and he desired desperately to taste every novel experience while he could. "The doctors tell me," he said of his cardiac condition, "I may live a month or perhaps half a year, but they know, and I know, that I may be struck down in half an hour."

To dare danger was his motto wherever he traveled. He explored the crater of a volcano in the Philippines, went on an elephant hunt in India, joined a caravan of slave traders on the African Gold Coast. He climbed the Andes of South America, lived on locusts in the deserts of Egypt, and was wasted by fever while roving about China. Bedouin bandits shot him in the leg when he ascended the Nile and a lance wounded him in the groin while he was leading a charge against guerillas in Mexico.

In his thirtieth year Kane's career of desperate adventure took a northward turn. He signed on as naval surgeon in a polar expedition financed by Henry Grinnell, an American shipping magnate who had made a fortune in the whale oil business. In 1850 Grinnell presented two ships, the *Advance* and the *Rescue*, to the United States Navy, so that they could join in the search for the missing Franklin expedition and help him do a little business on the side. No doubt Grinnell's motives were largely humanitarian and scientific (he was a founder of the American Geographical Society). But he made sure the instructions to the U.S. Naval Commander, Lieutenant Edwin Jesse De Haven, bore this explicit directive: "As the Whaling interest is becoming important in the Arctic Seas, you will obtain all the information in relation to it that you can."

As it turned out, the expedition produced little information about whaling or Franklin. The two little square-rigged brigs got trapped in the ice and spent the nine-month winter drifting aimlessly about Lancaster Sound and Baffin Bay. The voyage was mainly important because it served as Kane's personal apprenticeship in the northern latitudes. The first book that he wrote, *The U.S. Grinnell Expedition in Search of Sir John Franklin*, humanized the Arctic in terms that Americans could

appreciate; it introduced genuine Yankee idiom to polar folklore. His narrative brims with freshly minted phrases: some overstrained, some whimsical, some delightfully extravagant, like the early Mark Twain spinning yarns about *The Celebrated Jumping Frog of Calaveras County.*

"An odd cruise this!" Kane remarks. "The American expedition fast in a lump of ice about as big as Washington Square, and driving, like the shanty on a raft, before a howling gale."

Though wretchedly seasick, he sits on the heaving deck and draws watercolor sketches of the Fourth of July parade of floating icebergs. "There is not one of these smaller than our Washington Capitol, and one of them would fill the Capitol square. . . . About one o'clock today a fragment about as large as Independence Hall fell from it into the ice sea below. . . . At one time we had the whole Acropolis looking down upon us in silver; at another our Philadelphia copy of the Parthenon, the monumental Bank of the United States, stood out alone."

The ice hummocks created a terrific traffic jam in sea lanes no wider than the Delaware River. They collided, producing shrill noises that sounded like the whining of puppies, the humming of bees, followed by a "grinding, tooth-pulling *crunch*." The accidents left in their wake a litter of "bergy bits," some rising up like cones of crushed sugar forty feet high, others rattling past like a procession of prairie Conestoga wagons.

He went on for pages describing the wonders to be seen in the "long, staring day" of the midnight sun. It was, he said, like the phantasmagoria of an opium-eater's reverie. The artist in him was mesmerized by the play of light on the golden icebergs. It was as dazzling as the "spangled petticoats of a ballet dancer in full twirl to a boy on his first visit to the opera."

He went for nature rambles on the rubbery young ice (which he called "tickly-benders") and plucked wild flowers from the shore. An entire forest of shrubs, none higher than one's ankle, could be covered with a cloak. The fruit-bearing blaeberry bush (*Vaccininium uliginosum*) he could cover with a wine glass. "As for the wild honeysuckle (*Azalea procumbens*) of our Pennsylvania woods—I could stick the entire plant in my button hole."

The creatures he saw were a menagerie of grotesques. The tusky walrus was a Sphinx-like monster, "reminding me of stage hobgoblins, something venerable and semi-Egyptian withal." The yellowish polar bear appeared to be a colossal Puss-in-Boots, looking almost elephantine

from the rear. A speckled white beluga whale swam under his ship, and he vowed it performed an underwater concert—a medley of singing, whistling, barking and Tyrolean yodel.

The seal aroused his pity. "It has a countenance between the dog and the mild African ape—an expression so like that of humanity that it makes gun-murderers hesitate. They paddle in groups, like a party of schoolboys frolicking in the Schuylkill. At last, at long shot, I hit one. God forgive me!"

The prey was cooked up by the ship's French chef, Henri, and Kane played the role of fastidious gourmet, elegantly describing what it was to "arcticize" on such a Lucullan repast. "Seal is not fishy, but *sealy*," he maintained, "and with a little patience and a good deal of *sauce piquante* is very excellent diet." He found polar bear steak strong and rather capricious. "One day he is quite beefy and bearable; another, hircine, hippuric, and damnable." He smacked his lips over "seagull *à merveille*," while a filet of the snow white ivory gull was a *morçeau* between a spring chicken and an American canvasback duck. But roast guillemot! Ah, the maître d'hôtel of Delmonico's in New York had never for him trussed partridge as succulent. "They are very red in meat, juicy, fat, delicate, and flavorsome, something between a bluewing and a Delaware rail; in a word, the perfection of good eating."

He reserved his most extravagant hyperbole for the arctic winter. To use a cowboy phrase, he said, you had to rough it with no fancy trimmings. It was so cold you could pick your teeth with the handkerchief that froze when you pulled it out of your pocket. If you put out your tongue it became glued to your lip. Despite the heat of a stove, the bed clothes froze over your feet as though you were a mummy and a copy of the New York *Herald* at the head of your bunk became petrified with ice. He continued to cherish three luxuries that reminded him of warmer climes—silk next to his skin, a toothbrush for his teeth, and white linen for his nose. "Everything else is Arctic and hairy—fur, fur, fur."

The worst thing about the long winter twilight was the boredom; he felt as ennuied as though serving time confined in Sing Sing Prison. His active imagination found release in dreams. He dreamed of locating Sir John Franklin in a tropical polar cove lush with quinces and orange groves and watermelons, "and dreamed of being presented to Queen Victoria."

As his ice-cradled ship drifted southward, past Mount Raleigh of

*"Like blind men in the streets of a strange city" wrote Kane of groping across glassy ice hummocks.*

*"Like sleepwalkers moving on in a dream," he wrote of the ghastly perils of tumbling into a crevasse.*

Baffin Island all pearl-powdered with snow, he had more grandiose visions. "Meta Incognita," he reflected, "is still as unknown as in the days of Frobisher. . . . We have passed by the inevitable coercion of the ice, from the highest regions of Arctic exploration, the lands of Parry and Ross and Franklin, to the lowest, the seats of the early search for Cathay, the lands of Cabot and Davis and Baffin—all seekers after shadows. Men still seek Cathay!"

On Kane's return to New York in September of 1851, the shadow that the dreamer pursued was neither Cathay nor Franklin so much as the Iceless Polar Sea. In the lectures he delivered throughout the United States to raise funds for his next expedition, he somehow contrived to forge all these chimerical goals together. He appears to have been a spellbinding speaker, for he tells us that he competed on the Chautauqua Circuit with three powerful rival attractions. There was a magician named Blitz, an opera singer named Alboni, and the essayist and poet Ralph Waldo Emerson.

"We are all of one feather," said Kane, like a true showman. "No matter: so that I get my money I do not care."

It took him more than two years to raise the cash. Though he pledged his own naval salary, as well as his lecture earnings, the Second U.S. Grinnell Expedition was woefully underequipped for a jaunt to the Pole. He cadged a smattering of scientific equipment from the American learned societies. The U.S. Navy provided about two thousand dollars' worth of supplies, including salt pork, hardtack, and barrels of malt for brewing what was fallaciously believed to be antiscorbutic beer.

The merchant prince, Henry Grinnell, was somewhat less generous this time. He contributed just one of his ships—the one-hundred-and-forty-four-ton *Advance*. Originally intended for carrying castings from an iron foundry, she was a hermaphrodite, two-masted sailing brig built of white oak. She was roughly a third the size of the average British Admiralty discovery vessel and about as fragile as the figurehead on her prow—a little blue girl with pink cheeks nicknamed Augusta.

She sailed from New York on May 30, 1853. Aboard her was a very mixed crew of volunteers—seven civilians and ten from the Navy. Only three of them, including the land-lubberly Captain Kane, had previous Arctic experience. And three of them published journals of their own about the experiences they endured for two winters under the command of their sometimes capricious land sailor of a captain.

The most loyal of the diarists was William Morton. He was an

amiable if misdirected Irish steward who had allowed Kane to use his back as a drawing board for his sketch pad on the previous *Advance* voyage. He remained faithful to Kane until his commander's death. But afterwards Morton delivered lectures on the Chautauqua Circuit illustrating how he had personally reached a false northern latitude and seen a false open polar sea. Some critics claimed that the steward had hoaxed Kane and that his naive captain had been too willing to believe his steward.

Ship surgeon Dr. Isaac Israel Hayes was an ambitious man, a lean, dark, saturnine figure with a fierce no-nonsense moustache. He was just twenty-one, having recently graduated from Kane's alma mater, the medical school of the University of Pennsylvania. Kane hired the enthusiast because Hayes had a similar bee in his bonnet about the existence of an open polar sea. But Kane hired a rival. Hayes was one of the leaders of a party of deserters, and Kane described him in his unpublished diary as a "double-faced" ingrate. Hayes eventually wound up a successful politician after leading two unsuccessful expeditions of his own. In one of his books, titled *The Open Polar Sea*, Hayes brazenly exaggerated his figures to show that he had ventured farther north than Kane and had reached the illusory iceless ocean. A later book, written after Hayes was disproved, bore the title, *Cast Away in the Cold.*

William C. (Bill) Godfrey was a common seaman who wrote a book because he felt he had been maligned by Kane. A former New York East River boatman, he seems to have been a tough, independent-minded, saucy American. He was evidently quite a gay blade with the Eskimo ladies and entertained them with Negro minstrel songs. Although Kane acknowledged that Godfrey once saved his life, there was little love lost between them. Kane referred to him as a mutinous "wharf-rat" who had to be confined in the "Booby Hatch on bread and water," and he admitted he tried to shoot Godfrey for insubordination. Godfrey contended that Kane was an aristocratic fish out of water, playing the role of sea captain, who did not know how to administer balanced discipline.

At the Danish-Eskimo settlements on the southwest coast of Greenland Kane acquired two mainstays of the expedition who verified Godfrey's contention.

One was Carl Petersen. He was a gruff, stubborn, bearded Dane, who had spent most of his forty-five years serving as an Eskimo administrator in the Greenland whaling station of Upernavik. The King of Denmark later awarded him a silver cross for the Arctic services he per-

*Mutinous Bill Godfrey was one of eight deserters who abandoned ship.* METROPOLITAN TORONTO LIBRARY BOARD

*Hans Christian Hendrik was Eskimo hero of Kane expedition.*

formed for the British explorer, Sir Leopold McClintock. Petersen was equally diligent in helping Kane to outfit the *Advance* with dog teams and proper Arctic attire; but unfortunately there was a clash of temperament between the laconic, practical Dane and the volatile, idealistic American. In his confidential journal Kane described Petersen as a "cold-blooded sneak," a deserter who ought to be shot. In *his* journal Petersen called Kane an amateur commander, a bragging Yankee who did not have horse sense enough to pay heed to the advice of a seasoned Arctic hand like himself.

At the tiny settlement of Fiskernaes Kane hired a truly heroic figure. This was Hans Christian Hendrik, a Christianized Eskimo destined to save the lives of explorers on three other polar expeditions. Hans was just nineteen, but already an expert kayaker and hunter. "After Hans had given me a touch of his quality by spearing a bird on the wing, I engaged him," wrote Kane. "He was fat, good-natured, and, except under the excitement of the hunt, as stolid and unimpressionable as one of our own Indians."

Hans was not that unimpressionable. He was one of those rarities, an Eskimo who later recorded *his* impressions of the white strangers who blundered into his land. In his memoirs Hans was extremely fair when passing judgment on Docto Kayen—the Eskimo pidgin English for his *Kabloona* master. "He was very clever in not despising native food," Hans paid tribute to Kane's adaptability. To counterbalance this, Hans also perceived Kane's arrogance: "A pity it was that our Master behaved with haughtiness towards his crew."

One forgives Kane for his hauteur. If he made mistakes in judgment and leadership, it was understandable. This romantic was out of his element, taking one risky gamble after another with a divided crew. Yet somehow the gifted amateur managed to pull it off, and he did it with a pertinacity and gaiety that would have been beyond a more orthodox and sober-minded commander.

Certainly no conventional naval captain could have described the voyage with more verve. Crunching through the jewelry of ice—"one great resplendency of gemwork, blazing carbuncles, and rubies and molten gold"—his little brig nosed into Smith Sound. Overhead frowned the beetling cliffs of those Arctic Pillars of Hercules, Cape Alexander and Cape Isabella. "They look down on us as if they challenged our right to pass," he said. "Even the sailors are impressed, as we move under their dark shadow."

Soon a gale came roaring down the sound with lion-like fury. The manila ropes connecting the *Advance* with an ice ledge began to snap with a sharp twang! twang! "We could hear the deep Aeolian chant, swelling through all the rattle of the running gear and moaning of the shrouds," wrote Kane. "It was the death song!"

They were at the mercy of the slamming ice floes. By a miracle they hooked an anchor held by a tow line to a floating berg. It was, says Kane, a moment of old-fashioned suspense. "Our noble tow horse, whiter than the pale horse that seemed to be pursuing us, hauled us bravely on.... We passed clear; but it was a close shave."

The men were scared and wanted to turn back. Kane accordingly called a meeting of his officers and crew and, in the American tradition, took a vote. With the exception of one man, all were agreed on returning home immediately. Kane's ambitions were clearly stronger than his democratic ideals. He overruled the majority and decreed they should proceed to scout for a wintering harbor. They found it on the northwest coast of Greenland, at 78 degrees, 37 minutes north latitude, and Kane grandly named it after his ancestors Rensselaer Bay. The bleak coast itself—black with granite cliffs, white with glassy glaciers, brightened by the occasional tufts of purple saxifrage—he patriotically christened Washington Land.

Washington, D.C., seemed terribly far away that first winter. According to the observatory they built in an icehouse of a shack, the thermometer dipped as low as seventy-five degrees below zero. It was so cold that a bottle of good Monongahela whisky froze under a man's pillow. The weather played havoc on experimental teams of Newfoundland dogs that Kane had brought along. When hitched to American hickory sledges, the poor creatures scampered off "like a drove of hogs in an Illinois oak opening," and eventually more than fifty of them perished in the cold.

"The great difficulty is to keep up a cheery tone among the men," recorded Kane. He published a ship newspaper, *The Ice Blink*, and drew his most charming sketches for it. To encourage his men to exercise, he organized a tag-like game of fox chase around the deck, and offered his Guernsey shirt as a prize.

Christmas was celebrated with a bumper of champagne all around and the singing of *The Star Spangled Banner*. Dr. Isaac Israel Hayes delivered a Fourth of July style oration and read aloud from *David Copperfield*. Able Seaman Bill Godfrey crooned his repertoire of Negro

minstrel ballads. Carl Petersen told stories about life in south Greenland. Others played whist or chess and Kane staged a fancy masquerade ball.

But the men remained down in the dumps, and Kane tried to conceal his fear when the waxen faces of all but two of the crew members became mottled with scurvy. His attempts to get them to eat raw potato as an antiscorbutic proved futile. He added oil as a lubricant, and told them that some whalers actually got drunk on potato molasses. Yet, he worried, "It is as much as I can do to persuade the mess to shut their eyes and bolt it, like Mrs. Squeers' molasses and brimstone at Dotheboys Hall."

Even Eskimo Hans started to mope with homesickness. "He bundled up his clothes and took his rifle to bid us all goodbye," said Kane. "It turns out that besides his mother there is another one of the softer sex at Fiskernaes that the boy's heart is dreaming of. He looked as wretched as any lover of a milder clime."

Kane treated Hans's nostalgia successfully. He gave the lad "first, a dose of salts and, secondly, promotion. He has now all the dignity of a henchman. He harnesses my dogs, builds my traps, and walks with me on my ice tramps. He is really attached to me, and as happy as a fat man ought to be."

In mid-March Kane made a bad mistake in judgment. Over Carl Petersen's protests that it was too early in the season and the enfeebled men not up to a march, he persisted in sending out a sledge-hauling detachment. The party was to cache food depots for his planned exploratory expeditions up the Kane Basin. Eight men, headed by Petersen, set off in forty-nine-below-zero chill, fortified by Kane's last two bottles of port wine.

On March 31 three of them staggered back. They were speechless with cold. Only Christian Ohlsen, the ship carpenter, could talk, and he was so frostbitten that his toes had to be amputated immediately. What had happened to the other five members of their party? Ohlsen said they were lying in a tent about forty miles from the brig, awaiting a relief party.

Kane was at his best in an emergency of this sort. Poor Ohlsen, though his toes had just been cut off, would have to serve as guide for the rescue mission of nine men. He was sewn up in a fur bag and strapped on a sledge, and Kane led the rescuers in dragging him into the snow blizzard.

Kane fainted twice. The carpenter dozed off in a coma. They would have been lost in the whiteout except for the alertness of Eskimo Hans. He detected a half-obliterated sledge track. Beyond, they sighted a small American flag fluttering near a tent buried in snow.

Kane ripped open the tent flap and crawled in. The invalids, barely alive, greeted him with a gladsome outburst. "They had expected me," thought Kane. "They were sure I would come!"

The trip back to the brig was frightful. It was now fifty-five below zero, and the benumbed men threw themselves onto the snow and refused to rise. "It was in vain that I wrestled, boxed, ran, argued, jeered, or reprimanded," said Kane. "An immediate halt could not be avoided."

Able Seaman Bill Godfrey, the strongest of the group, pitched the tent and helped his comrades into their sleeping bags. "I was like the old woman in the shoe," recalled Godfrey, "having so many children to take care of."

The tent was not designed to hold so many campers. So Kane and Godfrey proposed to walk on ahead nine miles to another tent they had left as a halfway station on the outward journey. Drunk with cold, the captain and the sailor staggered through the snow drifts in a woozy stupor. Kane babbled of polar bears and presently fainted dead away. Godfrey hoisted him on his back and struggled on to the tent. There the able seaman cut off Kane's frozen beard with a jacknife, tucked him into a sleeping bag, and calmly prepared a breakfast of coffee and "scouse"—the naval hash which is a boiled mixture of salt pork and hardtack biscuit.

In the morning they were joined by the others. Their last lap to the brig was a madman's scene out of an Edgar Allan Poe horror story. Godfrey remembered that he felt like committing suicide; he could not bear to see his shipmates agonizing as their frozen limbs thawed out.

"I believe our whole company—myself included—were seized with frenzy," wrote Godfrey. "I know that all my companions were frantic; for they laughed immoderately, gibbered, uttered the most frightful imprecations, mimicked the screams and groans of the invalids, howled like wild beasts. In short, they exhibited a scene which I have never seen equated in any lunatic asylum."

Kane remembered it as a sleepwalkers' delirium in which they took turns at slumbering on the snow for three minutes each. "We moved on like men in a dream," he said. "When at last we got to the brig, still

dragging the wounded men instinctively behind us, there was not one whose mind was found to be unimpaired."

Christian Ohlsen, the unfortunate carpenter, was snowblind. Two crew members also required to have their frostbitten toes amputated. Two others died and Kane grieved as the chapter from Job was read and he sprinkled snow for dust over their pine coffins.

On the morning after one of their deaths, the deck watch hurried down into the cabin to report: "People hallooing ashore!"

Kane rushed on deck. There standing on the harbor ice, grouped together in a half-moon circle, "like the figures in a tableau of the opera," he saw the Polar Eskimos, come from their Etah village about seventy-five miles south. It must be said that Kane's initial response to the people who were to be his saviors was one of patrician condescension. They were "wild and uncouth" savages. They were lost in "barbarous amaze" at the sight of coal used as fuel—too hard for blubber, too soft for firestone.

And they were to be exploited. After buying some of their handsome dogs in exchange for a few cask staves, he demonstrated the white man's sorcery. "I tried to make them understand what a powerful Prospero they had for a host," he said, and chuckled as they watched his hand, "terrible with flaming ether, while it lifted nails with a magnet."

But despite their fear of the "boom, boom"—the gun which Kane ordered an officer to fire over their heads—the scamps persisted in pilfering a barrel of coal. Kane then took rather strong steps. He captured an Eskimo youth named Myouk and imprisoned the weeping boy in the hold as hostage. "Our Commander said to me that he intended to shoot him," says Hans in his memoirs. "I answered: 'What a pity.'"

Myouk escaped next morning. Kane, who had been merely play-acting, admitted, "There was a simplicity and *bonhomie* about this boy that interested me much; I confess I was glad my bird had flown." Subsequently the "agile, elfin youth," Myouk, became one of Kane's best instructors in arctic survival.

With the coming of spring Kane had not yet learned those techniques. Nevertheless he was determined to send out one sledge party after another to attain his *ultima Thule*—the Open Polar Sea. Three parties almost perished trying to locate it.

The first sledge detachment was led by Kane himself. He was hauled back in a state of collapse, after being seized with fainting spells and with his left foot totally frozen. Yet Kane felt the trek was worth-

while, for he had discovered the great Humboldt Glacier that swept along the Greenland coast for sixty miles. It was a "solid glassy wall," he marveled, "and its curved face vanished into unknown space at not more than a single day's railroad travel from the Pole." This was an exaggeration; so was his claim that the glacier was a "mighty crystal bridge, which connects the two continents of America and Greenland."

A second sledge party clarified his misapprehension a little. The party consisted of Dr. Hayes and Able Seaman Godfrey. They crossed the ice of Kane Basin and were the first white men to explore the interior of Canada's Ellesmere Island. They named it Grinnell Land and charted it for two hundred miles before planting the Stars and Stripes on a whipstock atop a table of ice. Dr. Hayes was painfully snowblinded. Even sturdy Bill Godfrey, who reputedly could sleep with his head in a bucket of ice water, admitted he suffered hardships. He fed the dogs shreds of his leather trousers. Then he made a meal of the tops of his boots, "which we cut into small pieces and dipped in lamp oil to render the morsels more savory."

A third party, consisting of the steward, William Morton, and Eskimo Hans, made the longest sojourn north. They groped through the mist and the maze of ice hummocks on the Greenland coast "like blind men in the streets of a strange city." Finally on June 24, 1854, standing on a high limestone cliff, Morton planted the American flag and a Masonic emblem and took possession of Cape Constitution. He reported that white-capped waves dashed at his feet; migratory birds flocked so thickly over the water that Hans could kill two of them with one shot; and not a spoonful of ice could be seen.

Kane named it Kennedy Channel after the U.S. Naval Secretary, John Pendleton Kennedy. He reported that this boundless expanse of water stretching toward the Pole "presented all the appearance of an open and iceless sea!" Furthermore, the wishful thinker accepted Morton's incorrect north latitude figure of 81 degrees, 22 minutes. In fact, it was about 80 degrees, 30 minutes; and the illusory Open Polar Sea was certainly not the ice-mantled Arctic Ocean, which lay nearly two hundred miles farther north. Still, Kane could be justifiably proud: his devoted steward and his Eskimo henchman had pushed midway up the American route to the Pole.

By mid-August Kane, the optimist, had to face grim reality. The brig was a virtual hospital of scurvy-riddled patients. The supply of salt pork and coal was fast diminishing. And the young ice threatened to lock them into Rensselaer Bay for another winter.

"I inspected the ice again today. Bad! Bad!" he noted on August 18. "It is *horrible*—yes, that is the word—to look forward to another year of disease and darkness. . . . I should meet it with a more tempered sadness if I had no comrades to think for and protect."

A few days later he faced a more agonizing dilemma. His comrades were holding secret meetings in the forward rooms of Dr. Hayes and Carl Petersen. There were whispers of mutiny.

Kane promptly called an open meeting of the crew to air grievances. Precisely what followed is clouded with ambiguity, for Kane and the malcontents gave conflicting versions of events in their journals.

The dissidents wanted to abandon the ship and head for Upernavik by sledge and longboat. As in a shipwreck, they contended they were no longer subject to the captain's orders; it was every man for himself. In any case, if they deserted, there would be fewer mouths to feed.

Kane argued that it was his duty to stick by the brig and the sick men aboard her. He preferred the familiar hardships of wintering where he was rather than attempting a journey so late in the season without the food and shelter which the *Advance* could still provide.

In democratic fashion he took a vote. He was dismayed when only six of the total company of seventeen volunteered to remain with him. It was a blow to his vanity. Ultimately just eight men abandoned the ship. Carl Petersen charged that Kane persuaded three others to stay "not without some menace, as it seems to me."

In his published journal Kane discreetly refers to the defectors as the "withdrawal party" and says it was an honest difference of opinion. In his confidential diary, however, they are double-crossing deserters, violating "everything gallant and honorable." It was good riddance to bad rubbish and he washed his hands of the whole rotten pack of them. The ingrates had deigned to "spit in my face. . . . If I ever live to get home—home!—and should meet Dr. Hayes . . . or the other low-minded sneaks . . . let them look out for their skins."

One cannot entirely blame the malcontents. Their captain had not given them firm leadership. At the same time one sympathizes with Kane, abandoned by most of his sturdiest men and left with the heavy burden of nursing a sickly crew.

How were he and the "faithfuls" to survive? Out of necessity he was driven to imitate the Eskimos. "I had studied them carefully," he wrote, "and determined that their form of habitations and their

*Nerves grated so badly in the cramped brig that Kane fired a gun at one seaman. The crew ate puppy dogs and rats. Left to right: Bonsall, Brooks, Kane, Hayes, and Morton.*

*Eskimos helped Kane's crew escape from the ice-beset ship in longboats, merrily joining in sea chanty, "Storm Along, My Hearty Boys!"*

peculiarities of diet, without their unthrift and filth, were the safest and best."

With certain American reservations, he gradually did adopt Eskimo techniques. He converted the brig into a form of igloo. A single compartment was bulkheaded off amidships as a dormitory, its walls lined with moss, and the Eskimo-like tunnel leading to it named New London Avenue, Pennsylvania. His dish lamps may have been fueled with pork fat rather than seal oil, but Kane was determined that his invalids learn to eat raw meat.

"The liver of a walrus (*awuktanuk*) eaten with little slices of his fat—of a verity it is a delicious morsel," Kane went into raptures. "Fire would ruin the curt, pithy expression of vitality which belongs to its uncooked juices. . . . I wonder that raw beef is not eaten at home."

Kane also gradually struck up a friendship with his Eskimo neighbors, although it must be said his *Kabloona* tactics were high-handed. Three hunters from the village of Anoatok (Eskimo for what Kane considered the poetically named "Wind-loved Spot") chanced to drop by. Kane invited them to sleep overnight in a tent below deck. Apparently considering them to be gifts, his guests departed next morning with Kane's lamp, cooking pot, and sled dog, Nanook.

Kane immediately dispatched his best walkers after them. The Americans pounced upon two Eskimo women in a snowhouse nearby; they had the booty with them as well as Myouk, the Eskimo lad whom Kane had imprisoned previously. "With the prompt ceremonial which outraged law delights in among the officials of the police everywhere," Kane wrote with mock humor, "the women were stripped and tied. Then, laden with their stolen goods and as much walrus beef besides from their own stores as would pay for their board, they were marched on the instant back to the brig."

He locked the two hostages for five days in the hold. There they sighed and wept, "with a dreadful white man as keeper, whose scowl, I flatter myself, exhibited a well-arranged variety of menacing and demoniacal expressions." Meanwhile Myouk was sent to the Wind-loved Spot to negotiate with the village headman for their release.

The villagers agreed to a peace pact drawn up by Kane. The "children of the snow," as he called them in the truce terms, promised to refrain from pilfering; to provide the white men with dogs; and to furnish fresh meat. In return, the "*naligak-soak*," or great white captain, pledged to desist from sorcery; to welcome them aboard ship; and to sell

them pins, needles and wood for high-quality seal and walrus meat.

The alliance seems to have worked out wonderfully well. "Our table talk at supper was as merry as a marriage bell," said "Docto Kayen," as he ratified the treaty at a banquet of walrus flipper. "Whatever might be the infirmity of their notions of honesty, it was plain that we have no lessons to give them in the virtues of hospitable welcome."

The withdrawal party of eight deserters likewise learned they had nothing to teach the Eskimos about hospitality, much less about civilized decency. On December 12, almost four months after they had abandoned the brig, the sorry lot of them returned, emaciated, frozen and quite chopfallen. Kane shook hands with Dr. Hayes and the others, and welcomed them back as though they were prodigal sons.

The story Dr. Hayes had to tell of their unsuccessful journey was a harrowing one, not unmixed with unwitting irony. The eight renegades had survived in an icy stone hut three hundred and fifty miles to the south. They would have starved on rock lichen and old caribou hide if it had not been for the generosity of a neighboring encampment of Eskimo hunters headed by a warm-hearted *angekok* named Kaluhtuna. The Americans were shamefully ungrateful. Because they were given such niggardly rations, they convinced themselves that their Eskimo hosts secretly intended murdering the weakened white men. So they hatched a scheme of drugging their benefactors with an opiate, stealing their dog teams, and driving back to Rensselaer Bay.

Dr. Hayes plotted the stratagem as though it were a Broadway melodrama, but it came off as semifarce. When Kaluhtuna and two Eskimo hunters came to visit Fort Starvation—the name given to the miserable hut—they brought with them generous chunks of bear and walrus meat. "It became our first duty to reassure them," says Dr. Hayes, "with friendly smiles."

And so, while the meat stew was boiling over the fire, Dr. Hayes entertained them. He showed pictures from his Medical Anatomy Textbook and ripped out illustrations from his copy of *David Copperfield* for them to take home to their children. Able Seaman Bill Godfrey further diverted their attention with a blackface minstrel show. He crooned his entire repertoire from his *Ethiopian Melodies* songbook—"Oh! Susanna" and "Uncle Ned" and "I'm Off to Charleston"—and plunked an imaginary banjo. Dr. Hayes meanwhile slipped into the soup unobserved a heavy dose of laudanum.

As soon as their drugged guests were snoring by the fire, the white

conspirators noiselessly crawled out of the hut. They took pains to sneak off with the sealskin boots, mittens and *kapetah* tunics of the sleepers. For good measure they plugged up the tunnel entrance with blocks of ice. Then they cracked the whip over the heads of the dog teams, and with a *Huk! Huk! Huk!*, made their escape aboard the three Eskimo sledges.

Here the scenario went a little awry. Dr. Hayes couldn't handle his dog team. His "wolfish herd" tossed him into a snowdrift and raced back toward the hut. Hayes got a lift with Bill Godfrey, who was more proficient at wielding the whip.

Presently they stopped at an ice cave for a rest. To their astonishment they saw gliding over the snow, hot on their trail, three semi-nude Eskimos on the abandoned sledge. It was Kaluhtuna and his two narcoticized hunters. They were garbed in the red, white and blue blankets from the hut, which they had cleverly fashioned into Mexican-style ponchos by cutting holes in the middle for their heads. Evidently the laudanum had only served to give the Eskimos a refreshing snooze.

The Americans brought their pursuers to a halt by aiming their rifles at them. "For a savage despises nothing as much as weakness," Hayes thought, "and respects nothing as much as strength." The Eskimos were understandably fearful of the "boom, booms" and threw their hands over their heads. "I took Kaluhtuna by the collar, and, after giving him a hearty shake in token of my displeasure, I moved him before me to the mouth of the cave," says Hayes. "Then, facing him around toward his sledge, I pointed to it with my gun."

By sign language Hayes indicated that if Kaluhtuna drove them to Rensselaer Bay, their dogs, sleds and clothes would be restored. Otherwise, Hayes signalled with his boom, boom, all three Eskimos would be shot forthwith.

The prisoners immediately agreed with an "Ee-ee-eeh" meaning Yes. "As a proof of our disposition to trust them, we restored their clothes," Hayes recounted. "And as they slipped into their jumpers and tied on their moccasins, I could not but reflect that this was a strange way to make people happy. A more grateful set of fellows I had never seen."

Hayes was in for another surprise. Out of sheer kindness Kaluhtuna took his captors to his own igloo for a feast and a rest. Hayes was perplexed by this display of turn-the-other-cheek Christianity from savages.

"The Esquimaux appeared to us more as our good angels than as our enemies," he wrote. "We received all manner of kind attentions from our host. The women pulled off our boots, mittens, coats and stockings, and hung them up to dry. My beard was frozen fast to the fur of my coat, and it was the warm hand of Kaluhtuna's wife that thawed away the ice. Meats of different kinds were brought in and offered to us in the only style known to the Esquimaux cuisine—that is, parboiled and raw; or as my shipmate elegantly expressed it, 'cooked with fire' and 'cooked with frost.' But our fatigue had destroyed our appetites, and the warmth of the hut soon so overcame us that we fell asleep in the very act of taking food from the hands of our hostess."

On their return to the brig Dr. Hayes had to have his frostbitten toes amputated by Dr. Kane. He was not the only one disabled that dreadful winter. Scurvy struck down all but Kane and two other men. There was a poignant scene when the boatswain looked at his wasted features in the mirror and burst into tears. They ran out of coal and were forced to chop the upper half of the ship into firewood. They were forced to eat puppy dogs and rats. The rats leaped into the bunks and bit the faces of the invalids. "Through the long winter night," says Kane, "Hans used to beguile the lonely hours of his watch by shooting them with the bow and arrow."

Nerves grated in the cramped quarters. Everybody suffered from the cabin fever that Bill Godfrey aptly termed the "blue devils." Kane became as testy as the others. At one point he formally accused Able Seaman William C. Godfrey of mutiny and fired a bullet that went whistling past the seaman's head. (Godfrey claims that he gave a burlesque bow and retorted with a cocky grin, "When your nerves are steadier, perhaps you may shoot with more effect.") Apparently Kane also threatened to shoot Carl Petersen if he did not obey orders. (Petersen claims he made the reply: "It would hardly be advisable for him to attempt the execution of any Yankee laws on a subject of Denmark, in particular if the question were about capital punishment!")

With the coming of spring Kane appears to have patched up these differences. He was on first-name terms with stubborn "Carlie" and impudent "Bill." Kane might well be excused for his lapses. Erratically aristocratic he may have been, but the gentleman from Philadelphia was also extraordinarily resilient. Although his background was so divorced from theirs, he cemented a genuine friendship with Kaluhtuna and the other Etah natives, and became, as he truly boasted, "more than half Esquimaux."

184

First of all, he looked like an Eskimo. He layered himself with furs "like the shards of an artichoke till I am rounded into absolute obesity."

He drove a sledge like an Eskimo. He cracked his sealskin whip over the heads of his favorite dogs, Toodlamik and Whitey, defying as he whimsically put it, the outrage of the Society for Prevention of Cruelty to Animals. He reveled in his speed, "a fox's tail held between the teeth to protect the nose in a wind." He enjoyed stopping when he was hungry to slice off a cold cutlet of the whale meat, hard as a plank, which often served as the runners and the driver's seat of the sledge. "Step by step," he said, "we went on reducing our sledging outfit, until at last we came to the Esquimaux ultimatum of simplicity—raw meat and a fur bag."

He lived in an igloo snowhouse like an Eskimo. He became accustomed to the "ammoniacal steam of some fourteen vigorous, amply-fed, unwashed, unclothed fellow lodgers, twined and dovetailed together like the worms in a fishing basket. I stripped like the rest, threw my well-tired carcass across Mrs. Eider Duck's extremities, put her left-hand baby under my armpit, pillowed my head on Myouk's somewhat warm stomach, and thus, an honored guest and in the place of honor, fell asleep."

He became as carefree as an Eskimo. "This life of ours—for we have been living much in this way for nine months—makes me more charitable than I used to be with this merry-hearted people, our Esquimaux neighbors. The day provides for itself; or, if it does not, we trust in the morrow, and are happy till tomorrow disappoints us."

He sorrowed like an Eskimo. He joined the members of the Wind-loved Spot in a traditional crying match after five of the villagers died of famine. "Mrs. Eider Duck (née Small Belly) looked up at me from her *kolupsut* (a hook suspended over the fire) and burst into a gentle gush of woe," he wrote. "I took out my handkerchief and, after wiping her eyes, wept a few tears myself."

And he began to think like an Eskimo. He assumed their values, and it surprised him how important it became in his eyes that he be accepted as a respected equal in the polar bear hunt. "It pleased me to find that I had earned character with these people," he said, especially with "Kaluhtuna—a man of fine instincts, and I think, of heart. He called me his friend—*Asakaoteet*, 'I love you well'—and would be happy, he said, to join the *nalegak-soak*, great white captain, in a hunt."

Yet Kane realized he could never be an Eskimo. His dreams were different from theirs. He kept dreaming of the Delectable Mountains. These were the blue cliffs and emerald-green glaciers to the north which the Eskimos called *Sermik-soak* or the Great Ice Wall. In Kane's imagination those uplifted hills became symbolically converted into the Delectable Mountains from John Bunyan's *Pilgrim's Progress*. All winter long he dreamt of the "orchards and vineyards and running fountains" that a pilgrim might discover somewhere beyond those mountains.

"I used to gaze upon them with an eye of real longing," he wrote of his mirage. "Very often, when they rose phantom-like into the sky, I would plan schemes by which to reach them, work over mentally my hard pilgrimage across the ice, and my escape from Doubting Castle to this scene of triumph and reward. Once upon your coasts, O inaccessible mountains, I would reach the Northern Ocean. . . . Leaning upon our staves, as is common with weary pilgrims, we would look down upon an Open Polar Sea, refulgent with northern sunshine. . . ."

By mid-May of 1855 Kane acknowledged that the American pilgrims could no longer aspire to attain the tropical marvels beyond his Delectable Mountains. They could not withstand another winter. The *Advance* was half burned up. They would have to drag their longboats on sledges as far south as Smith Sound. Then, if the water was ice-free, they might be able to sail around the middle pack of Baffin Bay to Upernavik.

As a good-luck omen the men insisted on taking with them the *Advance's* figurehead, the fair Augusta. She had lost one breast to the rude embrace of an iceberg and her nose had been nipped off; but the sight of Augusta cheered them on. So did the jaunty little American flag which Kane improvised from his discarded linen shirt, stripes from moldy stationery, and a bottle of ink. They had a woeful setback when Christian Ohlsen, the carpenter, died of a rupture. But high spirits were restored when the Eskimos of Etah—men, women and children—volunteered to give a hand with the dragropes and joined the sailors in a chorus of the sea chanty, "Storm Along, My Hearty Boys!"

On June 16, not far from the present American military base of Thule on the Greenland coast, the Eskimos were shouting "*Emerk! Emerk!*"—"Water! Water!" And Kane was recording thankfully: "We see its deep indigo horizon and hear its roar against the icy beach. Its scent is in our nostrils and our hearts."

There was much weeping and exchanging of gifts as he bade a last

farewell to the assembled Eskimo villagers. Little Myouk crowded fresh presents of raw auks on Docto Kayen. Mrs. Eider Duck was so moved she kept wiping her tears on a birdskin.

"My heart warms to these poor, dirty, miserable, yet happy beings, so long our neighbors, and of late so staunchly our friends," wrote Kane. "I blessed them for their humanity to us with a fervor of heart. . . .We have found brothers in a strange land."

More than two months later the pilgrims' longboats, *Faith*, *Hope* and *Red Eric*, neared the wrinkled hills of Upernavik. Carl Petersen was excited when a familiar Eskimo kayaker loomed out of the mists: "Paul Zacharias, don't you know me? I'm Carl Petersen."

"No! His wife says he's dead."

The kayaker paddled away fearfully as if he had encountered a ghostly spirit.

The disappointed crew sailed on for two more days. Then Kane heard a distant "Halloo!"

"Listen, Petersen," said Kane. "Oars! Men!"

Petersen was afraid to believe his ears this time. "What is it?" He listened quietly and then half-whispered to Kane: "Dannemarkers!"

Wringing his hands, he burst into a fit of tears. " 'Tis the Upernavik whale oil boat! The *Mariane*, the one annual ship, has come."

"Can it be a dream?" wondered Kane, as the Danes and Eskimos of Upernavik welcomed his pilgrims with coffee and warm hospitality. "Our habits were hard and weatherworn. We could not remain within the four walls of a house without a distressing sense of suffocation."

On October 12, 1855, Kane and his crew received a tumultuous welcome in New York City. There was no ticker tape, but the heroes were nineteenth century versions of moon-rocketing astronauts. They had discovered the Open Polar Sea. News of their arrival home, reported the New York *Times*, spread "with the rapidity of scandal in a country town." Even loan sharks "while skinning Wall Street with only three minutes between themselves and bankruptcy introduced their applications for a loan on call with the remark that Dr. Kane and party were just off Sandy Hook, safe and well."

The first American to profit from the enterprise, the *Times* added, was a Broadway impresario named James Wallack. The producer had rushed to a playwright asking him to deliver a melodrama ready to be performed that evening in the theatre. The thriller was to be titled

*Dangers of an Expedition to the Arctic Sea and Safe Arrival of Dr. Kane.*

Kane profited little from his voyage. Riddled with scurvy and racked by his chronic heart ailment, he worked feverishly for a year to produce the nine hundred pages and three hundred sketches for his best-seller. "My wish is to make it a centre-table book." he said, "fit as well for the eyes of children as of refined women."

*Arctic Explorations*, with its discreet downplaying of the ungentlemanly squabbles aboard ship, achieved that distinction. Within three years its sales were a phenomenal one hundred and forty-five thousand. Kane did not live to enjoy the plaudits that his gallantry, his courage and adventuresome spirit so richly merited. Within sixteen months of his homecoming, on February 16, 1857, while trying to regain his strength in the warm tropical climate of Havana, what he called his frail "life force" flickered out and he died of apoplexy. "The book, poor as it is," said the gentlemanly dreamer, "has been my coffin."

If so, his epitaph was contained in a letter he addressed to his patron, Henry Grinnell, subsequently made public by the United States Navy. In it he encouraged others to complete the American Highway to the North Pole.

"By dogs—the great blessing of Arctic travel—this whole area could be scoured," he predicted confidently. And then this "Eskimo-in-spite-of-himself" made a frank confession. "Strange as it may seem to you, we regarded the coarse life of these people with eyes of envy, and did not doubt but that we could have lived in comfort upon their resources," he said. "It required all my powers, moral and physical, to prevent my men from deserting to the Walrus Settlements, and it was my final intention to have taken to Esquimaux life, had Providence not carried us through in our hazardous escape."

This legacy inspired another American visionary even more romantic than Elisha Kent Kane. His name was Charles Francis Hall, and he was destined to make the pilgrimage beyond the Delectable Mountains and to lose his life while putting himself to the test of becoming a total Eskimo.

# Chapter 7

# The Eskimo
# from Cincinnati

At ten o'clock in the morning of July 7, 1860, the Eskimo kayakers of Holsteinsborg on the southwest coast of Greenland witnessed a peculiar sight. The New England whaling ship *George Henry* anchored in the harbor. Then a *Kabloona* hitchhiker from Cincinnati, Ohio, was rowed ashore. He was a bulky, bushy-bearded man of thirty-nine who might have passed for an American tourist of today. Instead of a camera, though, he carried a pair of opera glasses, a Colt revolver and a YMCA Bible, and there was a curious missionary gleam about his pale blue eyes. As soon as he landed on the beach he snatched up a handful of rocky earth and pressed it to his lips.

"Thank God, I am at last on Arctic land, where I have so long wished to be!" he apostrophized the crags around him. "Greenland's mountains, I greet you!"

Charles Francis Hall had arrived in the north. A more eccentric polar explorer it would be hard to imagine. If his American predecessor, Dr. Elisha Kent Kane, had been an improbable romantic, then Hall was a fantastical one. He was the first white man who deliberately set out to "Esquimaux-ise" himself. After becoming a complete Eskimo, he was determined to make a single-handed attempt to locate missing Franklin survivors. He would fill in stray links in the Northwest Passage. He would be first to set foot on "God's beautiful footstool"—the North Pole.

Hall failed in all these lofty missions. Yet it is a mark of his drive and will power that this unschooled former blacksmith achieved the success that he did. Before his mysterious death, by apparent murder, the would-be Esquimau roamed nomadically about the high Arctic for seven years with an Eskimo couple as virtually his sole companions. He almost reached the end of the American Highway to the Pole. He pushed past Kane's Delectable Mountains and raised the Stars and

Stripes just four hundred and sixty-four miles short of the top of the globe.

Hall worshipped Kane and tried to model himself after his idol. The two American visionaries were much alike, courageous and daunt-less to the extreme of foolhardiness, except that Hall was far more the extremist.

Like Kane, Hall was an effervescent enthusiast. Everything had to be done in bravura style; there were no half measures for Hall. When he climbed his first iceberg—"a mountain of alabaster resting calmly upon the bosom of the dark blue sea"—he tossed his felt hat high in the air and punctured it with his alpenstock. When he made his first geographical discovery, "I danced, and laughed, and made a complete somersault."

Like Kane, he was addicted to Yankee exaggeration. But Hall's tales were taller and more farfetched. He swore that polar bears played baseball, crushing the bulletproof skulls of walruses by pitching boulders at them from high cliffs, and he drew a sketch that allegedly proved it. To Hall, an Eskimo sorceress healed the sick because she sang an incantation, "her lips sounding like so many firecrackers in a Fourth of July festival at home." And the patriot vowed that the waters of the Sylvia Grinnell River he discovered on Baffin Island produced har-monious music that sounded exactly like *Yankee Doodle Dandy*.

Like Kane, he was a naive idealist. His compatriots were impressed by the positiveness of his convictions; by the almost childlike faith of this New England puritan, who abhorred profanity, drinking, and pro-miscuity. "Hall was a single-minded trusting man, who believed that others were like himself," wrote one of his Victorian biographers, Pro-fessor Joseph Everett Nourse of the United States Navy. "In this he often found an experience of disappointment.... He is full of hope, never desponding. He readily makes friends by his whole-souledness; and those who meet him once are happy to renew the acquaintance." A provincial hail-fellow-well-met, a sort of nineteenth-century Dale Carnegie fervent with Rotarian moral uplift, he was bound to meet dis-illusionment. One sometimes pictures him as the likeable, ingenuous ex-emplar of Mark Twain's *An Innocent Abroad*.

But there was a dark side to his personality, too. Like Kane, he was a high-strung individualist; his moods were as erratic as a weathervane; and he was inclined to erupt into rages if his authority and independ-ence were threatened. Like Kane, he fired a bullet at a seaman he suspected of mutiny; but unlike Kane, Hall killed the man.

There were other more vital differences between the two amateur sea captains. Kane had been a rather elegant, weedy, aristocratic figure with a frail constitution. Hall was a shaggy bear of a man. According to another of his contemporary biographers, Mrs. Euphemia Vale Blake, he had the powerful biceps of a former blacksmith, was five feet eight inches in height and robustly built rather than stout, though weighing not far from two hundred pounds. His massive, well-shaped head sprouted a profusion of wavy, reddish brown hair. His thick beard was a tangle of curls. "His general expression was pleasant, but somewhat dreamy withal," wrote Mrs. Blake, "but kindling into a brilliant enthusiasm when his favorite topics were discussed."

Easily his favorite subject was the region about the North Pole. He idealized it as a terrestrial paradise, according to Mrs. Blake. "Its glistening icebergs and snow-clad plains were as enchanting to his imagination as the fairy tales of younger days," she said. "And, above all, he had that impression of fatalism, that inspiration of a personal mission. It looked to some of his friends like a mania, but was a convincing voice to him."

Hall was, in short, a mystic. In his book, *Life with the Esquimaux*, Hall speaks of his evangelical mission. A religious vision urged him to convert the heathen Eskimos and, by gaining their confidence, to learn the whereabouts of the missing Franklin survivors. "It seemed to me," wrote Hall, "as if I had been *called*." It was as though God's voice were summoning him to the fabled "Far-off Land" known in the Eskimo tongue as *Wes-see-poke*.

He was a strange man, this polar evangelist. The motivating forces that drove him can be comprehended but dimly. By today's standards he would probably be regarded as just another crackpot, a rather pathetic religious zealot. Even in the melting pot of the United States frontier he was considered something of a misfit, a loner, an oddball. Yet, with all his idiosyncrasies, he somehow engages one's sympathy. He was the embodiment of the American Horatio Alger dream. He was the underdog who had to overcome poverty, lowly status, lack of scientific skill. Yet by sheer pluck—a favorite word in his vocabulary—he rose to the top of the heap among front-ranking polar explorers.

Charles Francis Hall emerged from a picaresque, if obscure, background. Most accounts agree he was born a poor New Englander in 1821, in either rural Vermont or New Hampshire. He dropped out of grammar school to become an apprentice blacksmith. The young village blacksmith then was seized with restlessness and roved westward until,

at the age of twenty-seven, he drifted into the "Porkopolis" of Cincinnati.

There he opened a stationery store and worked as a seal engraver. He dabbled in crank inventions and erratically published two tabloid newspapers, the Cincinnati *Occasional* and the *Penny Press*. Written in bombastic style, bristling with exclamation marks and underscored capital letters, they largely served to promote two of his pet hobbyhorses. For one thing, he was fascinated with American technology and its seeming ability to conquer nature. An entire edition of heated prose was devoted to balloons. He publicized so-called caloric engines so extravagantly that his readers, in a play on his initials, took to nicknaming him "Caloric Fool" Hall.

His other mania, of course, was the hero worship of explorers. He treasured uplifting maxims which he felt must have guided polar discoverers. One, which rationalized his own lack of scientific knowledge, read: "The question is not the number of facts a man knows, but how much of a fact he is himself." Another homily which he liked quoting was underscored: *"Our greatest glory consists not in falling, but in rising everytime we fall."*

Not long afterwards he printed an editorial headlined: "Does Sir John Franklin STILL LIVE?" Convinced by his own rhetoric, he persuaded himself that he had been selected by God to find the lost expedition on King William Island in the high Arctic.

He pursued his fantasy with whole-souled zeal. After reading every book in the Cincinnati library dealing with polar voyages, he decided he must first go into training to withstand the cold. So he equipped himself with a tent and spartan rations and commenced camping at night on a high hill. Unfortunately his experiment was rudely disturbed by a couple of local drunks. Incensed by his refusal to share whisky which they thought he must have on hand, the tramps fired a shotgun over his tent. Hall fled, barefoot and wearing little more than his nightcap. Cincinnati howled with laughter at newspaper reports of the escapade.

Hall's attempts to raise money in the East for The New Franklin Research Expedition were hardly more successful. His chief patron was Henry Grinnell, the New York shipping magnate, who had been so generous to Kane. Yet altogether Hall was able to collect no more than nine hundred and eighty dollars in cash. Undeterred, he scaled down his grandiose scheme to finance two ships; he settled for a twenty-eight-foot-long, one-masted sail boat which cost one hundred and five dollars.

He induced merchants to donate such things as pork cracklings, tobacco for his pipe, needles for barter with Eskimos, and a copy of *Bowditch's Navigator*, which the land sailor completely memorized. In return he promised to name geographical features after his expedition suppliers. The Cincinnati dentist, for example, who provided a tooth extractor is commemorated to this day by a lonely cove in Baffin Island named Hamlen Bay.

Perhaps the most pathetic contribution listed in Hall's itemized budget was twenty-seven dollars donated by his wife, Mary. We hear little of the long-suffering Mary in her husband's journals, except that she lived with him in rooms behind his engraving shop, bringing up their daughter, Anna. In May of 1860 Mary was pregnant with their second child, a son. But by the time Charles junior was born, Charles senior had abandoned his family.

Hall had hitched a ride aboard the whaling ship, *George Henry*. Her skipper, a crusty old salt named Captain Sidney O. Budington, was in a hurry to get to the whaling grounds; he had agreed to drop off Hall and his boat near Frobisher Bay on the southeast coast of Baffin Island. Although it was far from his destination of King William Island, Hall had grabbed at the chance of a free lift.

At last he was bound for the fabled Eskimo Far-off Land of *Wes-see-poke*. In mid-June, though heaving with seasickness and yet a good seven hundred miles from the Arctic Circle, the polar evangelist burst into anticipatory rapture. "Approaching the North Axis of the Earth!" he scrawled in his notebook. "I love the snows, the ice, the Fauna and Flora of the North! I love the circling sun, the long day, the Arctic night! . . . I am on a mission of love ready to do or die in the cause I have espoused."

Shortly after the *George Henry* berthed at Baffin Island, in a cove which Hall named Cyrus Field Bay after the American Atlantic Cable promoter, a disaster scuttled his cause. A gale dashed his little sailing boat to pieces. Hall was undismayed. He borrowed from Captain Budington a spare longboat. Though the craft was "frail, rotten, and not seaworthy," wrote Hall, "I determined that, God willing, nothing should daunt me; I would persevere. . . ."

God answered his prayers in the form of a remarkable Eskimo couple. The husband was Ebierbing, a thinly moustached, Baffin Island coastal pilot known to whalers as Joe. His wife was Tookolito, a twenty-two-year-old beauty known as Hannah. Hall's description of his first meeting with the pair has a lovely fairytale quality about it.

One snowy November morning he was intently writing in his cabin aboard the *George Henry*. Then he heard a soft, sweet voice behind him say, "Good morning, sir."

"The *tone* in which it was spoken—musical, lively, and varied—instantly told me that a lady of refinement was there greeting me," Hall recorded. Hall thought he was dreaming and turned his head. "A lady was indeed before me, and extending an ungloved hand."

A skylight concealed her features; but Hall could see that she was dressed in a flounced crinoline and a kiss-me-quick bonnet. He was certain this elegant vision could not be a Baffin Island Eskimo. For books had told him the female savages were "a link between Saxons and seals"—hybrids encased in furs and blubber "like a roly-poly pudding." And yet, when this dusky Broadway belle turned her face toward him, he marvelled, "Who should it be but a *lady* Esquimaux!"

Hannah politely introduced herself and her husband. Hall learned that a whaling captain, impressed by the couple's intelligence, had once taken them to England. They had spent almost two years there. They were a sensation in high society and had dined with Queen Victoria and Prince Albert. "Fine place, I assure you, sir," said Hannah, when Hall asked her about the royal palace. And Joe, with a finesse that would have done credit to any diplomat, avowed that Queen Victoria was quite "pretty."

The couple had obviously brought back the niceties of Victorian etiquette. A few days later Hall crawled into their nearby igloo for a visit and was enchanted when Hannah poured him a cup of imported English black tea. "Do you like your tea strong?" she inquired.

Over the tea cups he blushed as he heard his hostess tut-tut about the bad manners of American whalers. "Americans swear a great deal," she remonstrated, "and make our people swear. It is a very bad practice, I believe."

"How think you, beloved countrymen, I felt with these hot coals on my head?" exclaimed Hall in his book, *Life with the Esquimaux*. "Oh, that every swearing man could have heard that Esquimaux woman as she spoke thus!"

Hall immediately engaged the couple. It was the beginning of an oddly moving friendship that deepened into mutual lifelong affection. Hannah was to be his housekeeper and interpreter. He taught her how to spell and count and she in turn translated his *Progressive Reader* into an Eskimo vocabulary for him. Joe was to serve as his hunter and man Friday. Hall offered his umbrella as a gift (which the other Eskimos

*Charles Francis Hall, blacksmith turned explorer, roamed nomadically about the high Arctic for seven years accompanied by a devoted Eskimo couple, Hannah Tookolito and Joe Ebierbing. He died mysteriously after raising the Stars and Stripes 464 miles from the Pole.* METROPOLITAN TORONTO LIBRARY BOARD

called a "walking tent") and taught Joe how to play checkers and how to trim Hall's whiskers like a good barber.

Hall's adaptation to their way of life was somewhat more difficult. When sleeping in an igloo, he soon learned, the most important Eskimo term to know was *ik-ke is-si-kars*, meaning cold feet. One night he tried to sleep in the communal bed between Hannah and another Eskimo woman. Though wrapped in caribou furs, Hall shivered in the fifty-seven-below-zero chill. At length the low, musical voice of Hannah whispered, "Are you cold, Mitter Hall?"

Hall muttered that he was suffering woefully from *ik-ke is-si-kars.*

"Your feet are like ice," she remarked, "and must be warmed Inuit fashion!"

She twined her warm feet around his icy ones and asked, "Do your feet feel better?"

"They do," said Hall, "and many thanks to you."

"Well, keep them where they are. Goodnight again, sir."

It is doubtful if Hall engaged in sexual dalliance with Hannah. Close as he became to Hannah and Joe, he usually maintained a certain paternalism. "They were as children to me," he wrote, "and I felt toward them like what a parent would."

Hall appears, however, to have been more lecherous than avuncular in his relationship with a buxom snowhouse guest named Suzhi. When she leaned naked out of bed to chew a piece of blubber, he stared goggle-eyed at her immense breasts and wrote appreciatively that they reminded him of the image from the Robert Burns poem:

*Twa drifted heaps, sae fair to see.*

Rather less appealing was the prospect of dining on Eskimo fare, "rotten, strong, and stinking." Nevertheless Hall steeled himself and took an initial stab at joining his hosts in a feast of raw whale. He pretended that the uncouth black flesh was really roast white breast of poultry from Ohio.

"I peeled off a delicate slice of this spinal ligament, closed my eyes, and cried out, 'Turkey!' But it would not go down so easy ... it was tougher than any bully beef of Christendom! For half an hour I tried to masticate it, then found it was even tougher than when I began. At length I discovered that I had been making a mistake in the way to eat it. The Esquimaux custom is to get as vast a piece into their distended mouths as they can cram, and then, boa constrictor-like, first lubricate it over, and so swallow it quite whole!

"When you are in Rome, do as the Romans do," he concluded. "Therefore I tried the Esquimaux plan and succeeded—but that one trial was sufficient at the time."

He trained himself to grit his teeth and give an Eskimo cry of "*Pe-e-uke!*"—meaning "Good!"—no matter how repellent the titbit placed before him. And indeed in time almost everything on the Eskimo menu tasted wonderfully *pe-e-uke.* Like the Eskimos, he learned to avoid polar bear liver, whose excess vitamin A rendered it poisonous; but he found its two-inch coating of white fat as palatable as any beefsteak. Kelp (seaweed) mixed with *poung-nung* (blackberries) was a luscious appetizer. Vegetation in a caribou paunch had a nice acidic flavor, like a salad of sorrel. But the *pièce de résistance* was seal. "Be it remembered," Hall underscored, "*there is no part of a seal but is good.*"

A mother seal's milk was as creamy white as if it had come from a cow and tasted like coconut milk. Smoking hot seal blood, which you gulped down with "one long s-o-o-o-p mouthful," was fit for a king. "It is ambrosia and nectar! Once tasted, the cry is sure to be 'More! More!'" As for the whitish seal blubber, it was rich as butter, tangy as strong old cheese; Hall says he never tired of it, whether it was raw, frozen, or rendered into oil. He joked that he sometimes feared he might suffer the fate of a certain blubber gourmand. This Eskimo consumed so much of the nourishing, fuel-like stuff that the poor fellow allegedly was stricken with a permanent bellyache due to the formation of a huge tallow candle in his stomach.

Hall, one supposes, did not really believe the tall tale. He maintained that ultimately he could digest—and enjoy—everything eaten by the Eskimos, although he did not claim to match their camel-like capacities. "This I might challenge *any* white man to do," he said. "No human stomach but an Inuit's could possibly hold what I saw these men and women devour."

After nearly two years of dog sledding and paddling about Baffin Island with his Inuit guides, Hall was fairly happy with his accomplishments. He had not found any Franklin survivors, but he had unearthed twenty valuable relics of the Sir Martin Frobisher expedition conducted some three hundred years previously. In the process he had re-explored the one hundred and seventy-five miles of Frobisher Bay and conclusively disproved the myth that it was a strait. His other geographical discoveries were not startling, but they satisfied his patriotic fervor. In the "name of God and the Continental Congress," he had placed Uncle Sam's banner on top of a capital mountain that he proudly named the

President's Seat. Not only did he honor his dentist with a bay; the journalistic promoter also christened a Cincinnati Press Channel as well as a Harper Brothers' Island after the New York publishers of his forthcoming book.

His chief accomplishment was that he had conditioned himself, albeit superficially as yet, to arctic living. "Life has charms everywhere," he said, "and I must confess that Eskimo life possesses those charms to a great degree for me." He was charmed by the cold beauty of the north country and the warmth of its people. He was charmed by their hospitable greeting, "Welcome stranger, Father Hall." He was charmed by their mimicry when they joined him in whistling *Hail Columbia* at the sight of a spectacular aurora borealis. He was charmed by their courtesy when their *aya-ya-ya* dance drummer, using two iron spoons for drumsticks, honored him with a rendition of *Yankee Doodle*.

But he was moved, rather than charmed, to the point of tears when he had to say goodbye to the tribal elder, Toolookaah, who had served as his kindly mentor in Eskimo folklore.

"This noble, free-hearted *Inuit* loves me, I do believe; I know that I love him," wrote Hall. "We have now been acquainted more than a year; have voyaged together; have shared perils of storms and the glory of sunshine; have feasted together; slept beneath the same *tupic* covering together; have been, as it were, father and son. . . . At last we locked hands, and, with prolonged *terboueties* (farewells), tears started in his eyes, and rolling down his iron-ribbed face, we parted, probably never to meet again on earth."

In August of 1862 Father Hall returned to the United States bringing with him what he now termed his two "adopted children," Joe and Hannah. In fact, there were three of them, for Hannah had given birth to a son named Tukerliktu, meaning Butterfly. Regrettably little Butterfly died on the Chautauqua Circuit. To raise funds for his next expedition, Hall embarked on a lecture tour. One learns regretfully that Joe, Hannah and the poor baby, all dressed up in furred Eskimo regalia like freaks, were exhibited along with their sled dogs, Ratty and Barbekark, on the stage at Barnum's Museum in New York and the Aquarial Gardens in Boston.

"This is indeed bad business," complained Hall, "having dealings with 'show' people, whose sole business is to grasp and hold the Almighty Dollar."

It was a plaint to be echoed by many future polar explorers. Dollars poured into the boxoffice, but the lecture fee paid by impresarios was a drop in the bucket. It was nowhere near the twenty thousand dol-

lars that Hall needed for his new Combination Research and Whaling Expedition to King William Island. Because the Civil War had cut into the whaling business, Henry Grinnell could not afford munificent hand-outs either. At one low point Hall made this Chaplinesque entry in his journal: "Started down the Bowery, sold damaged old hat to make a raise of 37 cents!"

A less dedicated man would have given up, but not Hall. "Single-handed and alone, I will yet accomplish my purpose," he wrote, "or die attempting it." Once again he scratched together enough money to buy a small boat, the *Sylvia*, named after Henry Grinnell's daughter. Once again he promoted supplies from publicity-eager merchants: soap from Colgate & Co., rubber goods from Goodyear's India Rubber Co., medicine from McKesson & Robbins, biscuits from Borden's, a hat from Knox of New York. And once again he cadged a free ride aboard a New England whaling ship: this time it was the *Monticello*, skippered by Captain E.A. Chapel (Hall had quarelled with Captain Budington).

On July 1, 1864, accompanied by Hannah and Joe, Hall sailed from New London, Connecticut, for King William Island, "the Meta of my aspirations." It took him five years to set foot on it. During that time he made his main base at Repulse Bay, the whalers' rendezvous in the northwest corner of Hudson Bay, and sledged a total of almost three thousand miles with bands of itinerant Eskimos. He suffered one set-back after another; but it must be said that his problems sometimes stemmed from his own stiff-necked piety and combative temper.

He alternately socialized and feuded with the whaling captains. During their "gamming" recreational periods, he joined them in corn-popping and candy-making parties; in dances with neighboring Eskimo women all adazzle with beaded headbands and borrowed petticoats; and in theatricals where the so-called Hudson's Bay Theater Company staged *Damon and Pythias*. At the same time he was subject to sullen moods of suspicion and outbursts of almost childish tantrums. He broke off relations with Captain Chapel, accusing him of luring the wives of Hall's Eskimo party aboard ship "for his own *licentious accommodation*." He stormed off another vessel because he felt that her skipper "didn't care a d--n for all my previous arrangements" and was attempting to hire away Hall's native guides.

Perhaps Hall's restlessness was to blame. He was God's envoy on a mission and he could not abide waiting. When the Repulse Bay Eskimos kept delaying, he impatiently hired five whaling men, at five hundred

dollars each, to accompany him to King William Island. With these sailors Hall displayed the worst side of his impetuous nature. One day he berated them for shirking. They became surly and their burly leader doubled up his fists and threatened him with a fight. In a blind rage Hall reached for his revolver and shot him. Although Hall contritely nursed him, within two weeks the man was dead. And although Hall claimed he was defending himself against a mutineer, it was a black mark on his record. His act of violence betrayed a low boiling point in a highly unstable leader.

Hall's relationship with the bands of Eskimos was likewise erratic. There were periods when he was captivated by the wild freedom of these "noble children of the icy North." He became adept at whizzing over the snows on a sledge shod with the jawbone of a whale and cracking his thirty-foot-long sealskin whip over the curling tails of the dogpack. He became an accomplished snowmason and proudly flew the Stars and Stripes over the igloo he built. He was accepted as an able muskox hunter and was pleased by the compliments when he shot five caribou in five minutes. "Laughter, hilarity, joyous ringing voices abounded" at the feast.

He contributed to the hilarity by indulging his fellow hunters in a drinking wassail. The usually abstemious Hall served the men Hubbell's Golden Bitters (advertised as "Good for Dyspepsia") and spiked the punch with capital good bourbon whisky. "We talked, smoked and drank—talked, smoked and drank till every heart felt that it should be friendly to everybody," he wrote. "We were all gloriously drunk."

Next morning he suffered from an inglorious hangover. "When I awoke," he moaned, "I never had such a sick, terrible feeling in my life." The missionary was ridden with guilt: "I feel that I have neglected to teach these children of the North their religious duties . . . . May I learn from the glorious Bible my duty, and by the help of God perform it."

He read them the story of Joseph from the Bible and taught them to parrot prayers from his Book of Psalms. But the heathens stubbornly rebuffed Christian dogma. Even pious Hannah exasperated him by her adherence to Eskimo ritual. She gave birth to a son and allowed Hall to christen him King William. But then the infant died. Grief-stricken Hannah permitted Hall to buy her in exchange for a sled an adopted baby (a daughter named Puney) and to give her dead child a Christian burial under a stone cross. But it angered him when Hannah reverted with slavish obedience to the mourning taboos imposed by the tribal

*angekok*. She was forbidden to wear a warm tunic in a snowstorm, to dry her wet stockings, to repair her torn boots.

Hall once thought that Eskimos enjoyed greater freedom and independence than any American. "But I now know how mistaken I was," he wrote. "It is *custom—custom* of the old dead *Inuits* that must be followed.... How utterly impossible it is to knock or reason these absurd, superstitious ideas out of an *Inuit's* head."

His Christian morality was outraged when the *angekok* persuaded Joe to indulge in the traditional Eskimo practice of a friendly wife exchange for the night. Evidently virtue triumphed. Hall cunningly outwitted the *angekok* : he swathed Hannah in caribou skins as though she were "*mailed* from neck to ankles." Then Hall sat at the foot of the communal bed and gloated to see "how the fellow worked and puffed!" in a vain attempt "to get her skin tights open."

Apparently Hall was not entirely a prude. He seemed titillated by the scandalous stories of her past love life recounted to him by an old Eskimo woman named Erktua. Under the diary heading, ESPECIALLY PRIVATE!, Hall recorded her most lascivious exploit. She claimed to have taken as a paramour some forty years ago first that very proper English explorer, Sir William Edward Parry, and then his second in command, Captain George Lyon.

"Erktua furthermore says that, when Parry found out she had slept with Lyon, & learned she had done the same with Parry, they became jealous," Hall reported, "and for this Erktua ever after refused to sleep with either again."

A few months later Hall made another ESPECIALLY PRIVATE! notation in his diary: "Erktua is a notorious falsifier—in other words, a liar." The old crone, it seems, was now spreading the tale that Hall himself had tried to seduce her into becoming his inamorata.

This sample of Eskimo yarn-spinning did not diminish Hall's credulity. By putting forth leading questions, he elicited from the natives a sensational, though unlikely, piece of news: four of Franklin's lost expedition, missing now for almost twenty-five years, were said to be still alive on King William Island.

The Eskimos, of course, were not being mendacious; they were simply being obliging. If the foolish white man was so intent in his naive belief, why not please him by agreeing it was indeed so? In truth, Hall's trip to King William Island proved amply rewarding. He exhumed or bought from the natives one hundred and twenty-five authentic relics. Among them were: a silver fork bearing Franklin's crest, the skeleton of

a man later identified by his tooth filling as a lieutenant aboard the *Erebus*, a sword point, a pickle jar, and part of a mahogany writing desk being used, incongruously, by the Eskimos as a blubber tray.

At first Hall praised the natives; they were "noble, generous men" who had helped keep Franklin's party alive on seal meat. But then he heard gruesome tales of white cannibalism that he did not want to believe: of skeletons severed with a saw and boots filled with cooked human flesh. What shocked him still more was the discovery that the natives had not fed the four alleged survivors. In the brutal fight for survival, the Eskimos apparently *"would not stop even a day"* to catch seals for the starving white men; and the vandals had compounded their sin by robbing their graves as well.

Hall was bitterly disillusioned. *"Civilize, Enlighten and Christianize* them and their race," he exclaimed.

Hall was further disenchanted. His Eskimo band balked at helping him continue his seeming wild goose chase to locate a cement vault near Victory Point supposedly containing Franklin's remnants. This infuriated Hall, always an obsessively independent man. "Moral suasion with these creatures is entirely out of the question," he railed. *"Force* and *severity* . . . would soon bring them within the rule of Civilization!"

It especially rankled to take orders from his chief guide, a "hoggish" Eskimo, who kept him on mangy food rations and made him do menial women's work. "He," raged Hall, "acts the SAVAGE!"

It was with relief that Hall returned to the whalers' rendezvous and gorged himself on familiar American cooking. "O, what a glorious dinner for me!" he declared when Captain George Emory Tyson invited him aboard the *Antelope* for a repast. "Baked beans and pork, preserved beef . . . green corn, preserved cherries, mince pie, coffee and preserved milk!" Rather guiltily, like a reformed drunk going out on a binge, he confessed, "I like civilized food as well as any man."

His mission had failed. But he consoled himself that he had passed "my Arctic Collegiate education." Living on freshly killed fat meat—the best "fuel for the human stove"—he had survived five years without ever being tainted by scurvy. Although they had tried his patience to the utmost, he had learned that Eskimos must be accepted on their own terms. They could not be dismissed as simple children of the North. They were rather "a race of iron men—untameable eagles of the North," as free-spirited and as prone to human frailties as himself.

In September of 1869 "Father Hall" returned to the United States with faithful Hannah and Joe and little Puney. They were ready to

follow him to the ends of the earth. They had need of their devotion. Hall took them on lecture tours, preaching his new gospel. He argued that "God gave to man this beautiful world—*the whole of it*—to subdue." Just as the United States was later to take a proprietary interest in the moon, it was Uncle Sam's manifest destiny to be first to reach "the crowning jewel of the Arctic dome." Hall talked of establishing a colony on the North Pole and taking possession of rich whaling grounds there "in the name of the Lord, and for the President of the United States."

President Ulysses S. Grant, listening to Hall deliver his rhetoric in a speech at Lincoln Hall in Washington, could hardly resist. He signed a bill passed by Congress granting fifty thousand dollars for a U.S. Navy expedition to be commanded by Captain Hall. The former blacksmith-cum-journalist almost turned a somersault with joy. "North, *north*, farther and farther NORTH, I long to get," he wrote in breathless prose, "until I shall reach that spot of this great and glorious orb where there is no North, no East, no West. Of course, that mundane point is the one nearly under Polaris."

*Polaris* was the name he gave to his ship. She had served in the Civil War as the *Periwinkle*, a wooden gunboat of three hundred and eighty-seven tons. She was a combination of steam tug and sailing vessel, her twin masts dwarfing her squat smokestack. Now she was taken to the Washington Navy Yard to be replanked with thick oak and to have her hull sheathed with steel to combat ice.

On July 2, 1871, the day before she was scheduled to embark from New London, Connecticut, Captain Hall inspected her in company with a local Baptist congregation. He was pleased with what he saw. Below deck were enough provisions to last two and a half years, as well as an enormous library of books on the Arctic and an organ for playing religious hymns. "There is no desire in Uncle Sam," said Hall, "to give bad material or poor work to his Arctic devoted sons."

The optimist was deluding himself, for the human cargo of the ill-fated *Polaris* was an ill-assorted lot. Not counting the Eskimos, there was a roster of twenty-five officers and men, largely Americans and Germans, simmering with internecine hostilities.

Her sailing master was Captain Sidney O. Budington of Groton, Connecticut. He was the greybearded whaling captain who had given Hall his first free passage north aboard the *George Henry*. Hall had patched up his quarrel with him, but it was a truce. The veteran Arctic whaler drank hard and swore hard and it griped him to take orders from a landlubberly commander who was a prim teetotaller to boot.

Budington had no stomach for the "damned nonsense" of polar exploration. In his view, land sailors who risked their lives for science were "devilish fools." "I was sick and down-hearted," he later said of the whole confounded enterprise, and that drove him to drown his misery in drink.

Her assistant navigator, Captain George Emory Tyson, was the officer most devoted to Hall and his cause. He was the whaler who had played host to Hall on his second Arctic expedition. Like Hall, Tyson was a warm-hearted, thatch-bearded, pious and sometimes narrow romantic. Spurred by adventure stories of the polar explorers, he had run away from his job in a New York City iron foundry to become a Greenland whaler and had sailed the Arctic seas for twenty-three of his forty-two years. As a whaling captain himself, he resented having to play second fiddle to Captain Budington, whom he regarded as a "boozy" and disloyal incompetent; as for the expedition's German scientific corps, they were a pack of foreigners beyond the pale.

The chief scientist was Dr. Emil Bessels, a graduate of Heidelberg University and a former surgeon in the Prussian Army. Aged twenty-four, with a handsome dark beard and sardonic black eyes, he was said to be a meticulous naturalist, "sensitive" and with a "quick, nervous temperament." Others considered him dogmatic and ambitious, sleek and cold as a lizard, with a vaguely sinister air. He was openly contemptuous of Hall and the other Americans, whom he derided as his intellectual inferiors. On his deathbed Hall was to condemn Dr. Bessels as "that little German dancing master" and to accuse him of being his poisoner.

Bessels' meteorologist was Frederick Meyer, graduate of a Prussian military academy and a former lieutenant in the Prussian Army. He was a tall, ramrod-stiff figure with a "Kaiser" moustache and a matching imperious manner which won him the nickname of the "German Count." His service as a sergeant in the United States Signal Corps had not altered his arrogance or his sense of military punctilio. Meyer sneered that the democratic Hall "consulted with sailors and not with his officers" and was overheard complaining scornfully that "the sailors had command."

By the time the *Polaris* put into the Greenland whaling station at Disko these submerged dissensions had boiled up to the surface. Captain Budington had been severely reprimanded when caught stealing from the surgical supply of alcohol, and had blustered that he was ready to quit the voyage. Meyer had brazenly refused to help keep the ship's daily journal, and Hall had threatened to send him back to the United

States in irons. Dr. Bessels had stepped into the fray. If his assistant was forced to resign, so would Bessels—and take the German crewmen with him.

Hall, who would previously have flown into a violent rage, handled it with a measure of mature leadership. He compromised. Meyer would continue with his meteorological observations; another seaman would keep the ship's journal.

That Sunday Hall asked Dr. J.P. Newman, an American clergyman who chanced to be at Disko, to preach a special shipboard sermon. It contained this significant passage:

"May we have for each other that charity that suffereth long and is kind, that envieth not, that vaunteth not itself, that is not puffed up, that seeketh not her own, that is not easily provoked, that thinketh no evil, but that heareth all things, hopeth all things, endureth all things."

At Upernavik, the next stop on the west coast of Greenland, Hall welcomed aboard an Eskimo who needed no such sermonizing. It was Hans Christian Hendrik, plump and beaming as ever. He was the doughty seal hunter, who had been such a godsend on Kane's voyage to the so-called Open Polar Sea. Hans climbed aboard with his wife, Christiana; his children, Augustina, Tobias and Succi; his kayak and swarm of sledge dogs; and his omnipresent good cheer. Although some insensitive crewmen mocked at his verminous furs, Hans treated them with Christian forbearance. In his memoirs he speaks benignly of "the very kind and friendly" Master Hall and his "dear Westland comrades," Joe, Hannah and Puney, from the other side of Baffin Bay.

The eighty-horsepower engine of the *Polaris* made light work of the Baffin Bay obstacles that had bedeviled Kane's little sailing brig *Advance*. Northward she chugged. Past the Arctic Pillars of Hercules guarding Smith Sound. Past Kane's spectral Delectable Mountains shimmering ghostlike in foggy Kane Basin. Up through Kennedy Channel, past a rocky speck named Hans Island after Eskimo Hans, and then up into the unknown. Up into another saucer of icy water to be named Hall Basin. Up into Robeson Channel named after United States Naval Secretary George M. Robeson. Up and up she thrashed through freezing spume, past roaring walruses and clashing bergs and naked lunar landscapes until, at six AM, August 30, 1871, the *Polaris* established her record northing. She had steamed up to 82 degrees, 11 minutes north latitude and was at the very lip of the Arctic Ocean.

The sailors were frightened and some of the more superstitious

were afraid they might tumble off the edge of the world. Not so the expedition's two sovereign enthusiasts. "If the *Polaris* should get no farther," exulted Tyson from the crow's nest, "her keel has plowed through waters never parted by any ship before."

Hall felt strangely heady. Partly he felt the explorer's intoxicated thrill at having pushed so far up the American Highway to the Pole and partly he felt a curious letdown. He had always known he would one day attain the farthest reaches of *Wes-see-poke*, the Eskimo Far-off Land. Now he was at the fringe of it, and it was no more than the Lost Paradise which had once moved him to quote from John Milton's *Paradise Lost*:

> *. . . o'er the back side of the world far off*
> *Into a limbo large and broad, since called*
> *The Paradise of Fools.*

The Paradise he saw, through a veil of mist and falling snow, was a limbo of limitless white, laced here and there with a network of thin dark blue cracks like a giant cobweb. He named it the Lincoln Sea, but it was one vast floating continent of shifting, grinding, surging ice pack—a tangible mockery to the fools who had dreamed of an open iceless Sea.

Winds and floes and current were beating the *Polaris* southward. But Hall persisted in rowing to the Greenland shore in a longboat to hoist the Stars and Stripes in a token ritual at a spot he called Repulse Harbor. Then he called a meeting of his officers to determine what to do. They gave him conflicting advice. Tyson wanted to ram ahead north; Budington was obdurate about seeking refuge south.

"He was very set, and walked off as if to end the discussion," Tyson wrote of Budington's obstinacy. "Captain Hall followed him and stood some time talking to him."

The polar elements took the argument out of their hands. A gale and drifting floes whipped them back on their tracks into Hall Basin. Finally, on September 10, the ship dropped anchor in a mountain-rimmed Greenland fjord at 81 degrees, 37 minutes north latitude. Hall devoutly christened it Thank God Harbor and the protecting Gothic iceberg nearby he named Providence Berg.

There the *Polaris* prepared her winter quarters. Hall was now at his genial best. Though he issued orders forbidding profane language, he generated a true spirit of camaraderie among his festering and divided crew. He exchanged banter with his officers and encouraged the men to

compose a sea chanty, *We Are Going to the Pole.* To give more elbow room to the cramped English steward, John Herron, and the English Negro cook, William Jackson, Hall gave up his captain's stateroom and let them have it as a galley. He himself moved into a small cabin, just fifteen feet long and eight feet wide, where he bunked with six others, including the standoffish Bessels and Meyer. In a democratic spirit, he exhorted the officers and sailors to "all live together as brothers," and ordered the same kind of food prepared for both messes. The crew members were sufficiently moved to draw up a letter thanking him for his kind "disposition to treat us as reasonable men."

This unheard-of practice later drew a scathing denunciation from Sir Clements Markham, the British Admiralty historian. The critic said the Yankee expedition was bound to end in disaster, for "every man considered himself as good as his neighbour."

On October 10, as he set out on the last exploratory journey of his life, Hall felt no such forebodings. He was in buoyant good humor. He intended to make a two-week sledge reconnaissance northward. He would blaze the trail for the expedition's ultimate overland push to the Pole. His scouting party included his first mate, an eager Connecticut whaler named Hubbard Chester, and two sledges and fourteen dogs handled by Eskimo Hans and Eskimo Joe.

Tyson saw them off in a driving snowstorm and wished them a safe trip. In his journal Tyson made a notation about Hall's endearing absent-mindedness: "After all the time spent in preparing and packing, I have no doubt he has forgotten something; he is rather peculiar that way."

Sure enough Hans was dispatched back the next day bearing a long list of items that had slipped Hall's mind. Among other things he required his pair of sealskin pants, bearskin mittens, a candlestick, four onions and one snowshoe. "Tell Hannah and little Puney," he scribbled in a postscript, "to be good always."

His safari fifty miles to the north met formidable obstacles. Snow blizzards whirled into a "storm-roar upon the mountains." Winds slashed "cuttingly cold." The twenty-below-zero chill was so cruel that "our sleeping bags have to be coaxed a long time before we can unroll them they are so stiffly frozen." But Hall felt exhilarated. "These drawbacks are nothing new to an Arctic traveler," he wrote. "We laugh at them and plod on."

He was now fifty years old, an explorer in his true element. Part Eskimo, part scientist, he now felt able to draw upon all his hard-won

polar schooling over the past decade. He laughed as he rescued his poor fumbling first mate, who got lost floundering in a snow drift. He laughed as he helped Hans and Joe to build snowhouses and, like a seasoned arctic hand, blithely dried off his wet mittens and stockings by packing them next to his body as he slept. He laughed as he led the hunt for seals and muskoxen, and when the pickings were slim he laughed when he had to make do with a meal of raw pemmican. "Our standard provision and most nutritious of all foods," he described it, "and we now feel just as well as though we had been feasted by a New York City alderman."

He made careful scientific observations. He collected tufts of luxuriant orange lichen and nosegays of what looked like spider-walking *Andromeda tetragona*. He filled his mittens with specimens of coal-black slate and coral fossils, and set up his tripod in the misty mornings to attempt a sighting of the planet Jupiter.

Accompanied by his favorite dog, Wolf, and his trio of companions, he climbed up a steep limestone cliff. "On our way," he marveled, "grass and various species of flowering plants were seen, and they abounded even up to the mountain's top."

On the peak of his Lookout Mountain, gazing through his spyglass, he felt like Moses of the Old Testament surveying his promised land. To the east of his aery he could see the silvery glacier glow of the Greenland Icecap. About sixty miles westward, rising through the purpling mists like scoops of raspberry ice cream, could be dimly seen the alpine pyramids of Canada's Ellesmere Island (to be awarded the collective name of Grant Land). To the north, "a peculiar dark nimbus cloud hangs over what seems may be land," but Hall was reluctant to make any guesses. Below his vantage point, winding about thirty miles, were the open blue waters of a serpentine fjord, "having numerous seals in it, bobbing up their heads." Hall named it Newman Bay. Then he read aloud a prayer written for his sledge party by that worthy American clergyman. He regretted that he was as yet unable to recite an additional prayer which Dr. Newman had written for the occasion when Hall should first set foot on the North Pole.

Though a furious blizzard forced his sledge party to turn back to the *Polaris*, Hall was laughingly confident that his hardy sledgers were quite capable of reaching the Pole the next time out. "So long as we can forward the service we are engaged in," he wrote, "so long will we laugh at such obstacles. . . ."

Hall returned to the *Polaris* on October 24 and stopped to shake

hands with Tyson. "He said he was never better in his life," Tyson later testified at a naval court of inquiry. "He enjoyed the sledge journey, and was going right off on another journey, and wished me to go with him."

Hall then strode exuberantly to the small cabin he shared with Bessels, Meyer and four others. He asked for a mug of hot coffee. Within a half hour Hall was vomiting convulsively.

"I feel sick," he gasped, as the cluster of men helped him into his bunk. "There's bad stuff in that coffee. Burns your stomach." And he complained of its strange, sweet taste.

Dr. Bessels took his pulse (which beat erratically from sixty to eighty) and asked how he felt. "Bilious," said Hall. "I feel pain in the stomach and weakness in the legs."

As he was speaking Hall slumped into a comatose state. Dr. Bessels applied a mustard poultice and jabbed him with what appears to have been an injection of quinine. Hall recovered consciousness within twenty-five minutes. "His left arm and left side are paralysed, including his face and tongue," announced Dr. Bessels. He spooned out a purgative of castor oil and croton oil for his patient and then he took the others in the cabin aside.

"The captain is suffering from an apoplectical insult," diagnosed the doctor, "and I believe he will never get over it."

According to the testimony of others, it was no fit of apoplexy that had so suddenly stricken Hall. Some believed that he suffered from latent madness and some believed that he suffered from poisoning. For the next two weeks his behavior seemed to suggest both.

Always a deeply suspicious man, he now accused virtually everyone aboard of conspiring to murder him. Hannah and Joe were the only ones he trusted; he refused to take any medicine prescribed by Bessels unless it was first tasted by his faithful Eskimo retainers. In his dementia he saw weird hallucinations—flames darting from the mouth of Budington, blue vapor spouting from what Hall termed Dr. Bessels' "infernal machine."

"He talks wildly," noted Tyson, "seems to think someone meant to poison him." Almost everyone agreed that his suspicions focused on Dr. Bessels. "He appeared to spit out his whole venom on him," testified Budington. "That is, he appeared to think the doctor was the proper one."

By November 6 he had improved and spoke coherently. That night he summoned Budington, who found him seated in his berth, scribbling in his confidential journal. "Sidney," he wanted to know, "how do you spell 'murder'?"

Then his eyes took on a glassy look and he turned to face Bessels. "Doctor, I know everything that's going on," he said. "You can't fool me." And he spewed out a tirade against "that little German dancing master."

The next day he had a relapse. He sank into a coma and, as Dr. Bessels testified, "you could hear gurgling or rale in his throat." At 3:25 AM on November 8, 1871, while Bessels was smoothing his pillow and tucking blankets around him, Hall opened his eyes and spoke his last words.

"Doctor," Hall whispered a moment before he died, "you have been very kind to me, and I am obliged to you."

It is frustrating that nobody thought to record *how* those words were spoken. Was Hall expressing gratitude or was he expressing sarcasm? To this day the tone of his voice when he made that final utterance remains a mystery as inscrutable as the elusive smile of the Mona Lisa. One would like to think that the evangelist, so given to black moods and rages, died with Christian forgiveness on his lips. God knows, there was little Christian charity shown by most of his fellow officers.

Dr. Bessels, according to one seaman's testimony, suddenly appeared to be light-hearted. "Captain Hall's death," Bessels said with a laugh, "was the best thing that could happen for the expedition." Captain Budington felt relieved, and babbled drunkenly, "There's a stone off my heart." Meteorologist Meyer, the Prussian, was militaristic. "Maybe now," he told a group of sailors, "the officers will have something to say."

Captain Tyson, who thought of himself as Hall's protégé, was an exception. "Thus ends poor Hall's ambitious projects," he lamented. "Thus is stilled the effervescing enthusiasm of as ardent a nature as I ever knew. Wise he might not have been, but his soul was in this work."

Tyson led a few volunteers ashore to dig a grave. The ground was frozen hard as flint. They hacked at it with pickaxes for two days to reach a depth of twenty-six inches. Below that lay permafrost, impossible to dent.

Hall's corpse, wrapped in the Stars and Stripes, was laid to rest after an eerie funeral procession. Though it was not yet noon, the arctic night had set in and the pale stars shone through a weird boreal glow. The pine coffin, draped with a cotton American flag, was dragged on a sledge across the ice, and Tyson led the way for the funeral cortege, holding aloft a guttering lantern. The ship's bell tolled and the dogs howled and they lowered Hall into his grave with his face toward the

*On his deathbed Hall accused Dr. Emil Bessels, "that little German dancing master," of poisoning him.*

*In the fatal cabin, which he shared with Bessels, Hall suspiciously refused prescribed medicine unless it was first tasted by faithful Hannah and Joe.*

East and Resurrection, his back toward the iced waters of Thank God Harbor. They named that spot Hall's Rest, and it is recorded that its silence was broken by the wail of the wind and "by the sounds of the earth upon the coffin and by the sobs of Hannah."

In the end it was his Eskimo comrades who grieved most over Hall's death. "Captain Hall my friend," Eskimo Joe later testified at the hearings. "Captain Hall good man. Very sorry when he die."

"What mournful news, that he who loved us so kindly lives no longer!" wrote Eskimo Hans in his memoirs. And Hans tells of Joe wondering with him that now that their White Father was no more, "How shall we fare, for he is our only protector?"

They fared badly, and so did discipline aboard the *Polaris*. "The expedition died with Captain Hall," a sailor testified. Command was now divided between a rancorous Budington and Bessels, and the voyage degenerated into one long arctic saturnalia. Budington celebrated Washington's birthday by breaking open cases of Koesysbacher wine. Sailors swilled and staggered at the "North Pole Lager Beer Saloon." The demented ship's carpenter, aptly named Nathaniel Coffin, raved through the wild nights that now conspirators were plotting to murder him. Even Dr. Bessels seems to have been infected by the sodden *Sturm und Drang*. On Christmas he contrived a mad scientist's invention, so that branches of a pine Yule tree would bleed "sap" of pure alcohol.

"I wish I could blot out of my memory some things which I see and hear," worried Tyson. "It is enough to make Captain Hall stir in his ice-cold grave."

Hall's Eskimos were being maltreated. "We poor natives must be very careful," Joe warned Hans. "The white men despise thine and my customs."

Hans's wife, Christiana, was taunted for keeping her cabin like a dirty igloo. And the drunken crew threatened, apparently in sport, to punish Hans "man-of-war fashion" with a flogging and a hanging from the yardarm. "I fell a-weeping," wrote Hans. "Our little son asked: 'Why do ye cry?'" Tyson interceded with compassion and ordered the men to desist from their callous prank. "Whereupon, smiling, he petted our children," says Hans, "and a heavy stone was removed from my heart."

The seamen eventually gave up their Eskimo-baiting after a happy event. At 6 AM on August 12, Christiana gave birth to a son (apparently

her bad housekeeping was due to her pregnancy) and the crew celebrated by raising their cups and naming the baby, in honor of Hall and
the ship, Charlie Polaris.

Little Charlie Polaris was destined to be cradled on an ice raft, and
it was a saga that makes the last half of the *Polaris* expedition so singular
in Arctic annals. Anchored to a large floe, and left to the mercy of wind
and current, the leaky ship had been allowed to drift southward with
the pack from Hall Basin down to the neck of Kane Basin.

Then at 6 PM on October 15 catastrophe struck. A gale lashed the
pack with maniacal fury. Bergs walloped the *Polaris* and wrenched her
stern high in the air and she reeled over on her port side like a drunken
sailor. She shook and she trembled and her timbers cracked. A cry arose
that the gashed ship had started a fresh leak and panic set in.

"Throw everything on the ice!" yelled Captain Budington.

Boxes and barrels were instantly flung onto the floe. Captain
Tyson leaped onto the ice to take charge of the frenzied unloading. "It
was a terrible night," he later said, and so it was. The shriek of the wind,
the squealing of floes, the gusting of sleet, and the awful darkness—all
added to the terror and confusion. The crowning horror came when the
ice seemed to explode under Tyson's feet and the last anchor lines holding the ship to the floe snapped away. He looked down and saw a
muskox hide lying across a spreading crack in the ice. He grabbed it
just in time to rescue three of Hans's children wrapped inside the skin.
He looked up and saw the *Polaris*, with Captain Budington, Dr. Bessels
and twelve other men aboard her, disappear into the Arctic twilight like
a phantom.

"Goodbye, *Polaris!*" One of those left stranded on the floe with
Tyson gazed despairingly at the vanishing ship and kept uttering that
forlorn cry. "Goodbye, *Polaris!*"

In the morning Tyson took a roll call of his castaways. Counting
himself there were nineteen in all. Frederick Meyer, the Prussian
meteorologist, was the only other officer; his party consisted of nine
non-American seamen, including the steward and cook. The other nine
were all members of the two Eskimo families: Joe, Hannah and their
adopted Puney; and Hans, Christiana and their four children, including
the infant Charlie Polaris.

Tyson thought of all those mouths to feed as he took inventory of
the scant provisions. There were fourteen cans of pemmican, twelve
bags of hardtack, eleven dozen cans of soup, fourteen hams, one can of
dried apples, and a small bag of chocolate. In addition, they had saved

*Captain George Emory Tyson helped 19 castaways survive 1,500-mile drift on an ice raft.*

*"Goodbye, Polaris!" the castaways cried forlornly as the ship vanished in the hell-black night.*

two whaleboats, a scow, an A-tent, and the two kayaks and nine sled-dogs belonging to Hans and Joe. Their God-made raft, as he called the drifting floe, was about four miles in circumference. It was studded with ice hillocks as high as thirty feet, but it looked as though it might shatter under the hammer blow of the next storm.

What most distressed Tyson was the character of the "German party," as he termed the other white men. They seemed to be a pack of undisciplined grumblers. They exhibited their truculence that very first day. With infuriating deliberation the dawdlers would not set out in the whaleboats to look for the *Polaris* until they had a hot breakfast and changed their clothes.

They temporarily stopped dragging their feet when the *Polaris* suddenly hove into view. She seemed some ten miles away, and the castaways hallooed at the returned ghost ship, and hoisted flags and spread a dark India rubber canvas against the white of a snow hill. Tyson anxiously scanned the ship's movements through his spyglass. With bitter anguish he saw her slink away.

"God knows why, Captain Budington don't *mean* to help us," he thought. Then the reality of their plight struck him forcibly: "What shall I do with all these people if God means for us to shift for ourselves, without ship, or shelter, or sufficient food, through the long, cold, dark winter?"

It was a long melancholy winter, and if it had not been for Joe and Hans they would surely have perished. The two Eskimos supervised construction of an igloo village. Five snowhouses were linked by arched alleyways: a storehouse and a cookhouse, a hut for the sailors, a hut for Hans's family, and a hut for Joe's family. An additional compartment was to have housed Meyer and Tyson; it was quickly abandoned because the two officers clashed. Meyer shared quarters with the seamen; Tyson moved in with Joe and Hannah and little Puney.

And so the floating ice island — soon split asunder by a storm into a tenth of its size — likewise split psychologically into two camps. Tyson became the surrogate Father Hall to the Eskimos. Meyer set himself up as the substitute Bessels lording it over the white men.

The wrangling was constant over fuel and food. From the outset Tyson and the Eskimos used blubber lamps fashioned from pemmican cans and wicks of canvas. With reckless disregard for the future, Meyer and his seamen started breaking up the boats for firewood. The most improvident of them realized that, even with the occasional seals and dovekies speared by Joe and Hans, provisions would have to be rationed. With a pair of improvised scales weighted by ball shot, Tyson

and Meyer began by alloting eleven ounces of food daily for each adult and half that amount for each child.

But the seamen stealthily stole chocolate and hardtack from the storeroom. Dwindling rations were cut to nine and a half ounces for one daily meal. Gradually the dogs were killed and eaten one by one, with Joe reassuring the squeamish, "Anything is good that don't poison you."

Facing near-starvation, the seamen turned ugly. Although the sailors spent all their time in their quarters, playing cards and listlessly fretting, they treated their two Eskimo providers as subhuman lackeys. Once, when Joe and Hans caught a small seal, the seamen snatched it away and devoured the booty among themselves.

Tyson, helplessly outnumbered and without any firearms, was infuriated by this brutish show of white strength by the "German Count" and his brethren. "They were masters of the *Polaris* and wish to be masters here," he wrote. "They go swaggering about with their pistols and rifles."

Long afterwards Joe was asked why he and his Eskimos did not paddle away in their kayaks and leave the unfair white men to shift for themselves. "Cap'n Hall not like that," replied Joe. "Cap'n Hall good man; *good* man. If Cap'n Hall alive, *he* not run away. I not run away neither."

Tyson did his best to sympathize with his famished white shipmates. "The men are frightened," he wrote. "They seem to see Death staring them in the face and saying, 'In a little while you are mine.'" At the same time he was haunted by the fear that their desperation might turn them to cannibalism. Joe shared that concern. "I don't like the look out of the men's eyes," said Joe.

"I know what he fears," Tyson underscored in his notepad. "*He thinks they will first kill and eat Hans and family, and then he knows Hannah's, Puney's, and his turn would be next.* God forbid that any of this company should be tempted to such a crime! . . . If it is God's will that we should die of starvation, why, let us die like men, not like brutes, tearing each other to pieces."

He was a family man himself, and he thought of his own children suffering as did these starving brown-skinned children. His heart ached as he watched Christiana try to breastfeed baby Charlie Polaris while her four-year-old daughter, Succi, kept crying—"a kind of chronic hunger whine." Little Puney kept repeating over and over, "I am *so*

hungry," and he took no offence when she stared at Tyson and gravely remarked, "You are nothing but bone." Although it was true, Tyson could think of nothing but her skull-gauntness. "I can not resist," he said with compassion, "sometimes giving poor little Puney a part of my scanty rations."

He was striving, of course, to pattern himself after Hall. Yet ultimately he had to admit he could not match his mentor. His jaws ached when he chewed on dried seal skin, hair and all, and he was repelled when forced to gnaw on the refuse blubber of the oil lamp. "Captain Hall learned to enjoy it, but I can not," he groaned. "What filth and dirt I am compelled to eat!"

He was an extremely fastidious man; the vile smell of his own unchanged fur garments and the accumulated grease and grime of the igloo drove him to distraction. He kept after the seamen to clean up the squalid main passageway, and he reported with a certain delight: "Joe came back into the hut very indignant, saying, 'They talk about Esquimaux being dirty and stinking, but sailors are worse than Esquimaux.' His indignation was not without reason."

At times the tedium, the hunger, the cold and the dirt became too much for him. "If a man ever suffered the torments of wretched souls condemned to the 'ice-hell' of the great Italian poet, Dante," he wrote, "I think I have felt it here."

His love of poetry and his innate sense of humor helped to keep him from going mad. He missed desperately having no books to read, not even a two-year-old copy of *Harper's Weekly*. He found himself going for solitary walks to the edge of the ice floe, and admiring the "white waste of desolation around me, the terror and the beauty combined, with here and there a splendid spectacle of illuminated ice spears," and reciting aloud a paraphrase of the verses of Tennyson:

*Break, break, break*
*On these cold ice blocks, O sea!*
*And I would that my tongue could utter*
*The thoughts that arise in me.*

When cooped up by the forty-below-zero storms, "all snow and blow, blow and snow," he had to fall back on his own black humor. "I was thinking the other evening," he wrote with his stub of a pencil, "how strange it would sound to hear a good hearty laugh." He had nothing to do but pace back and forth in the igloo, just three feet

square, biting the hair of his beard and indulging in wild fancies. Sometimes he watched Hannah and Joe play checkers on an old piece of canvas, the squares being marked out with his pencil, and using his buttons for men.

"When I see people who don't know what else to do resorting to checkers," he reflected, "it always reminds me of what Dickens wrote of a forlorn old couple who tried to consider that it was a social way of spending the evening. He said it was more like 'clubbing their loneliness' than indulging in sociality. It is certainly so here."

Sometimes the loneliness became intolerable. The "German Count" and his foreign cabal, with apparent perverse rudeness, spoke German when Tyson was present; and he dearly wished he had more congenial company with whom to celebrate Washington's birthday and Christmas. "We shall not make many New Year's calls today," he noted ruefully on January 1, 1873. "Nor will the ladies of our party have any trouble in ciphering up their 'callers'!"

When he had just enough tobacco left for three more pipefuls, he consoled himself with philosophical whimsy: that perhaps being marooned had one redeeming feature: it might help him give up smoking. "But when that is gone, I shall feel more lonesome still," he mused over his pipe. "It is the only companion I have; and I think the most fastidious lady or the most inveterate 'anti-tobacconist' would hardly object to smoking on an ice floe. At any rate, I am not afraid of discoloring our curtains."

Alas, breaking the vile habit was as tough as hammering frozen seal entrails for lunch. "I have been out of the weed for twelve days, and I feel the deprivation very much! Joe has just given me out of his limited store two pipefuls, for which I am truly grateful."

In April he blinked at the returned sun, which looked as pale and sickly as his own haggard features, and tried cheering himself with mordant wit. "I think this must be Easter Sunday in civilized lands. Surely we have had more than a forty days' fast. . . . Well, a man can be trained to live on the rations of a canary; but I do not like the training."

They had been "fools of fortune" now for more than five months, drifting all the way down Davis Strait; and their little ice domain had melted away to a piece about seventy-five by one hundred yards. "This sort of real estate," he thought with forced hilarity, "is getting to be 'very uncertain property.'"

They would have to abandon the shrinking floe and sail to a larger one. But just one longboat remained, and nineteen people had to squeeze onto a craft designed to hold eight. With tenacious loyalty to

his commander, Tyson put up a fight to bring aboard his sole souvenir—a small portable writing desk that had belonged to Hall. It must have been a fierce tussle, for Tyson tells us that not only did the seamen protest; but they intimated as well "they would not have hesitated to throw over the women and children to save their own lives."

A gale raged and they were forced to take refuge on whatever tossing floes were available. Tyson's journal recounts one mounting horror after another.

*On April 6*: "The ice, with a great roar, split across the floe, cutting Joe's hut right in two. . . . We have such a small foothold left that we can not lie down tonight. We have put our things in the boat, and are standing by for a jump."

*On April 7*: "At six o'clock this morning, while we were getting a morsel of food, the ice split right under our tent! We were just able to scramble out, but our breakfast went down into the sea. We very nearly lost our boat—and that would be equivalent to losing ourselves."

Somehow they saved the tent, but sleeping in it, says Tyson, was as dicy as trying to catch forty winks on the crust of a rumbling earthquake: "Half of the men have got in under it to get a little rest, while the others walk around it outside. This is a very exciting period. If one attempts to rest the body, there is no rest for the mind. One and another will spring up from their sleep, and make a wild dash forward, as if avoiding some sudden danger. . . . I wonder how long we can fight through this sort of thing."

*On April 8*: "Worse and worse! . . . The ice split, separating the boat and tent, and with the boat was the kayak and Mr. Meyer. . . . We stood helpless, looking at each other."

Not everybody was helpless. Eskimo Hans tells us in his diary that Master Tyson asked the sailors to make a raft out of a piece of ice and try paddling it to rescue Meyer cast adrift in the boat. But the cowardly men refused. Hans knew that the loss of the boat and the indispensable hunting kayak would mean death for all. So he turned to his dear comrade, Westlander Joe, and said: "We *must* try to get at it."

And so the two Eskimos, paddles and spears in hand, leaped from one ice pan to another until, more than half a mile away, they sprang into the wave-tossed boat. Meyer took an accidental tumble and plunged into the icy sea. They rescued him and nursed him, but as darkness fell, he was too fatigued to help them launch the boat and he lay there benumbed and almost lifeless.

"He was like to freeze to death," wrote Hans. "I said to my com-

rade that if he remained so he would really die."

Laboring tirelessly through the night, the Eskimos succeeded in rousing the Prussian from his lethargy, forced him to exercise, and would not let him slump back into unconsciousness. At daybreak, when Tyson and three others finally reached them aboard floating ice cakes, the hapless Prussian's feet were totally frozen, but he acknowledged that his life had been saved by two heroic natives whom he had once scorned.

Hans was later to remember that all through the night he looked up at the stars and recited the prayer taught to him about mercy:

> *Jesu, lead me by the hand,*
> *While I am here below,*
> *Foresake me not . . . .*

This gesture of the Eskimos affected Tyson profoundly. He now looked at the humbled, skeletal German Count, once so arrogant in his strength, and he pitied him in his weakness. "If Doré had wanted a model subject to stand for Famine, he might have drawn Meyer," thought Tyson. "Poor Meyer looks wretchedly; the loss of food tells on him worse than the rest. . . . I have much sympathy for him, notwithstanding the trouble he has caused us."

The heretofore intractable seamen also won a measure of his respect. When it came to a tight pinch, they showed their mettle as true mariners. Tyson noted in his log: "The sea is running very high again, and threatening to wash us off every moment. The water, like a hungry beast, creeps nearer. Things look very bad. We are in the hands of God; He alone knows how this night will end."

Their crucial trial came at 9 PM April 20. Heavy swells of the sea surged over their tiny floe and swept away everything—tent, furs, food—leaving them destitute. "All we could do now, under this new flood of disaster, was to try and save *the boat*," chronicled Tyson. "So all hands were called to man the boat in a new fashion—namely, to hold on to it with might and main, to prevent *its* being washed away."

The men, as well as Hannah and Christiana, rallied smartly to every one of Tyson's commands. They held on for dear life as, every fifteen minutes, a battering wave would lift and drag them and the boat to the extreme opposite edge of the floe. Only poor Meyer, who was so weak, clutched at the boat as though to save himself from being swamped.

"The sea was full of loose ice, rolling about in blocks, some as large

as an ordinary bureau and some larger," wrote Tyson. "And with almost every wave would come an avalanche of these, striking us on our legs and bodies, and bowling us off our feet like so many pins in a bowling alley. After each wave had spent its strength, we had then to push and drag the boat back to its former position, and stand ready, bracing ourselves for the next battery. . . .

"Through the whole of that night it was as if we were the sport and jest of the elements. They played with us and our boat as if we were shuttlecocks. For twelve hours there was scarcely a sound uttered, save and except the crying of the children and my orders to 'Hold on,' 'Bear down,' 'Put on all your weight,' and the responsive 'Ay, ay, sir,' which for once came readily enough."

On April 30 while the half-drowned waifs of the storms were gorging on the raw meat of a polar bear shot by Joe and Hans, a faint light gleamed through a fog bank near Grady Harbour off the coast of Labrador. The watch shouted the electrifying cry, "There's a steamer! There's a steamer!"

The castaways shot off guns, and lit blubber fires on the floe, and Tyson ordered the Stars and Stripes to be flown from the mast of their crippled boat. Hans darted off in his kayak. He paddled up to the *Tigress* of Conception Bay, Newfoundland, skippered by a famous sealing and whaling man, Captain Isaac Bartlett.

"Who are ye?" cried out the Newfoundlanders.

"North Pole with *Polaris* people," Hans sang out.

"How do ye do?"

"Captain Hall dead," said Hans mournfully, and he guided the steamer toward the ice floe.

As soon as he stepped on board ship, Tyson was surrounded by a throng of incredulous questioners. The Newfoundlanders could not believe that nineteen castaways, including a new-born baby, had successfully survived a fifteen-hundred-mile drift over a period of six and a half months.

"How long have you been on the ice?" asked a seaman.

"Since the fifteenth of last October," said Tyson.

"And was you on it *night and day*?"

At last Tyson's pent-up craving for a justified belly laugh found release, and he laughed and he laughed as though the question were the funniest thing in the world.

The first serious thing Tyson wanted was a pipeful of borrowed tobacco, which was promptly offered. The next thing he sought was a

hot civilized meal. "I shall never forget that codfish and potatoes," he declared. "No subsequent meal can ever eclipse this to my taste, so long habituated to raw meat, with all the uncleanly accessories."

Finally he wanted God's vengeance wrought on those who had caused the death of Captain Hall. He thought back to what he had scribbled the past dark and dismal December when marooned on his God-made raft:

"The fear of death has long ago been starved and frozen out of me; but if I perish, I hope that some of this company will be saved to tell the truth of the doings on the *Polaris*. Those who have baffled and spoiled this expedition ought not to escape. They can not escape their God!"

Escape they did, from man-made justice at any rate. Budington and Bessels and the twelve seamen aboard the *Polaris* fared very well after deserting the nineteen castaways. From their testimony later, it seems evident they made the most perfunctory attempt to search for their abandoned shipmates. Instead they steamed away with unseemly haste toward a spot on the Greenland coast named Lifeboat Cove and beached the *Polaris* not far from the Eskimo village of Etah. There they built naval barracks named Polaris House and thanks to the hospitality of the Eskimo villagers—who remembered the previous kindnesses of Dr. Elisha Kent Kane—the seamen spent a relatively cozy winter.

They appear to have enjoyed most of the comforts of home. Budington drank; Bessels caught butterflies. On November 12, the day of the Presidential elections in the United States, they inaugurated the American practice in the Arctic of polling votes. Everybody was allowed to cast a ballot except Bessels; the German was excluded because he was not a naturalized American citizen.

In April they made history by introducing another American ritual. The sailors made a ball, bat and bases and played a baseball game in a ballpark consisting of the smooth ice of the bay. The official history of the *Polaris* records that the Eskimos were much interested in the sport, but could not learn to catch.

Indeed the official United States Naval historian, Admiral C.H. Davis, makes the entire *Polaris* expedition seem like a healthy baseball game played by the Boy Scouts of America. The foul balls and the fighting and the liquoring were left decorously unrecorded. The official Naval inquiry conducted in Washington seemed equally intent on preserving patriotic decorum. The *Polaris* party, after leaving their ship on June 3, 1873 in two flat-bottomed scows built of her dismantled timbers, were picked up in Baffin Bay twenty days later by the Scottish

*After more than six months adrift, the castaways were rescued by Newfoundland whaler.*

whaler, *Ravenscraig*. Then they were brought to Washington to face an umpire's decision notably muted and circumspect.

Budington got off with a mild rebuke. "Though he was perhaps wanting in enthusiasm for the grand objects of the expedition," the board of inquiry concluded, Captain Budington was "an experienced and careful navigator, and, when not affected by liquor, a competent and safe commander."

The suspicion that Bessels might have slipped Hall a lethal dose of poison was dismissed out of hand. "We are conclusively of the opinion that Captain Hall died from natural causes, viz, apoplexy," reaffirmed the Surgeon-Generals of the Army and Navy on December 26, 1873, "and that the treatment of the case by Dr. Bessels was the best practicable under the circumstances."

So the verdict rested until almost a century later.

In 1968 a party of investigators headed by Dr. Chauncey C. Loomis of Dartmouth College, New Hampshire, exhumed the flag-shrouded body, wondrously well preserved by the Arctic in its white pine coffin at Hall's Rest. Samples of Hall's fingernails and hair were then medically examined at the Centre for Forensic Sciences, a highly regarded crime laboratory in Toronto. Neutron activator tests proved that he had received during the last two weeks of his life an extraordinarily large amount of arsenic—as much as 76.7 parts per million of arsenic at the base of his fingernails alone. "Arsenic poisoning," concluded the director of the centre, Douglas M. Lucas, "is a fair diagnosis."

On the basis of that diagnosis Dr. Loomis wrote a brilliant psychological analysis of the case. Who had murdered Hall? Almost certainly it was Dr. Emil Bessels, and Dr. Loomis so names him as the prime suspect in his scholarly book, *Weird and Tragic Shores*.

Yet one wonders whether Charles Francis Hall would have appreciated being vindicated in a treatise bearing such a sombre title. Although he never did quite fulfil himself as a total Eskimo in the Arctic, the polar evangelist did not consider its shores weird and tragic, but rather he discovered a kind of beauty and serenity there. Just before he had embarked on the last voyage of his life, he had declared fervently: "The Arctic Region is my home. I love it dearly; its storms, its winds, its glaciers, its icebergs; and when I am there among them, it seems as if I were in an earthly heaven or a heavenly earth."

At Hall's Rest one would like to think that the tormented soul had finally found the Far-off Land of his dreams—his Eskimo *Wes-see-poke*.

# Chapter 8

# Hamlet on Skis

At the beginning everybody in Norway thought he was mad. The dreamer had conceived a plan that was suicidal. Not only that, he had the audacity to ask the government for five thousand kroner to help him accomplish his preposterous scheme. This twenty-six-year-old zoologist wanted to be the first man to cross Greenland from east to west, to conquer the heights of its unknown glacial Ice Cap; and he expected to do it on skis.

"Exhibition!" announced a Bergen comic newspaper in 1887. "In the month of June next, Fridtjof Nansen, Curator of the Museum, will give an exhibition of ski-running with long distance jumping on the Inland Ice of Greenland. Good seats in the crevasses. Return tickets unnecessary."

Fridtjof (pronounced "Freedyoff," an ancient Viking name meaning Disturber of the Peace) Nansen grew accustomed to being called a madman. Cynics were to call him crazy whenever he embarked on an exploratory expedition into the unknown, whether it was a journey across the polar ice or a voyage into the realm of untried ideas and idealism. Time and again he was to confound the cautious know-it-alls. Invariably the iconoclast proved them wrong. In 1895 he beat all previous Arctic records. With a single skiing companion he reached a point two hundred and twenty-six miles short of the North Pole. Later, following the First World War, he disproved skeptics in another arena. He showed that international compassion was possible. As High Commissioner of the League of Nations, who saved the lives of almost a million dispossessed refugees, he won the 1922 Nobel Peace Prize.

225

Nansen can not be classified with other polar explorers. With his exceptional qualities of heart and head, intuition and daring, he was unquestionably a genius, a towering mountain peak in the story of human adventure. Like most geniuses, he does not come within the ordinary range of assessment. There are dimensions to his richly poetic, mystical, sometimes discordant personality that continue to elude our understanding to this day.

Since his death in 1930 at the age of sixty-eight, his private letters and diaries have been published. They shed a certain amount of light on his complex character. The most surprising revelation is that the public hero who had triumphed in so many fields considered himself an abject failure. In his eyes he was a dilettante who had mastered nothing. He was a soul in pain torn by doubts and riven by what he called his "worm-eaten reflectiveness."

His daughter Liv, in her perceptive biography, *Nansen: A Family Portrait*, has truly portrayed him as a kind of Hamlet on skis. One part of him was the man of action: a competitive racer, a driving force, radiating energy and always testing his will power. The other part of him was the melancholy philosopher: an introspective brooder, a lyrical dreamer, acutely sensitive to human anguish, and an escapist whose sole release was his solitary communion with nature.

Nansen himself was aware of the split in his psyche. "It is as though thou wert formed of two beings from two different spheres," he once soliloquized darkly. One of the two demons warring within himself he named Master Irresponsible. This was the ego-ridden romantic who took risks for the sake of personal glory. It was the Viking who rashly burned his bridges behind him and sought excitement and immortality in the polar Valhalla.

"Let me climb the heights, let me have ski under my feet!" he wrote in his diary. "I would be the giant who stormed the heavens.... Why should one have a giant's longings and be created an ordinary soldier ant?... Ah, puny soul of man, how willing you are to deceive yourself, how prone to embellish your motives!... So it is vanity then, after all.... Your name must not die with you...."

The conflicting demon was the scholar *manqué*, the failed scientist who had not lived up to expectations. He might have been another Darwin, a Newton, perhaps a Louis Pasteur, Nansen reflected; but he had surrendered his intellectual gifts—to what?

A meaningless patchwork career, he thought, of "flightiness and

fumbling from one thing to another! Suppose I should win fame, or suppose I reach the North Pole, what good will it do?... I burn with longing to make new discoveries for mankind. Alas, I am not the great research genius I once believed. I lack the divine spark."

When these guilts and doubts became too overwhelming, he solaced himself with a parallel. Perhaps his endless quest after knowledge was motivated by the same drives that impelled his Norse ancestors to penetrate the horizons of an ever-beckoning Land of Beyond.

"Ah, courageous dreamer!" he addressed himself. "It is the same craving to go beyond the limits of the known, which inspired our people in Saga times.... To me the unknown has an irresistible attraction. Whether it is the unknown lands and seas of this globe, or the depths of the ocean and its currents, whether the unknown depths of the Universe or the secrets of the Atom, it does not make much difference—it is the Call of the Unknown.... And lo! far ahead, above the mist and the scud, rises your land of Beyond! We all have a Land of Beyond to seek in life—what more can we ask?"

He was frequently described as looking the epitome of the modern Viking. In the early years of his fame he enjoyed posing in that role, one of his few affectations. On world lecture tours he displayed his chesty, six-foot figure in a tight-fitting athletic costume of Jaeger wool designed by himself. He rarely wore an overcoat and covered his thinning blond hair with a picturesque slouch wool hat which won renown as the Nansen cap. "His body," wrote an American reporter, "was as well-trained and supple as that of a tiger." He was an expert figure skater, swimmer, hunter, snowshoer and ballroom dancer, and until the day he died his lanky legs would race up steps four at a time. He was very proud of the two nicknames given to him by the Eskimos: *Angisorsuak*, meaning the Very Big One, and *Uniformiut Nalagak*, meaning Leader of the Men with the Great Beards.

He himself was beardless. He sported a bristling yellow moustache. Searching grey-blue eyes set in a roughhewn face made him seem severe and forbidding. His intimates, however, spoke of the winning sweetness of his smile, of the tenderness underlying his powerful, resonant voice, of his moving manner of reciting poetry by the hour in English and Norwegian.

He had his faults. According to his detractors, he could be aloofly self-centred, excessively sentimental, provokingly stubborn. Happily he had the knack of disarming his critics with humor. "You know, people

*Fridtjof Nansen: explorer, painter, poet, humanitarian, Nobel Peace Prize-winner.* MITTET FOTO, OSLO

say I am very difficult to get on with," he once joked. "It's quite a mistake. Only give me my own way and I'm the easiest fellow in the world to get on with."

Generally his most likeable characteristic was his tolerance for dissenting opinion. He claimed it was a national trait. Of his epic voyage, when he intentionally set the *Fram* adrift with the pack across the Arctic Ocean, he said: "Only Norwegians are capable of undertaking such a task, because two Norwegians alone of all nations could sit face to face on a cake of ice for three years without hating each other."

Despite his disclaimers, he was extraordinarily gifted in many creative fields. He claimed to be a failure as a scientist. Yet he was the pioneering father of modern arctic oceanography. He claimed to be a failure in authorship. Yet scholarly books and trail-blazing articles poured out of him in five languages. Merely the list of his publications occupies three closely printed pages. His two-volume *Farthest North*, illustrated with his own photographs and lovely watercolor paintings, is among the most beautifully written journals in polar literature.

In common with his contemporary, the Norwegian dramatist Henrik Ibsen, he believed it was individual ruggedness of character that counted. Nansen often cited two quotations from that uncompromisingly honest playwright. One was: "The greatest victory is the conquest of self." The other was: "That man is strongest who stands most alone . . . a man's will is his heaven."

And yet, paradoxically, Nansen felt that his own vaunted steel-willed character was a failure, too. "I am myself of a weak nature," he claimed, "but what I have of character has come from my strict upbringing in youth."

Fridtjof Nansen, born on October 10, 1861, on the outskirts of Oslo, the capital of Norway, derived his strengths from two outstanding parents. It was a second marriage for both of them, and they complemented each other to provide a singularly happy home. His father was a Superior Court attorney, well-to-do, but with ascetic tastes. From him the son acquired logic, precision, a sense of justice and moral rectitude. But the elder Nansen was sternly religious and here the son differed with him. Young Nansen broke away from the national Lutheran Church to become an agnostic. "A commandment such as 'you shall believe' is immoral," the free-thinker later said. "It is to be tyrannized." He thus became one of the few polar explorers in the nineteenth century who refused to enforce religious worship on his expeditions.

His rebellious spirit and his love for the outdoors Nansen acquired

from his mother. She was a baron's daughter who outraged her aristocratic family by her first marriage to a common baker's son. Later she scandalized prim society by becoming the first lady of high breeding to take up the sport of skiing.

Fridtjof began skiing at the age of four and rapidly mastered it. He won national cross-country ski contests twelve times. As a boy he often spent weeks alone in the fragrant pine forests of Norway, content with the cheese and hard bread in his pockets, the game he shot with a bow and arrow, and the fish he broiled in the fire's embers. His solitary ramblings among the mountain peaks brought out a strong vein of poetry in him. "I loved to live like Robinson Crusoe up there in the wilderness," he said of his skiing excursions, "free as a bird under heaven."

At the University of Oslo he was an exceptionally studious and inquisitive youth, always asking: Why? Why? Why? "It was not enough for me to be first in my class," he said many years after of his high standing in science, mathematics, history and art. "I wanted to go deeper, to get behind it all, to the heart of things."

The turning point in his life came at the age of twenty-one. His zoology professor suggested that Nansen ship aboard a Norwegian seal-hunting sloop, the *Viking*, and spend four months as a research student gaining first-hand knowledge of the animal life near Spitsbergen. The first five days on a tossing deck were dreadful. "How gladly one would admire, and be uplifted, by the salt freshness of the deep," he wrote, "if the interminable, pitilessly rolling mountains of water did not make one feel so horribly seasick!"

The truth was that Nansen, the would-be Viking, was to be plagued for the rest of his life by seasickness. At the same time the cruise was the beginning of his life-long love affair with that bewitching mistress, the Arctic. The sensitive artist in him was at once captivated by the play of polar light on air, ice and sea. He became obsessed with trying to capture on canvas the delicate colors that lit up the sky: the milky white and sulphur yellow "ice blink" which reflected the dazzle of the ice pack; and the dark violet and lilac shades of the "water sky" which shimmered over open blue waters.

The riddles posed by the Arctic—its currents and its unexplored lands—likewise took possession of his inquiring mind. On her voyage home the *Viking* was frozen fast in the floes and drifted in the currents for twenty-four days alongside the jagged east coast of Greenland. Nansen in the crow's nest gazed with curiosity at one of the most massive glaciers in the world. Nobody had ever penetrated the some

million square miles of this mountain-rimmed bowl of snow said to be pitted with bottomless crevasses. Nobody had ever investigated its interior ice dome which rises almost imperceptibly to a height of more than nine thousand feet. Even the coastal Eskimos feared to venture too far into the spirit-haunted *Sermik-soak*—the Great Ice Wall.

But to Nansen it was the backdrop for scientific adventure. "I saw the mountains and glaciers, and a longing awoke in me," he wrote. "Vague plans revolved in my mind of exploring the unknown interior of that mysterious ice-covered land."

Five years were to elapse before his dream came true. On his return to Norway the brilliant young microbiologist was invited to become curator of zoology at the Bergen Museum. There, chained to his microscope, he prepared for his doctoral thesis—highly original concepts about the central nervous systems of primitive creatures of the sea.

There, too, his interest in the humanities was awakened. He lodged at the home of a certain Reverend Vilhelm Holdt, a compassionate man who served as minister to lepers. It was a home with a rich intellectual life. Nansen listened to the new national folk music written by the Norwegian composer, Edvard Grieg. He listened as the Reverend Mr. Holdt read aloud literature ranging from the works of the philosophers to the sagas of the Norsemen.

One day the pastor read aloud a newspaper report that electrified Nansen. It was about Greenland. Expeditions from four countries had tried to penetrate Greenland's ice plateau from its more hospitable west coast; all had been forced to turn back. Now a new attempt had been made. It was by the great Swedish explorer Baron Nils Nordenskjöld, who in 1879 was the first to navigate the Northeast Passage. Nordenskjöld had failed like the others to breach Greenland's spiky ice barrier. But the newspaper reported one striking fact: two Laplanders on his expedition had managed to make an incursion of some one hundred miles inland by skiing.

"The idea flashed upon me at once," wrote Nansen, "of an expedition crossing Greenland on ski from coast to coast."

His idea was risky to the extreme. It was dangerous enough to attempt such an exploit from the *west* coast of Greenland, where there were a few Danish-Eskimo settlements. But Nansen proposed to make his crossing from the uninhabited *east* coast. With a small party of five skilled skiers, he intended to disembark from a Norwegian sealer and get ashore by boat through the furious current of southward-drifting floes. Then he would trek about three hundred and fifty miles across the

inland ice fields by ski, snowshoe and sledge. Thus he would reach what he termed the western "flesh pots" of civilization. He was prepared to burn his boats irrevocably behind him, cut off all avenues of retreat.

"The order would be," he declared with a dramatic flourish, "Death or the west coast of Greenland."

Nansen applied to the Norwegian government for a grant equivalent to two hundred and seventy-five pounds. People were relieved when his seemingly insane "paper scheme" was rejected. "Creeping like a polar bear from one rocking ice floe to another on his way to shore," scoffed one Danish geographer, "shows such absolute recklessness that it is scarcely possible to criticize it seriously."

Luckily a Danish merchant interested in Greenland exploration, Augustine Gamel, was more open-minded. He contributed the necessary financial backing. Nansen in turn displayed a receptive mind when outfitting his expedition. He did his homework with scholarly thoroughness. He sought advice from Baron Nordenskjöld. He gleaned practical tips from every polar journal he could lay his hands on. He even took a short course in the Eskimo language. He immersed himself in polar research with such zeal that he scarcely had time to deliver his trial lecture for his doctoral dissertation, *On the Structure of the Sexual Organs in the Myxine.* "I'd rather have a bad degree," he quipped, "than bad equipment."

His scientific bent enabled him to design two novel pieces of equipment that were to bear his name in polar exploration. The Nansen cooker was a light, portable spirit-fuel stove. The Nansen sledge was a twenty-five-pound, nailless toboggan with ski-like runners.

After meticulous pretesting, he also took along such items as: Canadian Indian snowshoes; slitted Eskimo style wooden snow goggles; two doeskin sleeping bags calculated to hold three men each; a waterproof canvas tent; reindeer horns for signaling on mountain peaks; a two-and-a-half-pound American Eastman camera; his sketchbook and scientific apparatus; and plenty of tea, Parisian-made meat-powder chocolate, and Scandinavian *knakkebrod* biscuit. Although Nansen was himself a pipe-smoker and enjoyed his seidel of Norwegian beer, he believed these were debilitating on a tough Arctic hike. Therefore he permitted enough tobacco for only one pipe each on Sundays; alcohol he banished entirely.

Mistakes were made, but the errors were not of his doing. He had planned to take Eskimo sledge dogs; unfortunately this "meat on the hoof" could not be obtained in time to meet his schedule. An

experimental Iceland pony proved a poor substitute and was ultimately eaten raw. Nansen moreover had ordered a big supply of pemmican from Denmark; he was dismayed to discover that the blundering supplier in Copenhagen had removed all fat from the pounded dried meat. A small stock of butter and liver pâté was an inadequate substitute; the six travelers suffered a great craving for nourishing fat.

Just three of Nansen's five fellow travelers were really first-class skiers. But again it wasn't Nansen's fault.

Otto Sverdrup, later to become a celebrated explorer in his own right, was a perfect righthand man. He was a red-bearded Norwegian in the legendary Viking tradition. Among seamen he was known as "the king of ice navigators" and among Eskimos as *Akortok*, "He who steers the ships." There was nothing that this stoop-shouldered, tobacco-chewing, somewhat taciturn sea captain couldn't do well, whether it was skiing, hunting, fishing or carpentry. In a crowd he was rather shy, but with a few intimates on deck he was a matchless storyteller. He had left his father's farm at the age of seventeen to go to sea, and horizon-seeking was in his blood. Nansen, seven years younger than the thirty-three-year-old Sverdrup, showed respectful deference to the judgment of the seasoned Arctic hand; both comrades shared a spirit of romantic adventure. "Behind each bit of blue distance rises a new objective, luring you on," said Sverdrup. "It is the Princess behind the seven blue mountain ranges far away in fairyland all over again."

Nansen had no fault to find in his two other Norwegian skiers. His meteorologist was Oluf Dietrichson, thirty-four, a swashbuckling lieutenant from the Norwegian infantry. His general aide was Kristian Kristiansen Trana, twenty-four, a hardy forester's son. Lieutenant Dietrichson spoke for all the Norwegians when he coined the motto, "We have nothing to risk but our lives."

This attitude of daredeviltry was definitely not shared by the pair of Laplanders whom Nansen recruited sight unseen for the mission. He had advertised for two experienced mountaineers. They were to be in their physical prime between the ages of thirty and forty, and plucky enough to go on a dangerous journey from which they might never return.

The two Lapps who arrived from northern Finmarken—quaintly attired in yellow-trimmed reindeerskin skirts and high, square four-cornered caps—fell into none of these categories. They had enlisted their services solely for money. They admitted the entire project terrified them. Nansen had no time to replace the woebegone pair. He comforted

them as best he could. They turned out to be amusing fellows, Nansen later said, and they added a touch of comic relief.

Ole Ravna, who was forty-five or forty-six (he wasn't quite sure of his age) was a gnomish Lapp, almost dwarflike in stature. Nevertheless he was a surprisingly strong sledge-hauler, albeit a lazy grumbler. Poor Ole was continually sighing for his reindeer herd and wife and five children back in Finmarken, or bewailing his fate over his Lappish New Testament.

Samuel Balto, twenty-seven years old, was brighter, taller and livelier than his fellow reindeer-herder. He was also less pious. He tended to swear a good deal when in high spirits, and confessed that he had been drunk when he signed up for this lunatic expedition. Like Ravna, he vowed he would starve before eating raw meat and stubbornly resisted using snowshoes.

In his book, *The First Crossing of Greenland*, Nansen incorporated extracts from young Balto's diary. The contrasting viewpoints of their journals are entertaining to read.

On June 11, 1888, from the deck of the Norwegian sealer *Jason*, they caught their first glimpse of the sugar loaf mountains on the east coast of Greenland. "Dismal and hideous to look upon," wrote Balto. But Nansen had never seen a landscape of more savage beauty: "The sensation it gave me was nothing short of delicious. I had a sense of elasticity, as when one is going to a dance and expecting to meet the choice of one's heart."

On July 17 their two small boats, packed with equipment, were lowered into the sea about ten miles from shore. The two Lapps were in one boat, Nansen and his trio of skiers in the other. Crew members of the *Jason* waved goodbye. But soon the two boats were trapped in the tearing mill-race of the East Greenland current and they were locked in the grip of the southward-drifting pack. A storm blew up and they were forced to camp on a splitting floe. Nansen wondered how the poor Lapps were faring on the party's battered little ice island.

"I noticed some tarpaulins had been carefully laid over one of the boats," he wrote. "I lifted a corner gently and saw both the Lapps lying at the bottom of the boat. The younger, Balto, was reading aloud to the other out of the Lappish New Testament. Without attracting their attention, I replaced the cover of this curious little house of prayer which they had set up for themselves. They had given up hope of life and were making ready for death."

Nansen himself relished the danger. He sat up late at night sketch-

*Nansen (seated left), with his two Laplanders in quaint four-cornered hats and his three other Norwegian skiers, after they made the first Greenland crossing in 1888. Otto Sverdrup stands behind Nansen, second from left. Their diet included splinters from an extra pair of cherrywood snowshoes, all eaten up by the time they descended Greenland's 9,000-foot Ice Dome.*

ing and dreaming. "The sea is rolling in upon us, ruddy and polished as a shield," he wrote. "Raising their green, dripping breasts, the billows break and throw fragments of ice and spray far before them on to the glittering snow.... The evening is glorious, and the Inland Ice lay temptingly and enticingly before me. Strange that a narrow strip of drifting floes should be able to divide us so hopelessly from the goal of our desires! Is not this often the case in life?"

With crowbars, axes and hooked poles, they eventually forced a passage through the floes ashore. Then followed a laborious, thirteen-day boat trip northward to regain the two hundred miles they had lost on their drift. The Lapps alternately prayed and fretted; reindeer herders were not used to rowing. At length on August 10 they reached the twenty-five-hundred-foot slope of Mount Kiatak, the point of departure for their inland hike.

There Nansen was bemused by Balto's antics. The horrible boats would be cached and the young Lapp was so relieved that he leaped up on a crag and gave a mock imitation of a Finmarken clergyman delivering a sermon. Obviously the sinner had forgotten his previous penitence.

"He indulged in an oath or two," Nansen observed dryly. "He even went so far as to give back to Ravna the Lappish Testament which he had borrowed. He had no further use for it now."

"Don't be too cocksure," Sverdrup warned him. "There might be many a slip yet before the West Coast is reached."

Balto temporarily ceased his blasphemy. But for the rest of the journey his lapses became an index of their progress. If Balto uttered a few swear words, his bravado indicated they were making headway. If he was back to reading the Lappish Bible with Ravna, it was a sign the party had struck a crevasse-riddled region.

The crevasses varied in size from a mere slit to vast yawning abysses and they were treacherous. The skiers, pulling their sledge loads, never knew when they would plunge into a pit camouflaged by a crust of snow. Nansen and Sverdrup scouted ahead, gingerly probing with ski poles. They had to crawl over crevasse ice bridges flat on their stomachs. One or the other would sometimes tumble down only to be hauled back to safety by his companion to whom he was roped Alpine fashion. It gave you an odd feeling, wrote Nansen with nice understatement, to find your legs dangling in space.

Wind-whipped snow scratched at your face like cat's claws. Sledge tow ropes bit into your shoulders until you felt as though you were

being burned. But the worst hardship was an unquenchable thirst. Nansen tried chewing bits of tarred rope to keep the saliva flowing, but found it too vile-tasting. Sverdrup wondered whether their boot polish of linseed oil would disagree with him. The two then hit upon the idea of nibbling splinters of bird cherrywood from an extra pair of snowshoes. By the time they were through with Greenland, Nansen amiably remarked, the snowshoes were all eaten up.

For anyone who has flown over the appalling inland ice sheet of Greenland today, Nansen's unflagging good cheer seems amazing. His party advanced in forced marches of five to ten miles a day, sometimes bodily carrying the sledges up the ice hummocks, more often floundering like ants across the illimitable Sahara of snow. Yet to Nansen it all seemed like an "alluring" carpet of diamonds from the Arabian Nights stretching ahead.

It was wonderfully cozy, he says, loafing in their tent while a blizzard shrieked and raged around their guy ropes. Nansen would read aloud to his comrades a scientific paper on the fjords of Greenland. Sverdrup told stories of his sea adventures. The two other Norwegians filled in gaps in their diaries. Balto, the cook, was happiest when cleaning the stew pot after supper—licking it with his tongue or scraping it with his fingers.

Old Ravna, gloomily engrossed in his Lappish Bible, was the party's holdout pessimist. His face grew sourer and sourer. On September 14, after they had reached the summit of the ice plateau at an altitude of almost nine thousand feet above sea level, he could hold his tongue no longer.

"I am an old Lapp and a silly fool, too," he sulked. "I don't believe we shall ever get to the coast."

Nansen grew weary of his petulance. "That's quite true, Ravna. You are a silly old fool."

Ravna burst out laughing. "That's right. Ravna is a silly old fool." The Cassandra was consoled by the dubious compliment.

Yet it was Ravna who protested most vehemently when Sverdrup tried to speed up their descent of the Ice Cap. Their sledges were lashed together and their tent canvas rigged up on a ski pole as a sail. Ravna complained that he had lived his whole life in the north and a snow boat simply would not work. But work it did. "Our ship flew over the waves and drifts of snow," said Nansen, "with a speed that almost took one's breath away." And he marveled at the sight of the ski vessels gliding along, "with their square Viking-like sails showing dark against the white snowfield and the big round disc of the moon behind."

On September 24 they finally emerged from the ice desert and set foot on west-coast land. They romped and rolled like schoolboys in the grass and savored the resinous fragrance of mountain heather. When they came upon an alpine rivulet, they threw themselves down on the earth and sucked up the fresh water like horses.

Ravna, after drinking his stomach full, announced that it tasted like sweet milk. Then he inhaled the redolent scents of the valley, the reindeer moss and the dwarf willow and alder, and his small eyes puckered roguishly. "It does smell good here," he conceded. "Just like the mountains of Finmarken, where there is good reindeer pasture. I like the west coast well. It is a good place for an old Lapp to live in."

Balto was just as exuberant. He climbed up a grassy ridge and blew his reindeer horn and waved his hat in glee. He had sighted the blue expanse of the sea fjord known as Ameralik.

But Godthaab, the nearest coastal settlement, was still sixty miles distant and they had no vessel for sailing there. Sverdrup, the resourceful seaman, solved that problem. From willow branches and tarpaulin, an ash theodolite stand and thin pieces of bamboo, he improvised a crazy little rowboat shaped like a tortoise shell. It was barely eight feet long, just big enough to hold himself and Nansen. The pair decided to row to Godthaab with their willow branch paddles and arrange to have the four others picked up later.

Nansen and Sverdrup had an idyllic time on their six-day excursion down the fjord. It was marvelous to devour fresh food at last. They shot big blue seagulls and ate them ravenously, complete with head and feet. For dessert they demolished black crowberries, which they gobbled first standing, then sitting, then lying down. "At last we grew so torpid," Nansen says of their debauch, "that we had not the energy to pick the berries any longer with our hands. And so we turned on our faces and went on gathering them with our lips till we fell asleep."

As they neared the Danish-Eskimo whaling station, Nansen experienced the curious blend of elation and letdown so common to explorers once they have accomplished their goal. It was a strange mood, Nansen analyzed it, so devoid of a feeling of triumph. "To no other feeling could I attain than a sense of gross repletion. We had been kept waiting too long for our goal—there was too little surprise about its eventual attainment...."

There was one surprise in store for them. As they paddled ashore on the morning of October 3, they were welcomed good-humoredly by

Eskimos. Then Sverdrup said, "Here comes a European."

It was the Danish assistant superintendent of the colony. He was wearing a tam-o'-shanter which clearly marked him as an import from the King's Copenhagen. He approached the bedraggled pair officiously.

"Are you Englishmen?"

"No," said Nansen. "We are Norwegians."

"May I ask your name?"

"My name is Nansen, and we have just come from the interior."

"Oh, allow me to congratulate you on taking your doctor's degree."

This struck Nansen as so comical that he could hardly refrain from laughing. There were other incongruities at this remote outpost of civilization that seemed wondrously absurd. The first thing the official did—even before allowing his weatherbeaten visitors to wash up—was to play for them proudly on his music box a rendition of *The Last Rose of Summer*. And when Nansen met the Danish gentry of the colony that night at dinner, their pomposity tickled him. The ladies appeared in the longest of evening gowns and white gloves; the men wore black tuxedo jackets and shirt fronts of irreproachable stiffness.

Nansen felt far more at home with the colony's Eskimos. So did his traveling companions—although Balto was a bit put out by the two kayakers dispatched to pick them up at the fjord. Their rescuers were christianized natives; and Balto had endured enough of piety. Sharing his sleeping bag, the pair of Eskimos kept Balto awake by singing Sunday hymns and repeating Moravian missionary prayers. Balto uttered a round oath.

Because the next supply ship would not arrive for six months, Nansen spent the winter making an anthropological study of the Eskimos. He dwelt in their huts, hunted and fished with them, and became their friend and champion. *Eskimo Life*, his sympathetic account of their customs, was the first manifesto by an explorer to appeal to the conscience of their *Kabloona* exploiters.

"The greedy white men wish to get hold of their furs; but what do we give them instead?" asked Nansen. "Our products, some of which are of very doubtful value to them indeed; and then our ghastly, insidious diseases; and often our bad customs and morals. . . . Let there be no doubt about it; they are doomed if nothing really effective is done to protect them. The land of the great white silence will never more ring with the happy mirth of these lovable children of the twilight."

"*Pitsakase*!"—"How kind you are!" the Greenlanders said to Nansen. The Eskimos bade him farewell, saying, "You will soon forget us, but we shall never forget you." Nansen never did forget. Each Christmas he sent gifts and greetings in gratitude to the Eskimos who taught him how to handle a kayak—a skill which was to save his life on his next polar expedition.

But that was not to come for four years. Meanwhile Nansen and his fellow conquerors of the Ice Cap returned in the spring of 1889 to an overwhelming welcome home. Even Ravna, in his own way, was not unmoved by the cheering crowds massed in Oslo.

"Are not all these people a fine sight, Ravna?" he was asked.

"Yes, it is fine, very fine," answered Ravna. "But if they had only been reindeer!"

Three months later Dr. Nansen, newly appointed curator of zoology at the University of Oslo, proposed marriage to the great love of his life. It happened as such romances should—his bride-to-be literally fell head over heels for him. On a skiing holiday he observed a pair of shapely legs sticking out of a snow drift. Eva Sars, the darkhaired skier with the laughing dark eyes, lost her heart to the twenty-eight-year-old hero who rescued her from the spill.

It was a happy match. She was Norway's most famous concert singer; a member of an illustrious family of scholarly scientists; and, like Nansen, she was an ardent skier and landscape artist. She was a couple of years older than Nansen and her emotional stability provided ballast for her restless dreamer of a husband. He referred to her as his "all obliterating love," and when he was on lecture tours and scientific expeditions he sent her yearning love letters. She sent him teasing letters addressed to "My dear, blessed beast" and which ended, "A kiss on your mouth, for which I long so unspeakably." She insisted on continuing her career as a singing teacher during his long absences, for he had warned her when proposing marriage, "But I must take a trip to the North Pole."

His thoughts had long circled about the Pole, and his plan to reach it was as novel as it was bold. This was deliberately to wedge a discovery ship in the polar pack north of Siberia and then let her drift with the current-driven ice right across the roof of the world.

Nansen broached his proposal to the geographical societies of Norway and Britain. Once again the pundits ridiculed him as the mad scientist. The most caustic denunciation came from an American cavalry officer named General Adolphus Greely. He himself had led a dis-

astrous polar expedition plagued with starvation, murder and cannibalism. Now the military critic derided the folly of "Dr. Nansen's illogical scheme of self-destruction."

It seemed like madness because Nansen's scheme was mainly inspired by a pair of sealskin breeches from an American shipwreck, the *Jeannette*. She had been outfitted for a polar expedition by the New York *Herald* publisher, James Gordon Bennett, who earlier had financed Stanley's search for Dr. David Livingstone in Africa. This journalistic stunt, however, was not so successful. The *Jeannette* had sailed from San Francisco in 1879 headed northward past Bering Strait toward the Pole. Caught in the pack, she drifted northwestward in the current for two years until she was crushed by ice and sank near the New Siberian Islands off eastern Siberia. Her commander and a good part of her crew perished. But three years later sealskin breeches marked with the name of a hapless crew member were discovered washed up on the beach on the southwest coast of Greenland.

If a pair of breeches could ride with the pack over the cap of the world, reasoned Nansen, why shouldn't he? Furthermore he had the evidence of Siberian mud and larch driftwood which he had observed on both coasts of Greenland. By "taking a ticket with the ice," as he put it, his ship would clear up the mystery of the then-unknown circumpolar currents. At the same time, just possibly, he might be able to plant the Norwegian flag on that prized goal, 90 degrees north latitude.

What of the criticism that the ice pack would crush his ship to a pulp like a nut in a nutcracker? Nansen answered that he would design an uncrushable ship. When squeezed by the ice, her round hull would slip up and out of its grasp like the pip of an orange. Drawing on other parallels, Nansen said his vessel would drift for up to five years like half of a tough coconut; she would be as slippery as an eel; and she would serve the science of oceanography as a floating laboratory.

Working in concert with Colin Archer, a noted Norwegian ship designer, it took Nansen three years to get his coconut afloat. Financing the seemingly madcap project required so much persuasion that it won him the nickname of Fridtjof Finansen. A cautious Norwegian parliament eventually contributed two-thirds of the necessary twenty-five thousand pounds. King Oscar II, then the joint sovereign of Norway and Sweden, provided a nominal sum. Donors contributed the rest through a national subscription campaign headed by the Norwegian brewer, Ellef Ringness.

The completed ship was no beauty. She was a beamy tub with poin-

*Nansen and his skiing wife, Eva, a concert pianist who teasingly called her wandering genius of a husband "My dear, blessed beast."*

*Nansen's "floating coconut," the 402-ton Fram, left Bergen in 1893 and, cradled in the ice pack, drifted to a record highest northing.* NORSK TELEGRAMBYRA, OSLO

ty ends and a hull of "plump and rounded form." She was rigged as a three-masted fore-and-aft schooner, with an engine of two hundred and twenty horsepower. Ungainly she might be, but she was constructed of the stoutest Italian oak and greenheart of American elm. She had a capacity of four hundred and two tons gross, and her capacious holds were well stocked with everything from a fatty pemmican prepared specially by the Bovril Company to the finest Cadbury's chocolate.

Nansen took painstaking precautions. To combat the dark arctic winters, she was to blaze with electric lights powered by a deck windmill; and when the wind wasn't blowing, the men would get exercise supplying energy on a running treadmill. To help stave off boredom, he equipped her with a one-thousand-volume library and a harmonium organ. And to ward off homesickness, the communal living room (saloon) was decorated with gay paintings of Norwegian scenery. The chief ornament of his own cabin was a portrait of Eva and their six-month-old daughter, Liv (Norwegian for Life).

At the official launching it was Eva who smashed a bottle of champagne on the ship's curved bow and said: "I name thee *Fram!*"

*Fram* means "Forward" in Norwegian. The Norwegians who sailed forward with her—the "lucky thirteen," they were called—were handpicked men. Her navigator, of course, was Captain Otto Sverdrup. In good-humored tribute to his ancient age of thirty-seven, the youthful crew nicknamed Sverdrup's cabin "Old Age Retreat."

The luckiest young crew member was twenty-six-year-old Lieutenant Hjalmar Johansen. He was ultimately selected to be Nansen's sole companion on his ski dash for the Pole. Johansen was a short, muscular, genial athlete with many talents, among them the ability to play the accordion. He had been a champion skier and marksman in the Norwegian Army and while at university had become the country's most celebrated gymnast. At a Paris meet he had won a gold medal for turning handsprings over the backs of forty-two men and landing clean on his feet. As a lad he had read the adventure novels of James Fenimore Cooper and he was so eager to join Nansen's polar voyage that he signed on as engine room stoker. He smilingly remarked previous to sailing that he was lucky to get the hottest job on a polar ship.

On June 24, 1893, the *Fram* steamed out of Oslo Fjord bound for the New Siberian Islands. A brass band ashore gave her a sendoff with the rousing national anthem, *Yes, We Love the Land That Towers Where the Wild Sea Foams*. The foaming sea was at first too wild for Nansen. His ship, built primarily to ride on waves of ice, rolled like a barrel of

Ringness beer; so did her commander. "Seasick I stood on the bridge," he confessed, "occupying myself in alternately making libations to Neptune. . . ."

He soon regained his sea legs. As the ship plunged past Lysaker Bay, Nansen peered through his telescope. He was anxious to catch a last glimpse of his home. Clapping her hands at the window was little Liv, the baby who for the next three years was to say, "Daddy's at the North Pole." Seated on a backyard bench under the shade of fir and pine was Eva, and she was wearing a white summer frock and a big straw hat, and she looked sad and lonely. "It was the darkest hour of the whole journey," said Nansen.

In fact, the darkest hour of anxiety occurred after the *Fram* had stopped to pick up thirty-four Samoyed sledge dogs at a Siberian village and then tested her durability in the dreaded Kara Sea. She behaved beautifully, twisting and turning among the ice floes "like a ball on a platter."

By the end of September, 1893, the *Fram* was ready to mate with the pack off the New Siberian Islands. Nansen figured they were at 77 degrees, 44 minutes north latitude. They made fast to a gigantic ice block, the frost and the floes closed in, and the *Fram* yielded herself up to the embrace of the ice. Their polar drift had begun.

Preparations for what turned out to be a drift of thirty-five months were quickly initiated. The rudder was hauled up to avoid damage from its bed of ice. The six-knot engine was dismantled and stored away. Every conceivable kind of workshop, from a smithy to a watch repair shop, was set up to keep all hands busy. Nansen himself looked after the oceanography. He dredged up minute animals from the sea with a silk net; checked the salinity and temperature of the water at different levels; and made soundings. Significantly, he found that the Arctic Ocean was well over two thousand fathoms deep. He thus disproved the myth of a shallow polar basin.

Johansen, promoted to assistant meteorologist, helped scotch the notion of an unlivable polar cold. His journal relates that he spent the first winter fairly comfortably, although standing unsheltered on the ice and often removing his mitts to take instrument readings. When frostbite threatened, he walked on his hands, turned a few somersaults, and danced to the tune of the national anthem. A colleague actually dashed on deck to take a temperature reading at forty below zero in his underwear.

According to Nansen's journal, it was equivalent to taking a luxury

cruise on a floating sanatorium. The crew remained so disgustingly healthy that the ship surgeon, jolly Dr. Henrik Blessing, became desperate; he developed a headache in order to have a patient to treat. The doctor checked the weights of the men once a month and found they had all grown as fat as pigs; and among paunches, he gloomily reported, his own "corporation" was biggest.

It was little wonder that several sprouted double chins. Every birthday, saint's day, or national holiday was celebrated with a five-course banquet. Each sixty-mile degree of north latitude passed invariably was marked with a stupendous feast, Nansen handing out cigars and Dr. Blessing breaking open his best bottle of Norwegian brandy. (The most festive party, everybody agreed, was when Dr. Blessing poured Polar Champagne 83—referring, of course, to the degree of latitude attained and not the year when the vintage was bottled.)

It was a leisurely life. Usually the men turned out at eight to breakfast on freshly baked bread (rye and wholewheat), four different kinds of cheese (including Cheddar and Gruyère), corned beef, chocolate, tea or coffee. After breakfast they fed the kenneled dogs and went about their appointed tasks. Luncheon and dinner were often enormous repasts: Chicago tinned tongue, bacon, ham, caviar, anchovies, potatoes and baked cauliflower. Desserts sometimes included honey cake, pineapple, figs, bananas, strawberry glace, and marmalade, washed down with Ringness bock beer.

The evenings were given over to relaxed fun. Since tobacco was off limits in the saloon, the men gathered in the galley to smoke and spin yarns about their jousts with polar bears. After a siesta, the card players gathered in the saloon to gamble away imaginary fortunes. (I.O.U.s were wiped out when the imaginary debts became too supercolossal.) There were dart games and chess games and many a laugh at the jokes in the *Framsjaa*, meaning *Fram's Outlook*, the comic newspaper edited by Dr. Blessing.

Nansen joined in the merrymaking. He cranked out a tune on the organ, or gave poetry recitations, or on special occasions danced a waltz or a polka, democratically assuming the role of female dance partner for his men. And he often led his men in a singsong while Johansen squeezed out melodies on his accordion, the most popular ballads being "Oh! Susanna" and "Napoleon's March Across the Alps in an Open Boat."

Nansen, despite all the jollity, frequently felt stabs of guilt. He

would be lying comfortably in bed, smoking a Havana cigar, or perhaps nibbling a chocolate macaroon. Meanwhile he would be reading by the cozy light of an electric lamp all about the terrible hardships that had befallen Dr. Elisha Kent Kane. "I myself have certainly never lived a more sybaritic life," he thought. "I am almost ashamed of the life we lead, with none of those darkly painted sufferings of the long winter night which are indispensable to a properly exciting Arctic expedition. We shall have nothing to write about when we get home."

What he did write was lyrical prose-poetry, a sort of philosopher's paean to the arctic night. Time and again he would go for a stroll on the ice and try to capture in his sketch pad his conflicting feelings about himself, about life, about death, about his majestic surroundings.

"Here in this silent, starry Arctic night I stand in all my naked pettiness face to face with nature," he wrote. "I sit down devoutly at the feet of eternity and listen. It is all faint, dreamy colour music, a faraway, long-drawn-out melody on muted strings. It is dreamland painted in the imagination's most delicate tints. It is colour etherealised. Is not all life's beauty high, and delicate, and pure like this night?"

He gazed up at the sky, an enormous cupola, blue at the zenith and shading down into green, lilac, violet. The moon was a pale silver sickle dipping its blade into blood-red. The aurora fireworks display flickered and crackled, now like writhing serpents, now like flaming spears, "until the whole melts away in the moonlight, and it is as though one heard the sigh of a departing spirit. Here and there are left a few waving streamers of light, vague as a foreboding—they are the dust from the aurora's glittering cloak. And all the time this utter stillness, impressive as the symphony of infinitude. It is the infinite loveliness of death—Nirvana."

He stared for hours at the welter of ice masses, and glowing images filled his imagination. "O, Arctic night," he personified her, "thou art like a woman, a marvellously lovely woman. Thine are the noble, pure outlines of antique beauty, with its marble coldness. On thy high, smooth brow, clear with the clearness of ether, is no trace of compassion for the little sufferings of despised humanity, on thy pale, beautiful cheeks no blush of feeling. The proud lines of thy throat, thy shoulders' curves, are so noble, but oh! unbendingly cold; thy bosom's white chastity is feelingless as the snowy ice, chaste, beautiful and proud. But sometimes I divine a twitch of pain on thy lips, and endless sadness dreams in thy dark eyes."

But after months of endless drifting, he wearied of his Princess of

the Ice. "Oh, how tired I am of thy cold beauty! I long to return to life. Let me go home again, as conqueror or as beggar; what does that matter? But let me get home to begin life anew. The years are passing here, and what do they bring? Nothing but dust, dry dust, which the first wind blows away; new dust comes in its place, and the next wind takes it too. Truth? Why should we always make so much of truth? Life is more than cold truth, and we live but once."

The truth was that Nansen's adventurous spirit chafed at the monotony of his ship's interminable, zigzagging, crablike drift. By the winter of 1894, he estimated that the *Fram* would reach no nearer to the Pole than 85 degrees north latitude and that it might take eight years to arrive home. He cursed her painfully slow progress:

"Oh! at times this inactivity crushes one's very soul; one's life seems as dark as the winter night outside; there is sunlight upon no part of it except the past and the far, far distant future. I feel as if I *must* break through this deadness, this inertia, and find some outlet for my energies. Can't something happen? Could not a hurricane come and tear up this ice, and set it rolling in high waves like the open sea? Welcome danger, if it only brings us the chance of fighting for our lives—only let's move onwards!"

He therefore decided to court danger. The gloryseeker in him got the upper hand of the scientist. In the spring he would leave the *Fram* in the trusted hands of Captain Sverdrup and with a single companion strike out across the ice to the Pole. It would require an extremely venturesome comrade, for they would indeed be burning their bridges behind them. They would take three sledges, twenty-eight dogs, two kayaks, skis, a tent—and provisions for just one hundred days. They would have no food depots to fall back on. They would have no *Fram* to return to; for she would continue her northwestward drift. After planting the Norwegian flag at the Pole, the pair of over-ice adventurers would have to gamble on making their way back some five hundred and fifty miles to Franz Josef Land north of Russia and hope to be picked up in the vicinity by Spitsbergen whalers.

Nansen selected as his second man Lieutenant Johansen—"a fine fellow, physically and mentally," and unafraid of danger.

"If we fail," Johansen told his commander, "it would be no disgrace to die in such an attempt."

Nansen was by no means that resolute. What he termed his wormeaten reflectiveness filled him with hesitations and misgivings.

"Hundreds of times my eye wanders to the map hanging there on

the wall, and each time a chill creeps over me," he confided to his diary. "The distance before us seems so long. . . . Am I a coward? Am I afraid of death? Oh, no! But in these nights such longings can come over one.

"Ugh! These everlasting cold fits of doubt! Before every decisive resolution the dice of death must be thrown. Is there too much to venture, and too little to gain? There is more to be gained, at all events, than there is here. Then is it not my duty? Besides, there is only one to whom I am responsible, and she. . . ? I shall come back, I know it. I have strength enough for the task. 'Be thou faithful unto death, and thou shalt inherit the crown of life.'

"We are oddly constructed machines. At one moment all resolution, at the next all doubt. Today our intellect, our science, all our *Leben und Treiben* seem but a pitiful Philistinism, not worth a pipe of tobacco. Tomorrow we throw ourselves heart and soul into these very researches, consumed with a burning thirst to absorb everything into ourselves, longing to spy out fresh paths, and fretting impatiently. . . . Oh, mankind, thy ways are passing strange! We are but as flakes of foam, helplessly driven over the tossing sea."

He went on brooding morbidly. Was it sheer vanity that impelled him to attempt a dash to the Pole? Perhaps it was his duty to stick by the *Fram* and science. "Here I sit, whining like an old woman," he berated himself, and he began citing Shakespeare. "My thoughts come and go and carry me irresistibly ahead. I can scarcely make myself out; but who can fathom the depths of the human mind? The brain is a puzzling piece of mechanism: 'We are such stuff as dreams are made on.' Is it so? I almost believe it—a microcosm of eternity's infinite 'stuff that dreams are made on.'"

He finally overcame his doubts. In his diary one can almost hear the clang of a Viking sword. "Every night I am at home in my dreams," he pondered. "But when the morning breaks I must again, like Helge, gallop back on the pale horse by way of the reddening dawn, not to the joys of Valhalla, but to the realm of eternal ice. Like Helge, swimming in the dew of sorrow. . . . This is my life's *Gotterdammerung*, Twilight of the Gods. . . .

"H'm! As if dissatisfaction, longing, suffering, were not the very basis of life. Without privation there would be no struggle, and without struggle no life—that is as certain as that two and two make four. And now the struggle is to begin, it is looming yonder in the north. Oh! to drink delight of battle, in long, deep draughts. Battle means life, and behind it victory beckons us on."

On March 14, 1895, when the *Fram* was at 84 degrees north latitude, Nansen bade a last farewell to his company. It was a bitterly cold forty-five below zero, but he felt well prepared. He and Johansen were dressed in camel's hair coats, wool shirts, Norwegian tweed home-spun, woolen underwear, hooded felt hats, wolfskin gloves, and sealskin Lapp boots lined with warming sedge grass. Bags of pemmican were stowed in the two bamboo-frame Eskimo-style thirty-six-pound kayaks. About fourteen hundred pounds of supplies and equipment were stacked on their three twelve-foot-long maple Nansen sledges, one of which bore an odometer to register the distance traveled. There was a tearful eye or two and much gruff humor as Nansen passed along to his shipmates an old proverb. "Be happy," he said, "and if you can't be happy, take it easy; and if you can't be easy, be as easy as you can."

Sverdrup accompanied the two travelers for a few miles to speed them on their way into the Arctic wasteland and to share a final pipeful of tobacco with his commander. "The last thing Sverdrup asked me when sitting on his sledge, just as we were about to part," wrote Nansen, "was: If I thought I should go to the South Pole when I got home? For if so, he hoped I would wait till he arrived; and then he asked me to give his love to his wife and child."

As it turned out, Sverdrup patiently shepherded the *Fram* on her drifting odyssey up to 85 degrees, 57 minutes north latitude—the highest northing ever navigated by a ship. Nansen and Johansen hiked up to 86 degrees, 13.6 minutes north latitude—a record march that was to stand unmatched in the nineteenth century. The pair failed to step ski on the northern axis of the world by more than two hundred miles; but it was not for lack of trying.

They ran up against ice hummocks that crested like frozen waves of lava and they sweated like horses pushing and pulling their sledges over. The cold transformed their inadequate clothes into clanking suits of armor and the stiffened cuffs of Nansen's coat rubbed sores into his wrists to the bone. They slogged through freezing ice water at least ten hours a day and were so exhausted, says Nansen, "my head would drop and I would be awakened by suddenly falling forward on my snowshoes." By day they were forced to beat their wornout dogs with ash sticks and at night Johansen was still urging them ahead in his sleep, "Get on, you devil you! Go on, you brutes! *Sass! Sass!*"

On April 8, 1895, Nansen skied on alone to a high hummock. He gazed through his spyglass. "A chaos of iceblocks stretching as far as the horizon," he reported despairingly back to Johansen. With their limited

rations, they would have to give up. They made the best of it. They raised two Norwegian flags and celebrated with a "farthest north" banquet. Their feast consisted of bread and butter and stewed red whortleberries, topped by two delicacies—"lobscouse" (pemmican and potatoes) and a "polar mead" (limejuice and hot whey). Then they huddled together for warmth in "the dear bag, our best friend."

With heavy hearts next morning they turned their sledges southward. Ahead was a long journey of some four hundred and fifty miles down to those eighty-five hazily known islands since acquired by Russia, collectively called Franz Josef Land. Their retreat was toilsome, partly due to the blazing sun. They sometimes waded up to their waists in slush. They floated their sledges across narrow canals on ice pans. They leaped from one ice cake to another with a dexterity, said gymnast Johansen, "of which no acrobat need have been ashamed."

What shamed them was the need to gradually kill off their weakest dogs. The creatures had to be slaughtered one by one to feed the remaining Samoyeds, while the men, with provisions fast giving out, were reduced to drinking dogs' blood in a kind of hot mush porridge. Stabbing their faithful dogs, in order to save precious ammunition, revolted Nansen. He suggested they experiment with strangulation. They led poor Perpetuum behind a hillock out of sight of his mates. They tied a rope around his neck and, each taking an end, pulled with all their might. Perpetuum refused to die. His imploring eyes filled Nansen with guilt and self-reproach. Nansen could bear it no longer. Perpetuum's throat was slit with a knife. After that he left the distasteful, but necessary, task of dog murder to Johansen.

Over the curdled sea the men pressed on unremittingly, sometimes harnessed with their dogs to sledges, sometimes ferrying their teams across widening channels on kayaks. Hardship strengthened their friendship. Johansen tells us in his journal how they shared chunks of chocolate: "One of us arranged two portions on the kayak, while the other turned his back upon him and chose his lot by calling out 'right' or 'left.' We were quite fair to each other. Nansen, who was a bigger man than I, never made any difference in the rations."

And when Nansen strained his back, he describes how Johansen tenderly helped him remove his boots and socks, and nursed him back to recovery: "He is touchingly unselfish and takes care of me as if I were a child. Everything he thinks can ease me he does quietly, without my knowing it. Poor fellow, he has to work doubly hard now, and does not know how this will end."

It ended with Nansen saving Johansen's life. One day as Johansen stooped to pick up a hauling rope he received a cuff on the ear that made him see fireworks. It was followed by a bone-rattling wallop that laid him flat on his back. A female polar bear stood over him. She was, says Johansen, a tough customer. He seized her throat and held on for dear life.

"Get your gun," he cried out to Nansen who was several yards away.

Nansen's rifle was in its case stowed inside the kayak and he desperately struggled to extricate it. As he whirled around, cocking the shot barrel, he heard Johansen say quietly, "You must look sharp if you want to be in time."

It was an understatement. The bear was just about to bite Johansen in the head. Fortunately at that moment their two remaining dogs distracted the bear with their barking. As the bear lunged at them, Johansen rolled out of harm's way and Nansen killed her with a shot behind the ear.

They feasted on raw bear steaks as juicy as any porterhouse they had ever tasted at Oslo's Hotel Grand. Regrettably it was a last supper for the pair of surviving dogs—Nansen's favorite, Kaifas, and Johansen's favorite, Suggen. These two had been saved until this moment when the party had reached the open sea. Now, after lashing the two kayaks together with sledges and rigging up a Viking-like sail, the men had to discard all nonessential cargo. The loyal dogs were expendable.

"Destroy them in the same way as the others, we could not," wrote Nansen with remorse. "We sacrificed a cartridge on each of them. I shot Johansen's, and he shot mine."

Towards the end of August they landed on the western side of the Franz Josef archipelago. They were ecstatic. It was the first land they had felt underfoot in two years. Their senses reveled in sensations: the scent of yellow poppies and pink saxifrage, the mewing of the rare and lovely rose-breasted Ross's gulls, and the roaring of colonies of those basking "meat bergs," the walruses. The first two islands he saw, Nansen named Eva's Island and Liv's Island. The Soviet Union has since proposed renaming the entire archipelago Fridtjof Nansen Land because of Nansen's memorable wintering at a basaltic cliffed island a bit farther south.

Using a walrus shoulder blade and tusk as spades, Nansen and Johansen quarried rock for a moss-chinked, igloolike hut barely six feet

*Nansen and Johansen in two kayaks lashed together, after eating their dogs, dolefully headed south to Franz Josef Land.* MITTET

FOTO, OSLO

*Champion gymnast Hjalmar Johansen accompanied Nansen on his ski dash to within 200 miles of the Pole.*

high. They crawled in through a low tunnel covered with ice blocks and walrus hides. For furnishings they had blubber lamps, with gauze bandages for wicks, and a single bearskin sleeping bag. "When you lay across it, you kicked the wall on one side and butted it on the other," said Nansen. "However, even I could *almost* stand upright under the roof."

For nine months they hibernated in this smoky, fetid den, listening to polar bears and foxes scramble over their iced roof. Fresh meat was no problem. Incredibly, they ate up nineteen bears that winter. Each alternating week they took turns at acting as cook and waiter. Their two meals a day were simple: bear stew for breakfast and bear steaks for supper. A little burnt blubber fished out of the lamp sometimes served as dessert. The fatty diet agreed with them. Nansen wound up weighing two hundred and three pounds, twenty-two more than when he left the *Fram*; Johansen gained thirteen and was up to one hundred and sixty-five pounds.

Dirt and tedium were their main discomforts. Their filthy trail garments, layered with blood and grease, resisted washing. When they tried boiling and wringing their underpants, oil oozed out—promptly used to replenish their fuel supply. They yearned for soap. They longed for a Turkish steam bath. They lay staring at the lacy frost tapestries glazed on the frozen stone walls. They imagined themselves inside warm, bright shops and buying the cleanest and softest of linen clothes.

Killing time by sleeping was developed into a high art. Sometimes they slept twenty hours out of the twenty-four. Sharing the same sleeping bag did pose a few difficulties. "The worst part of it is when you've slept for a time on one side and want to turn over on the other," said Johansen. "You can't do it unless your sleeping partner wants to do the same. Both must turn at the same time. There was no help for it. One of us had always to rouse the other in order to turn around."

Another trial was Johansen's tendency to snore loudly. Nansen would then kick him in the back to hush him up. The kicks were not very effective. Nansen says his bedmate would merely shake himself a little, smile in his sleep, and sonorously drone on.

They dreamed of home constantly. Johansen dreamed of his mother looking after the cherry tree in their summer garden. Nansen dreamed of Eva sewing by the lamp and stroking the golden curls of their three-year-old daughter. "What good friends we shall be!" he dreamed of his reunion with little Liv. "You shall ride a cockhorse and I will tell you stories from the north about bears, foxes, walruses, and all the strange animals up there."

In their waking hours their thoughts wandered in trancelike nostalgia back to the splendid library of books they had left behind on the *Fram*. When departing, Johansen had been in the middle of reading one of the novels of Paul Heyse—was it *The Romance of the Canoness* or *The Maiden of Treppi?*—and he wondered how the plot had turned out. Nansen missed his shipboard reading of Darwin's *Origin of Species* and the plays of Shakespeare and the will-to-live broodings of the German philosopher, Arthur Schopenhauer, who had written of will power as the renunciation of desire. Yet how they desired books! The only one they had brought with them was the *Nautical Almanac*. They read it aloud to each other until they had memorized by heart its miscellany of information—all about the Norwegian royal family, self-help for fishermen, and how to render first-aid to people rescued from drowning.

And so the days passed. Christmas Eve was solemnly celebrated by turning their mangy shirts inside out and bathing in a quarter of a cup of hot water. For Christmas dinner they raided precious rations hoarded against their spring journey and they felt like kings dining on bread fried in blubber and a sliver of Cadbury's chocolate. New Year's Eve heralding 1896 was a touching occasion. Wrote Johansen in his diary: "Nansen proposed that we should begin to say 'thou' to one another as a sign of intimate friendship, like the French 'tu.' Hitherto we had called each other 'you.' " And in what he called his "black book"—a note book literally stained black with grease—Nansen gravely closed the year with a fatalistic, Omar Khayyám-like entry: "Once more a leaf is turned in the book of eternity, a new blank page is opened, and no one knows what will be written on it."

Six months later Nansen was recording in his journal with amazement Bret Harte's poem, *Heathen Chinee*:

*Do I sleep, do I dream?*
*Do I wonder and doubt?*
*Are things what they seem?*
*Or is visions about?*

He had reason to wonder if he was dreaming. After leaving their tomblike hovel in mid-May, the two wanderers had floundered about the maze of bleak ice islands, seeing and hearing nobody but bellowing walruses that almost gutted their kayaks. Then, on Wednesday June 17, 1896, there occurred a meeting as dramatic as the celebrated encounter

between Stanley and Dr. Livingstone. While Nansen was preparing a pot of walrus flesh for breakfast on the beach of Cape Flora, his ears suddenly pricked up.

"Johansen!" he shouted. "I hear dogs barking inland!"

Johansen tumbled out of the tent. "Dogs?" Surely he must be dreaming. Dogs were the companions of man. It was probably the cry of a loon or the scream of kittiwakes. Nansen nonetheless picked up his telescope and clambered to the top of an ice hummock.

With heart beating wildly, he thought he saw a pair of dogs and a human figure in the distance. He hallooed; an answering shout came back. He waved his hat; the man did likewise. Nansen rushed down to meet the approaching figure. And there, amid ice, glacier and mist, Nansen raised his hat and shook hands with the first white stranger he had seen in three years.

"How do you do?" said the man in English.

"How do you do?" replied Nansen.

Silence; a sizing up.

"On the one side," Nansen described the scene with a fine sense of comedy, "the civilized European in an English check suit and high rubber winter boots, well-shaved, well-groomed, bringing with him a perfume of scented soap, perceptible to the wild man's sharpened senses. On the other side, the wild man, clad in dirty rags, black with oil and soot, with long, uncombed hair and shaggy beard."

As if in a Noel Coward parody, the Englishman pursued the polite conversation.

"I'm immensely glad to see you."

"Thank you; I also."

"Have you a ship here?"

"No. My ship is not here."

"How many are there of you?"

"I have one companion at the ice edge."

Suddenly the stranger stopped, stared at Nansen's grime-masked face, and recognized him.

"Aren't you Nansen?"

"Yes, I am."

"By Jove!" he exclaimed, seizing Nansen's hand and pumping it again. "I *am* glad to see you!"

It was Frederick Jackson, an explorer sent by the English press magnate Lord Northcliffe, to survey Franz Josef Land. Soon Johansen, his grimy shirt and a Norwegian flag fluttering from ski poles, joined

*"By jove!" and "How do you do?" was Jackson's polite
English greeting — the first white stranger Nansen had seen in
three years.*

Nansen at an opulent hutted camp. While awaiting the arrival of the British supply ship, *Windward*, the pair enjoyed blessed soap and hot baths, cigars and port wine, and plenty of blubber-free food and sweet-smelling clean clothes.

Jackson later said he was too polite to ask the poor chaps what had happened to the rest of the *Fram* crew. It was the one unanswered question that agitated Nansen. In August 1896, a week after he landed at a Norwegian port, Nansen apprehensively ripped open a telegram. It was from Sverdrup. The *Fram* had completed her mission northwest of Spitsbergen. She had arrived safely at another Norwegian port. She was setting out at once to meet her commander at Tromso. "In my heart," wrote Nansen, "I sobbed and wept for joy and thankfulness."

As Nansen and his reunited *Fram* crew sailed triumphantly along the coast toward Oslo, the people of Norway greeted the heroes with fête after fête. There were torchlight parades, rivers of champagne, climaxed with a thirteen-gun salute. "I say, Nansen," said one of his shipmates, "this is all very well, but there's too much *racket*. I am thinking of the Arctic; we had a fine time up there."

Nansen agreed with him. Forever after he pined to be there once more, "to climb up on a hummock again, to spy out the way—that is real excitement. There's a life of action for you."

But he never did fulfill that dream. For the rest of his life, except for a trip he made to Siberia, his actions were taken up with being a scholar, statesman and humanitarian. He labored to fill six thick tomes with the scientific data accumulated on the *Fram's* circumpolar drift. He established the first chair of oceanography at Oslo University. He was instrumental in helping Norway to gain peacefully her independence from Sweden and served as his nation's first ambassador to Britain.

Then the First World War intervened and its horrors performed a kind of moral alchemy on Nansen's passion for discovery. Against all odds, as League of Nations Commissioner, he worked tirelessly to repatriate half a million prisoners of war; to put down slavery in Abyssinia; to find homes for more than a million Armenian, Russian and Jewish refugees. As his crowning achievement he persuaded fifty-two governments to recognize the Nansen Passport—a document bearing his portrait which was the only hope for people without a country.

The Good Samaritan to the world wore himself out in the task of easing human misery. Like the later Mark Twain, his private journals agonize over the follies of governing nations and man's inhumanity to man. A sampling reflects the inner turmoil of his melancholy:

"I laugh to myself until I chuckle out loud. Why? I think how thin is the veneer called civilization.... It seems to me that life and the world are rather absurd.... What a wonderful creature is Man! Plundering, robbing, at war with the animals, at war with his fellows. A beast of prey wherever he is found.... What a hell they can make of it.... My great discovery is that I have found hell, but there is no fire there. It is the land of clammy fogs.... The vast empty space envelopes me again, the terror. When the last vanity of life is gone, then life is a hell of fogs, empty space....

"Up man, you are sick. Fight or die for all that is beautiful. Remember your old kingdoms of beauty where everything was cool crystal, shining in the colors of the rainbow.... I must think of Hamlet's words: 'The time is out of joint; O cursed spite that ever I was born to set it right.'... But, oh, it is a hard life—and sometimes I long for the silent ice fields near the North Pole.... I must get some pure mountain air in my lungs again—to feel oneself like a bird as one rushes over the snowfields undisturbed by human feet and then, when the night comes, to sleep in the snow with the sky as a tent. Oh, you are so free...."

His interest in the polar regions never waned. In 1911 he published a monumental, albeit controversial, two-volume work, *In Northern Mists*, which probed into the blurred legends that shrouded early Viking voyages. In the last years of his life he was founder of an international scientific society, Aeroarctic, concerned with polar mapping by aircraft. When he died on May 13, 1930, to national mourning, he was planning to fly on the airship *Graf Zeppelin* over those frozen seas through which the *Fram* had drifted.

"That will be a picnic," he said. "Dogs and sledges will be taken, in case. But everything now is civilized and arranged and specialized. Very nice. Only romance has gone to glory. It won't return and the *Fram* won't return."

But the *Fram* has returned. Since his death the historic ship has been restored to her original glory in an exhibition hall near Oslo Fjord as a monument to his pioneering vision and genius. Nansen's drift aboard her inspired two other Norwegian giants of exploration, both of them his protégés.

In 1898 Captain Otto Sverdrup refitted the beamy, greenhearted *Fram*. For five years he conducted a scientific survey of one hundred and twenty thousand square miles of virgin Arctic land west of Canada's Ellesmere Island. He was poorly rewarded. The Norwegian parliament dismissed his discoveries as "of no more value than an ice

cellar." For his oil-and-gas-rich Sverdrup Islands the king of ice navigators received from the Canadian government a pittance of sixty-seven
thousand dollars.

Sverdrup died on November 26, 1930, six months after the death of
his beloved Commander Nansen. The two shipmates never did make
their planned expedition to the South Pole aboard the *Fram*. That feat
was accomplished by a younger Norwegian disciple of Nansen's, Roald
Amundsen, of whom we will read in our next chapter.

But here it is worthwhile telling the poignant story of how Nansen
relinquished his ship. In 1907, having navigated the Northwest Passage
and still eager for further achievement, the thirty-five-year-old
Amundsen had approached his mentor. He pleaded to accompany
Nansen on a proposed Antarctic voyage or borrow the *Fram* for his own
polar expedition.

Nansen, busy with his oceanography studies, had put him off for
nine months until this September day in 1907. Amundsen was sitting in
the library of Nansen's home anxiously awaiting his decision. Nansen
had half made up his mind to refuse to lend the *Fram*, and go to the
South Pole himself. But on the way downstairs to the library he stopped
to speak to his wife.

"I know what will happen," said Eva. "You are going to leave me
again."

That altered his decision. He went into the library and relieved the
look of suspense on Amundsen's face. "You shall have the *Fram*," he
said.

Amundsen did not embark on his voyage until three years later. In
the interim Eva died of catarrh of the lungs while Nansen was absent as
Norwegian envoy in London. Her last words to their five children were:
"I am not afraid to die. But poor him, he'll be too late."

His daughter Liv has described his anguish on his arrival home. "I
have never heard a human being cry so inconsolably," she said. "I
realized that if we children had lost eternally and incomprehensibly
much, Father had lost *everything*."

It was therefore all the more crushing when, on June 10, 1910,
Nansen watched the *Fram* sail out of Oslo Fjord. Amundsen was on the
commander's bridge and standing beside him was Nansen's former
polar ski companion, Lieutenant Hjalmar Johansen, now elevated to
captain. And Nansen himself was left behind.

"The bitterest hour of my life," Nansen said of this, his second loss.

He could not go back on his word; he thought he had renounced

personal glory for the sake of the advancement of science; and yet he felt torn by conflict.

"I must confess," he confided in a letter to Sir Clements Markham, president of the British Royal Society, "that it was with a bleeding heart that I thus cut myself off from doing the one thing I had planned and cherished for such a long time, and which should have been a winding up of my career as polar explorer, the masterpiece on which I should bring the blossom of my experience."

It is to Nansen's eternal credit that he was the first to stand by Amundsen in the controversy that raged over this last expedition of the *Fram*. The ship had been lent to Amundsen for a scientific drift through Arctic waters. But because the North Pole had already been attained, Amundsen changed plans midway. Instead he steered south and in his spectacular dash via dog sled and ski succeeded, on December 14, 1911, in planting the Norwegian flag on the South Pole. Nansen defended Amundsen wholeheartedly against criticisms leveled at him from England for stealing a march on Robert Falcon Scott.

The older explorer could understand the dreams that impelled his glory-bound young protégé. In the Viking spirit, neither could resist the call of adventure. As Nansen said nostalgically of his own quest after the Land of Beyond, "The ice and the long moonlit polar nights, with all their yearning, seemed like a far-off dream from another world—a dream that has come and passed away. But what would life be worth without its dreams?"

# Chapter 9

# The Polar Pirate

It was a black and squally midnight on June 16, 1903, and Captain Roald Amundsen stood on deck in a deluge of rain wondering whether he would be able to sail north before his creditors caught up with him. For months they had been hounding him persistently. They were demanding payment for supplies he had bought on credit for his little Norwegian herring sloop, the *Gjoa*. Somehow he had managed to put them off. Meanwhile, working part-time as a waiter in an Oslo waterfront restaurant, he had begged, borrowed and scrounged extra cash to buy sled dogs and pemmican and to hire a crew of six comradely polar seamen.

Now, as his one-masted discovery ship pitched and rolled alongside the pier in Oslo Fjord, his first mate scrambled up the gangway bringing the latest news. His principal creditor was on the wharf with a bailiff. They were waiting for the rainstorm's fury to abate before seizing the vessel and arresting her skipper for fraud.

Amundsen laughed. He seized an axe and, while thunder crashed overhead, he joyfully cut the mooring hawsers.

"When dawn arose on our truculent creditor, we were safely out on the open main, seven as light-hearted pirates as ever flew the black flag," he wrote, "disappearing upon a quest that should take us three years and that had baffled our predecessors for four centuries."

Thus did Captain Roald Engelbregt Gravning Amundsen set out to capture the grandfather of all geographic prizes, the Northwest Passage. Needless to say he captured it. He captured almost every major

geographical prize of his day. By ship he was the first to navigate the Northwest Passage. By dog sledge and ski he was the first to set foot on the South Pole. By open-cockpit seaplane he was the first to fly within one hundred and thirty miles of the North Pole. By dirigible balloon he was the first to make an intercontinental airship flight over the top of the North Pole. For good measure he also circumnavigated the Northeast Passage.

It is revealing that Amundsen likened himself and his crew on his first polar expedition to pirates. There was indeed a certain piratical gusto about him. The supreme man of action, he was not concerned with the subtleties of scientific discovery. Buccaneer that he was, Amundsen sought to be first to attain geographical goals because they were records to be broken, prizes to be won, each one a new piece of booty to be worn triumphantly at his belt. One sometimes imagines him as Douglas Fairbanks Senior starring in *The Black Pirate*, the silent movie made two years before Amundsen's heroic death in 1928. They were swashbucklers both, gallant and wonderfully athletic. They performed impossible feats of strength for the fun of it and the sport of it and the glory of it.

In real life it is psychologically interesting that Amundsen tried to model himself after Dr. Fridtjof Nansen, the Norwegian father figure whom he idolized. In most respects no two polar explorers could be more unlike. Yet their mutual respect was deep and abiding, possibly because each offered qualities that the other lacked.

Nansen admired his young protégé's cutlass-like directness. Here was no Hamlet, brooding with guilts and misgivings over slaughtering his sleigh dogs or stealing a march on his rival South Pole discoverer, the English Robert Falcon Scott. He was the iron man, resolved to be a winner at all costs. "There," Nansen said of him, "is a ring of steeled, purposeful human will—through icy frosts, snow storms, and death."

Amundsen, a confirmed bachelor, whose sole love was polar conquest, phrased it in romantic terms. He compared his aggressiveness with the blunt approach needed to master a beautiful mistress. "The deity of success is a woman, and she insists on being won, not courted," Amundsen liked saying. "You've got to seize her and bear her off, instead of standing under her window with a mandolin."

Amundsen admired Nansen's breadth of scholarship and idealism. The young disciple genuinely sought to emulate his mentor, but somehow the ambition to score a "sensational coup"—a phrase common in Amundsen's lexicon—tended to lead him astray. In 1907 Nansen lent

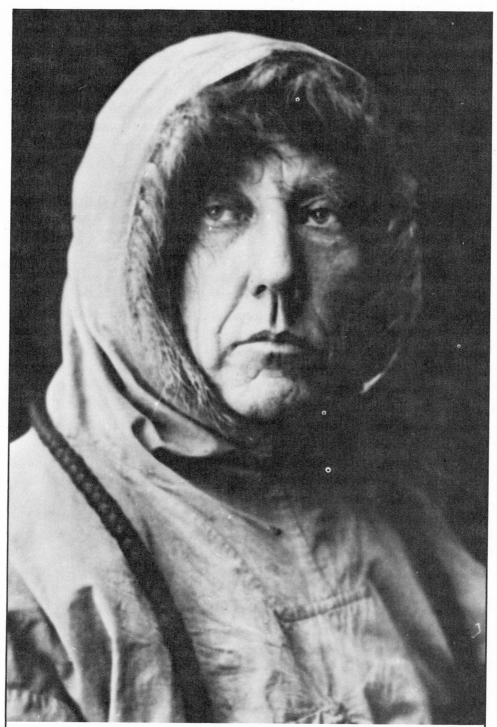

*Roald Amundsen: the piratical swashbuckler whose prizes included the South Pole and Northwest Passage.* WIDE WORLD PHOTOS

him the *Fram* on the clear understanding that Amundsen would make a scientific oceanographic drift toward the North Pole. Because that goal was seemingly attained by Dr. Frederick A. Cook, Amundsen changed course midway. Without informing Nansen, yet firing off a challenging telegram to Scott, "Am going South," Amundsen headed instead for the glamorous consolation prize at the bottom of the world.

"On this little detour," wrote Amundsen jauntily in his two-volume journal, *The South Pole*, "science would have to look after itself." And as he set out on his final ski-and-sledge dash, Amundsen noted semijocularly, "I tried to work up a little poetry—'the ever-restless spirit of man'—'the mysterious, awe-inspiring wilderness of ice'—but it was no good; I suppose it was too early in the morning."

When Nansen later heard of Amundsen's drastic switch in plans, he was at first inclined to scold the errant glory-seeker. "Well, I felt a little funny," confessed Nansen, for he himself had intended exploring the South Pole. But how could one upbraid a loveable pupil who had been so spectacularly successful? "It was evidently me he was most afraid of," said Nansen, and he voiced his sole regret: "If only he had told me, I could have helped him in so many ways."

Although he could not comprehend Nansen's broad tolerance and humanity, Amundsen never ceased worshipping "the man who from my childhood has embodied my highest ideal." On his Northwest Passage voyage he reverently hung Nansen's portrait on the cabin wall of the *Gjoa* and named a large Arctic promontory Cape Nansen. On his South Pole expedition his pet canary aboard the *Fram* was called Fridtjof and he named one of the loftiest Antarctic glaciers Mount Nansen.

If he could not aspire to Nansen's toplofty vision, Amundsen felt at least he could meet him on earthier grounds. "Nansen is too kingly," he once said in a rare criticism of his idol. "He will not hobnob with the common herd."

The same thing could not be said of Amundsen. His men adored him for his democratic comradeship and his boisterous high spirits; they volunteered to serve under his leadership time and again. Oscar Wisting, who was with him at both the South Pole and the North Pole, said of his Chief: "If we were in want of food and he said one must sacrifice himself for the others, I would gladly go quietly out into the snowdrift and die."

Amundsen himself set simple requirements for the Pole-hunters he chose to accompany him: "Courage and dauntlessness, without boasting or big words, and then, amid joking and chaff—out into the blizzard."

He endured so many blizzards during his long career that it was said of him that he looked like walking proof of the theory of weather erosion. In his later years of celebrityhood he was popularly known as the White Eagle. He certainly looked like an eagle, with his hooked beak of a nose, his long bald head, his snowy tufted brows, and his piercing blue-grey eyes. On his lecture tours he was sometimes billed as The Last of the Vikings. He looked like a Viking, too, with his trowel-shaped beard and his dramatically upswept moustaches, his magnificent six-foot-tall physique, and his seemingly arrogant, don't-give-a-damn stance.

If he seemed inordinately vain about his physical prowess, he had reason to be. In his fifties, after being mauled severely by a polar bear and suffering a heart attack, doctors warned him that he would die if he continued to indulge in strenuous exercise. Amundsen responded by running eight hundred miles through the heavy snow of Alaska, jogging at the rate of fifty miles a day. Then he wagered that he could outrun any man half his age. Evidently it was not an idle boast. A reporter-artist, sketching him for the New York *Times* a year later, was amazed by the explorer's springy stamina. He wrote that Amundsen had the body and quick step of a ballet dancer.

He was an imposing figure of a man, and some people considered his manner chilling and saturnine. They didn't really know Amundsen, according to his friends. Perhaps his most devoted intimate was Lincoln Ellsworth, the American millionaire's son who financed him and accompanied him on his two North Pole flights.

"He was like a child whose confidence has been betrayed so often that it finally trusts nobody," wrote Ellsworth in his memoirs, *Beyond Horizons.* "So he encased himself in a shell of ice. Win his confidence and melt that ice, and a different being emerged. Nobody was warmer-hearted, no boy could frolic more joyously than Amundsen."

Ellsworth gives us a delightful picture of some of the great man's idiosyncrasies. Evidently Amundsen maintained an aloof air in public for good reason: he never knew when one of his many creditors would pounce upon him. He was a terrible businessman; he was driven into bankruptcy partly because he splurged his money on his expeditions; and process servers kept harassing him.

At hotels, says Ellsworth, there seemed to be a perpetual rustling of paper on the floor. It would be another court summons for Amundsen being shoved under the door. Even in the midst of a civic banquet

honoring him—and nobody enjoyed public acclaim more than Amundsen—the explorer's after-dinner speech would be interrupted by the inevitable process server.

It got so bad that Amundsen developed a phobia—that he was constantly being trailed. A pack of little boys might stop to gawk at the celebrated explorer. "Ellsworth," he would whisper tensely, with a furtive glance over his shoulder, "we are being followed!"

According to Ellsworth, he had gargantuan appetites. He would gobble down four hardboiled eggs one after another without blinking. It was a ritual with him to have a good-sized drink of fiery *aquavit* brandy at precisely five o'clock each day. "His throat seemed to be lined with asbestos," Ellsworth recalled, "and his digestion was that of an ostrich." He would gulp mug after mug of scalding hot chocolate or Horlick's malted milk that would sear the throat of any other man. "That is good," he would say as he finally set down the empty mug. "There are two times when a man is happy up in the north—when his belly is full of hot liquid and when he is in his sleeping bag."

He had the gifts of a carnival showman. Ellsworth suggested they modestly slip off on their joint flight to the North Pole without informing the press. Amundsen was horrified. "You can't do it that way," he rebuked his naive partner. "You *have* to have the publicity." Ellsworth soon learned from the master the tricks of polar promotion. The New York *Times* paid fifty thousand dollars for the exclusive story of their polar flight. Moreover they sold ten thousand post cards, at one dollar apiece, so that people could boast of having received the first piece of airmail ever delivered over the Pole.

Ellsworth felt that Amundsen's most endearing trait was his ability to laugh at himself. He was a wonderful raconteur, and could spin funny stories by the hour, usually directed at his own foibles. He would tell how he had absentmindedly neglected to bring a snow shovel with him to the South Pole; how he failed miserably to devise a wind protector that would cover his mountain peak of a nose; how embarrassed he felt to see an Oslo bootmaker make a window display of the mammoth-sized ski boots specially designed for an Amundsen expedition. "We are all a trifle vain, and dislike having our own shortcomings shown up in electric lights," said Amundsen. "If I had ever cherished any illusions on the subject of 'a dainty little foot,' I am sure the last trace of such vanity died out on the day I passed the shoemaker's window. . . . I used to go a long way round to avoid coming face to face with these monsters in public."

Ellsworth said Amundsen was not above telling a "white fib" now and then to embellish a good story. "In all matters relating to his own achievements, however, he was scrupulously truthful," Ellsworth maintained. Once they were both seasick on a wildly pitching ship heading for Spitsbergen. Ellsworth turned as chalk-white as Amundsen, who was gritting his teeth and muttering one of his fatalistic maxims, "Life is a ball in the hands of chance." Finally Ellsworth groaned, "You know, Captain, I don't like the sea." Amundsen, the Norseman who posed on the lecture platform as The Last of the Vikings, moaned with him: "I don't either. It is something we have to put up with."

It must have been a difficult confession to make. Roald Amundsen, born on July 16, 1872, on the outskirts of Oslo, came from a long line of seafaring Norsemen. His father, the co-owner of a shipping business, was a former captain who loved the salt tang of the sea. Indeed he took his Swedish bride on a honeymoon trip to China aboard a small ship which he skippered.

The father was reputed to be a strict but just disciplinarian. He died when Roald was fourteen. By that time Roald's three older brothers had left home and the teenager was left to live alone with his mother. He was a lonely boy, a mediocre student at school, because he daydreamed over romantic books of adventure. The book that shaped his life was the narrative of Sir John Franklin, the English explorer who met his doom seeking the Northwest Passage. In his later memoirs, *My Life As An Explorer*, Amundsen gives us a fascinating insight into the masochism that impelled him to follow in Franklin's footsteps.

"Strangely enough the thing in Sir John's narrative that appealed to me most strongly was the sufferings he and his men endured," wrote Amundsen. "A strange ambition burned within me to endure those same sufferings. Perhaps the idealism of youth, which often takes a turn toward martyrdom, found its crusade in me in the form of Arctic exploration. I, too, would suffer in a cause . . . in the frozen North."

He lost no time in hardening himself for his chosen profession. To improve his stamina, he played football which he detested, went skiing on barrel staves, snow-shoed for hours in the most rugged Norwegian mountains. He thus developed a physique which astonished every physician who examined him. To build up his tolerance for cold, he became, to his mother's great distress, a fresh-air fiend. He slept with his bedroom windows flung wide open in the middle of winter.

His mother, who had no sympathy for such shenanigans, induced him to study medicine at University of Oslo. He didn't have his heart in

it, but the indifferent scholar persevered for her sake; he didn't want to hurt his mother's feelings. She died when he was twenty-one. "With enormous relief," says Amundsen, "I soon left university to throw myself wholeheartedly into the dream of my life."

He served his Arctic apprenticeship by sailing for three years with Norwegian seal-hunters. At twenty-five he was first mate aboard the *Belgica*, which was conducting a scientific survey of the south magnetic pole. This Antarctic voyage taught him a lesson in leadership. When the ship got locked in the ice for thirteen grim months, her commander went berserk. He refused to let his scurvy-sick crew eat seal meat, took to his bed, and made out his will.

First mate Amundsen, though nominally next in command, took no credit for rescuing the crew from their plight. He paid generous tribute to the ship's surgeon, Dr. Frederick A. Cook, the American destined to become embroiled with Robert E. Peary in the race for the North Pole. It was Cook, said Amundsen, who nursed the sick back to recovery, compelled them to eat blubber, and ingeniously used explosives to extricate the *Belgica* from her ice trap. "He, of all the ship's company," wrote Amundsen, "was the one man of unfaltering courage, unfailing hope, endless cheerfulness, and unswerving kindness."

Years later, when Cook was branded a swindler and thrown into prison, Amundsen's own loyalty was unswerving. He visited Cook in the federal penitentiary at Leavenworth and publicly commiserated with the unfortunate explorer who was reduced to doing needlework. "Only this I know," said Amundsen. "Cook pulled us all out of the Antarctic with his good spirits and his medical care. That is all the Dr. Cook there is for me."

It was a noble act of defiance on Amundsen's part. He thus aroused the ire of Peary's powerful backers at the National Geographic Society; they revengefully exerted pressure to cancel Amundsen's lecture contracts in the United States. But the gesture was characteristic of Amundsen. He measured a man by his actions; not by his bluster.

It was for this reason that young Amundsen, on his return to Norway, approached with trepidation the one he termed the Grand Old Man of Arctic exploration. From boyhood he had revered Fridtjof Nansen for his deeds. He had stood with the Oslo crowds welcoming back Nansen from his polar expeditions; and a voice seemed to whisper to him, "Just imagine if *you* could penetrate the Northwest Passage!" Now he was seeking support from the great public hero himself.

"I think it is Mark Twain who tells of a man so small that he had to

go twice through the door before he could be seen," Amundsen was to recall the awesome moment. "But this man's insignificance was nothing compared to what I felt on the morning I stood in Nansen's villa and knocked at the door of his study. 'Come in,' said a voice from inside. And then I stood face to face with the man who had loomed before me as something almost superhuman."

The Grand Old Man was most amenable. Nansen induced his protégé to not only search out the Northwest Passage, but to relocate the vagrant north magnetic pole as well. That would take the voyage out of the realm of derring-do and lend it a gloss of scientific value. He arranged to have Amundsen study terrestrial magnetism at Berlin and Hamburg. More important, Nansen pulled strings to help raise the barebones minimum of some seven thousand pounds needed to buy a ship and scientific equipment.

Today one can't help but marvel at Amundsen's courage and audacity. The scope of his achievement becomes all the more awe-inspiring if we compare his *Gjoa* with the S.S. *Manhattan*, which lumbered through the Northwest Passage in 1969.

The American oil tanker was a colossus of one hundred and fifty-five thousand tons. She was more than one thousand feet in length—almost as long as the Empire State Building is tall. Her steel decks sprawled in width over three acres—massive enough to accommodate a helicopter landing pad plus a few football fields. Her gigantic propellers were driven by turbines of forty-three thousand horsepower—affording enough momentum to shatter iron-tough icepack. She carried one hundred and twenty-six persons aboard, including some of the most expensive scientific and navigational brains available.

Amundsen's oak-sheathed little herring fishery smack was a forty-seven tonner seventy-two feet in length—tiny enough perhaps to pass muster as one of the *Manhattan's* lifeboats. Her decks were eleven feet wide—offering just enough space to accommodate a bit of a cabin fore and aft. She was driven by a thirteen horsepower kerosene motor plus three hundred square yards of sail billowing from a single mast of Norwegian pine. And her total complement of seven men, including her skipper, did everything from swabbing the deck to stoking the engine to feeding the twenty Greenland sled dogs.

Nevertheless, as he sneaked out of Oslo Fjord that rainy June midnight in 1903, Captain Amundsen was sublimely pleased with his herring sloop and his six piratical conspirators. The *Gjoa*, loaded down with enough provisions to last five years, might look like a moving van

afloat. But she was the same age as himself—thirty years old—and he thought this was a splendid omen.

His handpicked crew, all dashingly moustached, were experienced seamen in northern waters. Equally important to Amundsen they were all good companions. "We constituted a little republic on board the *Gjoa*," he fondly recollected. "And the voyage was more like a holiday trip of comrades ... full of good humor, song, and laughter."

Much of the light-heartedness was generated by two crew members who later accompanied their Chief on his South Pole expedition. One was second mate Helmer Hanssen, who wrote a book about his experiences, *Voyages Of A Modern Viking*. The short, wiry, convivial thirty-three-year-old had sailed the Arctic seas aboard Norwegian whalers since the age of twelve. "He knew no fear," Amundsen said of him, "and was as nimble as a squirrel." Hanssen was a crackshot hunter, who thought nothing of bagging thirteen caribou in an outing. He was a superb ice navigator, reputedly able to smell out the ice ahead. He was a first-class dogteam driver, who sometimes engaged his shipmates in a duel testing the toughness of their hickory dogwhip handles. And when he wasn't playing *Ta-Ra-Ra-Boom-De-Ay* on the *Gjoa's* gramophone, he was playing practical jokes.

The butt of the horseplay was cook Adolf Henrik Lindstrom. He was a plump, jovial thirty-eight-year-old Norwegian with an enormous moustache and a paunch to match. Lindstrom had served as cook on the *Fram's* second voyage to the eastern Canadian Arctic skippered by Captain Otto Sverdrup—and later he could boast that his hot wheat cakes had satisfied the palates of Pole-hunters on the top and bottom of the world. If they claimed not to be satisfied, he would point to his immense girth and say, "It's all the same to me. I am just as round, I am." Henriki, as he was known to the Eskimos, was an amateur collector of arctic fauna for an Oslo zoology professor; he was also an expert whist player and a heavy gambler. In a pinch, he made meteorological observations, took soundings, attended the engine, and entertained the crew as well with a wind-up toy doll, petticoated Olava, who displayed her naked bottom as she turned somersaults.

The four other sailors were equally versatile. Meteorologist Gustav Juel Wiik, destined to come to a tragic end on this voyage, was the youngest of the crew at twenty-five. First mate Anton Lund, a veteran arctic harpoonist and ice pilot, was the "old man" of the group at age thirty-nine. Both were talented violinists, and diverted the Eskimos with their rendition of the "Apache Waltz."

Peder Ristvedt, thirty, the baldish engineer with the sweeping moustachios, was a jack-of-all trades; he was an accomplished meteorologist, hunter, instrumentmaker and blacksmith. First Lieutenant Godfred Hansen, a twenty-seven-year-old Danish Navy officer, had navigated ships to Iceland and the Faroes; he was proficient in astronomy, photography, geology; in mending gloves on the ship's Singer sewing machine, and spinning amusing yarns about his past voyages.

"All of us were travelled men," summed up Helmer Hanssen, "who could both lie and tell true tales from life."

Amundsen was singularly candid about his feelings as his ship threaded through ice-strewn Baffin Bay and steered for Lancaster Sound, the traditional gateway to the Northwest Passage. Relieving the watch one chill August night, he stood at the helm and shivered in the damp fog. "Perhaps as an Arctic traveller, I ought not to admit this, but anyhow I did feel perishing with cold," he wrote in his two-volume journal, *The Northwest Passage*. "For the sake of my comrades, I maintained a calm demeanour as usual."

At twilight on August 22 he anchored reverentially at Beechey Island. It was the barren speck of rock where Sir John Franklin's *Erebus* and *Terror* had made their last known winter harbor more than half a century previously. Amundsen walked up the shingly beach. He straightened a cross marking a grave of one of the mariners who had died of scurvy while seeking the Passage. "I had a deep, solemn feeling that I was on holy ground," said Amundsen. At the same time a chill ran up his spine. The sadness of death and failure hung over the place and he wondered if his luck would be better. "Were we and the *Gjoa* to meet the same fate?"

Resolutely he steered southward down Peel Sound and Franklin Strait. He was heading for King William Island, that diamond-shaped cemetery where more than one hundred of Franklin's men had perished. In "virgin waters," as he put it, he was prepared to put to the test the speculation of previous Passage theorists. If he attempted to sail straight down along the *west* side of King William, he would undoubtedly butt against the impenetrable icepack that had crushed Franklin's ships. His sole hope was to detour around the *east* side of the diamond-shaped island. Then he would have to pray that the *Gjoa* could slither through those narrow, rocky corridors, James Ross Strait and Rae Strait and Simpson Strait.

On his perilous detour Amundsen, not a particularly religious man,

indeed found himself praying. "In my distress I sent up (I honestly confess it) an ardent prayer to the Almighty," he wrote.

They were in one tight spot after another. First a fire broke out in the engine room; it threatened to blow up cases of fuel and explosives. Feverishly scooping up buckets of sea water, they extinguished the blaze in the nick of time. Then, in the shallow, uncharted waters, the *Gjoa* was grounded on a huge shoal of jagged rocks. Amundsen ordered cases of dogs' pemmican thrown overboard to lighten the ship; hoisted sails; and then prayed for a stiff breeze that would help them ride over the reef. But it was a sleety gale that blew up and the *Gjoa* almost foundered in its fury.

"The spray was dashing over the ship, and the wind came in gusts, howling through the rigging," wrote Amundsen. In the high choppy sea, the *Gjoa* seemed to "dance from one rock to another," and then, with her timbers shrieking and groaning like a wounded animal, she seemed permanently pinned on the last ledge of reef.

Amundsen says he struggled, with great inner turmoil, to reach a decision: "I had to make my choice—to abandon the *Gjoa*, take to the boats, and let her be smashed up; or to dare the worst, and perchance go to meet death with all souls on board."

He gathered his crew on deck and consulted them. His heart was gladdened when, with one voice, they all volunteered to throw further provisions overboard and make a last attempt to save the ship. "Hey-presto!" wrote Amundsen. "We went for the deck cargo and cases were flung over the rail like trusses of hay."

Not everything was heaved overboard. Second mate Hanssen tells us that cook Lindstrom shouted, "Here's something that must not go to the bottom!" He held up a bottle of champagne and a bottle of wine from the Oslo Oyster Cellar restaurant. Let the storm blow; the jolly Pole rovers wouldn't let anything prevent them from polishing off the two bottles.

After less precious cargo had been discarded, Amundsen climbed up to the crow's nest in the flying spray and freezing spume. The keel gave a convulsive shudder, he says, "the mast trembled, and the *Gjoa* seemed to pull herself together for a last final leap. She was lifted up high and flung bodily on to the bare rocks, bump, bump—with a terrific force. . . . Yet another bump, worse than ever, then one more, and we slid off."

The gale continued to lash them for five days and five nights.

*It took him from 1903 to 1906, but with six fellow crew members and a 47-ton herring fishery smack, The Gjoa, Amundsen captured the grandfather of all geographic prizes, the Northwest Passage. His ship is shown here grounded on a shoal of rocks before being safely berthed in Gjoa Haven on the southeast coast of King William Island.* NEW YORK PUBLIC LIBRARY PICTURE COLLECTION

When it was over, Amundsen and his crew celebrated with a bowl of smoking hot toddy.

It was now the second week of September, 1903, and the long arctic night was drawing near, and Amundsen knew they must soon batten down for the winter. At the entrance of Simpson Strait he was therefore relieved to hear Helmer Hanssen cry out from the crow's nest: "I see the finest little harbor in the world!"

Through his Zeiss binoculars, Amundsen scanned the landlocked bay on the southeast coast of King William Island and agreed it was perfect. Circling limestone hills sheltered it from the winds. Caribou roved near the sandy, moss-clad beach, making it a veritable arctic paradise. Furthermore it was about ninety miles west of the north magnetic pole, and therefore an ideal campsite for a meteorological station. He named it Gjoa Haven, and it was to be their snug wintering home for two years.

The shacks they built ashore were likewise appropriately named. The magnetic observatory was christened Variation House. It consisted of forty wooden cases held together by copper rather than iron nails, so the delicate recording instruments could not be disturbed. Nearby young meteorologist Gustav Wiik and his assistant, Peder Ristvedt, made their living quarters in a hut constructed of sixty cases. It was grandly named Villa Magnet. Amundsen felt that its interior, filled with the operatic strains of Wiik's violin and warmly insulated with sand, was cozier than the damp quarters aboard ship. "Every night during the winter," said Amundsen, "we had to chop large icebergs out of our bunks."

To keep his men fit, Amundsen recommended that each spend an hour a day skiing up in the hills. During these excursions the sportsmen, led by Helmer Hanssen, collectively bagged more than two hundred caribou.

One October morning, while chatting on deck with his second mate, Amundsen noticed some far-off specks on top of the hill. "Well, Hanssen," he said, "don't you feel like hunting reindeer today?"

The second mate, who had uncommonly sharp eyesight, squinted at the moving figures. "Ah, yes," he said quietly, "but not *that* sort of reindeer over there. They walk on two legs."

Amundsen rushed to fetch his binoculars and trained them on five approaching men. "Eskimo!" he said.

Amundsen described his first meeting with the Netsilik Eskimos as an almost burlesque affair. He had read in Franklin's narrative that the

"Arctic barbarians" were sometimes hostile. Supposedly they were most impressed by British military pomp. So Amundsen dragooned his two best rifle-shots, Helmer Hanssen and first mate Anton Lund, to accompany him as he sallied forth to subdue the enemy. His recruits were to be covered by marksmen from the deck in case an army of Eskimo cohorts was lurking behind the hill.

Amundsen says he meticulously inspected his brave troops. Cocking their rifles, Hanssen and Lund did a splendid job of standing at attention, clicking their heels, and saluting. "I myself," he wrote, "threw out my chest, made a regulation right-about-turn, and gave the command, 'Forward—march!'"

He was a trifle annoyed that cook Lindstrom and the others on deck were grinning at his charade of a military parade. "Well, I thought, it is easy enough to be gay when standing well-sheltered on board, while we were going forth to meet the uncertain, possibly death, here on the open field." Nevertheless, he wrote, "I advanced in my best martial style, and behind me I heard the tramp of my men in well-timed cadence."

General Amundsen was taken aback as he deployed his ranks within two hundred yards of the furred enemy. They weren't impressed either. With their bows and their arrows, and their copper-colored features, they reminded him of the Indians he had read about in James Fenimore Cooper's *Deerslayer*. But they didn't behave like warlike Mohicans. They were openly laughing.

"*Tima!*" cried Amundsen. It was one of the few Eskimo words he knew. It meant "Peace!" or "Good friend!"

The Eskimos bettered him. "*Manik-tu-mi!*" they roared with laughter. Amundsen understood it to mean, "Happy to make your acquaintance!"

"In a moment we flung away our rifles and hastened toward our friends," says Amundsen, "and with the universal shout of '*Manik-tu-mi! Manik-tu-mi!*' we embrace and pat each other, and it would be hard to say on which side the joy is greater."

By and large it was a happy mutual acquaintanceship. Soon Amundsen found himself mayor of a miniature town of sixty Eskimos camped in the vicinity of Gjoa Haven. At first, it must be said, he ruled rather autocratically. To prevent them from pilfering, he gave a demonstration of *Kabloona* sorcery. He arranged to have a charge of explosives buried in a snowhouse some distance from the ship. Then he gathered the natives on board and delivered a lecture on the terrible

punishment the godlike white men could inflict if angered. Giving the signal to ignite the concealed powder train, he pointed to the igloo. "See what we can do if you misbehave!" he said. The igloo blew sky high; the Eskimos quaked with fear.

Gradually, however, he won their respect and friendship by more legitimate means and they learned from each other. Though he never did completely "go native," he mastered the art of snow igloo masonry, became a fairly good kayaker, and recognized the superiority of their arctic survival techniques. Of sledge runners, for example, he acknowledged: "One can't do better in these matters than copy the Eskimo and let the runners get a fine coating of ice; then they slide like butter."

He used his university training to doctor their illnesses with *Kabloona* medicines. But he learned on his part the absurdity of the traditional white man's remedy of rubbing snow on frostbitten skin. Eskimos were not that foolish; they massaged the spot with a warm hand.

The cultural interchange produced its comic episodes. Amundsen learned to appreciate Eskimo hospitality from an aristocratic, almost haughty-looking fellow named Atikleura. Everything about this luxuriantly bearded grandee was superior and choice—his clothes, his dogs, his spotlessly tidy igloo. Even his well-bred, tattooed wife was a charming and dignified hostess. They generously presented their *Kabloona* guest with a fine bearskin and an artistically fabricated caribou tunic.

"In my eagerness I wanted to strike while the iron was hot," said Amundsen, somewhat ashamed of his boorishness, "and hinted that I should greatly value a suit of underclothing as well." To his astonishment, Atikleura promptly undressed, took off his own underwear, and handed it to his guest. "I must say I was not in the habit of exchanging underwear in the presence of a lady," wrote Amundsen; he felt embarrassed and chastened, but recognized it would be impolite to offend. "I quickly seated myself, veiled my charms as well as I could with the bed clothes, and was soon clad in Atikleura's still warm underclothing."

For a buccaneering explorer, Amundsen seemed unusually prudish. He claims that he sternly resisted sleeping with the pretty Eskimo maidens offered to him in barter for a few needles. He further maintains that wife borrowing, "though not quite unknown in *Kabloona Land* either," was a practice virtuously shunned by his crew.

Evidently they were taught to quell what he termed their "baser

passions" after witnessing the downfall of their ship handyman, Talurnakto. He was a good-natured Eskimo hired by Amundsen because he seemed so eager to imitate the white men. He did odd jobs aboard ship, bustling about with his newly acquired ragged blue sweater, discarded shirt collar, and old cycling cap. From Helmer Hanssen he learned how to smoke and swear, "Well, I'll be damned." From Amundsen he learned how to use a fork and wash and dry a cup after using it, although, Amundsen was amused to note, Talurnakto licked the cup clean with his tongue and used his shirt as a towel. "Take him all round, he was really a regular 'Arry, and always cheerful," said Amundsen. "He was perpetually singing—invariably one note, like a bumble bee in a bedroom at night."

Alas, Talurnakto succumbed to his baser passions. He ran off with another man's wife, a veritable Amazon, says Amundsen, named Pandora. Unfortunately for Talurnakto, he was compelled to run off with Pandora's husband, too. The Amazon was insatiable in her demands and liked to have two spouses around to henpeck.

Talurnakto returned to his job as ship handyman a woefully changed man. As Amundsen tells the morality tale: "He had plainly had a very trying task as a lover. His round face was thin and drawn out and bore the stamp of the deepest despondency. He had no cherished mementoes of his amorous adventure. All his property, knife, spear and pipe, had been given over to his beloved—or rather to the husband, who required some recompense for his liberality. Poor Talurnakto returned from his escapade stripped of almost everything."

Talurnakto soon regained status, lording it over the other Eskimos who came to visit the ship. He had privileged sleeping quarters and they didn't. Usually Amundsen held open house each evening between seven and nine o'clock. He traded needles and nails for their artifacts which he was collecting for the Oslo Museum.

When the weather was extremely cold, he felt sorry for his visitors and invited them to stay overnight. Some nights he had as many as thirteen guests in his aft cabin. They lay on the bare floor, blanketed with caribou skins and wedged together, he says, like Norwegian herring in a barrel.

Cook Lindstrom, who bunked in the forecabin, turned up his nose at the house guests. He felt they smelled terribly of seal oil. To hurry them on their way past his cabin, he developed a ruse. He turned up the stove, counting on the heat and their bulky fur clothes to make them feel unwelcome.

Amundsen was more tolerant. "I never thought they suggested Eau de Cologne, violets, or new-mown hay when they took off their *kamiks* (sealskin boots) at night," he said. "But we were putting up with a little inconvenience in order to proffer hospitality, which was a simple matter to us and also inexpensive."

The only time Lindstrom would open his cabin door to Eskimo visitors was when they brought specimens for his cherished natural history collection. His collecting passion led to the cook's comeuppance. Helmer Hanssen relates in his memoirs the wry story of how word got around among the Eskimos that Lindstrom was paying fantastically high barter prices for arctic *pediculi*, vulgarly known as lice. The natives produced such a surplus that the market was swiftly flooded, but the amateur collector kept being besieged by bearers of *pediculi*.

One Sunday, while Lindstrom was trying to catch an after-dinner snooze in his cabin, two Eskimo women hammered on the door. When Hanssen opened it, one woman held up her fist. "*Ellipsi koma pelliti?*" she exclaimed, meaning, "Do you want lice?"

His cabin mates aroused Lindstrom with a fervent cry: "Here are some more *pediculi*. You will have to get up."

"I don't *want* any more lice!"

"Well, you better come and take them anyhow, or else they'll throw them into the berths."

"Lindstrom had to get up and explain to the ladies that not only was there a slump in the lice market, but there was no demand for them whatsoever," wrote Hanssen. "The ladies then sat down, opened up their fists, and ate the lice—one by one, with obvious relish."

The fastidious chef was aghast, but not Amundsen. In the interests of gustatory science, he founded a Polar Gourmet Society dedicated to tasting every Eskimo delicacy. Peder Ristvedt had to serve as cook for the Society; for Lindstrom vowed, "I'd rather throw myself into the sea than prepare such stuff." To Lindstrom's chagrin, the Society gourmets solemnly proclaimed fox steak and seal flipper superior to any of his concoctions and they announced he would have to improve in the culinary line before matching caribou tripe à la Eskimo.

Thus challenged, Lindstrom surpassed himself on Christmas Eve. Wearing a paper cap lettered "To the fattened Polar pigs," he served a prodigious banquet of roast duck and ptarmigan, honey cakes and wheat cakes and plum puddings galore, hot toddy and punch and *aquavit*. He topped it all by marching into the mess with an artificial Christmas tree festooned with colored paper and blazing with candles.

Wrapped toys which Amundsen had brought from home were then drawn by lot, and the men played with the games as gleefully as if they were children. Wiik and Lund got out their violins and serenaded the Eskimos with Christmas carols. And the sled dogs howled and the Norse buccaneers wept as they joined in crooning the chorus of the hymn, "Now Mother Lightens All the Lights, No Corner Shall Be Dark."

And so two Christmases passed. Amundsen shivered through the sixty-below-zero chill of January, which the natives called *Kapidra*, translated as meaning, "It is cold, the Eskimo is freezing." Presently the spring ice in Simpson Strait was a bright bluish green, and the temperature was up in the seventies, and bees buzzed over the sprouting yellow poppies. The June month of *Kavaruvi* ("The seals are shedding their coats") swiftly merged into the August month of *Ichyavi* ("The young birds are hatched") and Amundsen felt it was time to leave and complete "the hitherto unsolved link in the Northwest Passage."

He had clearly fulfilled his scientific obligations to Nansen. He had relocated the north magnetic pole—not far from where it had first been detected more than seventy years ago by Sir James Clark Ross. His men had made herculean sledge expeditions—on one eight-hundred-mile trip mapping the eastern coastline of Victoria Island up as far as Cape Nansen. He had amassed enough Eskimo artifacts to delight the soul of any anthropologist.

One thing he had not done: truly mastered the Eskimo language. As Helmer Hanssen wittily phrased it, "When we talked Eskimo, they thought we were talking Norwegian, and when they tried Norwegian, it sounded to us like Eskimo." Amundsen wanted to bring a Netsilik Eskimo back with him to Oslo for a thorough ethnological study. At first his ship handyman, Talurnakto, agreed to serve as that candidate. But then, a few weeks before the scheduled departure, the usually cheerful fellow burst into tears. He pleaded with *Amekjenna* (pidgin Eskimo for Chief Amundsen) not to take him away to *Kabloona noona* (Land of the White Men). He had been shown horrible book illustrations depicting the bloodshed of the Boer War and he wanted no part of that so-called civilization.

Amundsen understood and was in complete sympathy with his point of view. "We were able to compare those Eskimo who had come into contact with civilization with those who had not," he later recorded. "And I must state it as my firm conviction that the latter—the Eskimo living absolutely isolated from civilization of any kind—are undoubtedly the happiest, healthiest, most honourable and most con-

tented among them. . . . My sincerest wish for our friends, the Nechilli Eskimo, is that civilization may *never* reach them."

However, he was pleased when a bright, seventeen-year-old Eskimo orphan named Manni volunteered to accompany them to *Kabloona Land.* Manni had an engaging manner that won everybody's heart. Amundsen paid his foster father a knife and a file for him. The lad was scrubbed with soap and his long hair doused with insect powder and neatly combed. When he was dressed up in white stockings, knee breeches, and a pale blue bathing cap that Amundsen had once picked up at a summer resort, everybody thought he looked exceedingly handsome.

On August 13, 1905, Amundsen took leave of Gjoa Haven amid laughter and tears. The laughter came from his Eskimo lady friends. He had set up hundreds of empty tin cans on the brow of a hill and, after a count of "One! Two! Three! Go!", he had allowed the female contestants to race up the hill for these trophies. As he watched them scramble gleefully after the prizes, he thought what a joyous race they were, content with so little. "Taking them altogether," he considered, "they were the merriest people I have met."

The tears came from the many friends he had made, among them Atikleura, the aristocrat, and the amorous handyman, Talurnakto, who wisely preferred Gjoa Haven to civilization. They had all assembled in the misty morning on shore to wish Amekjenna a last *Manik-tu-mi!*—"Happy to make your acquaintance!"

"Talurnakto accompanied us in his kayak out towards Fram Point," wrote Amundsen, "and we could hear him calling out his '*God-da! God-da!*' ('Good day! Good day!') long after he was lost in the fog."

For Amundsen the next two weeks were a purgatory. The strain of negotiating the "Arctic Zigzag," he wrote, aged him so that he looked like a haggard old man in his sixties. It was nerve-wracking to tiptoe the *Gjoa* around the unsurveyed, rock-studded shallows of Simpson Strait; at times there was only one inch of water under the ship's keel. And it was hellish snaking about the tortuous, berg-riddled channels of the sea he named after Norway's Queen; at times he was so bewildered by the hairpin twists and turns of Queen Maud Gulf that he was forced to swivel back on his tracks.

"We bungled through Zigzag as if we were drunk," he said. "I was at the helm and kept shuffling my feet out of sheer nervousness. . . . The lookout man jumped about in the crow's nest like a maniac. . . . We barely managed to scrape over."

When the *Gjoa* finally weaved her way into the relatively safer waters of what has since been named Amundsen Gulf, her skipper had a curious reaction. Amundsen felt ravenously hungry. Knife in hand, he clambered up the rigging into the shrouds where carcasses of caribou were hanging. He slashed furiously at the raw meat and thrust the frozen chunks down his throat like a famished animal. He ate and ate until he felt sick. He vomited and devoured more. His rapacious appetite satiated, he staggered to his bunk and enjoyed his first rest in two weeks.

At 8 AM on August 27, 1905, Lieutenant Godfred Hansen rushed into the cabin and woke him with a thrilling cry: "Vessel in sight, sir!"

"I suppose it was weakness on my part," wrote Amundsen, "but I could feel tears coming to my eyes. . . . The words were magical."

He hurriedly dressed himself. For a moment he paused in front of Nansen's portrait hanging on the wall. "It seemed as if the picture had come to life, as if he winked at me, nodding, 'Just what I thought my boy!' I nodded back, smiling and happy, and went on deck."

The black two-masted schooner he saw through his binoculars flew the Stars and Stripes. She was the American whaler, *Charles Hanson*, out of San Francisco. Amundsen boarded her. On the quarter deck he was greeted by her white-whiskered skipper, Captain James McKenna, the first white stranger he had seen in two years.

"Are you Captain Amundsen?"

"Yes," said Amundsen, surprised that his name would be known in this desolate region.

"Is this the first vessel you have met?"

"Yes."

The old whaling captain shook his hand heartily. "I am exceedingly pleased to be the first to welcome you on getting through the Northwest Passage."

Amundsen gratefully received such luxuries as a year-old San Francisco newspaper, a sack of onions and a sack of potatoes. More immediately to the point he was glad to get the newest American chart of the ice-strewn waters that barred his way on his last lap across the roof of Yukon and Alaska.

His troubles were not yet over. At King Point, on the north shore of the Yukon, just beyond the brown mudflats of the Mackenzie River delta, thick ice closed in. The *Gjoa* was trapped for a third winter. Amundsen was disappointed, but he made the best of it. He arranged for meteorologist Wiik and the other crew members to build a sod hut

magnetic observatory ashore. And he instructed Lieutenant Hansen to look after young Manni aboard ship.

Then he had a trip thirty-five miles across the ice west to Canada's Herschel Island, where five American whalers were also holed up for the winter. There he learned that the whaling captains had chipped in to send an experimental dog sledge post five hundred miles inland to Eagle City, Alaska, where a telegraph station was located. The conqueror of the Northwest Passage was naturally eager to convey word of his success to the outside world, and so he offered his services.

It was a bizarre journey. The postal inspector in charge was a fat, bandy-legged incompetent, who had shipwrecked his own whaler. He refused to take along nourishing pemmican, scornfully arguing, "Such food is not fit for a dog to eat." Instead, he sat on the sledge all the way, feasting on sacks of cooked beans, while urging Amundsen to run ahead in the deep snow breaking trail. Amundsen gritted his teeth and made the trek in six weeks, arriving at his destination in sixty below zero weather.

On his way back north with a congenial Eskimo dog-sledder named Jimmy, Amundsen encountered a white mailman destined to become a legend in the Arctic. "Look," said Jimmy, pointing to a black dot jogging on the frozen Yukon River. "A man traveling alone without a dog."

It was Hubert Darrell, a Klondike gold-rusher who had turned northern mail carrier for the Hudson's Bay Company. Amundsen considered the quiet, unassuming Scot the bravest man he had ever met. All alone, dragging his toboggan, Darrell trudged hundreds of miles, distributing letters to the gold camps and Mountie detachments and Arctic whalers, and thought nothing at all of his exploits. Amundsen says they became warm friends at once and he was later dismayed to receive news that this undaunted man of action was lost in a snowstorm near the mouth of the Mackenzie. "I stood looking after him as he disappeared from view," Amundsen recalled their last meeting, "and I thought if you got together a few more men of his stamp, you could get to the moon."

On Amundsen's return to the iced-in *Gjoa* in March of 1906, two tragedies struck at his shipmates and made him realize all the more how the Arctic could be a cruel adversary. Meteorologist Gustav Wiik, the youngest white crew member, was the first victim. Wiik complained of sharp abdominal pains and chills and fevers. After consulting *Uckermann's Medical Guide*, Amundsen assumed it must be pleurisy or

pneumonia. He first applied cooling bandages and then a mustard plaster. These seemed to help, lowering the patient's temperature from 104 degrees to 101. Amundsen thought he was improving; for the youthful fiddle-player was laughing and joking in the small cabin ashore when Amundsen retired for the night aboard the *Gjoa.*

But later that evening, while a blizzard raged outside, Wiik awoke shivering violently. Lindstrom the plump cook sharing the bed with him, covered him with additional furs and fired the stove. Wiik continued to shudder and cold perspiration beaded his deathly pale face. He begged Lindstrom to lie on him. The cook did so, pressing the warmth of his fleshy girth onto his sick shipmate's body until the attack subsided.

Amundsen was now alarmed. He asked Jimmy, the Eskimo dog-team driver, to run over to Herschel Island nearby and fetch a doctor from a whaling ship. But the snowstorm was blustering so fiercely that even the hardy Eskimo could not venture to make the trip until five o'clock that afternoon.

At 5 PM, the bell in the captain's cabin aboard the *Gjoa* rang ominously. Amundsen had strung it up between the ship and Wiik's hut for such emergencies, and now he rushed over through the driving snow. He was in time only to hear Wiik breathe his last. There was silence in the room except for the crackle of the stove and the shriek of the wind outside. "I closed the eyes of our late comrade," he said, "and we remained sitting there for a while in silence and sorrow."

The ground's skin of permafrost was so tough they could not bury poor Wiik until May. Then the black-painted coffin containing his remains was sledged to the sod hut which had served as his magnetic observatory. Amundsen read the Lord's Prayer. Then they walled up this makeshift mausoleum with driftwood, and spread turf over it, erected a wooden cross over the hut, and blanketed it with forget-me-nots. Who would have thought, grieved Amundsen, that when Wiik was digging sod for his observatory he was digging his own tomb?

Two months later tragedy overtook its next victim. By July Amundsen had managed to wrestle the *Gjoa* over to Herschel Island to await the final ice breakup. It was partly to give Manni a foretaste of the pleasures and perils of *Kabloona Land.* Though a bachelor, Amundsen dearly loved Eskimo children (he later adopted an orphan Eskimo girl and had her educated in Oslo) and now he treated Manni as though the teenager were his son. He encouraged the boy to take regular lessons in reading and writing from Lieutenant Hansen; scolded him for acquiring

the nasty habit of chewing rank tobacco; gave him a carbine shotgun as a reward for performing the chore of sweeping the cabin so tidily; and to make sure he wouldn't catch cold, helped him change clothes whenever Manni returned from hunting eider ducks.

His fatherly concern extended to the boy's visits to the little Eskimo/white colony that had developed on Herschel Island. An Anglican missionary school and a detachment of the Royal North West Mounted Police had been established there, as well as a Jersey Island Grand Opera Company set up by the whalers. This was all to the good, Amundsen pointed out to Manni. At the same time, he didn't want Manni to mingle too freely with the local Eskimos; they had become dependent on the white man's flour, sugar and whisky, and they had picked up other *Kabloona* vices. "I did not care to have him infected with any of the Eskimos' various diseases with which civilization had gifted them," wrote Amundsen. "For instance, syphilis was very prevalent."

One morning Amundsen left the ship, paternalistically advising Manni to stay away from the roughhouse whalers and to confine his duck-hunting to the waters near the *Gjoa*. Meanwhile the skipper and his first mate rowed a few miles along the shore, scanning the ice and hoping for an open channel. As they were returning to the *Gjoa*, Amundsen was chilled by the sight of the ship's flag flying at half mast. "What can it mean?" he wondered, and he had a terrible premonition. "I at once thought of Manni."

He was met on deck by a white-faced Lieutenant Hansen, the other crew member who loved the cabin boy almost as much as Amundsen and had taught him his ABCs. The lieutenant's announcement was stark. Manni was dead.

The lad had gone out duck-hunting in a canvas boat, wielding Amundsen's shotgun and proudly wearing the blue bathing cap that Amundsen had given him. The lieutenant had last seen him standing upright in his little boat and taking aim at a bevy of eider ducks. When he next glanced in that direction, all the lieutenant could see was Manni's boat rocking in the waves, empty and half filled with water, the oars drifting in the icy sea. A search party could find no trace of the boy. Amundsen lamented that he had never taught the orphan lad how to swim, and now the Arctic had taken its toll, and Manni would never learn how to survive in *Kabloona Land*.

Amundsen broke free of the ice and steered the *Gjoa* on the last leg of her journey with a heavy heart. He could not reconcile himself to

*Amundsen wept at the death by drowning of his adopted Eskimo son, Manni, shown wearing the explorer's hand-me-down blue bathing cap.*

*The strain of negotiating the "Arctic Zigzag" so aged him, said Amundsen, that he looked like a haggard 60-year-old.* NORSK
POLARINSTITUTT

those two deaths on the threshhold of victory. His spirits did not revive until the night of August 31, 1906. With an ice-smashed propeller and a broken mast gaff, his little herring sloop at last completed the North-west Passage, linking the waters of the Atlantic and Pacific. She limped into the gold rush town of Nome, Alaska, amid the blaze of a powerful searchlight and the jubilant roar of welcome from a thousand throats ashore. Amundsen gathered his crew on deck and they quaffed a drink of the best Norwegian Lyshom's *aquavit.* Tears came to his eyes as he stepped ashore to the cheering and the whistling and the shouting. The frontier boom town went wild over him. Amundsen always did like a good party, and at the flossiest saloon in Nome's largest hotel, Helmer Hanssen tells us, "there were beautiful ladies and dancing and fun till far into the morning."

The gala celebrations were repeated two months later when the *Gjoa* sailed into San Francisco. Amundsen presented his gallant little ship to Golden Gate Park, and she was exhibited there until July of 1972. Then, on the centenary of Amundsen's birth, she was returned home to Oslo Fjord, and she can be seen there today, after being buffeted by ice and storms, quietly at peace with the sea and her immortality.

Her glory-bound captain did not come so easily upon tranquility. It seemed as though the explorer's insatiable need for exciting conquest could never be fulfilled, and for the rest of his life he was responding to the siren call of what he personified as the Polar Enchantress: "Inviting and attractive, the fair one lies before us. Yes, we hear you calling, and we shall come. You shall have your kiss, if we pay for it with our lives. . . . We always go back, we polar travellers, and that is exactly how it is for me."

Time and again he went back, despite one turbulent crisis after another. He had a fiery temper and craved adulation, and his outspoken candor frequently engendered criticism. He was often envied or cheated or misunderstood. Yet he would not be beaten and he continued to add to his string of triumphs.

On December 14, 1911, using all the hard-won travel techniques he had learned from the Netsilik Eskimos, he and four Norwegian comrades unfurled their flag on King Haakon VII Plateau at the very bottom of the globe. "Five weatherbeaten, frostbitten fists they were that grasped the pole," wrote Amundsen, "raised the waving flag in the air, and placed it as the first at the geographic South Pole."

His coup outraged English patriots and dog-lovers. The foreign in-

terloper had poached on what was deemed a British preserve; he had made his sledge dash of some seven hundred miles seem like a holiday lark, placing frozen fish in the snow to mark his food depots; and the heartless fellow had the gall to name one spot the Butcher's Shop where he had slaughtered his dogs and eaten them as though they were succulent cutlets. They felt it was manifestly unfair to poor starving Robert Falcon Scott. That gallant Englishman, depending upon Shetland ponies, had arrived heartbroken thirty-five days later to find the Pole pre-empted and a note in a silken tent which Amundsen brazenly asked him to forward to King Haakon.

The Royal Geographical Society never forgave Amundsen for his buccaneering bad manners. At a London banquet supposed to honor him for his indisputable geographic feat, Lord Curzon, the nominal president, ended his speech with the derogatory piece of sarcasm, "I therefore propose three cheers for the dogs!" Amundsen resigned in a huff from the Society, declaring, "The British are a race of very bad losers."

The low point in his tempestuous career came with his laborious negotiation of the Northeast Passage. He squandered close to a quarter of a million dollars on building an egg-shaped, one-hundred-and-sixty-foot-long ship. He named her the *Maud* after Norway's Queen, and christened her with ice rather than champagne, saying it was more fitting, since she would have to drift through ice water and not wine. The jinxed ship took from 1918 to 1925 to complete her drift north of Russia to Alaska; but it was financial hot water that largely plagued her skipper. His business manager embezzled funds until Amundsen was forced to declare bankruptcy. His own brother, Leon, sued him for twenty-five thousand dollars and attempted to seize Amundsen's home near Oslo. The Norwegian press turned against him and printed the slander that the Eskimo girl he had adopted was his own illegitimate child.

Amundsen was an embittered man. He was yesterday's hero, a seeming has-been, vainly trying to pay off his debts by lecturing to half-empty halls in the United States. Then one day out of the blue the telephone rang in his hotel room at the Waldorf-Astoria in New York.

"Mr. Amundsen?"

"Yes. Amundsen speaking."

"Lincoln Ellsworth here."

"Who are you?"

"I am an amateur interested in exploration, and I might be able to supply some money for another expedition."

Ellsworth, the American millionaire sportsman, was clearly a god-send. He enabled Amundsen, down-and-out in his fifties, to embark on a new career in the pioneering age of the flying machine.

With ninety-five thousand dollars donated by Ellsworth, Amundsen acquired two sea planes which they planned to fly six hundred miles from Spitsbergen to the North Pole. One must remember that it was 1925, two years before Charles Lindbergh made his transatlantic flight. Therefore Amundsen's two Dornier "flying boats," as his N24 and N25 were then called, seem by today's standards the flimsiest of flying machines. They were radioless, open-cockpit crates, which meant that the three occupants in each were exposed to the direct blast of the polar winds. And since neither Amundsen nor Ellsworth was a trained pilot, they had to depend on others to handle the primitive instruments.

On May 21, 1925, the two amateur aviators and their four technicians took off from King's Bay on the northwest tip of Spitsbergen to perform what the world press called the first "hop to the Pole." Parachutes were buckled on their backs and their flying attire was picturesque. They wore sun goggles, leather-lined flying helmets, hooded parkas, heavy gloves, wool underwear, oversize canvas shoes stuffed with hay, and white scarves jauntily tucked around their necks.

For eight hours everything seemed to go well on their flight over the endless expanse of hummocky, shifting ice and cracks of blue-green water. Then one of their Rolls-Royce engines, which had carried them at an average speed of seventy-five miles per hour, began to cough and choke ominously. At close to 88 degrees north latitude, some one hundred and thirty miles from the Pole, a forced landing was necessary.

The prospect was terrifying. "It was like trying to set down a ship on the bottom of the Grand Canyon," Ellsworth remembered. "Great blocks of ice were upended or piled one upon another. Ice pressure ridges stood up like fortress walls."

They managed to pancake down on a relatively ice-free lagoon. But one plane was totally disabled, the floes were closing in menacingly, and they held the dubious distinction of being the first polar explorers to be shipwrecked in a plane. They attached skis to the underside of the remaining hydroplane and for the next twenty-four days labored like madmen to clear off a five-hundred-yard runway on the piled-up drift ice. Amundsen estimated they removed three hundred tons of protruding ice and snow using sheath knives and pocket axes. On June 15 they taxied across their air strip and flew up in the air; by a miracle, when

they sputtered down on a patch of water off King's Bay, Spitsbergen, they had just twenty-three gallons of fuel left in their tank.

King's Bay was the jumping off point for Amundsen's epic polar flight the following year aboard the airship *Norge* ("Norway"). Ellsworth had bought her for seventy-five-thousand dollars from Benito Mussolini, the dictator of Italy. She was a semi-rigid, cigar-shaped, silver-skinned cross between a blimp and a zeppelin. The Eskimos who saw her thought she was a giant whale floating in the sky. To Amundsen, she was a "gas bag"; and in his jaundiced view, so was the fascistic designer-pilot, Colonel Umberto Nobile, whom he was virtually compelled to hire in order to fly her. Evidently Nobile embodied the qualities that Amundsen most disliked: he was an ostentatious braggart given more to big talk than action.

Relations between Commander Amundsen and his Italian pilot were frosty even before the huge gas bag rose ponderously up into the sky on the chill morning of May 11, 1926. Nobile swaggered on the scene with five Italian mechanics and his white terrier, Titina—the first dog to fly over the Pole. Nobile stirred up a tremendous fuss about the Norwegian passengers that Amundsen wanted aboard—especially Frederick Ramm, the first journalist to dateline his radioed dispatches as emanating from the North Pole. As one Norwegian technician after another was stricken from the rolls, on Nobile's claim that the dirigible would be overloaded, Amundsen turned to Ellsworth with a grim smile. "If this keeps up," the commander whispered to his partner, "one or both of us may be left behind."

Amundsen ultimately settled on a total complement of sixteen. He flatly rejected as insolent the demand that the Norwegian crew members take an oath of personal allegiance to Nobile, who was, after all, the hireling of the Amundsen-Ellsworth expedition.

The seventy-hour flight to Alaska, at an average cruising speed of fifty miles per hour, was uneventful except for a few serio-comic incidents. After fifteen hours, the mammoth airborne silver fish with her four ice-sheathed gondolas, floated over ninety degrees north latitude. "Here we are!" somebody exclaimed. Sixteen pairs of eyes glanced downward. They were disappointed in what they could detect through the woolly ocean of clouds. The North Pole was nothing but a crinkled sea of ice. Amundsen ritualistically dropped a small silken Norwegian flag. Ellsworth let a pocket-sized Stars and Stripes flutter down. Nobile, despite his cautions about overloading, startled them by his nationalistic hoggishness.

*Amundsen acquired the airship Norge (top) for $75,000 from Italian dictator Benito Mussolini (above) and feuded bitterly with fascistic "gasbag" Col. Umberto Nobile (left) who piloted her over the North Pole. The explorer died nobly later trying to rescue his former foe.*

"Imagine our astonishment to see Nobile dropping overside not one, but armfuls, of flags," wrote Amundsen. "For a few moments the *Norge* looked like a circus wagon of the skies, with great banners of every shape and hue fluttering down around her. Nobile produced one really huge Italian flag. It was so large he had difficulty in getting it out of the cabin window.... Before he could disengage it we must have been five miles beyond the Pole."

According to Amundsen, the "fatuous colonel" almost made a tragic fiasco of the piloting. At one point Nobile apparently went to pieces and was wringing his hands and shedding tears in panic. The airship would have plunged into the ice if the Norwegian navigator had not thrust the weeping Italian aside, taken over the instruments, and raised her to a safe elevation.

Over northern Alaska the airship, coated with about a ton of ice, groped blindly through fog and sleet and missed her destination — Nome. "Could we make a landing here?" asked Amundsen.

Yes, replied the colonel; he was positive he could see a whole troop of cavalry waiting to receive him below.

Amundsen reached for his binoculars and peered down and lost his temper. The hallucination that his ego-ridden pilot had seen was a cluster of rough indentations on the coast.

Finally at Teller, a tiny Alaskan community about sixty miles northwest of Nome, the red-colored ripcords were pulled, and the big gas bag crumpled into a limp, deflated envelope, and her thirty-one-hundred-mile cruise was concluded.

But, with the ending of the flight, the colonel's egomania appears to have expanded. In direct violation of the contract he had signed, the airship's paid chauffeur radioed press dispatches to the world taking full credit for the success of the mission. At one civic reception Amundsen was flabbergasted to find himself ignored while the crowds cheered the "strutting, epauletted colonel," who had smuggled aboard his heavy military uniform all plastered with fascistic medals. The unkindest cut of all occurred when Amundsen tried to recoup his losses by going on an American lecture tour later in 1926. He found that his "upstart" of a pilot had covered the circuit ahead of him and was declaring that it was Benito Mussolini, Italy's Minister of Aviation, who had originated the idea of the *Norge* polar expedition.

The feud between the two piratical glory-seekers ended in tragedy. Amundsen retired from polar exploration, jokingly telling reporters that there were no more thrilling adventures left for him to achieve, ex-

cept possibly trying marriage, "if I can find the right girl." On his part, Nobile was determined to prove to the world that he could accomplish a polar flight without assistance from Amundsen, whom he felt had belittled his superior aviation abilities.

So on May 23, 1928, General Umberto Nobile—elevated in rank by *Il Duce*—set out for the North Pole on a new dirigible named the *Italia*. The airship and her crew of sixteen had been blessed amid much fanfare by Pope Pius XI. "You will consecrate the summit of the world," said the Holy Father, as he presented Nobile with an enormous oaken cross. "It is a bit large, and like all crosses, it will be heavy to carry."

Shortly after midnight on May 24, General Nobile dropped the Pope's cross, *Il Duce's* flag and a medal of the Virgin of the Fire over the sanctified axis of the globe. "The standard of Fascist Italy," read the message radioed to the Italian dictator, "is floating in the breeze over the ice of the Pole." While the *Italia* circled over the consecrated spot, eggnogs were served, a phonograph played *The Bells of San Giusto*, and the general made the Fascist salute as the crew cried, "Long live Nobile!"

Nobile was one of the eight who lived after the *Italia* crashed down in the dense ice about one hundred and eighty miles northeast of Spitsbergen. The other eight met death in various ways. Some were instantly killed during the thousand-foot plunge; some were annihilated when the hydrogen-filled airship caught fire and exploded; and some, it was later alleged, were devoured by their cannibalistic crew mates. The fate of crippled Nobile, his dog Titina, and the other survivors remained a mystery until early June, when the Russians caught a faint S.O.S. transmitted from a handpowered radio which had been set up in a red tent on the ice.

Amundsen was attending a testimonial dinner at Oslo when he received word of the international search for his missing rival. He read the message and said quietly, "I'm ready to leave at once to do anything I can to help."

On June 18, 1928, Amundsen set off from Tromso, Norway, on his last polar journey. With him aboard the blue Latham seaplane was his loyal Norwegian pilot, Lief Dietrichson, who had been with him on his previous plane hop to the Pole, and four volunteer members of a French crew. The twin-engine amphibious Latham was an experimental model, relatively untested, but Amundsen didn't care. At the age of fifty-six, the White Eagle of exploration could not resist another daring exploit.

"Ah, if you only knew how splendid it is up there in the North!" he

is reputed to have said before he set off. "That's where I want to die, and I wish only that death will come to me chivalrously."

The plane roared off toward Spitsbergen and was never seen again. In September, 1928, long after the disgraced Nobile and the other *Italia* survivors had been rescued, a seven-foot-long blue pontoon was fished out of icy waters near the Barents Sea. Aviators identified it as a pontoon ripped by ice from the doomed blue seaplane and the trophy was added to the fifty-one gold medals and many geographic prizes that Amundsen had collected during his stormy career of heroics.

It was somehow a fitting end. Amundsen, the buccaneer, who had always sought to emulate the humanity and compassion of Fridtjof Nansen, had at last matched his mentor on an ennobling mission of mercy. And Amundsen, the romantic, who had pledged conquest of his polar mistress, whether by sea, ski, dog team or flying machine, had fulfilled himself responding to the siren's beckoning call.

"Yes, we hear you calling and we shall come," he had said. "You shall have your kiss, if we pay for it with our lives."

The White Eagle had sacrificed his life giving her a last kiss.

# Chapter 10

# The Race to the Big Nail

The Etah Eskimos were mystified. There were no more than two hundred and fifty of them living in the vicinity of Anoatok— the poetically named "Wind-Loved Spot"—among the blue glacier tongues and violet mountain peaks and ice-scarred valleys on the far northwest shores of Greenland. Yet almost every year, around the turn of the twentieth century, the mad white men sailed to their remote igloos to seek help.

To the Eskimos they were the *Oopernadleet*—the "visitors who come in the Spring." And the visitors were surely *piblokto*—"robbed of their senses." They were willing to hire entire Inuit villages, not to hunt for seal or polar bear, but to guide them on an insane quest. The lunatics wished to leave the safety of coastal land in search of an imaginary point. They said it was some seven hundred miles to the north and somewhere in the centre of five million square miles of ice-strewn ocean. They referred to it as the North Pole.

The white men tried to explain that it was purely geographical and mathematical. No sign would indicate that they had reached the end of their dog sled march over the terrible sea of drifting ice. But from the way the white men's eyes glowed as they spoke of this much coveted prize the Eskimos would not believe them. Not even a *Kabloona* could be so unhinged as to risk death for such an intangible thing. The Pole must be a giant metal spike shining at the top of the world. And so the Eskimos called this most precious of all hunting trophies *Tigi-su*—the Big Nail.

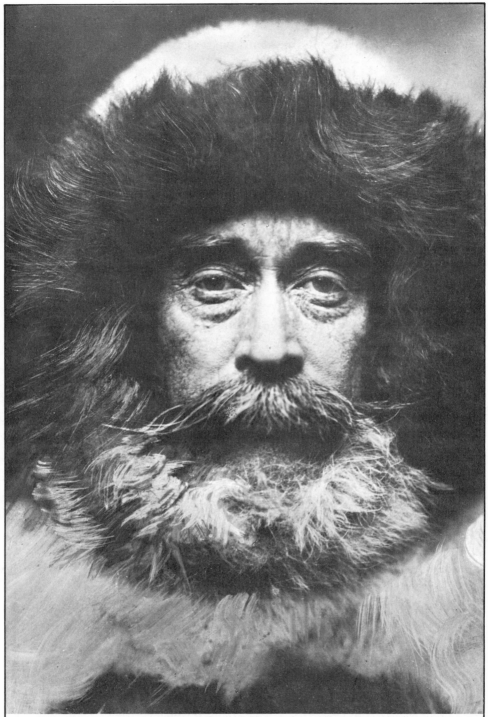

*Robert Peary, ruthless, monomaniacal, but gutsy, claimed to have set foot on the North Pole on April 6, 1909.* BROWN BROTHERS

Two American explorers each claimed to be the first to attain the Big Nail. And perhaps the Eskimos were not far wrong in thinking that each was touched with madness and possessed by the great Devil Spirit that was *Tornarsuk.*

One was Lieutenant Robert Edwin Peary. He was known to the Eskimos as *Pearyaksoak,* meaning Big Peary. The other was Dr. Frederick Albert Cook. He was known as *Doto,* pidgin Eskimo for Doctor. Both were obsessed men, haunted by private demons and fantasies.

Peary, the U.S. Navy career engineer who claimed to have set foot on the Big Nail on April 6, 1909, was undoubtedly the maddest. The "weatherbeaten fanatic" was called many vile things during the virulent feud that raged between himself and Cook, and there was a measure of truth in all the epithets. He was ruthless. He was egocentric. He was tactless. He was a slovenly geographer. He was jealous of other explorers. He arrogated to himself his rivals' discoveries. He was absolutely overweening in his ambition. Even the most worshipful of his contemporary biographers, Commander Fitzhugh Green, author of *Peary, the Man Who Refused to Fail,* conceded he was a brutish leader of men: "Many in Peary's command used to return hating him in a way that murder couldn't gratify."

Peary was, it seems, something of a monster monomaniac.

And yet, despite his twisted personality, Peary must be ranked among the titans of polar exploration. If for nothing else, he ought to be remembered as the discoverer who braved the hellish blizzards and crevasses of northeast Greenland and put Peary Land on the map. He was like a primitive force of nature, a throwback to that roughhewn Elizabethan slave driver, Sir Martin Frobisher. If he was arrogant and overbearing, he was also the embodiment of endurance and courage and adamantine pertinacity. He was consumed by an *idée fixe* and for more than two decades he simply would not give up pursuing his North Pole mania. One will always think of him crippled in a wooden shack in the high Arctic, his eight frostbitten toes snapping off like icicles. Yet the indomitable man painfully managed to scratch on the wall his credo from Seneca: *Inveniam viam aut faciam*—"I shall find a way or make one."

Melodrama was a way of life to him. His speech often sounds like the titles from a silent movie and it smacks of oldfashioned ham. The important thing was that he believed in the heroic phrases he cited from "Horatius at the Bridge" and Tennyson's "Morte d' Arthur," and he strove to live up to them. "The Fates and all Hell are against me," he once wrote in his journal. "But I'll conquer yet!" He meant it.

Cook, the Brooklyn doctor who claimed to have reached the Pole almost a year before Peary on April 21, 1908, was afflicted with a more subtle form of madness. He was as ambitious and as glory-hungry as Peary; but his was a kind of madness of the intellect and the imagination. "Cook was a liar and a gentleman," ran a famous aphorism of the period, "and Peary was neither." Like most witticisms, it was just partly true. Cook and Peary were equally given to exaggeration. Cook's poetic licence with the facts of reality, however, was of a very special kind. It was, first of all, literally poetic. He was a doctor-poet with a flair for the bizarre; he was daring enough to invade the mental borderland between sanity and fantasy. Significantly, he embarked on his polar sledge trip bearing with him two books: the tragedies of Shakespeare and the nightmare horror tales of Edgar Allan Poe.

What strikes one on reading Cook's lurid yet hauntingly beautiful journals, *My Attainment of the Pole* and *Return from the Pole*, is their introspective quality. Although he was an experienced surgeon and geographer, Dr. Cook was not concerned with furthering orthodox hard science. Rather, as he tells us, it was "a crazy hunger I had to satisfy." It was a journey into his spiritual psyche "to prove myself to myself." It was a voyage into the unknown frontiers "between the ears and behind the eyes. Therein is the greatest field for exploration."

Dr. Cook was, in short, the Arctic's first Dr. Sigmund Freud.

During the great North Pole controversy he was variously labeled a humbug, a confidence man and a charlatan—terms frequently hurled at an original thinker, ahead of his time. He was a pioneer psychiatrist constantly scrutinizing the "glimmer from the mirror of self," the subconscious "other-world life" of dreams and illusions. His very language was thus Freudian. "I was puzzled below the realm of consciousness, where, they say, the secret service of the mind grasps the most elusive things." He hoped to dissect "every hidden recess of gray matter . . . to interpret the biographies of self-analysis." He says that "the very air was charged with madness" in the high Arctic, and lent itself to macabre mirages and hallucinations. For that very reason he found this Zero Land of satanic polar night an ideal laboratory. There he could pose the elemental questions of human survival to himself and his two Eskimo companions close to perishing in an ice cave: What does it feel like to freeze to death? To starve to death? To eat human flesh?

"Life after death—what dies at the end?" he pondered, as though it were some detached clinical riddle. "Again and again this thought seeks an answer in the twilight of our death wake."

Cook was, furthermore, an ethnologist far in advance of his time. Historians have neglected to give him full credit for his pioneer anthropological probing. To be sure, it may have been a superb athletic feat for him to survive for fourteen months on his polar trek with just two Eskimo companions. But his real achievement was his adjustment to the thought processes of those two Eskimo companions. He gave them compassion and understanding, and he treated them as human individuals.

This was a genuine breakthrough in polar literature, and it establishes the chief difference between Cook and Peary. From all accounts Cook was an ingratiating, whimsical, sweet-natured fellow, naive and unworldly perhaps, but still a likeable charmer. He appears to have been an almost Charlie Chaplin figure, unassertive and rather dreamy. People loved him for his lack of pretentiousness. "He never complains, never swears, don't care whether his shoes are tied or not, but he just keeps plodding along," said John R. Bradley, the sportsman who gave him a lift on his yacht for the first leg of Cook's North Pole expedition. And explorer Roald Amundsen, who accompanied him on his South Pole voyage, had nothing but admiration for the unassuming way that surgeon Dr. Cook assumed leadership when the commander of the iced-in Antarctic ship ran amok.

"Of all the ship's company, Cook was the one man of unfaltering courage, unfailing hope, endless cheerfulness, and unwearied kindness," Amundsen wrote affectionately in his memoirs. "When anyone was sick, he was at his bedside to comfort him; when anyone was disheartened, he was there to encourage and inspire. And not only was his faith undaunted, but his ingenuity and enterprise were boundless. . . . Cook was the most popular man of the expedition, and . . . won the respect and devotion of us all."

Even Peary was to admit, albeit grudgingly, that Cook was "the perfect gentleman." In contrast, most contemporaries agreed that Peary was as tough as Bessemer steel and inspired awe rather than friendship. His worshipful biographer, Fitzhugh Green, made this revealing comment about Peary: "He was not the born leader, in the sense of being automatically able to inspire his men by that hypnotic charm some men have, the weaker more often than the strong character. There was always too much iron in his will to soften its outer surfaces into a blurred and fuzzy humaneness." Whether it was blurred or fuzzy, Cook had humaneness and Peary had not.

Paradoxically, despite this fundamental difference in character, the

two archrivals had much in common. Privately, both were rather reserved and withdrawn men, each a lone wolf and a romantic, dreaming private dreams of glory. Publicly, they were flamboyant showmen. Possibly because each had to overcome the handicap of a lisp, they enjoyed wringing tears and evoking shudders from thrilled crowds on the lecture circuit who came to listen to their gaudy rhetoric. Cook earned $3,000 a performance in the vaudeville theatres of the Shubert Brothers. Peary raised more than $10,000 from a Buffalo Bill Wild West Show. They were adroit promoters. Cook organized America's first luxury travel cruises to the Arctic, and was eventually jailed for his alleged high-pressure oil stock promotions. Peary had no compunctions about being a huckster, endorsing the advertised brands of cereals, razors, tobaccos and disinfectants, and shrewdly massaged the egos of the multimillionaire patrons of his Peary Arctic Club. His financial backers were supplying the "sinews of war," and their general would perpetuate their names in history by naming after them his northern battle fields of conquest. In an age of rampant American patriotism, both were flag-waving jingoists. Victory over the Pole, said Cook, was an exploit "peculiarly adapted to American dash, and it should be achieved under the Stars and Stripes." Peary actually wrapped the Stars and Stripes around his body on sledge expeditions, and snipped off diagonal strips of Old Glory to mark his farthest northings.

Physically, they looked somewhat alike, too. Both had blue eyes: squinting and wrinkle-ridged as a result of having weathered so many Arctic blizzards and dazzling suns. Cook's were a pallid and milky blue; Peary's penetrating and icy. Each sported a reddish-blond moustache. Cook's was droopy and Chaplinesque; Peary's walruslike and theatrical in the style of Ben Turpin of the silent screen. Each had a sturdy physique: broad in the shoulders and narrow in the hips. Cook was five feet nine inches and weighed about one hundred and sixty pounds; Peary was six feet tall and weighed roughly the same.

Finally, both emerged from strikingly similar backgrounds. Each bore the scars of emotional or physical deprivation.

Peary was born on May 6, 1856, in the backwoods farm community of Cresson, Pennsylvania. His New England forebears were barrel-stave makers of French descent. (The family name was an American modification of the Gallic Pierre.) His father died when he was three years old and Peary was raised on the slender widow's resources of his mother, Mary. He was an only child and she was a possessive, demanding and singularly insensitive woman. She dressed him in girlish clothes and

sent "Bertie" out to play wearing a sunbonnet. Regarded as a sissy by his peers, he was a lonely, reclusive youth. He was given to taking solitary hikes in the woods and made money by stuffing the hawks and eagles that he shot. At an early age he was thrilled when he read the polar adventures of the American explorer, Dr. Elisha Kent Kane, and he was determined to become even more famous.

He seemed obsessed with fame. "I shall not be satisfied until my name is known from one end of the world to the other," he declared. "Remember, Mother, I *must* have fame."

Fame was a constant spur when he was studying civil engineering at Bowdoin College in Brunswick, Maine. He informed his mother that he was resolved to outshine all rivals. He was highly competitive in sports, drama and oratory, and kept dreaming his heroic dreams. Significantly, at the masquerade party of his college fraternity, he posed as Sir Lancelot. And, for the graduation exercises, he wrote an epic poem in which he imagined himself to be Sir Roland, the peerless "knight in sable armor, with a waving snow white crest." The villain of the piece is cursed bombastically:

*Curse thee, curse thee, Roncesvalles!*
*Curse, O curse thee, fatal valley!...*
*And the fiercely howling storm winds,*
*Round the lifeless peaks,*
*Echo "Curse thee, Roncesvalles!"*
*As it were the fiend who speaks.*

Peary was destined one day to use the same sort of florid language when he cursed his polar antagonist as "that blackguard ... that dastardly cur," that "cowardly dog of a sordid imposter."

Frederick Cook, who was to denounce Peary as his "brutally selfish, brutally unscrupulous rival," was born on June 10, 1865, in the backwoods farm community of Hortonville in upstate New York. He came from a long line of physicians of German descent. (The family name was an Americanization of Koch.) His immigrant physician father died when Cook was five years old. The burden of supporting five children fell on the widow Magdalena; she was ultimately reduced to taking in sewing from the sweatshops of New York City.

"My boyhood was not happy," wrote Cook. "As a tiny child I was discontented, and from the early days of consciousness I felt the burden of two things." One was "an innate and abnormal desire for exploration." The other was "the constant struggle to make ends meet, the sting

of poverty" which drove him to accomplish "some extraordinary achievement."

At an early age he, too, was attracted to the polar exploits of Dr. Elisha Kent Kane, but largely because the American physician had been a healer among the Eskimos. He was a quiet, reticent youth, an escapist, who used to go on long nature tramps in the Catskill Mountains, where "the voice of the wild became a lifelong study." He was studious at high school, a prize-winning scholar in geography. But he had to earn his keep and he remembered his childhood labor as a Dickensian grind. At thirteen he worked in a glass factory. Later he helped support his family in their Brooklyn slum home by getting odd jobs at the Fulton Fish Market. He earned his way through medical school at New York University as a door-to-door milk delivery man, working through the night until it was time to attend lectures at 10 A.M.

Six months after he graduated, just three patients had sought out his medical services. Then one day the twenty-five-year-old physician was reading the New York *Herald* in his empty office, when a news announcement riveted his eyes. A certain Lieutenant Robert E. Peary, then stationed at the Philadelphia Navy Yard, was looking for a surgeon to serve without pay on an independent expedition to north Greenland.

"It was as if a door to a prison cell had opened," said Cook. "I felt the first . . . call of the Northland."

The thirty-five-year-old naval civil engineer who signed him on had already answered the first siren call of the North. In 1886 Peary had obtained a summer's leave of absence from the Civil Engineering Corps of the United States Navy; he borrowed five hundred dollars from his mother; and with a Danish skiing companion he had made a one-hundred-mile journey over the inland ice from the southwest coast of Greenland. He had carved out a minor reputation for himself as an explorer. Now he was eager to write his name large across the Arctic. He would solve the mystery of the blank space on the map that was north Greenland. Fame would be his if he could determine whether Greenland was an island continent or whether, as some geographers believed, its interior Ice Cap thrust right up to the North Pole.

He had little trouble securing an eighteen months' leave of absence from the Navy and ten thousand dollars from financial backers. He had become versed in the fine art of string-pulling and persuading influential people with his grandiloquent language. He always sounded militaristic and exuded enormous self-confidence. His strategy, as he called his plan, was to take with him a wintering party of six

*Dr. Frederick Cook, the gentle but persevering Sigmund Freud of the Arctic, claimed he reached the Pole on April 21, 1908.* THE BETTMAN ARCHIVE

"campaigners" aboard the chartered Newfoundland sealer, the *Kite.* Then he would conduct a "White March" over the "Great Ice" of northeast Greenland and claim for Uncle Sam an "imperial highway to the North."

Cook was greatly impressed when the *Kite* sailed from Brooklyn for the northwest coast of Greenland on June 6, 1891. He sized up Peary as "a thoroughly decent fellow and a strong character." Peary was to wind up the trip praising his surgeon as an "always helpful and indefatigable worker" with "unruffled patience and coolness in an emergency."

The campaigner aboard ship who attracted most newspaper copy was Peary's wife, the first white woman to winter at such a high latitude in Greenland. The former Josephine Diebitsch, the daughter of a professor at the Smithsonian Institute, was a tall, spirited, firm-jawed woman, who closely resembled Peary's mother. The two women were equally possessive of Peary and never got along well. Mary Peary accompanied her son and his "Washington belle" on their honeymoon; and the mother moved in with the newlyweds for at least a year after their marriage in a quarrelsome *ménage à trois.* Josephine soon realized she was married to an obsessed man who was really married to the Arctic. She was eager to accompany him on this trip because it gave her a rare opportunity to be with her footloose husband.

Josephine wrote a book about her experiences entitled *My Arctic Journal: A Year Among Icefields and Eskimos.* It gives us an insight into the developing characters of Peary and Cook. We catch a glimpse as well of the human problems that beset a polar explorer's wife. The *Kite* was ramming a passage through the rubble ice of Baffin Bay when a blow from the iron tiller broke both bones of Peary's lower right leg just above the ankle. Cook set the fractures in splints; Josephine helped him to relieve the patient's pain with a shot of whisky and doses of morphine. Her husband was a fretful patient. When she asked how she could make his leg more comfortable, Peary growled, "Oh, my dear, pack it in ice until someone can shoot it!" Wrote Josephine: "Dr. Cook, who has been more than attentive, has made a pair of crutches for the poor sufferer."

On July 30 the party of six men and one woman landed at their destination—the foot of the steep, red, lichen-covered cliffs in Inglefield Gulf immediately north of the modern United States Greenland military base of Thule. Peary was strapped to a plank and carried ashore to a tent. There the engineer demonstrated his outstanding organizational skill. Though painfully crippled, he supervised the erection of a

prefabricated, two-room, tar-papered cabin named Red Cliff House that was to serve as their wintering quarters.

As the party settled in for the long polar night the Etah Eskimos flocked from hundreds of miles away to gaze at the first white woman they had ever seen. Josephine was shocked by the outlandish customs of the "huskies," as she termed the natives, but on the whole handled herself with aplomb. She declined gracefully when one admiring Eskimo offered to exchange mates and make Josephine his *koonah*, or wife, for the night. What really bothered her was their amiable tolerance for *koomakshuey*, or vermin. Like a housewife striving to convert Greenland into a suburb of Washington, she occupied herself each day sprinkling the cabin with lice disinfectant and vigorously sweeping the floor with a silver-handled whisk broom.

On New Year's Eve she issued cards inviting guests to join Mr. and Mrs. Peary at an "at-home party in the south parlor of Red Cliff." She served apple pandowdy, crullers, chocolate ice cream and Sauterne wine cocktails. "It was amusing," wrote Josephine of her Eskimo guests, "to see the queer-looking creatures, dressed entirely in the skins of animals, seated at the table and trying to act like civilized people." It must have been equally amusing for her visitors to stamp in from the forty-five-below-zero cold and be greeted by a hostess (clad in a low-cut canary-yellow silk tea gown, trimmed with black lace) languorously waving a palm leaf fan.

Eventually her pioneer spunk appears to have won the respect of the Eskimos. Brandishing a parasol, warmed by double flannel skirts and a muff, and armed with a cartridge belt and a .38 calibre Colt revolver, she fearlessly climbed the cliffs alone to inspect her own line of fox traps. She didn't flinch either when the men in the party were shooting a herd of ferocious walrus while aboard the *Mary Peary* whaling boat. Josephine sat in the plunging stern for hours calmly reloading their empty Winchester rifles, meanwhile protecting with her skirts her husband's mending outstretched leg.

Peary soon threw away his crutches, and within three months, Josephine tells us, the amazing man was running foot races with Dr. Cook. His hardihood was truly remarkable. He took snowbaths in near-zero temperatures. To demonstrate to the Eskimos his superior endurance, he scorned igloos and sleeping bags and slept out in the open all night in his hooded parka and caribou socks.

Peary's attitude toward the Eskimos was ambivalent. He had the intelligence to recognize the superiority of their arctic survival tech-

niques. He adopted for his expeditions their use of dogteams, sledges, nourishing fatty meat, and light fur garments. But while he made use of their skills, he could not accept them as his equals or as people. Sometimes he referred to them in proprietary terms as "my Eskimos," "my boys," "my dependants," or "my dusky children of the Pole." More often they were "my human instruments," cogs to be exploited in "my North Pole traveling machine." He was their benefactor and they were to be treated as sulky children of an inferior race. He never really learned their language, and he even scorned the warmth and hospitality of their snowhouses.

"Often, in winter traveling, I have been obliged to sleep in one of these hospitable igloos," he was to write derisively in *The North Pole*. "On such occasions I have made the best of things, as a man would if compelled to sleep in a tenth-rate railroad hotel or a slum lodging house, but I have tried to forget the experience as soon as possible. . . . A night in one of these igloos, with the family at home, is an offense to every civilized sense, especially that of smell."

Cook, on the contrary, was captivated by the Eskimo people from the very beginning. On this trip he became the first explorer to take systematized anthropological measurements and photographs of their body structure. He took a careful census of their families. He lent a sympathetic ear as he recorded their customs and folklore, and became proficient in their language. He regarded them as "primitive artists" of a very high order, and marveled at their ability to survive "in a state of happiness, comfort, and peace, not contaminated by Caucasian vices." Even Peary was infected by his zeal. "In his special ethnological field," Peary generously proclaimed, Dr. Cook had compiled a "mass of most valuable material concerning a practically unstudied tribe."

In May of 1892 Peary set out on his epic White March eastward across the Ice Cap of north Greenland. Cook headed the advance sledge party beating trail for the first one hundred and thirty miles, until they reached the rim of the great Humboldt Glacier, which wound "like cold molasses" around the feet of glassy cliffs. At that point, though Cook eagerly volunteered to go ahead, Peary sent him back to look after Josephine at Red Cliff. The Eskimos, believing that the interior was haunted by the evil *Tornarsuk*, returned with him. Peary snowshoed on with thirteen dogs, two sledges, a good supply of pemmican especially packed for him by Parke, Davis & Company of Detroit—and a single traveling companion. This was Eivind Astrup, a twenty-year-old ski champion from Norway, plentifully endowed with the Horatio Alger-

esque qualities that Peary most admired: "true grit" and "sand" and "pluck."

Peary himself displayed these attributes admirably on this trek. In sixty-five days he and his ski mate struggled across six hundred miles of unexplored terrain. It was a herculean athletic feat: teetering over crevasses, battling sleet squalls, crawling up alabaster ice slopes. Peary took it all in his stride. He marched ahead carrying in his hand a blue-starred silken banner made for him by Josephine. At night, after luxuriating in a nude snow bath, he would set his little alarm clock and disdaining his sleeping bag, but clothed, he says, sleep blissfully on a couch of ice. By day, after smearing his sunburnt skin with vaseline and slipping on a pair of heavy smoked sunglasses, he would commonly indulge in a little reading as he trudged on. "Bareheaded and in my undershirt," he wrote, "I read *Exiles of Siberia* as I drove the dogs."

The landscape seemed Siberian to him. The "strident sibilation" of the hissing snow drifts, he wrote, "became as maddening as the drop, drop, drop of water on the victim's head in the old torture rooms." The bald ice mountains reminded him of crouching lions ready to spring. The northern lights bristled with rapier points "which leap and flash like the uplifted sabres of charging cavalry."

At length, under a steel blue sky and a yellow sun whose glare seemed as cutting as sword blades, the campaigner stood on the summit of a reddish bronze mountain more than three thousand feet high which he named Navy Cliff. He was certain that he had reached the northernmost shore of Greenland and proved its insularity. Peary Land, which appeared to be a rocky island, loomed northerly out of the mists of a channel at his feet which was called Peary Channel. Since the day was the Fourth of July, he patriotically named an easterly inlet Independence Bay. And this harbor, at close to 82 degrees north latitude, appeared to him to stretch out into the broad, ice-strewn expanse of the Arctic Ocean.

"I could now understand the feelings of Balboa," Peary exulted, "as he climbed the last jealous summit which hid from his eager eyes the blue waves of the mighty Pacific."

Peary planted two American flags. He buried in a rock cairn copies of the New York *Sun* and *Harper's Weekly* which had publicized his expedition. He triumphantly produced a little silver flask of brandy. Before turning back home, he and his companion celebrated the glorious occasion, he wrote, by swigging a thimbleful of Brandy Cocktail à la Fourth of July.

His total roundtrip march of twelve hundred miles was a truly magnificent achievement, which earned him deserved fame. But unfortunately Peary's cartography was riddled with erroneous wishful thinking. It was not the Arctic Ocean he had seen from Navy Cliff. He was actually one hundred miles from the coast. His so-called Independence Bay was not a bay but a deep fjord. And Peary Channel did not mark the northern boundary of the mainland of Greenland; it was a tragic error which later cost the life of a Danish scientist attempting to confirm Peary's jump to false conclusions.

In 1915 the United States government was compelled to withdraw Peary's disproved maps of that part of Greenland. But by that time Peary had long established his reputation as an Arctic authority, and had set a reckless pattern of unscientific behavior. The opportunist became accustomed to making extravagant claims to the Peary Arctic Club. He gambled on his prestige to carry him through if his maps were questioned. He seemed to care only that the alleged records he broke would further his money-raising campaigns for his next Arctic safari.

"The time to prepare for your next expedition," he told Roy Chapman Andrews, his biographer, of the American Museum of Natural History, "is when you have just returned from a successful trip."

Back in "God's Country," as Peary called the United States, he quickly realized twenty thousand dollars on the lecture circuit for his Second North Greenland Expedition. Cook did not accompany him on this new expedition. He resigned when Peary jealously refused to let Cook publish a scientific paper on his ethnological Eskimo findings. No member of his expeditions was allowed to publish anything except in a book bearing Peary's name alone as author. The break was cordial. Cook later said: "There really was no lingering malice between us."

For the time being this appears to have been true. Though he was organizing his own tourist cruise to Greenland, Cook took time off in June of 1893 to give medical examinations to Peary's departing campaigners once again bound for Inglefield Gulf.

Peary's strangely assorted party included, besides himself, pregnant Josephine; a nurse; a temperamental artist paying his own way; ten other men; eight burros from New Mexico; and a flock of carrier pigeons. On September 12, 1893, the number was increased by the birth of a nine-pound baby, the first white child to be born at that high Arctic latitude. She was christened Marie Ahnighito Peary. Her middle name was that of the Eskimo woman who chewed bird skins for her diapers, and the Etah Eskimos traveled for miles to see this blue-eyed "Snow Baby" swaddled in the Stars and Stripes.

That blessed event was the only happy one arising from the expedition. Evidently Peary's martinet manner rankled and caused discord. He now regarded Eivind Astrup, the young ski champion, as a glory-seeker and weakling. That brave Norwegian suffered a nervous breakdown, and ultimately committed suicide on a glacier. Most of the other men could not tolerate Peary's bulldozing demands, and returned with Josephine and her infant and nurse on the next supply ship to the United States. Peary and two others pushed north toward Peary Land with forty-two sled dogs. They were defeated by furious blizzards, and after terrible hardships the trio of frozen and wind-whipped cripples limped back to the Greenland coast with just one sled dog left.

Peary was undaunted. In the years between 1898 and 1906 he wrote a superb record in terms of the territory he explored. One cannot help but be overwhelmed by the magnitude of his accomplishments and the distances traversed by this half-mad, demon-driven traveler. But in Peary's eyes it was a record of failures he chronicled, for he had not succeeded in attaining the Pole. Using Eskimo families as work gangs, he endeavored to set up a series of Pole-hopping bases along the northeast rim of Canada's dragon-shaped, ice-tortured Ellesmere Island. He was frustrated by desertions, dying Eskimos, the amputation of his eight frostbitten toes, and especially, he felt, by the "trespassing" on his domain by the great Norwegian explorer, Captain Otto Sverdrup.

On one occasion, chancing to meet Sverdrup on the lonely windswept wastes of Ellesmere Island, Peary brusquely refused to share even a cup of coffee with that scrupulously scientific-minded mapmaker. On another expedition, Peary attempted to usurp for himself new land already surveyed by his rival discoverer. He marched across Ellesmere to the north end of the island which Sverdrup had called Axel Heiberg Land in honor of a Norwegian consul. Peary planted the American flag and renamed it Jesup Land, after one of his Peary Arctic Club patrons. Peary then climbed the headland which Sverdrup had called "Svartevoeg" (meaning Black Wall) and renamed it Cape Thomas Hubbard, for another Peary backer. Not content with this, Peary stood on the black cliff, peered through his binoculars, and claimed he saw an undiscovered land lying in the Arctic Ocean to the northwest. It may have been a mirage, but nevertheless he named it Crocker Land, after another wealthy sponsor. And then, giving vent to his incredible neurotic need for acclaim, he wrote in his diary:

"What I saw before me in all its splendid sunlit savageness was *mine*, mine by the right of discovery, to be credited to me, and associated with my name, generations after I have ceased to be. . . . *Mine!*"

His single-minded lust for fame has no parallel in the history of exploration. Here he was a "maimed cripple," as he privately termed himself in self-pitying moments; he put pemmican tincan lids in the soles of his boots to protect the stumps of his amputated toes and wore the tins down to the size of a Canadian nickel; the pain he endured on the march was so searing that his jaws ached from grinding his teeth together. Yet his compulsion was such that all he could think about was that he had merely reached (according to his suspect reckoning) a highest northing of 87 degrees, 6 minutes north latitude—still one hundred and seventy nautical miles short of the North Pole.

"Twenty years last month since I began, and yet I have missed the prize," he berated himself in his diary. "To think I have failed once more . . . I felt that the mere beating of the [northing] record was but an empty bauble compared with the splendid jewel on which I had set my heart for years, and for which, on this expedition, I had almost literally been straining my life out. . . . I sometimes think I would almost sell my soul . . . by such a bargain as used to be effected in the good old times when souls were a marketable commodity and always on demand by the devil. . . ."

His family did not need to be told that he had long sacrificed them in his Faustian bargain with the polar devil. In 1902 his fatherless Snow Baby, Marie, wept at home, "I want my father. What's the use of having a father if you can only see him in spots?" Then she wrote a touching letter to "My dear, dear Father":

"I have been looking at your pictures, it seems ten years, and I am sick of looking at them. I want to see my father. I don't want people to think me an orphan. Please think this over. Your loving Marie."

Josephine's letters were more pitiful. She learned that Peary had fathered an illegitimate son, Kahdi, after a passionate love affair with a beautiful Etah Eskimo woman named Allakasingwah. He had been insensitive enough to publish nude bathing photos of the "bright-faced Allakasingwah," depicting her in his book, *Northward Over the Great Ice*, as his "*cafe-au-lait* hostess" of the Greenland igloos. The rogue went on to write piously that Ally, as his mistress was nicknamed, was one of "five buxom and oleaginous ladies, of a race of naive children of nature, who are hampered by no feelings of false modesty or bashfulness in expressing their tender feelings. My years, and at present semi-crippled condition . . . will, I trust, protect me."

Despite her humiliation, Josephine forgave him for his sexual escapades, and wrote him heart-wringing letters. "Come home and let

Marie and I love you and nurse you," she beseeched her philandering husband. "Don't let your pride keep you back. Who will *ever* remember it ten years from now?... Oh, Bert, Bert. I want you so much. Life is slipping away so fast—pretty soon all will be over."

For his adulterous misconduct Dr. Cook was later to give Peary the mocking nickname, the "Sultan of the North." But for the time being he felt sorry for Peary. In the summer of 1901 Cook volunteered to sail north as surgeon on the Peary Arctic Club relief expedition.

"Peary's failure is sad news," remarked Cook. "He has fought hard and against tremendous odds to accomplish something. He deserves sympathy."

Cook gave a thorough medical examination to the man he had not seen for almost a decade. "The first impression," he wrote, "was that of an iron man, wrecked in ambition, wrecked in physique, and wrecked in hope."

Cook commiserated with Peary and gently told him, "You are through as a traveler on snow on foot. For without toes and a painful stub, you can never wear snowshoes or ski."

Peary turned his head away and would not listen. He confided to his journal, "Has the game been worth the candle? And yet I could not have done otherwise than to stick with it.... Besides, a few toes aren't much to give to achieve the Pole.... I believe that this is the work for which God Almighty intended me.... I am going now in God's name."

Cook did not claim divine sponsorship, but for years he himself had privately nursed similar Polar ambitions. In 1893 and 1894 he had organized the first tourist pleasure cruises to Greenland. As a result he became a founder and president of the Explorers Club of New York. Between 1897 to 1899 he had served as surgeon-ethnologist aboard a Belgian Antarctic expedition surveying the south magnetic pole. His skill in extricating the *Belgica* from her iced-in prison had won him a gold medal conferred by King Leopold; his book, *Through the First Antarctic Night*, had won him respect in scientific circles because it dealt with the psychological effects of spending a winter in polar darkness. In 1906 he took credit for being the first to ascend Mount McKinley in Alaska, North America's highest peak. His narrative, *To the Top of the Continent*, established him as a drawing card on the lecture circuit.

By the summer of 1907 Cook felt he had served his apprenticeship and quietly prepared to enter the contest to attain the North Pole. No polar expedition was organized with less fanfare. A gambler-sportsman from Palm Beach, Florida, named John R. Bradley invited Cook to ac-

company him on a yacht trip to hunt polar bear in Greenland. Cook agreed, and at lunch at the Holland House in New York City one June day he said casually, "Why not try for the Pole?... You and I could make it, John—with two Eskimos."

"Not I," said Bradley. "Would you like to try for it?"

"There is nothing I would rather do." Cook's pale blue eyes shone fervently. "It is the ambition of my life."

It was as simple as that. Cook scraped together eight thousand dollars and bought equipment and provisions for his Poleward trek. If he failed to find Greenland Eskimos to accompany him, it would be written off as an unpublicized big-game hunting trip and he would return quietly home again.

Peary, then spending a fortune donated by his millionaire clique to mount his elaborate and final North Pole campaign, later could not believe that Cook could pull it off with such simplicity. Bradley retaliated: "This was no harum-scarum dash for the Pole by a man in a straw hat. Dr. Cook is one of the ablest men with all kinds of appliances I ever met."

Moreover, said Bradley, Cook was a master at winning the confidence of Eskimos: "He knew their capabilities and their sensibilities. He can speak their language. They know he is a square and honest man. He could get them to go with him anywhere."

And so it proved to be. On July 3, 1907, the white and gold *John R. Bradley* slipped unobtrusively out of Gloucester, Massachusetts. She was a converted fishing schooner of one hundred and eleven tons and Cook had arranged to have her clipper bow sheathed with white oak and steel. Aboard her was Cook's family: his wife, Marie Fidele, a handsome, socially gracious, well-to-do widow of a Philadelphia surgeon, and their two daughters, Ruth, aged nine, and Helen, two. He kissed them good-bye when they got off at Sydney, Nova Scotia, and then proceeded to brush up on the use of his sextant as the *Bradley* headed for northwest Greenland.

Her skipper, Captain Moses (Moe) Bartlett, of the famous whaling family of old salts bred in Argus, Newfoundland, had not been informed of Cook's polar plans. But Captain Moe was a pretty shrewd guesser. He eyed the nearly one thousand pounds of pemmican which Cook had bought from the Armour Company of Chicago.

"Got enough pemmican here to feed a tribe of Eskimos," the skipper remarked to Bradley.

"Oh, yes," said the gambler, playing his cards close to the vest. "Might need it in case we are shipwrecked."

Then Captain Moe poked his thumb at the crates of tough white hickory wood, which Cook expected to use for fashioning sledges and building a wintering base at Anoatok. "Quite some hickory wood aboard," observed the skipper.

"Quite so. We may need it to erect houses with when we get crushed in the ice."

"Well," drawled the captain, "if I didn't know you were going on a hunting trip, I would say you were going to find the Pole."

As the ship spumed northward Cook's imagination caught fire. Despite the purple patches of his prose, he was a superlative verbal scene-painter. He had the gift of dramatizing himself and his surroundings with vivid phrases far more polished than the histrionic outbursts of Peary.

The icebergs were a Coney Island carousel of diamond-eyed steeds and they whirled about in a sea of molten glitter. Greenland, that "eerily, weirdly beautiful land," was a glow of frosty blue and lilac and lavender. Its storm-chiseled cliffs were whalebacks of terra cotta and buff and seal-brown. The glacier valleys were gashes of topaz and sapphire and old gold. The sky was as rose-colored as his dreams.

"As we sped over the magical waters, the wild golden air electric about me, I believe I felt an ecstasy of desire such as mystics achieved from fasting and prayer," he wrote. "For years I had felt the lure of the silver glamor of the North, and I can explain this no more than the reason why a poet is driven to express himself in verse. . . . Spiritually intoxicated, I rode onward."

At Anoatok he came down to earth. He had no trouble whatsoever persuading the colony of friendly Etah Eskimos to help him unload his equipment and build his wooden-box wintering cabin.

On September 3 Bradley prepared to return on the *Bradley* to the United States with his hunting trophies. Cook then revealed to the crew his carefully thought-out plan for a North Pole expedition. Without counting detours, he explained, it would be a one-way trek of at least nine hundred and twenty miles. With a band of Eskimos he would take a sledge trip of some four hundred miles across central Ellesmere Island; for explorer Otto Sverdrup had reported it to be rich in herds of muskoxen. With two selected Eskimos he would then make his Poleward dash of some five hundred and twenty miles from the north end of Axel Heiberg Island; for it was believed that the Arctic Ocean currents north of that jumping-off point would make for relatively easier over-ice travel.

Meanwhile Cook wanted one white man to winter with him at his Anoatok camp headquarters. Virtually the whole crew volunteered to stay. Cook selected steward Rudolph Franke. He was a strong, blond, German-born Arctic enthusiast, thirteen years younger than the forty-two-year-old Dr. Cook. It was a good choice. Franke was as companionable as the good-humored cluster of Etah Eskimos. The Eskimo men fashioned Cook's pliable fifty-two-pound, twelve-foot-long sledges lashed together with seal thongs. The Eskimo seamstresses sewed his bearskin pants, birdskin shirts, hareskin stockings, caribouskin parka, and sealskin boots.

"Fortunately, tea was one of the supplies of which I had brought a good deal for the sake of pleasing the natives," Cook related. "It was not long before I had a very large and gossipy afternoon tea party every day in this northernmost human settlement of the globe."

Cook was struck by the incongruity of his Christmas Eve celebration: half civilized, half primitive. He and Franke consumed the last delicacies left behind by the yacht and mixed them with such Eskimo titbits as frozen blubber. "As I sat eating, I thought with much humor of the curious combination of caviare and caribou steak, of the absurd contradiction of eating green turtle soup beyond the Arctic Circle," he mused. "I ate heartily with more gusto than I ever partook of delicious foods in the Waldorf Astoria in my faraway home city."

After dinner he went for a stroll to the nearby igloos, gave presents to the Eskimos, and gazed up at the sky. "As I looked at the star-lamps swung in heaven, I thought of Broadway, with its purple-pale strings of lights, and its laughing merrymakers on this festive evening." He felt a twinge of loneliness. "Returning to the box-house, I ended Christmas evening with Edgar Allan Poe and Shakespeare as companions." Before falling asleep he thought of his two children and their jubilation next morning when they unwrapped gifts around the Christmas tree. "I think tears that night wet my pillow of furs. But I would give them, if I did not fail, the gift of a father's achievement, of which, with a glow, I felt they should be proud."

At sunrise of February 19, 1908, he left Anoatok on the first leg of his long march to the Pole. Crossing the glacial ridges of Ellesmere Island with him were Franke, nine Eskimos, eleven sledges, and one hundred and five dogs. Almost a month later, on March 16, they reached the lip of the Polar Sea, under the beetling black cliffs of Cape Svartevoeg, on the north tip of Axel Heiberg Island. "My heart leaped," wrote Cook. He was at 81 degrees, 38 minutes north latitude.

*Josephine Peary (top left) accompanied her husband on two expeditions to Greenland. Marie Ahnighito Peary (right) was the first white "Snow Baby" seen by Etah Eskimos.*

*Rudolph Franke accompanied Cook on the first lap of his Pole dash.*

Now his Poleward dash was ahead of him, and he had to reduce his party to the absolute minimum.

Like Peary, Cook has been criticized for not taking a white man with him to verify his observations. In his book, *My Attainment of the Pole*, he rationalized, "From past experience I knew it was impossible to control adequately the complex human temperament of white men in the Polar wilderness."

Whether this was true or not, Franke appears to have accepted it gracefully when Cook sent him back with most of the Eskimos to Anoatok. "He was the commander of the expedition, and I obeyed without hesitation," said the steward, who was to remain Cook's lifelong friend. He was instructed to guard the ten thousand dollars' worth of blue fox furs and narwhal tusks in the box shack. If Cook had not returned by June, Franke would attempt to get a lift down south with a whaling ship.

From the Eskimo party Cook selected two youths to accompany him to the Pole. Each was twenty years old, unmarried, though with girl friends back in Anoatok, and both were excellent igloo builders and hunters. Etukishook—called Etuk for short—seemed much older because of his steady nerve and his slow, mature method of speaking. Ahwela—known as Wela—was quick-thinking and quick-acting and more volatile. "My two savage companions," Cook at first addressed them. As he came to know them better they were simply his two close human companions.

On March 18 the trio set out on the fields of heaped drift ice "glimmering in the rising sunlight with shooting fires of sapphire and green." They traveled with twenty-six dogs hauling two sledges, one silken tent, two caribouskin sleeping bags, and a twelve-foot-long folding canvas boat for crossing canals. Their sixteen hundred pounds of provisions were to last for eighty days. Each man was to be apportioned one pound of pemmican a day. Cook counted on killing off dogs en route to serve as extra food and reducing the number to six for the home stretch.

Cook glanced back at the scowling black cliffs of Axel Heiberg Island. Through the dull blue haze they seemed like marionettes dancing a wild farewell. "Our heart pulls were backward," he wrote, "our mental kicks were forward."

By Cook's account, it took him thirty-five days to come within gunshot of the Big Nail. His daily marches, according to his sledge pedometer, averaged about fourteen miles. His greatest distance covered in one day near land was twenty-nine miles. He kept a daily

meteorological record and took at least seven sextant readings on his outward journey. Unlike Peary, his observations of the sun were for longitude as well as for latitude. For day-by-day travel he navigated by compass. Some days he could not travel at all. He was knocked off course by the eastward-drifting ice pack, detours around yawning crevasses, and furious blizzards.

No explorer has captured so well the ghostly, nether-world atmosphere created by the arctic haze. The mirages wove a web of marvelous delusional pictures, says Cook, and sometimes drove him to the verge of madness. "Huge creatures, misshapen and grotesque, writhed along the horizon. . . . They filled me almost with horror, impressing me as the monsters one sees in a nightmare."

He imagined he heard the spirits of dead explorers shrieking in the wail of the wind and the gusting snow. "Disembodied things—the souls of those, perhaps, who had perished here—seemed frenziedly calling me," he wrote. "I felt the terrible oppression of that raging, life-sucking vampire force sweeping over the desolate world. . . . I felt the goad of their hopes within me. I burned to justify those who had died here; to fulfill by proxy their hopes; to set their calling souls at rest."

Etuk and Wela were not inspired by these wraiths, but their faith in Doto Cook was unwavering. They never grumbled, he says, and "we tried to be equals in the sharing of the burdens of life." Each night the trio built a snowhouse. If you were the last to wiggle into a two-man sleeping bag, Arctic courtesy sanctioned the warming of icy hands on the stomach of your bedfellow.

The morning ritual seldom varied. Each took turns at being chef and waiter. Leaning on elbows, those being served would breakfast on two mugs of hot tea, a Nabisco biscuit, a chip of frozen meat, and a "boulder of pemmican." They would creep out of their sleeping bags and thrust shivering legs into the cold cylinders of their bearskin pants. Someone would kick out the door of the igloo. With chattering teeth they would dance about to warm up. Dog teams would be hitched to sledges. Then they were off for another march, at an average pace of two and a half miles an hour, across drifting ice fields that would wobble and crack and rumble under their feet.

On March 23 they were temporarily delayed by the two-mile-wide snaking Arctic Ocean river known as the Big Lead. Cook described it as "mottled and tawny-colored, like the skin of a great constrictor." They stepped gingerly across the thin, yellowish, rubbery young ice that formed its skin.

On March 30, at close to 86 degrees north latitude, Cook gazed

westward and saw another spectacle. Though snow-covered and ice-sheeted, it appeared to be an expanse of fifty miles of undiscovered land. "I felt a thrill such as Columbus must have felt," declared Cook. He named it, in honor of his gambling sponsor, Bradley Land.

Contemporary critics contended the island must have been a mirage, like Peary's nonexistent Crocker Land. But the Canadian geographer, Moira Dunbar, has since credited Cook with perhaps having discovered one of the floating glacial ice-and-rock islands now known as T-1, T-2 and T-3.

Whatever it was—an illusion or a floating island—the prospect of encountering land further north helped Cook to goad on his Eskimo companions. Whenever they felt dispirited, he would encourage them with the idea that a murky cloud on the horizon indicated *noona* or "land" ahead. But by April 13 that spur no longer worked. Etuk stared despairingly at the endless plains and ridges of ever-shifting dead-white ice. Wela's face was streaked with frozen tears.

"It is well to die," wept Wela. "Beyond is impossible! Beyond is impossible!"

"Cheer up!" said Cook, coaxing them with the Eskimo term *igluc-too*: "Beyond tomorrow will be better."

"The land is gone," said Wela. "Our loved ones are gone. The signs of living are gone."

"A little further come," pleaded Cook. "Only a little further. Come walk a little further. The Big Nail is near."

He stirred them out of their lethargy. They gripped their whip handles. They yelled, *Huk! Huk! Huk!* The dog teams leaped forward like chariot horses.

Soon Cook calculated they were within one hundred miles of the Pole.

"Then felt I like some watcher of the skies, when a new planet swims into his ken," he wrote, quoting a line of poetry from John Keats. "In this land of ice I was master. I was sole invader. I strode forward with undaunted glory in my soul."

At noon of April 21, 1908 his excitement quickened. His calculations showed "with reasonable certainty" but not within "pinpoint accuracy" that he was a half mile from the centre of the earth. With his Tiffany watch, sextant, compass and chronometer, he took seven complete observations of the sun, one every six hours, until midnight of April 22. He conceded that his longitude reckoning was "at best only a rough guess." Ice drift, refraction of the sun, and compass corrections to

take into account the vagrant north magnetic pole—all made astronomical readings "difficult and unreliable." Nevertheless he was convinced he was within gunshot of 90 degrees north latitude. One factor convinced him more than any other. He used Etuk and his tent pole as a kind of shadow dial. The length of the shadow cast was the same at all hours of the day. This was corroborative evidence, he explained to Etuk and Wela, that they had just about hit the Big Nail on the head.

"We all were lifted to the paradise of winners," wrote Cook in a burst of rapture. "At last we step over colored fields of sparkle, climbing walls of purple and gold. . . . We touch the mark! The soul awakens to definite triumph; there is sunrise within us. . . . We are at the top of the World! The flag is flung to the frigid breezes of the North Pole!"

Etuk and Wela were understandably puzzled. Doto Cook asked them to pose beside the Stars and Stripes planted to mark this important spot. But the Big Nail seemed to have vanished underneath the ice. Cook noted that his bewildered Eskimos frequently stopped cutting igloo snow blocks to scan the horizon in search of the lost spike. They finally gave up and hung up their sodden fur garments to dry on ice axes and alpenstocks and crawled exhausted into the igloo.

"Hanging out wet clothes and an American flag at the North Pole seemed an amusing incongruity," wrote Cook in *My Attainment of the Pole*. He felt jubilant but "so tired and weary! How we need a rest!"

The next day he suffered the inevitable emotional letdown. He buried in the snow a brass cylinder which contained a small silk flag, a dated record of his arrival, and his medical calling card. Then he gazed at the bleakness about him.

"What a cheerless spot this was, to have aroused the ambition of man for so many years," he thought. "A sense of the utter uselessness of this thing, of the empty reward of my endurance, followed my exhilaration. . . . As my eye sought the silver and purple desert about me for some stable object upon which to fasten itself, I experienced an abject abandon, an intolerable loneliness. . . . Why, for so many centuries, had men sought this elusive spot? What a futile thing, I thought, to die for! How tragically useless all those heroic efforts—efforts, in themselves, a travesty, an ironic satire, on much vainglorious human aspiration and endeavor!. . . I was victorious. But how desolate, how dreadful was this victory! We were the only pulsating creatures in a dead world of ice."

He could hardly wait to get back to the solid land of Anoatok. It took Cook, Etuk and Wela twelve months to get there. *Return from the Pole*, his account of the "brotherly sympathy" that bound white man

and Eskimos together, is surely one of the most moving sagas in polar literature.

On April 23 the troupe headed for home on a zigzag route that swung west of their upward trail. They were three pieces of human flotsam adrift on shifting ice on an ever-moving Polar Sea and they could not backtrack. They averaged eleven miles of sledging a day. They got lost in blinding fog and snowstorms, and for twenty days Cook candidly admitted his observations to determine their location were pure guesswork. "We seemed like souls in torment," he wrote, "traveling in a world of the dead, condemned to some Dantesque torture that should never cease."

By mid-June an orange sun burned at last through the purple mists. Cook was able to calculate they were nearing the Sverdrup Islands at 79 degrees, 32 minutes north latitude, just west of Axel Heiberg Island. His comrades needed no nautical instruments.

"I smell land," said Wela.

"I do not smell," said Etuk, "but I *feel* land ahead."

They scrambled ashore and were enraptured to feel gritty sand under their feet and they reveled in the scent of yellow poppies and rejoiced to hear a snow bunting trilling its song. Wrote Cook: "It seemed as divine as the bird that came of old to Noah in the Ark."

They fed the chirping thing their last crumbs of biscuits and played on the seashore like children. They stripped off their soggy fur clothing and the "Arctic nudist cult," as Cook phrased it, sunned themselves like summer bathers at Coney Island.

Cook described an interesting conversational exchange about their nudity. By now their sunburned faces were all equally wrinkled and colored like winter-withered russet apples. The skin color of his body, though, aroused the curiosity of the Eskimos.

"Our skin is yellow," said Wela. "Yours is less yellow. I thought your skin, like that of white men, was white. But now you are yellow. In another year it will be as dark as ours."

"Yes, my skin is yellow," said Cook. "The skin of all white men is yellow, less yellow than yours. Under the skin all men are yellow. But the human heart is red in the people of every race and color. All men are brothers. All women are sisters. Humanity is, or should be, a family circle."

"Yes, but why do men kill each other?" Etuk interjected. "Why do the Indians hate us and why do we hate the Indians?"

No matter how idealistic, Etuk's query strikes one of the few

seemingly false notes in Cook's narrative. Conceivably Indian-Eskimo enmity may have been a tradition handed down by Etuk's ancestors; but the fact remains that there are no Indians in Greenland. One might suspect Cook of spinning fiction. His credibility is buttressed, however, by the realistically detailed account he wrote of their wintering in a cave at Cape Sparbo on Devon Island.

The wanderers reached the granitic, dun-colored cliffs of that cape, on the south shore of Jones Sound, after paddling their canvas boat some five hundred miles around the maze of the Sverdrup Islands. They stopped en route to hunt for game. Since Cook had just four reserve cartridges left in his Remington and Sharpe rifle, Etuk and Wela amazed him by their ingenuity in improvising makeshift weapons. "The Eskimo is by habit an explorer with the capacity for invention and imagination," he wrote. "He gets as much pleasure from the shaping of a new device to secure animals as a poet or painter does from creative work." His Eskimos snared hares with the equivalent of shoelaces. They stoned gulls with slingshots. They contrived to lasso muskox bulls with whale lines which was, he marveled, "tantamount to attacking an elephant with pocket knives."

By mid-September, to use Cook's colorful phraseology, the thickening piecrust ice of Jones Sound and the gunshot wads of wintry wind forced them to hole up in a dungeonlike den on Cape Sparbo. Their wintering quarters were located on a bleak headland, immediately south of Ellesmere Island, and nearby are two landmarks which Canadian geographers have since named, in Cook's honor, Cook Creek and Cook Falls.

For one hundred days and nights Cook and his two Eskimo comrades lived like Stone Age cavemen in an underground pit, three feet high, roofed with sod and stone and whalebone. Their bed was a platform of rocks, six feet by eight feet, barely wide enough for three prostrate men. A hole in the earth permitted them to stand upright, one at a time, to move their stiff and aching limbs.

Cook spent the interminable hours stooped over a stone slab writing desk scribbling his field notes. His writing lamp was a moss wick dipped in a tin plate of burning muskox fat. Using four pencils, he wrote one hundred and fifty thousand microscopic words. He squeezed them between the lines of three already filled notebooks; he crammed them on a small pad of prescription blanks, on two memo pads, even on toilet paper. The minute details that he got down about ethnology, about animal and bird life, and, above all, about the day-by-day life of

the three cooped-up prisoners, later convinced sceptics who doubted his story.

Cook says that writing was the only thing that helped preserve his sanity. Etuk and Wela at first diverted themselves by shooting arrows and poking torches through roof peepholes at ravening bears that came to plunder their slim rations. But then the prowlers lumbered off to their own caves, and his two fellow hermits were left without any sport.

Cook observed their growing melancholy. They became listless and yearned for home. A family of glossy black ravens cawed over their hovel in October, and Etuk and Wela talked to the *too-loo-ah* (Eskimo for ravens) as though the birds were human.

Would the *too-loo-ah* fly to Anoatok and deliver messages to their loved ones? "Ka-ah," replied the ravens, which was interpreted as meaning "Yes."

"Go and take the tears from the eyes of my loved one, An-na-do-a," called out Etuk. "Tell her I am alive and well and will come back to her soon."

"Ka-ah," replied the ravens.

"Tell my father I am in *Ah-ming-ma Noona* (Muskox Land)," said Etuk. "Bring us some powder to blacken the bear's snout."

"Ka-ah."

"Dry the tears of my mother's cheeks," said Wela.

"Ka-ah. Ka-ah."

"Then go to my sweetheart, Sir-wah. Tell her that Wela's skin is still flushed with thoughts of her. That he will return to claim her in the first moon after sunrise."

"Ka-ah. Ka-ah. Ka-ah." The ravens flew off, and the Eskimos felt that the *too-loo-ah* had surely departed for Anoatok.

Their craving for company, human or animal, was answered one midnight with the arrival of a little blue lemming. She was a pretty thing, with pink eyes and soft fluffy fur, but very shy. They were touchingly eager to keep her as a permanent tenant, and they went out into the forty-eight-below-zero cold to dig up mosses and willow roots for her. She returned two days later with her mate, and the tailless rodents became steady boarders in a berth arranged just above Cook's head. "We learned to love the creatures," says Cook, and it became a daily ritual to feed them on a little footlighted stage in the centre of their rock bed. But not long after the sun sank on November 3, the pets went to sleep in their nest and did not awaken for more than a month.

Cook, Etuk and Wela were left utterly alone together in the blank

mental torpor he called Zero Land. He analyzed their moods, which ranged from crazed hysteria to calm acceptance of impending death.

"We were condemned to die," he noted. "And yet there was something almost pleasing in our abject resignation. It was not gladness nor happiness. Something like a divine wine of action drove our feeble hearts. 'So this is the end,' came to me often while the motor vehicles of the brain slowed down."

He recognized that they were doomed if they continued to sink into this apathetic state and so he began firing provocative questions at them. "The more gruesome the theme the more intense became the interest in these first experiments of thought entertainment: 'How does it feel to freeze? When people starve what thought and action precede death? What does human flesh taste like?'"

Their flagging spirits quickly revived as they debated these vital questions. Said Etuk, "When people freeze to death, it begins in the fingers and toes. This is why we always guard and protect the ends first. We bare our stomachs and backs to extreme cold, but never the hands and feet. Cold first dulls the feeling of the skin. Then the eyes, the ears and nose fail. After that the head gets dark and then the end is not far off."

Wela agreed, "In the last days of starvation, as in the last days of freezing, the head becomes dark. There is then no pain, no thought, and no feeling."

They hesitated to speak of eating human flesh, but both implied they had known the horrors of eating a body. After some silence, Wela said with tears in his eyes, "Man flesh tastes like that of dogs and wolves and foxes and gulls and ravens. Even the flesh of the bear has a human aroma and taste."

This taboo subject seemed too close to their present situation, and so Cook directed them to more light-hearted topics. Why did the Eskimo dog have a long tail? They solemnly considered Cook's answer: it was inherited from the southern wolf. Without a tail, neatly coiled around its snout when sleeping in the snow, the sleigh dog could never breathe. Was the world round? Here they politely but firmly disagreed with Cook. "How could people hold on to the bottom of a round earth?" argued Wela. "How could birds fly upside down? How could ships sail bottom side up? No, the earth is flat, because we can walk on it."

They ended the lively discussion by agreeing on the wisdom of the Eskimo saying, "Friendship supplies the mental meat."

On February 11, 1909, Cook recorded, "The sun has burst nature's dungeon." He and his two Eskimo comrades rejoiced at the prospect of escaping from their underground cell. Anoatok was more than three hundred miles northeast. They prepared to complete the last lap of their journey with a single dogless sledge, a patched-up canvas boat, and a ripped Shantung silk tent. En route the starving men were reduced to eating bits of their boots, a chunk of candle and leather lashings.

Though he broke some of his teeth while masticating a piece of tough walrus hide, Cook didn't mind. "I was Eskimo by this time," he remarked stoically. "It was hard on the teeth, but easy on the stomach."

His troupe staggered on, at a tortuous seven miles a day, and paused at two rocky islands about two miles east of Cape Tennyson on Ellesmere Island. Here Cook took immense pleasure out of naming the larger island Etuk and the smaller one Wela.

"These rocks will stand as monuments to the memory of my faithful savage comrades when all else is forgotten," he wrote. Were they really savages? "My two savage companions taught me more than I could ever teach them," he reflected. "They rose to an emergency requiring a high order of intelligence. I reverted and reacted to the basic urgency of the primitive. Together we suffered and worked as brothers to feed and shelter and protect each other.

"We speak of the brotherhood of man, but only among savages is this love and helpfulness most effectually expended. . . . The most enduring and the most agreeable memories which linger with me from this journey to the End of North center in the splendor of co-ordinated brotherly love of my two savage companions."

On April 18, 1909, so weak that they had to drag themselves up on hands and knees, the three comrades clambered to the top of an ice hummock overlooking the igloos of Anoatok. The Etah villagers saw them and came swarming up with dog sledges.

With them was a blond stranger. The white man glanced at Cook—by now an emaciated Robinson Crusoe of a figure, with bony face caked with dirt, unkempt hair hanging down to his shoulders, the haggard eyes of a man who had survived a fourteen-month, two-thousand-mile trek in the Arctic wastes.

He shook Cook's hand warmly. "I am Harry Whitney," he said. "You are Cook, of course. We feel honored to greet you."

The stranger was a wealthy American sportsman, destined to gain a reputation as a "one-man reception committee for returning discoverers of the North Pole." Harry Whitney explained to Cook that he

was hunting for polar bear at Anoatok. He had received ship passage there a year ago from Robert E. Peary. The last he'd heard Peary was now at the north end of Ellesmere Island with a sledge expedition that had made a dash for the Pole.

The culture-shocked Dr. Cook listened to these words in a daze. He was in a state of collapse and was more interested in making sure his Eskimo comrades were looked after.

"We had been so long in the chill of impending death that, compared to Whitney and to the Eskimos about, we were but half alive . . . something like a resurrection from suspended life," he wrote analytically. "Having borrowed from each other all ideas that could be used in a long-continued hermit life, we acquired unconsciously merged personalities. . . . We had become exotic. . . . Henceforth we were native to Nowhere. We were strange to ourselves and strange to others."

Cook and his Eskimos were scrubbed in several tubs of soapsuds, but the hot water remained inky. "Doctor, either you have turned black in ugly spots," said Whitney, acting as his nurse, "or you are still very dirty."

"Yes, but on with the food," said Cook. "This bathing must be taken on the installment plan."

He warned Whitney to feed them just a little at a time in their starving condition. If they demanded more, Whitney was to tie them up. For Cook there was first coffee with fresh biscuits and butter. For Etuk and Wela there was meat broth with a few slices of liver. The Eskimos were then anointed in fresh seal blubber, their skin polished with corn meal, and massaged with a hare forepaw. Cook luxuriated in one hot bath after another, dry clothes, and more and more food.

The one thing that disturbed him was the news about Rudolph Franke. His faithful steward had been allowed to sail south aboard Peary's ship tender, the *Erik*. But Peary had first demanded, "like ransom sought from an enemy," that Franke hand over the ten thousand dollars' worth of fox furs and narwhal horns which the steward had been guarding for Cook.

Though this disturbed him, Cook kept his emotions in check. One piece of news he could no longer conceal. Shyly he told Whitney: "If you keep this quiet for the present, I will tell you some great news. I have reached the Pole."

Cook later wrote: "Uttering this for the first time in English, it came upon me that I was saying a remarkable thing. Yet Mr. Whitney showed no great surprise and his quiet congratulation confirmed what

Cook was acclaimed a hero in Copenhagen, but denounced by Peary for handing the public a "gold brick."

Picture postcards were sold hailing both Americans for hanging the Stars and Stripes on the Big Nail.

"STARS AND STRIPES NAILED TO THE NORTH POLE"

DR. FREDERICK A. COOK
APRIL 21 1908.

COMMANDER ROBERT E. PEARY
APRIL 6 1909.

TWO DAUNTLESS AMERICANS WHO REACHED THE GOAL OF A THOUSAND YEARS AND PLANTED THE STARS AND STRIPES UPON THE AXIS OF THE WORLD.

was in my mind—that I had accomplished no extraordinary or un-believable thing; for to me the Polar experience was not in the least remarkable, compared with our later adventures."

Nevertheless he was eager to reveal news of his accomplishment to the outside world. Whitney urged him to wait at Anoatok and hope for a lift home aboard Peary's expedition ship soon due to arrive from north Ellesmere Island. This was a chilling prospect, and Cook wouldn't wait. Instead he left under Whitney's protection a box containing most of his instruments and original field astronomical records—a decision he was later to regret bitterly. Then with a single Eskimo companion he made the long sledge journey of more than six hundred miles to the Danish whaling station of Upernavik on the southwest coast of Greenland. There he was offered passage to Copenhagen on the Danish govern-ment steamer, *Hans Egede.*

On September 1, 1909, the ship anchored briefly at the Shetland Is-land port of Lerwick. Cook handed the telegraph operator a cable to be sent to his wife: "Successful. Well. Address Copenhagen." He sent another cablegram to the International Polar Commission in Brussels, informing them he had reached the Pole on April 21, 1908. Almost as an afterthought he cabled the New York *Herald* that he was leaving a two-thousand-word dispatch about his expedition with the Danish consul at Lerwick. If the *Herald* was willing to pay three thousand dollars, plus ca-ble tolls, the newspaper would get a world scoop.

Cook arrived in Copenhagen to find himself acclaimed an interna-tional hero. He was besieged by the press. He was lionized by King Frederick at the palace. He received an honorary degree from the University of Copenhagen. And the Royal Danish Geographical Society presented him with its gold medal certifying him as the dis-coverer of the Pole.

Within a week, while Cook was being feted at a Copenhagen ban-quet, he was handed a message. It was a copy of the triumphant cable which Peary had dispatched to the news wire services:

"Stars and Stripes nailed to the Pole April 6, 1909."

It was soon followed by another Peary broadside:

"Do not imagine *Herald* likely to be imposed upon by Cook story, but for your information Cook has simply handed the public a gold brick. He's not been at the Pole April 21, 1908, or at any other time."

The Big Feud over the Big Nail had begun.

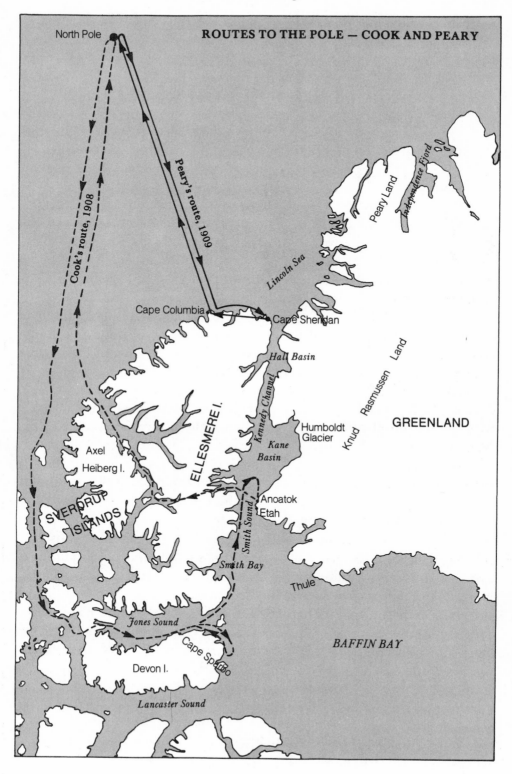

ROUTES TO THE POLE — COOK AND PEARY

North Pole

Cook's route, 1908

Peary's route, 1909

Independence Fiord

Peary Land

Lincoln Sea

Cape Columbia

Cape Sheridan

Hall Basin

Kennedy Channel

Humboldt Glacier

Knud Rasmussen Land

GREENLAND

Kane Basin

ELLESMERE I.

Axel Heiberg I.

Anoatok
Etah

SVERDRUP ISLANDS

Smith Sound

Smith Bay

Thule

Jones Sound

Cape Sparbo

BAFFIN BAY

Devon I.

Lancaster Sound

# Chapter 11

# North Pole or Bust

On April 6, 1909, Robert Edwin Peary claimed that he stood at the top of the world and he wrote in his diary: "The Pole at last!!! The prize of three centuries. My dream and goal for twenty-three years. *Mine* at last. I cannot bring myself to realize it. It all seems so simple and commonplace."

It was not that simple and the world controversy that raged over his claim was not commonplace. The dispute persists to this day. Books continue to pour out which keep the Great Polar Debate alive. Partisans wrangle over the issues almost as heatedly as they did more than a half-century ago. Was Peary the first man to reach the Pole? Was it Dr. Frederick Albert Cook? Or were both men colossal hoaxers who never got within a hundred miles of striking what the Eskimos called the Big Nail?

We shall never know. Neither explorer took a scientifically schooled witness and neither kept verifiable records. All we have to go by is the word of each claimant, and their words were highly colored.

The great feud was slow to begin. It did not really start to flicker until early in 1908. Heretofore Commander Peary, the imperious U.S. Navy career engineer, had not regarded Dr. Cook, the Brooklyn physician, as a serious contender for that "splendid frozen jewel of the North." In Peary's view, he was an insignificant amateur not worth considering. To be sure, Cook had been an affable fellow when he served as surgeon-ethnologist on Peary's second Greenland expedition of 1891/92. It had helped Cook win the presidency of the New York Explorers Club, of which they were both members. Apart from that, Peary dismissed him as a likeable bumbler who had done a little mountain climbing in Alaska and had got stuck in the ice on an expedition to the South Pole.

But then word got back to the Explorers Club via John R. Bradley. He was the big-game hunter who had given Cook a lift on his yacht to

Anoatok in north Greenland in the summer of 1907. "I have hit upon a new route to the North Pole," Cook wrote casually to his fellow members. "So here is for the Pole. . . . Kind regards to all."

Peary did not take it kindly. He told the Explorers Club it was an unpardonable breach of Arctic etiquette: "I wish to say that I regard Dr. Cook's action in going north 'sub rosa' . . . for the admitted purpose of fore-stalling me as one of which no man possessing a sense of honor would be guilty."

Peary had similarly rebuked those Norwegian interlopers, Fridtjof Nansen and Otto Sverdrup, for daring to poach on his domain.

Cook later retaliated. With perhaps understandable iciness he asked, "Who had the power to grant a licence to seek the Pole? . . . If Mr. Peary had a prior lien on it—it is still there. We did not take it away. We simply left our footprints there."

Yet Peary's chagrin was perhaps understandable, too. Here he was preparing for his eighth expedition northward. Time and again he had failed to attain the Pole. In his melodramatic phrase, it was "my dream, my destiny, the goal of that irresistible impulsion which had driven me for twenty-three years to hurl myself, time after time, against the frigid *No* of the Great North."

His past failures had left him a cripple for life. He had lost eight of his frozen toes. He had sacrificed his family and his career for his obsession. Now he was fifty-two—a greying "weatherbeaten fanatic" his ill-wishers termed him—and it was intolerable that this upstart might snatch the prize from under his nose.

Peary could not bear to think of that possibility. He frantically stepped up his campaign to mount the most powerfully backed polar expedition in American history.

In terms of prestige and wealth behind him Peary certainly looked like a sure winner and his rival like the puniest underdog. The thirty-one millionaire members of the Peary Arctic Club—an élite circle including magnates of the Colgate Soap Company, the United States Steel Corporation, the Atlantic Mutual Insurance Company, and the Bankers Trust Company—pledged three hundred and fifty thousand dollars to see their man through. The New York *Times* paid four thousand dollars in advance to publish the exclusive story of his expected Polar coup. He had the sponsorship of the National Geographic Society of Washington. He had the blessing of the American Museum of Natural History in New York. The United States Navy, which had released him repeatedly from his civil engineering duties, lent its massive support to him.

Finally President Theodore Roosevelt, who could recognize a chip hewn from the same granitic block, approved mightily of this kindred aggressive spirit. Peary thanked the President for personally pulling strings to extend his leave of absence from the Navy. "I believe," Peary wrote him, "I shall win this time."

Peary outfitted his tough, black-hulled, schooner-rigged steamship named after the President. The *Roosevelt* had been built in 1905 at a cost of one hundred thousand dollars according to Peary's admirable design specifications. She was an ingenious precursor to the modern ice-breakers. Her raking bow did not bore through the pack on direct impact; rather it glided up and over the opposing ice mass and cracked it by vertical pressure. Mixing his metaphors a little, he referred to his ship as a "fifteen-hundred-ton battering ram" that "fought like a gladiator" and sprang over obstacles "like a steeplechaser taking a fence."

Unfortunately Peary's book about his epic voyage aboard her, *The North Pole*, is an unsatisfactory account. It was ghost-written by a novelist-playwright, A.E. Thomas, who believed in spirit messages for inspiration. Therefore we must rely in part on the journals of the six Pole dashers he selected. They were to accompany Peary at least part way on his Poleward push from Ellesmere Island across the frozen wastes of the Arctic Ocean. They formed a magnificent team, the most loyal troupe he had ever assembled.

Most devoted of the six was the man accorded least recognition for his extraordinary achievements. On seven Arctic expeditions he sweated and slaved for Peary. He nursed him through sickness. He frequently saved his life. Yet ultimately Peary tossed him aside like a worn-out old sealskin boot. For Matthew (Matt) Henson was a Negro.

Matt was as durable as rawhide, thickly moustached, cocoa-colored, uncomplaining and self-educated. As a twelve-year-old orphan he had run away from the Maryland tobacco fields to become a ship's cabin boy. He was clerking in a Washington hat shop when Peary first hired him to be his valet. He was now forty-one. For eighteen years he had proven himself more than the equal of his master. To Eskimos he was a great *Maktok Kabloona* (Black White Man) because he was such an accomplished dog team driver and igloo builder. More often they called him their beloved *Miy Paluk* (Dear Matty) because he had mastered their language and treated them affectionately. But to Peary he remained "my colored boy," "my bodyservant," and "dark-skinned, kinky-haired child of the Equator." We doubtless shall never know why

*Matt Henson, the black American who accompanied Peary on his Pole dash, was treated shabbily by his master. He died in 1955 an impoverished Brooklyn car park attendant and $17-a-week messenger boy.* BROWN BROTHERS

Matt accepted these degrading slurs with such Christian forbearance and never uttered a harsh word against an employer who demanded such subservience. "He was never understandable," said Matt with a shrug, and the non-pareil Negro explorer took solace in his Bible and the works of Charles Dickens.

Captain Robert (Bob) Bartlett, skipper of the crew of thirteen hardy Newfoundlanders, was the hardiest and most celebrated Newfoundlander who ever sailed out of the Canadian whaling port of Brigus in Conception Bay. Almost as well-known was his cousin, Captain Moses (Moe) Bartlett who had earlier carried Cook aboard the *John R. Bradley* to Anoatok. Captain Bob was a breezy, lantern-jawed, thirty-two-year-old veteran of two previous Peary Polar thrusts. He was almost as gifted a sledgeman as Henson; but in the art of inventing colorful profanity he was matchless. Peary reputedly could swear for five minutes and enunciate each piece of blasphemy with distinction; but Captain Bob could cuss a blue streak for hours and never repeat himself.

Yet despite his earthy Billingsgate, Captain Bob was a nondrinking seaman and a reader. He carried the *Odyssey* and Omar Khayyam's *Rubaiyat* on all his voyages. Though Peary was to deprive him of fame on this trip, Captain Bob never held it against him. "That man, he was never downed," Captain Bob said admiringly of his Commander. "He wasn't heartless; he was just businesslike. He was always that way."

Professor Ross G. Marvin, twenty-seven, had also served as a Peary Pole-hunter on a previous expedition. He was a baldish, taciturn six-footer, a meticulous scientist who taught civil engineering at Cornell University. He was an odd man, loved by the other white members of the party, but inclined to liquor up the Eskimos with gin and watch them erupt into *piblokto*—arctic madness. On this journey he evidently went *piblokto* himself and was destined to be murdered.

The three other party members were Arctic novices—gay-spirited tenderfeet, who, in Matt Henson's phrase, were "the life of the funeral."

The oldest of the polar tyros was Dr. John W. Goodsell, known as "Doc." He was a stout, genial, thirty-five-year-old surgeon from New Kensington, Pennsylvania, where he was a specialist in clinical microscopy. An avid natural scientist, he had come on the trip largely to collect specimens of arctic rocks, flowers, and the beautiful snow-white species of caribou named after Peary—*Rangifer pearyi*. Doc delighted the education-hungry Henson (whom he called Othello) by reciting Shakespeare as they marched across ice fields.

Donald Baxter MacMillan, known as "Mac," was a tutor of another sort. Thirty-four years old, he was a short, ebullient athlete, later to make a reputation as an Arctic explorer in his own right. Peary chose him because Mac was a graduate of Peary's alma mater, Bowdoin College, where he had excelled in track and field and as a halfback football star. Mac taught mathematics and physical training at Worcester Academy in Massachusetts. On this trip he gave Matt Henson lessons in navigational maths; he instructed the Eskimos in high school gymnastics; and for good measure taught the natives to repeat after him in Latin the first six lines of Vergil's *Aeneid*.

George Borup, at twenty-two the "kid" of the expedition, was also its most entertaining enthusiast. He was chosen because he was an outstanding college athlete and a cheerful morale booster. He was a graduate of Yale, where he had been a champion wrestler, golfer and sprinter; he had finished second in the six-hundred-yard track tournament at Madison Square Garden. Borup enlivened the expedition with his "Golly-Gee-Whiz" college slang; unquestionably he was the first Arctic traveler who taught the Eskimos an Inuit-cum-American variation of the Yale football cheer: "*Timah! Timah! Timah!* Rah! Rah! Rah! Yea! Team!"

The flag-decorated *Roosevelt* got a rousing sendoff as she prepared to sail out from New York Harbor on the steamy afternoon of July 6, 1908. Manhattan's sweltering heat wave may have melted together the stock of Yankee chewing gum in the hold. It did not deter thousands of New Yorkers who gathered on the East River pier and cheered on Peary to bring back the Pole on board.

The three-masted steamer was surrounded by a flotilla of yachts. About one hundred moneyed guests of the Peary Arctic Club visited on board. They drank champagne and inspected their investment—especially Commander Peary's luxury yellow pine cabin, with its private bathtub, its autographed portrait of President Roosevelt, and its pianola which played ragtime music. "You couldn't spit," as Captain Bob said, "without hitting a silk hat."

President Theodore Roosevelt himself, teeth glistening and voice booming, offered his namesake vessel a vigorous Rooseveltian bon-voyage when she paused briefly near his summer home at Oyster Bay, Long Island.

"The first thing T.R. said when he came aboard," Captain Bob Bartlett recalled in his memoirs, "was: '*Bully!*' in a loud voice."

The President insisted on shaking hands with every member of the crew.

*Peary aboard the Roosevelt, the steamer which scored a record highest northing at Cape Sheridan.*

"It's ninety or nothing," said Bartlett, when it came his turn for a hearty hand clasp. "The North Pole or bust, this time, Mr. President."

At Sydney, Nova Scotia, the *Roosevelt* was joined by her auxiliary coal tender, the *Erik*. There Peary said goodbye to his wife, Josephine, and kissed his two children—five-year-old Robert junior and his "Snow Baby" born in Greenland, Marie, now fourteen.

"Another farewell," mused Peary sentimentally, "and there had been so many."

At Anoatok on the northwest coast of Greenland he was greeted by the Eskimos. "You are like the sun," they told him. "You always come back."

The news they imparted to Peary was not so cheering. Seven months earlier Doto Cook with a band of Eskimos had sledged westward across the ice toward Ellesmere Island for an expected march to the Big Nail.

Peary was shaken. Clearly he was competing with a rival who must be taken seriously and treated like a marauding enemy. He gave short shrift to Rudolph Franke, the steward assistant who had been guarding Cook's ten thousand dollars' worth of furs and ivory in a box shack at Anoatok. Franke was sick with scurvy and pleaded, "Please, Mr. Peary, let me go home with your other vessel, the *Erik*."

Peary grudgingly agreed, but only on condition that he hand over Cook's cabin and the plunder inside. (A single narwhal tusk he seized, worth one thousand dollars, was later polished by Peary and presented as his personal gift to President Roosevelt.) A sign he tacked up on the door showed that Peary could be a pretty mean antagonist:

"This house belongs to Dr. F.A. Cook, but Cook is long ago dead, and there is no use to search for him. Therefore, I, Commander Robert E. Peary, install my boatswain in this deserted house."

Peary left ashore at Anoatok Harry Whitney, a wealthy sportsman, who had paid fifteen hundred dollars as a passenger to the Greenland bear-hunting grounds. The *Roosevelt* took aboard a potpourri of human and animal cargo: forty-nine Etah Eskimos hired to sew fur garments and make sledges; two hundred and forty-six yapping dogs; seventy tons of odoriferous whale meat; and ripe blubber from fifty walruses.

Captain Bob Bartlett was heard muttering inelegantly that his decks smelled like a Chinese stinkpot. He reserved his more pungent phrases for the navigational task ahead. Peary ordered him to put on the steam full blast. The *Roosevelt* had to ram through three hundred and fifty miles of perilous ice pack before reaching Cape Sheridan, her pro-

posed wintering berth on the northeast corner of Ellesmere Island.

Aloft in the crow's nest, peppering his speech with his spiciest flow of invective, Captain Bob kept hollering through his four-foot megaphone: "Rip 'em, Teddy! Bite 'em in two! Go to it! That's fine, my beauty! Now—again! Once more!"

Her twisting and dodging and hammering through blue snarling floes was an exciting spectacle. Peary never forgot the "sheer brute force" of the thing. "Ah, the thrill and tension of it, the lust of battle," he recalled years later. "I can see Bartlett up in the crow's nest, at the head of the swaying mast, jumping up and down like a mad man, swearing, shouting to the ship, exhorting it like a coach with his man in the ring."

George Borup, the sophomoric Yale sports enthusiast, thought it was more thrilling than the Big Game against Harvard: "The *Roosevelt* was just like a good fast-dodging halfback running a punt through a broken field. . . . Hully Gee! It shows great nerve, to say nothing of fine piloting."

Though she was kicked about by the floes as though she were a football, the *Teddy* slid forward like a greased pigskin. On September 5 she scored her touchdown. She reached her goal of 82 degrees, 30 minutes latitude—a record highest northing for a ship under her own steam on the American Highway to the Pole.

Their wintering at Cape Sheridan was not without its periods of Yankee nostalgia and high hilarity. Christmas was a nifty occasion, you bet, said Borup. Physical training instructor Donald MacMillan had the crew pickaxe a smooth seventy-five-yard track on the ice for the first meet of the North Polar Athletic Club.

At twenty-one below zero, Mac was certain it was the coldest track meet he had ever organized. The Eskimo women, even with babies tucked into their sealskin pouches, were first-class sprinters in the fifty-yard dash. The Eskimo men put on a good show of boxing, thumb-pulling, and wrestling. In the rope tug-of-war, Matt Henson was effective but rather too light in weight; the two-hundred-pound Dr. Goodsell was a bull in strength; and everybody agreed that muscular Captain Bob could pull the side off a ship. Borup, of course, was a shoo-in winner of the white man's sprinting heat, and MacMillan put on a dazzling display of handsprings and somersaults.

Neckties were obligatory at dinner. The meal included roast muskox, plum pudding, iced chocolate sponge cake, brandy and champagne, and Christmas packages of nuts, candy, and chewing gum.

Afterwards there were raffles and disc-throwing contests. Prizes most sought by the Eskimos reflected the incursion of civilization: the men preferred cigars, the women scented soap. The highlight of the festivities was a dance exhibition staged by the Floradora Sextette. A giggling chorus of six Eskimo beauties kicked up their furred legs in a cancan number while the pianola played ragtime tunes as well as "Annie Rooney" and "McGinty" and "Home Sweet Home."

Soon sledge parties, bearing lanterns to light up the great Arctic dark, were dispatched ninety miles northwest to high-cliffed Cape Columbia. It was the northernmost point of Ellesmere Island. Therefore, Peary figured, it was the ideal jumping-off spot for the ultimate dash across the four hundred and thirteen nautical miles of Arctic Ocean ice northward that separated him from his White Grail at the apex of the world.

The tenderfeet in the party seemed to have acclimatized themselves well to the searing cold. According to George Borup, if you dosed a flask of malt whisky with red pepper and Tabasco, the hot stuff warmed you up fine. The "pickaxe biz" of laying food depots was a dandy proposition if you simply thought of it as setting up a chain of Childs' lunch counters, cached with a few of the "fifty-seven varieties." As for walrus-shooting, it involved "the snappiest kind of team play," and was terrific sport.

"Holy smoke! You may spiel of your lion shooting in Africa," he wrote at his slangiest in *A Tenderfoot with Peary*. "But if you want the real thing, try a scrimmage with walrus.

"Giving their battle cry of 'Ook! Ook! Hold on to your seats, you fellows; we're going to sing the second verse!' they charged us. Our magazines were as empty as a Princeton man's pocketbook after the Yale football game. The ammunition hoist was on the bum.

"Our huskies (Eskimos) didn't like the look of things. They grabbed the oars and banged them on the gunwhale of the boat, yelling like Broadway on the night of December 31; but as well try to head off the New Year. Mac and his automatic were having a bully time and we cut loose ... Mazzazza, pazzazza, it was grand!"

To Matt Henson, teaching the neophytes to construct igloos on the trail to Cape Columbia was a little trying. However, the novices made light of the rigors with much joking. Matt remarked to Dr. Goodsell that the long arctic night had given Doc's skin a greenish-yellow tinge.

"*My* complexion reminded him of a ginger cake with too much baking powder in it," Matt amiably recalled in *A Black Explorer at the North Pole*. "We laughed and talked and I taught him a few tricks for

keeping himself warm. . . . Though the tumpa, tumpa, plunk of the banjo was not heard in the igloo, and our camp fires were not scenes of revelry and joy, I frequently did the double-shuffle and an old Virginia breakdown, to keep my blood circulating."

There was also a certain knack to catching forty winks when your Eskimo companions were snoring on either side of you. "The only way to get asleep," Matt advised Doc, "is to wake them up, get them good and wide awake, inquire solicitously as to their comfort, and before they can get to sleep fall asleep yourself. After that, their rhythmic snores will only tend to soothe and rest you."

Peary had his own technique for dealing with the Eskimos. Realizing they were reluctant to leave the safety of coastal land on the white man's strange mission over the frozen sea, he resorted to bribery. One day in mid-February he heaped the mess table with two Winchester rifles, steel knives, lance heads and tobacco. He covered these treasures with a tablecloth and summoned the Eskimo dog team drivers.

After delivering a speech and explaining with match sticks a little bit about his plans, he dramatically whipped up the cloth. The Eskimos gaped. They coveted what they saw. That was just a sample, Peary announced. Four Eskimos would ultimately be selected to accompany *Pearyaksoak* and one other *Kabloona* on the last stage of the sledge trip to the Big Nail. The fortunate four would receive a duplicate of everything on the table—plus a whale boat, sledge wood, and many steel hatchets. To others who drove sledges part way, he would give whatever he thought each deserved.

The sight of all these riches, we are told, put heart and muscle in reluctant "huskies" who suffered from cold feet.

Peary spoke far more bluntly to his six non-Eskimo Pole dashers. On Saturday night of February 27, 1909, he assembled them in the igloo encampment under the snow-veiled bluffs of Cape Columbia and delivered a final pep talk.

"The Peary discipline is the iron hand ungloved," recalled Matt Henson. "From now we must be indifferent to comfort, and like poor little Jo in *Bleak House*, we must always be moving on."

"It reminded me somewhat of the way a football team gathers around its leader just before trotting out on the field for a big game," wrote George Borup. "He told us he wasn't a believer in hot air, but in action."

The football coach analogy was apt. Their Commander outlined his "Peary platoon system" strategy for scoring a touchdown. The North Polar Flying Squadron would consist of five separate sledge pla-

*George Borup, the 22-year-old Yale athlete, enlivened the expedition with his "Golly-Gee-Whiz" college slang.*

*Captain Bob Bartlett, the breezy, profane, poetry-reading Newfoundlander, wept when Peary sent him back.*

toons, in addition to Peary's main rear headquarters party. The five detachments would break trail, build igloos, and deposit supply caches in rotation. Periodically the exhausted units would drop back to Peary's main rear party and then be sent back to land. Within about one hundred and thirty miles from the Pole, Peary would make the last spurt with four of the best Eskimos and a single yet-to-be-chosen platoon leader.

His master plan sounded foolproof in theory. Regrettably, it was indeed riddled with hot air. Years later Peary testified before a Congressional hearing that he considered longitudinal reckonings on the Arctic Ocean a "waste of time": he did not require a single sextant check of his wanderings to the left or right on his journey. Hence his ludicrous map shows him taking an arrow-straight course along the 70th meridian of longitude directly to the Pole. In his calculations he largely dismissed detours created by huge ice hummocks. Most implausible of all, he did not take into account ice drift caused by the surging ocean currents.

The modern scientist, Dennis Rawlins, author of *Peary at the North Pole: Fact or Fiction?*, has expressed his scepticism in a single devastating phrase. To swallow Peary's tall navigational tale, he writes, one would have to believe that the Arctic Ocean's ice stood as still as Joshua's sun for thirty-six days straight.

Nor was this the only flaw in Peary's story. As we shall see, when he had no white witnesses to verify his record, the ego-driven traveler claimed that he virtually ran to the Pole and back. In fact, as Matt Henson innocently revealed in his memoirs, his crippled Commander was practically "a dead weight" riding on a fur-lined sledge most of the way.

One strongly suspects that Peary was behaving like a desperate, aging coach on his last legs. Gambling on his immense past prestige, he expected his word to be accepted unquestioningly by his trusting supporters. On his previous Polar thrust three years before, the toeless fifty-year-old had sighed in his diary: "Oh, for the untiring energy and elasticity of twenty years ago. . . . It seems as if I deserved to win this time."

On his present punishing Poleward dash, one cannot help but sympathize with the broken and obsessed old cripple. He felt a stab of pain in his right leg, which had been smashed on his second Greenland trek eighteen years ago, and he confided to his journal:

"This was my final chance to realize the one dream of my life. The morning start would be the drawing of the string to launch the last arrow in my quiver."

His platoon leaders, poised on the edge of the frozen Polar Sea and eager to take off in the morning, were not aware of the desperation that gripped their Commander. Before going to sleep that Saturday night, they gathered in Bartlett's igloo.

"After a fine talk, I suggested each man sing a college song, Marvin from Cornell, Borup from Yale, and MacMillan from Bowdoin," wrote Captain Bob. "After this all joined hands and each fellow gave his college cheer. Honestly I began to be sorry I hadn't gone to college when I heard the way those fellows could yell."

They pledged to help Peary plant the Stars and Stripes at the Pole whatever the cost. "We wanted him to win, and he deserved to," said MacMillan. "We were to give him our best, perhaps our hands, our feet, or even our lives. . . . Peary never knew how loyal we were."

They shook hands and parted and wondered, as Borup said, "When shall we four meet again?"

At dawn the next morning Captain Bob sniffed the fifty-below-zero cold, discarded his plug tobacco in favor of his cherished copy of the *Rubaiyat*, and set out with his pace-setter platoon of Eskimos. Soon all the platoons were strung out on the undulating skin of Arctic Ocean ice like a wriggling centipede. There were twenty-four men, a hundred and thirty-three dogs, and nineteen sledges.

Captain Bartlett and Matt Henson appear to have been the supermen of the expedition. They plodded on over humped white icefields with heads bowed, eyes half closed and squinting, against the barrage of icy particles flung in their faces like broken glass. The air, says Peary, was "keen and bitter as frozen steel." It was so cold that the Three Star Brandy in a flask under Peary's caribouskin parka froze solid. His pace-setters hewed and hacked a path through the chaotic ice ridges, accomplishing an average march of approximately thirteen miles a day. In the pickaxed passes they left behind a trail of leaky fuel tins, smashed sledges, and the rigid carcasses of frozen dogs.

"You had to fight for every yard gain," said Borup, "as you'd do on the football field."

In his rear headquarters division, rather like a coach or a general, Commander Peary felt secure that he had anticipated almost every contingency to be met by his North Polar Flying Squadron. In most respects he had indeed demonstrated his great organizational skill. He had devised an ingenious alcohol fuel lamp, useful for lighting and cooking. He was the first Arctic explorer to dispense with heavy sleeping bags. He felt a party sleeping in one was in danger of drowning in

case the Polar Sea ice under him cracked open during the night. Instead he designed a hooded caribouskin coat containing rawhide drawstrings which were pulled taut at night and cleverly enabled the traveller to sleep in a self-contained garment sleeping bag.

Finally Peary was intelligent enough to reduce travel provisions to the absolute essentials. Daily rations per man consisted of sixteen ounces of pemmican, sixteen ounces of biscuits, four ounces of condensed milk, and one half an ounce of tea. It was an admirably balanced diet of proteins, fats and carbohydrates.

Yet superb as he was as an organizer, Peary was surprisingly derelict in more ways than one. His vanity was such that he claimed to have invented a "Peary sledge" infinitely superior to those perfected by the Eskimos. It was a thirteen-foot-long, ninety-five-pound monstrosity of solid oak; Cook later said derisively it was as clumsy at navigating ice hummocks as a Mexican ox cart. Furthermore, unlike Cook, Peary neglected to supply his expedition with a canvas folding boat for crossing lanes of open ice water that Arctic whalers call leads.

On March 5 this lack of foresight caused much grief to the North Polar Flying Squadron. They were unable to tackle the notorious Big Lead. Peary nicknamed it the Grand Canal—a malevolent Styx of "inky black water, throwing off dense clouds of sullen vapor."

It stalled them for six days as they impatiently waited for a film of young ice to cement a bridge over it. Peary kept pacing up and down, in his shuffling toeless gait, and seethed like the boiling Styx. In his diary, Peary let off steam: "God damn K—to hell."

K—was evidently Koodlooktoo. He was one of the mutinous Eskimos who watched the witch's cauldron of vapor rising and felt it was stirred up by the dreaded Devil Spirit, *Tornarsuk*. Two others became so fearful that Peary took the drastic step of sending the two "quitters packing back to Eskimo land."

Though loyal to Peary, Matt Henson and MacMillan felt pity for the pair of abandoned Eskimos. MacMillan expressed their feelings:

"One could not help but sympathize with those two silent figures as they drove away in the half-light over the drift ice of the Polar Sea with a tin can for a lamp and a little food to sustain them until they reached land. Worse still, they had their orders not to stop at the ship, but to take their wives and children and leave immediately for home, some three hundred miles south. . . . I would not say that Peary was loved by these people of the North, or that there was even a deep feeling of friendship between him and a single member of the Smith Sound

*A giggling chorus line of six Eskimo beauties, dubbed the "Floradora Sextette," kicked up their legs in a cancan number while the pianola aboard the Roosevelt played ragtime tunes.* COPYRIGHT NATIONAL GEOGRAPHIC SOCIETY, COURTESY ROBERT E. PEARY JR. AND MARIE PEARY KUHN.

*Allakasingwah, shown thus in Peary's book* Northward Over the Great Ice, *was Peary's Eskimo mistress in Greenland and mother of his illegitimate son, Kahdi.*

tribe. But he was certainly deeply respected ... even to the point of fear."

It was MacMillan's friendly attitude that averted a wholesale desertion of the Eskimos. The gym teacher diverted their attention by organizing athletic contests in boxing, wrestling and native games. He promised the Eskimo winners fantastic prizes which they could later claim on the *Roosevelt*.

Henson was amused to note that Koodlooktoo won the ship's anchor after winning the thumb-pulling championship. "At least," Matt jokingly told Mac, "you would have to salvage the rudder for our voyage home."

"I can't," said MacMillan with a grin. "Ootah won it yesterday."

Eventually ice closed over the Styx and the squadron plunged on. By mid-March Peary began sending his support platoons back to land. First to return was the party headed by Dr. Goodsell. His medical services were needed back on the ship. Everyone was sorry to see the genial Doc go.

MacMillan was the next to return. Ice had buckled under him while he was taking a sounding with a lead line and plunged him into the sea. Peary, to his credit, had thrust the schoolteacher's freezing feet under his own red flannel undershirt against the warmth of his bare chest. But one of Mac's heels remained severely frozen, and he couldn't take any more. Before leaving, he joined Borup and Marvin in singing a college song in Latin, *Amici Usque ad Aras*.

But Borup and Marvin were likewise plagued with frozen and bleeding feet and in their turn were sent back.

"I would have given my immortal soul to have gone on," said young Borup. "I never felt so bad in my life as when I turned my footsteps landward.... Still, it was part of the game. When the captain of your eleven orders you to go to the sidelines, there's no use making a gallery play by frenzied pleas to go on."

Three years later, in a burst of athletic enthusiasm, the youthful Yale graduate was doomed to die by drowning while on a canoe trip on Long Island Sound.

Professor Ross Marvin died much sooner. The usually taciturn Cornell engineering instructor seemed strangely agitated when Matt Henson gave him a fraternal handclasp. "I'm sorry to see you leave, Professor," said Matt.

"I'm not, I'm glad," said Marvin, according to Matt's recollection. "I'm sick of this ice. Everywhere, everything—ice, ice, ice! I sometimes think the only reason it doesn't drive you and Peary crazy is that it must flow in your veins."

Captain Bartlett said goodbye to the professor with the fatalistic phrase, "I'll see you again in one of three places, Heaven, Hell, or the *Roosevelt.*"

Neither Captain Bob nor Matt Henson saw Marvin again. Koodlooktoo confessed he killed him because on the way back the high-strung professor went *poblikto* and threatened to murder another Eskimo sledge driver.

On the nippy morning of April 1—April Fool's Day, as some historians have noted—there was madness in the air. Captain Bartlett took a seaman's quick observation and fixed a north latitude of 87 degrees, 47 minutes. He took no longitudinal reading, which meant that the accuracy of his reading was dubious; but it convinced Peary he was one hundred and thirty-three nautical miles on a direct beeline to the Pole. It was then that Peary ordered the captain to return to the ship. Peary would sledge on with four Eskimos, five sledges, forty dogs—and with Matt Henson.

What happened next has been violently disputed. Bartlett later told a New York *Herald* reporter that he argued, begged, and quarreled with Peary, for he had been unaware until that moment he wasn't going to the Pole.

"I don't know, perhaps I cried a little," said Captain Bob. "I guess perhaps I was just a little crazy then. I thought that I could walk on the rest of the way alone. It seemed so near. Here I had come thousands of miles, and it was only a little more than a hundred more to the Pole. . . .

"It seemed as if I could make it alone even if I didn't have any dogs or food or anything. I went along for five miles or so, and then I came to my senses and knew I must go back . . . . But my mind had been set on it for so long I had rather die than give it up then."

In *The Log of Bob Bartlett* the sea captain was more restrained. "The American public has held it against Peary for not taking me," he wrote. "But don't forget that Henson was a better dog driver than I. So I think Peary's reasoning was sound; and I have never held it against him."

Peary's reasoning for not taking along a nautically trained witness, who might verify his observations, was variously stated. When that question was raised by the New York *Times*, Peary offered one explanation: "Because after a lifetime of effort I dearly wanted the honor for myself . . . the only white man who has ever reached the North Pole."

In his book, *The North Pole*, Peary put forward the sorriest of his rationalizations. Henson was a mere Negro cog in his "traveling machine." Therefore "he would not have been so competent as the

white members of the expedition in getting himself and his party back to land. . . . He had not, as a racial inheritance, the daring and initiative of Bartlett, or Marvin, MacMillan, or Borup. I owed it to him not to subject him to dangers and responsibilities which he was temperamentally unfit to face."

Peary was not content with disparaging the Negro sled driver who had been the backbone of so many of his expeditions. He belittled as well the initiative of the four Eskimos he chose. They were "members of an inferior race," he wrote in *The North Pole*, "as loyal and responsive to my will as the fingers of my right hand. . . . Whatever pace I set, the others would make good; but if I played out, they would stop like a car with a punctured tire."

For the record, the human tires supporting the Peary machine were the most unpuncturable of Eskimos. Ootah, the oldest at age thirty-four, had been a pace-setter on a previous Peary expedition. He was a strong, sinewy *angekok*, at five feet eight inches unusually tall for an Eskimo. "Ootah was regarded as the best all-around member of the tribe," Henson described him, "a great hunter, a kind father, and a good provider." On the last sprint of this trip, Matt found himself floundering in a lead about to drown.

"Before I could give the 'Grand Hailing Sigh of Distress,' faithful old Ootah grabbed me by the nape of the neck, and with one hand he pulled me out of the water, and with the other hurried the team across," wrote Matt. "He had saved my life."

Ootah's brother, Egingwah, aged twenty-six, was a stocky fellow weighing about one hundred and seventy-five pounds. He and twenty-four-year-old Seegloo were both veteran Peary campaigners. On a former expedition the pair had subsisted cheerfully for days on sealskin boots. The youngest was Ooqueah, nineteen. According to Matt, he had "an open, honest countenance, a smile that was 'childlike and bland,' and was spurred on by the shafts of love." Ooqueah hoped that the promised rewards offered by Peary would help him win the hand of a certain demure Miss Anadore back in Anoatok.

Peary says that after he dismissed Bartlett, the Peary "traveling machine" made amazing progress which took him straight to the Pole in five marches. His flying squadron doubled Bartlett's speed, Peary claims, averaging twenty-six miles a day, and on the last march achieving a stupendous thirty miles. The faster they went the more grandiose his prose became. He was the heroic knight in armor at last, about to slay the "dragon which guards the Rhinegold of the Arctic" and "the

end lay with that Destiny which favors the man who follows his faith and his dream to the last breath."

Peary says that he pridefully took his proper place at the head of his picked campaigners. "The joy of again being in the lead affected me like wine. The years seemed to drop from me. . . . I felt the keenest exhilaration, and even exultation, as I climbed over the pressure ridge and breathed the keen air sweeping over the mighty ice, pure and straight from the Pole itself. . . . The floes were hard and level, with patches of sapphire blue ice. While the pressure ridges surrounding them were stupendous, some of them fifty feet high, yet they are easily negotiable, either through some convenient gap or up the gradual slope of a huge drift of snow."

The last lap, he went on, was "a glorious sprint with a savage finish . . . the dogs galloping along and reeling off the miles in a way that delighted my heart. . . . On, on we pushed, and I am not ashamed to confess that my pulse beat high, for the breath of success seemed already in my nostrils."

One would like to believe Peary. The man had guts; and if anyone deserved victory, surely it was this battle-scarred Arctic campaigner. Yet it must be said that Matt Henson's version of events punches holes in Peary's highflown romanticism and breathes an air of reality into it. Without meaning to, honest Matt unwittingly proved the truth of the maxim that no man is a hero to his valet.

"Every man and dog of us," boasted Peary, "was as lean and flat-bellied as a board, and as hard." No doubt this was true of his fellow travelers. But Matt recalled in his memoirs that his fifty-three-year-old Commander, far from racing at the head of his dogs, was virtually a dead-weight cripple forced to ride on Egingwah's sledge "for the greater part of the journey as he did upon the return." Moreover, because Peary was "heavy for the dogs to haul," the party was lucky to accomplish "as much as eighteen miles" on a single march. Neither were the marches an easy cakewalk through convenient passes. Rather, it was hellish pickaxing through walls of rough, hummocky drift ice and zigzagging on detours around floebergs and dangerously thin-coated leads. "We marched and marched, falling down in our tracks repeatedly, until it was impossible to go on," Matt remembered. "We crossed lead after lead, sometimes like a bareback rider in the circus, balancing on cake after cake of ice."

Finally Matt innocently disclosed one fact that was most damning of all: "He made no observations in the five days." This hard truth was

dragged out of Peary himself years later when he was being grilled as a witness by a Congressional investigating committee.

Congressman Macon: "Then you took no observations, longitude or otherwise, for a distance of 133 miles after you left Bartlett at 87 degrees, 47 minutes?"

Peary: "No, Sir."

Congressman Macon: "And without that you managed to make a straight course to the Pole without anything except conjecture or estimate to guide you? Is that it?"

Peary: ". . . I am satisfied that I made that distance."

Assuming that he made that distance by some intuitive means, the attainment of his goal was something of a letdown for Peary's Pole hunters. At 10 AM on April 6, 1909, Peary camped on the threshhold of what he claimed was the summit of the world. Henson and the four Eskimos began building igloos on the jumble of cracked drift ice. What happened in the next thirty hours is a matter of controversy, for the various versions given by Peary and Henson are confusing and contradictory and sometimes laughable.

Despite the dense mist overhead, Peary apparently was able to take thirteen observations of the sun. Then, according to Matt, by miraculous coincidence, "when the Flag was hoisted over the geographical center of the earth, it was located just behind our igloos!"

Ootah stared about blankly when ordered to pose with the others holding five flags planted beside the Big Nail. "There is nothing here," cried the Eskimo, offering perhaps the most perceptive observation made about the *Kabloonas'* vainglorious race for the Pole. "Just ice!"

Peary ignored the remark. He solemnly cut a diagonal strip from the Stars and Stripes which he had wrapped around his body on his previous Pole hunts. Then he deposited the silk taffeta piece of Old Glory in a glass jar along with a note proclaiming that he had formally taken possession of the axis of the earth on behalf of the President of the United States of America.

Before leaving the spot, he performed one last act. He wrote his wife a message on a postcard bearing the address of 90 North Latitude.

"My dear Jo," he wrote. "I have won out at last. Have been here a day. I start for home and you in an hour. Love to the 'kidsies.' Bert."

At 4 PM on April 7 he turned to his homeward-bound campaigners and issued his command: "From now on it was to be a case of big travel, little sleep, and hustle every minute."

If Peary is to be believed, it was a hustle that broke every record of

sledge travel in polar history. In the first two days alone he allegedly raced at a breakneck speed of seventy-five statute miles per day. "We were coming down the North Pole hill in fine shape," he wrote as though it were a smooth toboggan slide. "So far we seemed to bear a charm which protected us from all difficulties and dangers.... It had seemed as if the guardian genius of the Polar waste, having at last been vanquished by man, had accepted defeat and withdrawn from the contest." And when they reached Cape Columbia on April 23, Peary claims that the Eskimos danced with glee and Ootah exclaimed: "The devil is asleep, or having trouble with his wife, or we should never have come back so easily."

Henson had a drastically different recollection of the journey back to land. To him it was a "horrid nightmare" crawl across raftering, piled-up ice mountains. It left his Eskimo companions with "lean, gaunt faces, seamed and wrinkled, the faces of old men."

Peary, with deeply trenched, haunted eyes, was "a bent figure, shuffling awkwardly . . . a frightening, walking corpse."

What most shocked Matt was the cruel change in Peary's attitude toward him. It was as though the Old Man now wanted to shun him, was frightened that Matt might betray a secret that Peary was concealing. "From the time we were at the Pole," said Matt, "Commander Peary scarcely spoke to me. Probably he did not speak to me four times on the whole return journey to the ship.... It nearly broke my heart on the return journey from the Pole that he would arise in the morning and slip away on the homeward trail without rapping on the ice for me, as was the established custom...

"On board the ship he addressed me a very few times.... I would catch a fleeting glimpse of Commander Peary, but not once in all that time did he speak a word to me.... Not a word about the North Pole or anything connected with it."

Matt solaced himself at night by reading the twenty-third Psalm in his Bible: "Yea, though I walk through the valley of the shadow of death, I will fear no evil: for thou art with me; thy rod and thy staff they comfort me." And he read in the fifth chapter of St. Matthew: "Blessed are the meek: for they shall inherit the earth."

Meek Matthew inherited nothing from his Commander except a brusque dismissal and his expedition salary of twenty-five dollars a month. The great Negro explorer was destined to eke out a sparse living as a Brooklyn car park attendant and then as a seventeen-dollar-a-week messenger boy for the Customs House of New York. He died at the age

of eighty-eight on March 9, 1955, so impoverished that he could rarely visit the Explorers Club because he could not afford to pay for his lunch.

The unmeek Peary inherited far more. After returning to the *Roosevelt,* and keeping strangely mum about his alleged Polar conquest, he gloated in his diary how the world might most fittingly pay him tribute: "Have my North Pole eyeglasses gold mounted?... Monument or mausoleum? Faced with marble or granite?... Bronze figures, Eskimo, dog, bear?... Or bronze tablet of flag on North Pole and suitable inscription. Bust."

But when Peary's ship touched Anoatok, he heard alarming news that threatened to shatter his dreams of glory. Sportsman Harry Whitney informed him that Dr. Cook had apparently beaten him to the punch. Cook claimed to have attained the Pole a year before Peary; he had left his field notes and instruments in Whitney's care; and had proceeded down south with an Eskimo to make his announcement to the world.

Peary was frantic. He threatened to leave Whitney stranded in Greenland unless the sportsman gave Peary his "word of honor, as a gentleman, not to take a thing belonging to Dr. Cook aboard this ship." Whitney complied and thus was compelled to bury vital evidence of Cook's expedition in a cache which somehow mysteriously vanished.

Peary ordered Captain Bartlett to speed south to the nearest telegraph station. On September 6, from Smoky Tickle on the coast of Labrador, Peary began sending out a blizzard of cables announcing that he was the first man to nail the Stars and Stripes to the Big Nail. He seemed fixated by the word, nail. After wiring his wife, Josephine that he had successfully struck home the "D.O.P."—Damned Old Pole—he assured her: "Don't let Cook's story worry you. Have him nailed."

However, he switched his Yankee idiom when dispatching his celebrated denunciatory telegram to the New York *Herald*: "Cook has simply handed the public a gold brick."

The great polar slanging match was thus initiated, and, in the grand tradition of American ballyhoo, the American press and public got zestfully into the spirit of the thing. President William Howard Taft set the wisecracking tone. He received a Peary cable that read: "Have honor to place North Pole your disposal." Replied Taft: "Thanks your generous offer. I do not know exactly what I could do with it."

POLE WAR HOT cried the headline in the New York *Herald*. The subhead read: "Peary Aims a Knockout Blow, but Cook Prepares to

Block It—Scientists Are Marking Time to See Which Has the Best of It."

Cook, surrounded by an army of refereeing newsmen in Copenhagen, responded to Peary's opening haymaker with a series of disarming feints. He assumed the stance of the gentlemanly pugilist. "If Peary says he reached the Pole, I believe him," said Cook. "There is room enough and honor enough for two American flags at the Pole."

Cook's magnanimous behavior infuriated Peary. The more generous his opponent became, the more recklessly did Peary swing out with wild accusations. Claiming that Cook had never left land, Peary and his supporters jabbed away: "Dr. Cook is a fraud. . . . His witnesses for his far journey were simple-minded Eskimos. . . . He must offer proof that he reached the Pole." Peary fumed to an English geographer: "I pulled the thing off finally, and then have had the whole matter soiled and smirched by a cowardly cur of a sordid imposter." And Josephine Peary got into the fray, charging that Cook's two Eskimos "could not tell the Arctic Pole from a barber's pole."

Cook sailed to New York to receive the keys of the city and to be feted in a big ticker-tape parade. He continued to wear an air of amiable humility, but he stepped up his attack a trifle.

"Peary's comments indicate to me that he is getting peevish," he told press interviewers. "To Peary the explorer I am still willing to tip my hat. But Peary's unfounded accusations have disclosed another side to his character which will never be forgotten."

He raised the logical question: "Why should Peary be allowed to make himself a self-appointed dictator of my affairs? Commander Peary has as yet given to the world no proof of his own case."

Both explorers took to the Chautauqua lecture circuit, demanding a fee of up to ten thousand dollars per performance, to present their case to the American public. Pugnacious Peary, who had branded his rival a liar in advance, was generally regarded as an unsporting bad loser. Cook, the self-effacing underdog, won the vote of the common man. A popularity poll conducted by the Pittsburgh *Press* showed more than seventy-three thousand rooting for Cook as opposed to two thousand for Peary.

American press-agentry entered the great polar sideshow. Chicago milliners styled a fur hat two feet high and touted their North Pole bonnet as the latest fashion rage. A dahlia at a New York flower show was named after Cook. A copy of the New York *Herald* containing Cook's serialized version of his exploits was enshrined in the cornerstone of a

Long Island church. A Broadway bar concocted a so-called Cook Cocktail, whose ingredients included a tablespoon of Maraschino and a pony of gin. After imbibing three Cook Cocktails, said the New York *Times*, drinkers were apt to begin mushing blindly in the direction of the North Pole.

At the height of the furor, it seemed as if the entire United States was divided into two acrimonious camps, each faction claiming its champion. It was also a newspaper circulation war, and in the long run Cook didn't stand a chance. Because the New York *Herald* had obtained the exclusive world syndication rights for the Cook story, most rival publications took a stand against him. Peary, on the other hand, had a powerful propaganda mill on his side. The mighty New York *Times* had been his newspaper sponsor. His financial backers controlled the New York *Globe*, the Brooklyn *Standard Union*, the *National Geographic Magazine*, and the Northcliffe chain of British newspapers as well. In addition, the multimillionaires behind the Peary Arctic Club put together a war chest of more than three hundred thousand dollars to persuade newspapers to slant their editorials.

Press wits had a field day. Quipped the Wall Street *Journal*: "Never before was there such a hot argument about so cold a subject."

*Punch* took to verse:

*In rival type it almost looked*
*As if the whole account was Cooked!*

The Washington *Times* jested: "England is raising $200,000 to send Captain Scott to the South Pole. About $183,000 of that had better be used to get a good umpire."

Scientific umpires were not much help in resolving the dispute. Peary refused to let unbiased geographers in Europe adjudicate. Instead he submitted his findings to a so-called subcommittee of the National Geographic Society in Washington. Cook scaldingly called the trio a "scrub team" of kitchen geographers. They had never seen a piece of arctic ice. And the National Geographic Society was neither national nor geographic nor a society, but rather "a kind of self-admiration society." It was a privately owned publishing firm, which ran a lecture bureau on the side. Peary was its star lecturing turn. Moreover the society had contributed one thousand dollars to back Peary on his Pole expedition.

The predisposed subcommittee was hardly objective. After a per-

functory examination of Peary's trunk full of instruments—conducted in a railway baggage station in the middle of the night—the trio unanimously agreed that Peary was the discoverer of the Pole.

Commander Peary would have been wise to let the verdict rest there among his friends. But he was greedy for honors, and the civil engineer wanted to be named a rear admiral in the U.S. Navy. It would be the capstone of his career with an accompanying retirement salary of six thousand five hundred dollars a year.

The appointment required approval by Congress, and several members of the Congressional investigating committee were not as gullible as Peary's adherents. They raked him over the coals, pointing out one flaw after another in his dubious testimony: his slipshod geography, his ridiculous sledge speeds, his miraculous ability to steer on a straight line up to the Pole without taking a single longitudinal reading. Peary twisted and turned in the witness seat. But he refused pointblank to reveal the raw data of his original field records—evidence which has not been disclosed to this day.

Thanks to Peary's heavily financed Washington lobbyists, Congress passed the bill granting his appointment. Significantly, though, the words "discovery" and "discoverer" of the Pole were stricken from the record. And Peary never forgot the humiliation he suffered under the tongue-lashing of Representative R.B. Macon of Arkansas, who filed a minority report. On the floor of the House, Macon set off a brilliant fireworks display of Yankee vituperation. The "titbit editors of yellow journals" who espoused Peary's spurious story were derided as "weazen-brained sapheads, pea-eyed, pinheaded and putrid-tongued infinitesimals." Admiral Peary was lambasted as "a willful and deliberate liar, dirty little pilferer, and contemptible little ass."

Cook, with remarkable Christian forgiveness, sent a letter to the Chairman of the House Committee lending his support to Peary.

"My object in writing you is to clear the way for Mr. Peary," said Cook's gracious letter of January 10, 1911. "Give Mr. Peary the honors—the retirement with increased pay. His long effort in a thankless task is worthy of such recognition.

"My claim of the attainment of the Pole is a personal one. . . . I ask for nothing. Within my own bosom there is the self-satisfying throb of success. . . . My reward will come with the reward that our children's children will give."

Certainly Cook never received that reward in his lifetime. His case was weakened because his original field calculations had been buried by Whitney. Nevertheless he submitted copies of his observations to five

disinterested scientists at the University of Copenhagen. The jury had no other recourse but to bring down a verdict of "Not proven."

The *Journal* of the Royal Geographical Society of London remarked that the decision was neither an endorsement nor a repudiation. But to the Peary-manipulated press, it was an outright dismissal of Cook's claim. The New York *Times* unleashed five pages of vicious diatribe. Among other things, Cook was branded "a monster of duplicity," "shameless swindler," "greatest imposter of all time" and "king of the thimble-riggers of all time."

The hounding and the heckling were too much for Cook. The Peary Arctic Club set detectives on his track. So he disguised himself (wielding a pair of scissors to trim his moustache, using black paste to touch up his face, and wearing a black slouch hat) and fled the country.

"I was like a deer that had been driven into a cold stream," he was to write of the abuse hurled at him. "My spirit was broken. In the bitterness of my soul, I felt desirous of disappearing to some remote corner of the earth, to be forgotten."

Meanwhile Peary made a triumphal tour of the European capitals. He picked up more than a dozen medals from learned societies. They assumed that the National Geographic had the same unimpeachable concern for scientific accuracy as the Royal Geographical Society of London. To its credit, when presenting Peary with its gold medal, the English society took pains to point out that its award was not made necessarily for his Pole dash, but for "all the long years of toil and trouble which he has devoted to polar exploration."

Nobody would argue with that tribute. Especially not one member of the audience who listened attentively when Peary delivered his lecture before that august English body. It was Dr. Cook, now a nonperson, disguised in a Vandyke beard, a clipped moustache and a bobbed haircut.

"I stood twenty yards from Peary," Cook was to recall with a sad smile, "and none recognized me. I was very much interested in Peary's lecture."

In later years Cook said he could not remember much of what Peary said in his speech. All the physician could think of as he caught this last glimpse of his belligerent antagonist was that the signs of pernicious anemia were so pitifully engraved on Peary's face.

On February 20, 1920, Peary died of that affliction at the age of sixty-four. "In the last year of his life," said his daughter, Marie, the former Snow Baby, "he spent most of the summer lying in the sunshine

on a muskox skin spread out on the lawn of our island home in Maine."
He was buried at Arlington National Cemetery in Washington amid
much military pomp. His casket was draped with the remnants of the
Stars and Stripes with which he had swathed his body on his Arctic expeditions. The monument placed upon his grave by the National
Geographic Society was a huge globe of white granite representing the
earth. Inscribed on it was Peary's motto, "I shall find a way or make
one," and a legend proclaiming him "Discoverer of the North Pole."

Cook was not destined to be buried amid such splendor. The cabal
of moneyed Peary advocates maintained an unrelenting campaign of
vilification and slander that was to follow the discredited Cook to his
grave twenty years later. After emerging from a self-imposed exile in
South America, he tried to redeem his tarnished reputation on the
American vaudeville circuit, billed as the "American Dreyfus Case."
But the Peary adherents preceded him in whichever city he was booked
to appear and supplied local newspapers with a damaging press kit.

As his supporters gradually abandoned him, Cook attempted to
make his living as an oil explorer in Texas. Eventually he was charged
with allegedly defrauding the public by exaggerating the prospects of
the oil lands his company controlled. His wife divorced him; but she remained loyal during the trial and raised ten thousand dollars from oil
men for a defense fund. The Peary money men appear to have exerted
pressure on the judge. Cook was condemned by the bench as a bunco
artist the equal of Ananias, Baron Munchausen and Machiavelli, and
sentenced to fourteen years and nine months in Leavenworth Penitentiary—the longest sentence on record for misrepresentation. Ironically, as
it turned out, Cook had not misrepresented at all. The wells of his oil
land in Winkler County, Texas, which were seized by the U.S. government, ultimately gushed black riches worth millions of dollars.

Cook almost seemed resigned to being cast in the role of scapegoat.
"I reviewed my career in vivid dreams," he reflected while awaiting the
jury's verdict. "I saw the flag and the snow hut at the Pole, the ...
mirages ... the tall cliffs at Cape Sparbo ... the walrus sprawled on the
drifting pans."

Incredibly, when he became eligible for parole, the Peary forces
organized a campaign protesting his release. He walked out of prison a
broken old man of sixty-five, pauperized and near blind, but with the
blessings of the Leavenworth inmates and officers. He had organized a
prison night school, worked in its hospital, and edited the Leavenworth
newspaper, *New Era*. His successor's parting editorial lauded him as "a

*Peary took this blurred photo of Henson and the four Eskimos hoisting flags at the so-called top of the world which he located, coincidentally, on their igloo encampment. Evidence of modern geographers indicates that neither Peary nor Cook got within 100 miles of striking the Big Nail.*

NATIONAL GEOGRAPHIC SOCIETY

man meek and loving, asking for nothing more than an even break from his fellow men."

The only break he got was a pardon granted to him by President Franklin D. Roosevelt three months before Cook's death. He spent his last days writing *Return from the Pole*, though he was paralyzed and could hardly speak. One of his last visitors was Rudolph Franke, his loyal comrade who had wintered with him in Greenland before Cook had made his dash for the Pole. Franke reminded him of the Christmas they had spent together at Anoatok. "You and I did the best to make that day cheerful for one another," Franke said. He reminded him how wonderful it had been to watch the stars glittering like Broadway lights in the Arctic sky. Then Franke spoke a few words to him in Eskimo. Cook's blue eyes seemed to smile in reply. He died on August 5, 1940, at the age of seventy-five, managing to whisper two words, "Thanks. Happy."

Like his great antagonist, Peary, Cook died happily convinced that he had won the race to the North Pole. Did either of them ever reach the Big Nail? It is doubtful. In the 1930s Dr. J. Gordon Hayes, the English geographer, investigated both their claims in what is probably the most scrupulously fair scientific inquiry ever conducted about the affair. In *Conquest of the North Pole* he concluded that Peary's claim was impossible and Cook's story more plausible, but the chances were that neither of them got within one hundred miles of striking the Big Nail. "Thus the North Pole may be said to have been besieged for several years," according to Dr. Hayes' final analysis, "but emerged from the infantry attack like a virgin fortress."

While Cook never won due recognition for his athletic feat, his assault of the Pole yielded a far greater victory for humanity. He broke through the barriers of *Kabloona* prejudice. He prepared the way for two outstanding explorer-ethnologists, Vilhjalmur Stefansson and Knud Rasmussen. They were to follow his trail and, like him, strive for a genuine human and scientific understanding of the people of the north. Perhaps Cook's *My Attainment of the Pole* did not live up to its title. It was, however, the first book by an Arctic explorer whose title page offered a dedication to the Arctic's aboriginal pathfinders:

*To the Indian who invented pemmican and snowshoes;*
*To the Eskimo who gave the art of sled traveling;*
*To this twin family of wild folk who have no flag*
*Goes the first credit.*

# Chapter 12

# Knud: Champion of the Eskimos

*"Who are you? Are you a trader come to buy foxes?"*
*"I have come to look at you, and see what you are made of inside."*

—Knud Rasmussen, reporting a conversation with a Canadian Eskimo in *Across Arctic America.*

In the early 1900s there were two white men roving across the Arctic who at first puzzled the Eskimos. Clearly both were a different kind of *Kabloona*. They were neither whalers, nor missionaries; neither sportsmen, nor foolish seekers after the Big Nail.

Surprisingly both were virtuosos in Eskimo survival techniques. They were accomplished sledge drivers. They were skilled hunters. They considered Eskimo food appetizing. They spoke the Eskimo tongue fluently. Most astonishing, they did not ridicule Eskimo superstitions, songs, and folktales. Rather they loved listening to them and spent years recording the ancient lore of the *Inuits*.

They were, of course, ethnologic anthropologists. This meant they were social scientists who made a study of primitive people. Yet Knud Rasmussen, the Eskimo-Dane, and Vilhjalmur Stefansson, the Icelandic-Canadian, were not just pioneer students of Eskimo folklore. They were also the last of the great sledge explorers, possibly the greatest of them all. And they were not merely concerned with delineating new places on the map (although the discoverers did their share of filling in blank spaces and were prodigious travelers both). Other things

interested them far more. They tried to understand the teeming life of the Arctic, and to treat respectfully the human beings who were its splendid inhabitants.

The two interpreters of the north country, exactly the same age, were not rivals. They admired each other's work. But they were markedly different in approach and personality. Knud Rasmussen was the intuitive one. Vilhjalmur Stefansson was the brainy one. They thus complemented each other, and by their joint efforts were the first to make the Arctic and its people truly comprehensible to the outside world.

Knud (pronounced "Kunoot") Rasmussen was known to the Eskimos as *Kununguak*, meaning Little Knud, and they adored him. Wherever he went, whether crisscrossing Greenland or sledging across the roof of North America, the Eskimos almost invariably recognized their beloved *Kununguak*. When Knud was the first to traverse the Northwest Passage by dog team, relates Helge Larsen, chief curator of the Danish National Museum, "they knew about him long before he arrived. When he came to the Netsilik tribe at the north magnetic pole, for example, the Eskimos tried to cut a lock of his hair, tear a piece from his notebook, get anything that belonged to him, for use in their amulets."

Some of his hosts found their hawk-nosed, pale-faced guest frankly ugly in appearance. One woman invited Knud inside her igloo for a special reason. She thought her daughter would appreciate meeting "someone just as ugly as herself." But most thought him handsome because of his Eskimolike attributes. He was a powerfully chested five-foot-five, with raven-black hair, high cheekbones, and merry brown eyes. Usually he was seen puffing a pipe fixed in his wide, boyishly grinning mouth—an Eskimo artist drew a charming portrait showing his pipe converted into his nose.

He mesmerized people with his brand of irresistible charm. "Talk to us! Talk to us, *Kununguak!*" the tribal elders would say; and in exchange for the *angekok's* own local legends, he would recite wonderful tales picked up from other villages. "Dance with me! Dance with me, *Kununguak!*" the old women would cry; and in exchange for demonstrations of their swaying drum dances, he would foxtrot the old ladies about to "Alexander's Ragtime Band" played on his creaky phonograph.

He was something of a ladies' man, something of a dandy, and very much the *bon vivant*. According to his best friend, Peter Freuchen, Knud

had at least one Eskimo mistress. He flattered Eskimo seamstresses so outrageously that they vied to equip him with the most beautiful footwear; he always carried a pair of scissors for cutting his hair; no matter how biting the cold he washed his face daily. He was such an enthusiastic organizer of igloo parties that Freuchen titled him the Elsa Maxwell of the Arctic.

"Knud was an Eskimo at heart," said Freuchen. Like most Eskimos, he was a gifted mimic and had a keen ear for music and language. Whenever the dusky polar night made him feel blue, he would play Mozart's *Don Giovanni* on his phonograph; or he might reread Byron's *Don Juan* and Kipling's *Jungle Tales* in English; or, better still, dip into his favorite book of heroism, Xenophon's *Anabasis*, in the original Greek.

He was not much of a mathematical scientist. He never could determine his location with navigational instruments, because he had been humiliated as a boy by a sarcastic maths teacher who called him a dunce. But when it was a matter of locating the hearts of people, Knud was a genius as unerringly sensitive as a seismograph. His books, notably *The People of the Polar North* and *Greenland by the Polar Sea*, give us a greater insight into Eskimo thought and feeling than any other chronicles in polar literature. And his *Across Arctic America* is a delightfully fresh-eyed narrative equalled for its readability only by "my private gossiping journal" written by that Victorian-Age charmer, Captain George Francis Lyon. No matter how tough the hardships, Knud's prose almost always seemed to be smiling. His happiest moments, he wrote, came when "hungry and shrunk from lack of meat, we espied distant settlements with the smell of unknown people."

And on one of his Bunyanesque sledge treks across the northern Ice Cap of Greenland, he was capable of belittling his achievements with a few enchanting phrases: "The outlines of our work, however, were drawn by our predecessors, and we therefore knew beforehand that we could not expect any great geographical surprises. It was only the crumbs from the table of the rich expeditions we were to gather, and the role we were to play would be comparable to that of the little polar fox, which everywhere on the Arctic coast follows the footsteps of the big ice-bear, hoping that something good may be left for it. But our task was not an ungrateful one, for we came to lift the stones which the others had let lie."

Knud Johan Victor Rasmussen spent his happy boyhood hunting the little polar foxes. He was born on June 7, 1879, at the Danish whal-

*Knud Rasmussen, Eskimo-Danish anthropologist, criss-crossed Greenland and was first to traverse the Northwest Passage by dog team.* ARKTISK INSTITUT, CHARLOTTENLUND, DENMARK

ing station of Jakobshaven, the great breeding place of icebergs, on the southwest coast of Greenland. His maternal greatgrandfather was a pureblood Eskimo named Paulus Sealhunter. Knud's part Eskimo mother, Sophie, told the boy many stories of the redoubtable Sealhunter's deeds. Knud's father, Pastor Christian Rasmussen, was a scholarly Danish missionary. The linguist helped compile an Eskimo dictionary and grammar and passed on to his son an abiding affection for the native Greenlanders.

At the age of eight, Knud was driving his own dogteam. At ten, carrying his own rifle, he joined his Eskimo playmates in hunting forays. His sole regret was that his father forebade him to own a kayak. The local schoolmaster complained that the parson's mischievous son played hooky too often. But Knud was gaining a first-hand knowledge of Eskimo traditions and legends.

His imagination was fired by tales of "The New People." They were supposedly ferocious, man-eating Eskimos who wore polar-bear skins and lived somewhere on the north tip of Greenland, in the dark Kingdom of the North Wind, at "the very end of the world." These myths about the un-Christianized Neighbors of the North Pole excited his curiosity. "When I grow up," he promised himself, "I will go see for myself."

When Knud was twelve, the Rasmussens moved to the vicarage at Lynge on the outskirts of the Danish capital of Copenhagen. At the University of Copenhagen he was a poor scholar. He felt like a caged polar bear and never completed his academic studies. He quit to take a brief fling at opera and drama. (An early photo shows the young actor wearing a rakish fedora and looking as intensely theatrical as a junior John Barrymore.) Then he tried his hand as a freelance journalist. He wrote colorful human-interest features, and he had no trouble getting newspaper assignments as foreign correspondent in Iceland, Lapland and Sweden.

At the age of twenty-three he found his true *métier*. He was hired to be interpreter and literary historian for a Danish expedition that planned an eighteen-month trip to northwest Greenland. He returned to Copenhagen as the Boswell and cultural advocate of the Etah Eskimos of the "Kingdom of the North Wind." His first book, *The People of the Polar North*, captured in fluid story style the humor and the hardships of a maligned and misunderstood race. They were not fierce man-eaters at all. Never had he met "more cheerful, more amenable and good-humoured people" than his bear-trousered, faun-like hosts. "I

have learned to love them," he said, "as highly as I admire their remarkable ability to live the life of these harsh regions."

But the people he had adopted were in a dilemma. The American explorer, Robert Peary, had paid them with rifles, ammunition, steel hatchets and wooden utensils. Then, after having "developed in them the white man's brain," as Knud phrased it, Peary had simply left them flat. The Etah Eskimos now felt the white man's means of hunting were economic necessities; some were suffering because they could not revert to their former Stone Age way of life. The Danish government turned a deaf ear to Knud's plea that it establish official trade channels with the north Greenland fur hunters and take an interest in their welfare. Knud therefore resolved to raise money independently and assume that task himself.

Knud was not quite a one-man trade and cultural ambassador to his Kingdom of the North Wind. He was fortunate to hire as his second in command a gay, yarn-spinning Danish newspaperman destined to become almost as heroic a figure in Greenland as himself. Peter Freuchen, sometimes nicknamed Peter Summerwhiskers, was a bearded giant of a man. He was a dropout from Copenhagen medical school; a sometime sailor; a part-time explorer who had shipped as a stoker with a 1906 Danish expedition to Greenland; and mostly he was a born showman. Film scripts, novels and adventure stories poured out of him, glamorizing his legalized marriage to an Etah Eskimo wife named Navarana. Later, after he had his frozen left leg amputated, he commercialized on it. He stumped around the lecture circuit on a magnificent hollow leg made of narwhal horn as he told of his thrilling escapades with Knud.

According to Freuchen's memoirs, *I Sailed with Rasmussen*, he and Knud tried to raise funds for their Greenland mission via a semifarcical lecture tour throughout Denmark. Knud was supposed to deliver a travelogue lecture explaining the lantern slides he had accumulated in Greenland. Freuchen was to operate the second-hand projection machine he had acquired on credit. But at the first lecture hall the projector did not work properly. It showed only a few black splotches on the screen.

Knud, with his theatrical background, adlibbed masterfully. "Yes, ladies and gentlemen," he bluffed, "I'm sure you've all seen pictures of Greenland taken during the summer midnight sun. But for the first time you have the privilege of viewing *realistic* pictures shot during the long dark winter night."

*Young Knud posing as an actor.*

*Knud at Thule with Peter Freuchen.*

*Knud with his missionary father, Pastor Christian Rasmussen, who compiled an Eskimo dictionary.* ALL THREE PICTURES: ARKTISK INSTITUT, CHARLOTTENLUND, DENMARK

Freuchen flashed on a fuzzy scene of dancing Eskimo women.

"A night polar bear hunt," Knud improvised. "Isn't it dramatic?"

It was followed by a series of flickering lights and shadows that looked like nothing at all.

"A brave Eskimo," declaimed Knud. "He's standing over a seal's breathing hole for hours in the polar gloom, so he can bring home the bacon for his starving children."

There was a burst of applause for the brave Eskimo. But the audience began to fidget. They had enough of midnight photography. Now they clamorously demanded to see how Greenland looked in the daytime.

Like Mark Twain's mountebank Dauphin and Duke in *Huckleberry Finn*, the pair of vagabond troupers were virtually run out of town. For the rest of the tour they hired a professional projectionist. Apart from the fun they had, it netted little cash. Fortunately Knud's father persuaded a committee of church and mercantile friends to contribute funds.

Knud received support as well from the beautiful Copenhagen heiress he married. The former Dagmar Andersen was an ideal explorer's wife. She was a concert pianist who shared Knud's love for operatic music; she was to present him with two daughters and a son; and apparently she seldom complained about the years that her husband spent in the world's northernmost station in the Kingdom of the North Wind.

On August 19, 1910, Knud and Freuchen established their remote outpost in North Star Bay on the northwest coast of Greenland, not too far from the Etah Eskimos' Wind-Loved Spot of Anoatok. Except for a bathtub which they later installed, the shack was hardly palatial. Nevertheless Knud gave it a grand name—Thule (pronounced "Toolee"). It is derived from the *Ultima Thule* of the ancient geographers, meaning the farthest north land known to be inhabited by man. It has since become the United States Thule Air Base: among the world's most northerly ballistic-missile early warning systems, equipped with a weather and radio station and streamlined aircraft. But for the Etah Eskimos toward the beginning of the century it was a combination trade, medical and social centre. For Knud it was the base from which he launched seven major dog sledge expeditions over a period of twenty-one years.

The first one was initiated for humanitarian reasons. Three explorers had died while trying to verify Peary's erroneous map of the

northeast corner of Greenland. A fourth Danish explorer, Ejnar Mik-
kelsen, after landing by ship on the east coast of Greenland, had gone in
search of the missing trio into the interior. Now it was feared that he
had suffered the same fate.

In mid-April of 1912 Knud set out on his rescue mission determined to make a swift direct march across the evil ice dome on the cap
of north Greenland. He was taking an audacious gamble. He intended
to live off the land Eskimo-style, provisioned with just one month's supply of dog food for his total five-month, sixteen-hundred-mile journey.

Fifty-three dogs would pull four sledges. His sole companions
would be Freuchen and two Eskimos. Knud laid down the dictum from
the outset that for all of his expeditions "there must be no difference in
standing between the Eskimos and ourselves, the Eskimos being members with equal rights and duties." The two he selected were courageous
men, for heretofore few coastal Eskimos had dared to venture too far
over the spirit-haunted *Sermik-soak*—the Great Ice Wall. One was a
champion sledge driver named Uvdluriarq. The other's name was so
unpronounceable that he rejoiced in the nickname of Harrigan, after
the title of a popular American vaudeville ballad.

"A beautiful and exciting time, with races from morning till
night," wrote Knud. "One sledge after another shoots across the ice like
a swift bird flying out into the darkness . . . and ahead beckon the skull-
capped peaks and slit glacier tongues."

The four broke all records for overland snowshoe-ski-and-dogteam
travel, averaging a speed of thirty-five miles per march. According to
Freuchen, the chief chronicler of this trip, they were able to keep up the
breakneck pace because of Knud's incessant good cheer. At an altitude
of seven thousand feet, Freuchen said, the sun's rays were like white-hot
metal poked in their eyes. Ice needles ripped through dog booties.
Blizzards of blinding, sugarlike snow blew with hurricane force so that
an entire team of dogs was lifted into the air and three of the creatures
were lost in a crevasse. Yet, like a cheerleader, Knud kept urging his
team forward with a chorus of American football songs, Danish ditties,
and snatches of Wagnerian opera.

When their food ran out, they were reduced to eating the strips of
frozen walrus hide which they had been using as sleigh runners.
Resourceful Knud had taken the precaution of bringing along copies of
a women's housekeeping magazine. Each night, as they sipped tea and
gnawed walrus skins, he would read aloud succulent menu recipes.

"Scrambled eggs and bacon!" he would shout. "That's what we're
dining on tonight."

*Family customs of the Eskimos were enchantingly chronicled on Knud's 20,000-mile sledge trek across Arctic North America.* MANITOBA ARCHIVES

*Knud elicited ancient lore from Eskimo storytellers in exchange for playing "Alexander's Ragtime Band" on a gramophone.* MANITOBA ARCHIVES

"Right you are!" Freuchen would sing out. "With pancakes!"

Harrigan and Uvdluriarq accepted the prospect of starvation with much levity. They doubled up with laughter as they spoke of the vast amounts of seal meat and blubber they had cached back home on the west coast. Knud marveled at their amused contempt for death and took a lesson from it. "When one has decided on the hazards of a journey," he concluded, "one must take everything that occurs like a man—that is, with a broad grin."

Things improved when they reached their destination on the east coast. South of Peary Land (which proved to be a huge peninsula, instead of the island which Peary had mistakenly reported) they came upon an oasis of alpine flowers blossoming yellow and gold among the bluey-white glaciers. Knud promptly called it Poppy Valley. It was rich as well in grazing muskoxen. They were so tame that Knud attacked the shaggy creatures as though in a mock bullfight. Freuchen played the role of picador, distracting their attention by pelting them with pebbles. Meanwhile Knud, as matador, crept up stealthily from behind and plunged a long knife between their shoulders.

"We lay down and sucked the fresh milk from the udders of the cows," said Freuchen. "The taste was heavenly."

Their high spirits turned to gloom when they found camp traces of the Danish explorers who had lost their lives as a result of Peary's cartography. Still intact after twenty years was the stone cairn which Peary had erected on top of reddish bronze Navy Cliff. But his "Peary Channel" turned out to be nothing but a glacier-filled valley; it clearly was not washed by the waves of the Greenland Sea, as Peary had claimed.

It was Freuchen who had to climb to the peak of Navy Cliff. Knud had developed sciatica in his left leg and could no longer walk. The journey back was sheer torture for him. Freuchen carried him on his back across glaciers and rivers. But the jolting of the sledge which bore him over ice hummocks left him in agony. His face was ghost-white; he bit a piece of hide to conceal his pain and he fainted several times. Sometimes the sledge turned over and he spilled onto the ice. He merely winced and said quietly, "This is unpleasant."

Freuchen suggested they rest for a few days. Knud would not hear of it. He lay with his eyes closed and muttered cheerfully, "Shut up, and go ahead."

Happily, by the time they neared Thule, with just four scrawny dogs left, Knud recovered and could outrun the whole party. He was pleased with what his expedition had accomplished. Besides disproving

Peary's false map, he had refuted the notion that the coastal Eskimos were too superstition-ridden to attempt crossing Greenland's interior Ice Cap.

"The Eskimos are a roaming people, always longing for a change and a surprise," he decided. "A people who like moving about in search of fresh hunting grounds, fresh possibilities, and 'hidden things.' They are born with the explorer's inclination and thirst for knowledge; and they possess all those qualities which go to make an explorer in these latitudes."

On the outskirts of Thule, it pleased him to see how his plucky explorers decided to share their few remnants of tobacco, so the troupe could make a grand entrance with pipes in their mouths. On their arrival, Harrigan took enormous pride in reaching for his tobacco pouch and greeting the Thule villagers with the casual remark, "Have a smoke?"

"And then there was feasting in Thule!" wrote Freuchen. "All-night dancing and heavy eating! People came running with huge slabs of whale hide and rotten bird meat and other kinds of delicacies, and Knud dissolved all of the journey's difficulties into laughter and gay stories."

There were more tears than laughter on Knud's Second Thule Expedition. With two other specialists, he planned a six-month survey of the vast stretch of north Greenland coast now known as Knud Rasmussen Land. Knud himself would do the anthropological research; he hoped to discover encampment ruins, which would indicate the trail of ancient Eskimo migrations. Specimens of plant life would be collected by Dr. Thorild Wulff, an eminent Swedish botanist; he was a rather frail, thirty-nine-year-old Arctic tenderfoot, whose past experience had been largely confined to the more exotic flora of Japan, China, and India, Sumatra and Java. Yet he was determined to be the first scientist to investigate north Greenland's vegetation. He was intensely dedicated to it. Freuchen, who wasn't coming on this expedition, tells us he took Dr. Wulff out on a preliminary toughening-up snowshoe run across ice hummocks. Whenever the botanist faltered, Freuchen snapped his whip at him.

Dr. Wulff was most appreciative. "It proved I could do more than I had believed myself capable of doing," he said, "and I thank you for forcing me to do it."

The second scientist was twenty-four-year-old Lauge Koch, a Danish geologist, who hoped to discover coral specimens, as he did; the

ambitious youth also took a course in cartography, for he knew the maps of north Greenland were very deficient. "Broad of shoulder," Knud described Koch, "strong of build, tough, and showing the consciousness of his strength in the swing wherewith he walks, like a young Great Dane." Koch was to need all the strength he could muster on the gruelling trip ahead.

This time Knud had no trouble recruiting four Eskimos to help drive the six sledges with seventy dogs to *Akia*—Eskimo for "The country on the other side of the Great Glacier." There was Harrigan, the pipe-smoking veteran of his previous expedition. There was Bosun, so nicknamed because he operated the motorboat at Thule. There was Ajako, just twenty years old, but a nimble hunter with marvelous endurance. And there was an amiable, Christianized hymn-singer known as "Happy" Hendrik Olsen, destined to come to an unhappy end on this journey.

The expedition started out happily enough. In early April of 1917, before tackling the great glassy Humboldt Glacier on the west coast, Knud staged an all-night ball. He called it a musical debauchery. Knud joined Enrico Caruso and Adelina Patti in singing their *Rigoletto* arias on the phonograph; he led the Eskimos in dancing tangos and one-steps.

"One goes out to meet one's fate and adventures filled with joyful expectations," said Knud, and he did. He had an appreciative eye for the luminous beauty of the glacier-swathed peaks, looming like iced wedding cakes, all along the west coast. He had a feeling of reverence as he came upon abandoned encampments of explorers who had preceded him. He paused reflectively at Rensselaer Bay, where Dr. Elisha Kent Kane had undergone such dreadful hardships. "Tall, elegant, and proud sandstone mountains stand on both sides of the bay, like a majestic porch leading to the cove," he wrote. These cloud-plumed pyramids seemed to symbolize Kane's courage.

He camped at Thank God Harbour and took off his hat as he contemplated the grave of Charles Francis Hall. Nearby he found an opened bottle of port wine which had preserved its bouquet after more than a half century of frosty nights.

"It was, of course, drunk in a mood of devotion," he wrote. "The ground on which we stand is dearly paid for; its exploration has cost the life of many a brave man of iron will. But for each one who fell there were others who offered to take his place; thus our knowledge of the northernmost regions of the earth moves farther and farther north."

His party pushed northeastward, across "endless white ice-steppes," mapping wherever they went. The dogs wore down their claws fighting for a foothold on glassy ice slopes. They were swallowed up by clammy fogs. They were lashed by gales. Knud remained cheerful. He named a cape, in honor of "my beautiful and hearty friend," who had been left minding the store back home, Peter Freuchen Land. Poor Peter was missing all the fun, Knud thought, as his party camped near Mount Punch, "with its genially sounding name, lifting its snowy cap rakishly towards the clouds."

It was May 27, a blustery Whitsun Day at ten below zero Centigrade. Knud, the inveterate party-thrower, had the members of his party celebrate the occasion, though they were consuming almost the last of their civilized provisions.

"Here on the skull of the world," he wrote with a flourish, "we eat a tin of Mauna Loa pineapple, the only one we possess, tinned at Hawaii. . . . And as we see before us the dark-eyed, garlanded girls who picked the fruits, it is as if we cut through all horizons and conquer the world.

"Hawaii and the Polar Sea, North Latitude 82 degrees!

"So we cook muskox meat from Nares Land, drink coffee from Java, after the tea from the Congo, and smoke tobacco from Brazil!

"A glorious Whitsun!"

But soon he had changed his tune. They were near starvation. Their pemmican supply was fast running out. Their poor dogs, with ice lumps frozen to their lacerated paws, were leaving a trail of blood in the snow. The snow itself, dry and powdering, was too soft to be traversed by either ski or snowshoe, and the drifts raged and gusted like a tornado of flour.

"There is nothing for it," Knud tried to cheer up his men. "We must, like the little saxifrage which sometimes winters in full bloom, sleep everything away and let the storm pass over us as if we did not exist."

By the end of June they were forced to turn back home. Muskoxen were not to be found anywhere. They were eating their dogs one by one. The creatures were so emaciated that Knud didn't have the heart to celebrate Koch's twenty-fifth birthday with a party of stringy dog flesh.

"It appeared to me not only unaesthetic and unappetizing, but akin to cannibalism," Knud confided to his diary. He put on a good face and did his best to convince the white men in his party that dog meat was as delicious as fresh mutton. "What the devil!" he argued plausibly.

"The dog is merely a domestic animal, and all the world over one eats domestic animals!"

But try as he might, he could not convince himself that this was true. In his diary he described a recurring dream:

"I am at my father's vicarage at Lynge, standing with my mother in the larder, where is to be found a drawer which is always full of cakes. Mother has just finished baking and put two lovely warm Christmas cakes into the drawer, sweetly fragrant with delicious ingredients, bristling with raisins and citron. She cuts a couple of thick slices for me, saying in her gentle voice: 'There you are, my boy; eat as much as you like!'

"As I raise the delicious cake to my mouth, I wake up to all our misery. My comrades are lying asleep, the wind is whipping the drifting snow around our tent, and an exhausted dog is lying out in the drifts, whimpering pitifully. . . . Again I awake from the mocking dream, and as compensation we make coffee from the old grounds and distribute half a rye biscuit to each man."

Knud realized they were doomed if he couldn't buck up their morale. So he organized a singsong of football songs, had Dr. Wulff give a lecture on the nature of lichens, and encouraged them to crack jokes.

"We try to stimulate each other by poking fun at the miserable appearance many of us present," he wrote. "There is nothing for it but sucking nourishment from one's humour during these days."

Eventually even his omnipresent good humour began to flag. Sometimes they were wading up to their knees in icy water. Sometimes the winds were so violent they tottered like scarecrows on their skis. The glacier ravines were "like waves stiffened in horror" and the howl of two faroff white wolves sounded like an eerie duet of lamentation.

To Knud the Ice Cap crowning Knud Rasmussen Land was as barren as a Libyan desert. "No sign of life, not a bird, not a plant, softens the impression of this utmost desolation," he wrote. "A land without a heart. . . ."

Those last words seemed prophetic. On July 21st Happy Hendrik Olsen crossed the rotting ice over to an island to shoot hares for his famished companions. He never returned. For seventy-two hours they searched for him, but in vain. Knud surmised that the Eskimo had perhaps stumbled and accidentally shot himself with his Winchester rifle and had possibly been devoured by wolves. The saddened party built a stone cairn, and lowered the flag, and Knud delivered a memorial address, first in Danish and then in Eskimo, mourning the loss of the happy hymn-singer.

"The little orphan boy from Rittenbenk was to die not merely as a Greenlander, but altogether as the man who traversed and learned to know the greatest stretch of his Fatherland's coast," said Knud. "The Polar Eskimo has a proverb. It says no man will settle down and take up a new land for good until death overtakes him and ties his body to a stone mound; first then is it possible to attach a man to a country.

"I therefore propose that we hold to his idea, born by the enormous spirit of liberty of primitive man, and to this island, where Hendrik found his grave, give his name. . . . We all know how fond he was of singing his hymns. We will say the Lord's Prayer, in his own tongue, as a final farewell from his old comrades."

The pitiless Ice Cap was to snatch another victim. Towards the end of August Knud acknowledged they were fighting for their lives. They had eaten their last dog. They possessed a single spoonful of tea. Harrigan carried his swollen arm in a sling as a result of pulling sledges over ice hummocks. Koch was dizzy with fatigue and his body was covered with painful boils. Dr. Wulff was suffering most of all. Not only was he tormented by boils, but he looked like a limping skeleton. He had tumbled through the ice crust of a crevasse and had been barely able to hang onto the ledge with his arms until Knud had rescued him. In his exhaustion the botanist said he couldn't take another step through the frothing, paralyzingly cold mountain rivers.

"This is the end," he said. "I cannot go any farther."

Knud called a council meeting. It was almost two hundred miles to Anoatok, the nearest Etah Eskimo village on the west coast. They all agreed that Knud and young Ajako, the most robust members of the expedition, would walk there and send a relief party back. Harrigan and Bosun would remain behind to hunt for hares and do what they could to help the weakened botanist and geologist proceed in slow marches.

Knud was to remember that Dr. Wulff seemed resigned and almost happy and jocular when he left him. Resting on a rocky ledge, the botanist waved goodbye to the pair of hikers and said with a sad smile, "Now don't forget to send some pancakes with the relief sledges."

Sixteen days later the relief sledges returned to Anoatok with just three survivors: Koch, Harrigan, and Bosun.

"Koch sat down on a stone, pale and without a word, and the tears which rolled down his cheeks told me everything I needed to know," wrote Knud. "A catastrophe had overtaken the expedition. Wulff was dead, fallen in the last fight for life."

When Koch regained his composure, the geologist had a moving

story to tell. Sleet, hail, and lack of game had compelled the invalids to move away from the barren glacial valley to a better hunting ground. Koch had crawled on with them for a few days, and they were subsisting on the occasional raw hare, willow roots, and even caribou excreta. In their enfeebled state they began to discard their scientific equipment. Dr. Wulff said he could proceed no farther. He had neither the strength to go on nor the wish to abandon his cherished botanical collection. He had lost the will to live and was quite content to die in the field.

"This walk is worse than death," he said. "It is like walking to one's own funeral."

He begged to be left behind. All he wanted was a grass-and-flower-strewn couch where he could lie down and rest. So desperate was their situation that Koch was forced to comply.

Dr. Wulff lit his pipe and calmly dictated to Koch his last will and testament as well as a summation of the sixty flowering plants he had discovered.

"Well, dear comrades, here I will rest," he finally waved them off. "I wish for you personally that you may reach your goal. When you meet difficulties, remember that now it is you that must save our results. May good fortune follow you. And now farewell."

Until the very end, his fingers frozen stiff with cold, Dr. Wulff was scribbling in his diary notes on the flora and fauna of the Arctic:

"Veget. finished for the year, everything yellow and brown, ready for winter's rest. . . . We make fire of Cassiope or better still with old dry branches of *Salix arctica*, finger-thick. . . . A loon, geese, terns, buntings in flocks. Midnight gloom, gneiss knolls, tracks of reindeer. . . .

"Cold. Fog. Falling snow . . . *Selago, Rhododendron*, red-polls in flocks, terns, falcons, plenty of animal life and rich plankton in several little lakes. *Sax. cernua*, foot high with top leaf. *Myrtillus ulig.* blood-red, very common, always without fruit. . . . Ate entrails of young hare raw, warmth in body. . . .

"I am half-dead, but found *Woodsia ilv.* Lay down at 7 PM, for I will not hamper the movements of my comrades on which hangs their salvation. . . .

"I await death with a perfectly calm mind and in my heart is peace. Up to the last I have honestly striven to honour our name and hope that the results of my work may be saved."

The death of the dedicated scientist affected Knud profoundly. It inspired him to conduct the most ambitious scientific study of Eskimo culture ever performed. He would investigate no less than every major

tribe across Arctic North America, and in the process make the longest sledge journey in polar history.

On June 17, 1921, the famed Fifth Thule Expedition sailed out of Copenhagen aboard the especially built, one-hundred-ton motor schooner, *Sea King*. Knud was to focus his research on the spiritual and intellectual life of the almost mythic people known to Greenland Eskimos as *Akilinermiut*—"those who dwell on the land beyond the Great Sea." His party of fellow Danish scientists included the distinguished anthropologist, Dr. Kaj Birket-Smith, and the illustrious archaeologist, Dr. Therkel Mathiassen. Peter Freuchen (destined to lose his left leg on this expedition when he found himself frozen fast to his icy bed under his sledge and apparently escaped by using his own frozen excreta as a hatchet) was to serve as cartographer and naturalist. Knud's veteran sledge comrade, Bosun, headed the contingent of seven Eskimos picked up en route at Thule.

For two years they headquartered at windy "Blow Hole" (now known as Danish Island, at the top of Hudson Bay, south of Melville Peninsula), and they fanned out on explorative treks in five directions. Then on the morning of March 10, 1923, Knud said goodbye to his colleagues, cried *"Huk! Huk! Huk!"* to his team, and set out on his Great Sledge Journey to the Pacific Ocean.

It was a stupendous trip. He was to traverse in one and a half years the entire coastline of the Northwest Passage. He would thus weld together the regions it had taken Sir John Franklin, Sir John Richardson, Dr. John Rae, Thomas Simpson and other great travelers more than a century to explore piece by piece. And Knud would accomplish this mammoth feat with two twenty-foot-long ice-shod sledges, twenty-four dogs, and only two Eskimo companions. One was Miteq, meaning "eider duck," a cheery twenty-two-year-old, whom Knud had known since the youth had been a baby at Thule. The other was Anarulunguaq, a pretty, round-cheeked widow of twenty-eight, whom Knud jokingly referred to as "my little woman." King Christian X of Denmark, patron of the expedition, was to present her with a gold medal for keeping Knud's Eskimo travel outfit so neatly mended during the long trek.

Knud was aware of the historic import of his pilgrimage. He made a point of sledging up to the King William Island region, the graveyard of the Sir John Franklin expedition. On the east coast of Adelaide Peninsula he came upon human bones and scraps of white men's clothing—doubtless, he thought, the last mortal remains of Franklin's

*Eskimos drew this charming sketch to illustrate one of their legends.* ARKTISK INSTITUT, CHARLOTTENLUND, DENMARK

*Anarulunguaq, Knud's "my little woman" companion on his Arctic America sledge trip.*

*Botanist Dr. Thorild Wulff, who died bravely listing Greenland's flora and fauna.*

doomed men. He buried the forlorn remains under a cairn, and lowered a British and Danish flag at half mast.

"Here on this lonely spit of land," he said in tribute, "weary men had toiled along the last stage of their mortal journey. Their tracks are not effaced, as long as others live to follow and carry them farther."

He did indeed extend their sledge tracks. The body of water southeast of King William Island, separating Rae Strait and Simpson Strait, has since been named in his honor Rasmussen Basin.

Furthering geography, however, was not his principal concern. Knud was more interested in enshrining in his thirty large notebooks the ancient folkways and philosophy of "our contemporary ancestors," some of whom had never before seen a white man.

The very first Eskimo he met on the northern rim of Hudson Bay typified for Knud their unfailing cordiality. A caravan of sledges approached him on the ice, headed by a man bearing a harpoon. Knud sprang on his sledge, and urged his team forward toward the furred Eskimo. The yammering dogs tore along at such full speed that Knud was virtually hurled into the arms of the harpoonist.

" 'Stand still!' I cried; and, taking a flying leap out among the dogs, I embraced the stranger after the Eskimo fashion," wrote Knud. "So there we stood, laughing and shaking each other. I had yelled at the dogs in the language of the Greenland Eskimos. And, from the expression of the stranger's face, in a flash I realized that he had understood what I said."

The harpoonist promptly introduced himself as Papik, meaning "Tail Feather." He stood there with his face covered with rime, his hair thick with icicles. Characteristically, his gleaming white teeth showed as he flashed a warm smile.

"Their gums," Knud was to write, "were always dry with smiling."

The other members of the caravan came shyly forward to be introduced by Papik to the white man who understood their language. "As soon as they saw we were friendly folk, as interesting to them as they were to us, they went wild with delight," Knud wrote. "There was a shouting and laughing and cracking of jokes."

Soon they were building a snow dance house for a party, and Knud, of course, felt right at home.

Throughout the entire course of his sledge trek, Knud found that he could communicate with each tribe using his Greenlandic Eskimo language. This seldom failed to astonish his hosts.

"At one village, having no idea that we can understand everything

they say, the people jest about my big nose and Arnarulunguaq's fat cheeks," Knud observed with vast amusement. "Our appearance, our clothing, all our possessions are subjected to expert appraisal, as if a traveling circus were about to open."

Like the impresario of a carnival freak show, Knud then delivered a long spiel in perfect Eskimo. They gaped. Then they shrieked with laughter. "The *faux pas* is buried beneath noisy and mutual merriment," he wrote, "and we are at once friends with a proper respect for one another."

It was not all sweetness and merriment that he recorded in his notebooks. He did not flinch from describing cannibalism and murder. In one encampment alone he noted that out of fifteen families there was not a single full-grown man who had not been involved in the killing of another. Yet with innate sympathy he could comprehend the fear and deprivation that sometimes drove them to violence. "It ought not to be forgotten," he wrote, "that a life amid a raw and stern climate does not make for hothouse plants."

He had a marvelous capacity for digging through the façade and extracting their innermost feelings. One old patriarch revealed:

"Oh! You strangers only see us happy and free of care. But if you knew the horrors we often have to live through, you would understand, too, why we are so fond of laughing, why we love food and song and dance. There is not one amongst us but has experienced a winter of bad hunting, when many starved to death in front of our eyes."

It was true, for in the old man's region twenty-five persons had recently died of hunger. The reality of their precarious existence was brought home to Knud most poignantly in their songs. He was deeply moved by the anguish expressed in one litany entitled *A Dead Man's Song, Dreamed by One Who Is Alive:*

*Here I lie, remembering*
*How stifled with fear I was*
*When they buried me*
*In a snowhut out on the lake,*
*Ayi, yai, ya.*

*In fear I lie, remembering:*
*Say, was it so beautiful on earth?*
*Glorious was life in winter*
*But did winter bring me joy?*

*No! Ever was I so anxious*
*For soles to our footwear*
*Or skins for our boots.*
*Would there be enough for us all?*
*Yes, I was ever anxious.*
*Ayi, yai, ya.*

*In fear and horror I lie,*
*But was I not always troubled in mind?*
*Glorious was life in summer*
*But did summer bring me joy?*
*No! Ever was I so anxious*
*When the hunting failed*
*And there was dearth of skins*
*For clothing and sleeping*
*Yes, I was ever anxious*
*Ayi, yai, ya.*

*Say, was it so beautiful on earth?*
*Now I am filled with joy*
*Whenever the dawn rises over the earth*
*And the great sun glides up into the sky....*
*Ayi, yai, ya.*

Another ballad, untitled, reflected the tense drama that filled their lives:

*The autumn comes blowing;*
*Ah, I tremble, I tremble at the harsh northern wind*
*That strikes me pitilessly in its might*
*While the waves threaten to upset my kayak.*
*The autumn comes blowing;*
*Ah, I tremble, I tremble lest the storm and the seas*
*Send me down to the clammy ooze in the depths of*
*the waters,*
*Rarely I see the water calm,*
*The waves cast me about;*
*And I tremble, I tremble at the thought of the hour*
*When the gulls shall hack at my dead body.*

And yet life was not all grim. Knud noticed that they were constantly singing and humming, and their humor was infectious. Once, Knud was sledging into an encampment and an elderly Eskimo put her hand on his shoulder.

"Tell me, stranger," she said. "Are you the sort of man who has never a smile for a woman?"

"I laughed aloud," said Knud in his diary. "I could not help it. And with that the ice was broken all round."

Never had he seen so many "poets and philosophers unawares." Though things might seem desperate, they were essentially celebrants of life rather than doom-criers. The verses they composed could find joy in the simplest blessings:

*Cold and mosquitoes*
*These two pests*
*Come never together ...*
*Ayi, yai, ya.*

And the word, joy, itself kept recurring in their lyrical salutes to the world:

*Joy bewitches*
*All about us*
*Skin boats rise up*
*Out of their moorings....*
*The great sea*
*Has sent me adrift,*
*It moves me as the weed in a great river.*
*Earth and the great weather*
*Move me*
*Have carried me away*
*And move my inward parts with joy.*

As he trekked westward, Knud was able to discern why these nomads derived so much pleasure from roaming. One bright spring day, while his dogs gamboled in the fields of budding flowers, he burst into a paean himself:

"Over the sappy-green meadows there was the song of thousands of birds, one continuous tremulous tone of joy and life. I saw geese, ducks and eider ducks swimming about in all the lakes, and every time I ap-

proached they rose noisy and cackling. The swamps were full of wading birds building their nests and laying their eggs, and all these voices joined into one great chorus singing that once again the earth lived. On a sunny day like this there is no feeling of being in the world's most rigorous regions."

Winter, too, could be a jubilant time, because of his expectation of the feasting for himself and his dogs at the next Eskimo encampment. "And from my heart I bless the fate that allowed me to be born when polar research by dog sledge was not yet a thing of the past," he reflected. "So all our experiences lie in the sweetness of the many camps and stopovers. And again I see clearly before me the lines of the little sledge tracks through the white snow."

As he neared the end of the trail, on the north coast of Yukon and Alaska, he could not help but feel somewhat saddened. American whalers had introduced a "tinpot store and canned provision culture" with its attendant vices. Knud was now obviously in the Land of the Almighty Dollar. Though they had no use for them, the exploited Eskimos, just to be fashionable, were buying such things as typewriters. Some of the younger Eskimos were peddling their parents' wonderful blubber lamps to tourists for thirty dollars apiece. A self-styled specialist in folklore offered his services confidently at twenty-five dollars a day. Knud could not blame them for being hard bargainers, like the white man; but yet it was saddening.

"Here, if I wanted folk tales, I found myself confronted with salesmanship," sighed Knud. "I felt, indeed, something of an old fossil myself among all these smart business folk; legend and myth and ancient traditions were things they had left far behind. Many a time during these first few weeks did I think wistfully of the eastern tribes, where men and women still had some respect for the wisdom of their forebears."

He was especially distressed by a young woman who had discarded her beautifully crafted caribouskin garb in favor of a horrible print apron. She sat cross-legged in her igloo amidst her Hudson's Bay Company blankets and tin cooking pots. Her hands, Knud noted, were covered with cheapjack rings. A Lucky Strike cigarette was held between her two fingers. She breathed out smoke from her nostrils as she leaned back with the languid air of a film star and greeted Knud with a world-weary "How do you do?"

Knud thanked his lucky stars that he had come before the white man's "civilization of enamel chamberpots" had taken over completely.

In August, 1924, he completed his epic twenty-thousand-mile sledge trek with a brief boat trip across the Bering Strait to catch a glimpse of the Eskimos on the East Cape of Siberia, and then he turned homeward. Looking back, he felt the finest compliment he had ever received came from a sledge driver of the Caribou Eskimo tribe who had told him, "You are the only man we have ever met who was both a white man and an Eskimo." The philosophy that had touched him most profoundly had come from a mystical tribal *angekok*: "All true wisdom is only to be learned far from the dwellings of men, out in the great solitudes; and is only to be attained through suffering. Privation and suffering are the only things that can open the mind of man to those things which are hidden from others."

And he thought back to old Ivaluartjuk, the first story-teller and ballad-singer he had met three years ago on his arrival in Hudson Bay. The old man's recollection of his youth seemed no different from any other old man's nostalgia: "Then all meat seemed juicy and tender, and no game too swift for a hunter. When I was young, every day was a beginning of some new thing, and every evening ended with the glow of the next day's dawn. Now, I have only the old stories and songs to fall back on, the songs I sang myself in the days when I delighted to challenge my comrades to a song contest in the feasting house."

Knud returned to Copenhagen to be feted like a hero. He brought back twenty thousand ethnological and archaeological treasures exhibited today at the Danish National Museum. He and his colleagues produced thirty-two monographs in ten thick volumes, *Report on the Fifth Thule Expedition*—perhaps the most exhaustive pioneer treatment of Eskimo legendry, poetry and philosophy extant. Knud condensed his own findings in his popular volume, *Across Arctic America*.

"The Eskimo is the hero of this book," he wrote with simple eloquence. "Their culture is a witness in itself to the strength and endurance and wild beauty of human life.... The Eskimos, intimately studied, are much more spiritual-minded, much more intelligent, much more likeable than the average man has been led to expect. They prove to be human beings just like ourselves—so like, indeed, that we cannot avoid drawing them into the fold and saying, 'These people belong to our race!'"

Knud spent the rest of his life crusading on behalf of the Eskimos. The Canadian government invited him to Ottawa as a consultant for the improvement of its far-flung Eskimo settlements. In Thule he helped native Greenlanders organize a Council of Hunters; their rules

dealing with such matters as sanitation and animal conservation were written into law on his fiftieth birthday.

"There is no end to exploring people," he said, and until the very end he continued to explore the mythology of his beloved Greenlanders. In 1933 he conducted his seventh and last Thule expedition. In east Greenland he was making a documentary film titled *Palo's Wedding*, based on local folk legends, when he contracted a rare kind of meat poisoning. When his ship docked in Copenhagen a few weeks later, he was fatally ill. But when he heard the cheers of the waiting crowd, his actor's instinct impelled him to spring up from the stretcher. He walked down the gangplank, waving to his fans with that charming, boyish grin of his before being driven to the hospital. When he died on December 21, 1933, at the age of fifty-four, all Denmark joined Greenland in mourning the loss of a truly lovable man.

Today one finds his picture hanging on the walls of schools named after him in the most remote settlements of Greenland. On the outskirts of Copenhagen a thirty-ton granite statue of Knud stands looking out at the sea. The inscription bears the words of an Eskimo song he recorded in his notebook while making his Great Sledge Journey across the Arctic:

> *Only the Air Spirits know*
> *What I shall find beyond the mountains*
> *Yet I urge my sledge team on*
> *Drive on and on*
> *On and on!*

# Chapter 13

# Stef: Champion of the North

On his lecture tours around the world in the late 1930s, reporters invariably asked Vilhjalmur Stefansson, the last of the great sledge explorers, "Surely you have been to the North Pole?"

"No," he would reply with a glint of sardonic amusement. "I'm a scientist, not a tourist."

Stef, as he was universally known, was up to his old tricks of baiting the public. It was true that he never did make a dash to the Pole. The point was that he considered that athletic marathon pointless. He had already proved himself the equal of any other Arctic traveler by adding one hundred thousand square miles to the maps of the Canadian Far North. What engrossed him far more was shaking up people's misconceptions about the land and the people he had explored.

Knud Rasmussen, his fellow ethnologist-explorer, once paid him this generous tribute: "Few have understood the Eskimo as well as Stefansson, or had the power of living their life and entering into their thought. . . . He raised the standards of exploration, from the barren breaking of records, as in a sport, to the study of the Nature People. . . . He rescued the Arctic countries from their supposed horrors by describing their real, as opposed to their assumed, climate and resources. . . . A courageous explorer and splendid writer."

Stef, who had a healthy ego, probably would have agreed with this assessment, except for one thing. He would have hooted at the word, "courageous." The great debunker of the Frozen North always claimed that exploring the cozy, comfortable, warm Arctic required as much

courage as driving a taxicab in New York City. Danger, he maintained, was practically nonexistent there for a prepared traveler, and a visitor who got lost in a blizzard undoubtedly would have been run over by a truck back home.

He was once asked to deliver a lecture on the topic of "Courage." Stef got up and said, "I know nothing whatever about courage. I'll talk instead on the vastly more important virtue of adaptability. Everything you add to an explorer's heroism you have to subtract from his intelligence."

It was one of the beliefs of a deliberately provocative educator. Stef was essentially a teacher, and a most engaging and brain-proud schoolmaster he was. The entire world was his classroom; he took on the task of correcting its ignorance of the untapped bounties of the north country. Cool logic, sweet reason, scientific facts, unblinkered vision—these were the principal weapons of his arsenal when he attacked the strongholds of orthodoxy. He thrived on controversy, because it stimulated people to re-examine their long-held stereotypes, and he hoped to reach them through their minds.

His own intellect was formidable. He was a scholar fluent in ten languages before he mastered the Eskimo tongue. He was erudite in all branches of science; he was a pioneer—almost a crank—advocate of the high protein, all-meat diet; he was thoroughly steeped in polar literature and knew the strengths and weaknesses of past Arctic explorers. His favorite was Dr. John Rae, after whom he modeled himself. Like that Hudson's Bay Company Scot, he was a lifelong exponent of the need to live off the land in the manner of the Eskimos.

Indeed Stef and Rae had much in common: a whiplash wit, incisive originality, and a love for Arctic hiking and hunting. Away from the Arctic milieu, however, Stef deviated from Rae, the virile, hairy-chested sportsman. He would take a cab rather than walk three city blocks; he said he was behaving like his friends, the Eskimos, who never engaged in unnecessary exercise. He shunned hunting as a leisure sport; anybody who believed in killing helpless beasts for sheer pleasure, said Stef, ought to get a job in the stockyards in Chicago.

He was a man of ascetic tastes. He did not drink, smoke, swear, dance, play athletic games, or gamble. Totally dedicated to polar scholarship, he worked at his typewriter twelve hours a day almost until the day of his death at the age of eighty-two. He was not completely monkish. He was known to have an Eskimo wife (about whom he kept discreetly mute). Publicly at any rate he remained a bachelor until he

was sixty-one; then he unexpectedly married a beautiful Jewish actress, Evelyn Baird, aged twenty-seven.

Stef never did fit into any pigeonholes, even in his physical appearance. A colleague said he looked like a well-fed missionary rather than the public concept of an Arctic explorer. He had a heavy frame five feet, eight inches tall; warted, high-cheekboned Scandinavian features; and the blue eyes behind his tortoiseshell spectacles always seemed to wear an amused expression. An abundant, swirling shock of blondish-brown hair erupted from his domelike head; Stef claimed that the salubrious arctic climate and his diet of uncooked fatty meat prevented his hair from falling out. Though he spent ten winters and thirteen summers in the Canadian high North between 1906 and 1918, Stef's skin was surprisingly pale; the undersides of his wrists were almost lily-white.

"I didn't wear my skin out in the open," Stef would expostulate. "I had it covered with fur. Like the Eskimos, I really lived in a tropical heat up there. Out of doors we dress in a fur thermos bottle. Inside the snug snowhouse we sit naked as if in a Turkish bath or like chickens in an incubator."

Then he would go on for hours, expounding on the hospitable warmth of his beloved Arctic. "If you spend an entire year at the North Pole, you will never see the temperature fall below −58 degrees," he liked saying, "while three American states, which are *inhabited*, have more intense cold: Wyoming, −67 degrees; Montana, −62 degrees; and North Dakota, −58 degrees."

Stef would have been an impossible pedantic know-it-all, if it weren't for his redeeming sense of humor. His lucidly written books, notably *The Friendly Arctic* and *My Life with the Eskimos*, are among the most entertaining journals in polar literature. Like his lectures, which were delivered in an easy conversational style, they crackle with epigrams and glitter with stiletto thrusts of wit. His better-known bon mots include: "False modesty is better than none," "A polar adventure is a sign of incompetence," and "A land may be said to be discovered the first time a European, preferably an Englishman, sets foot on it."

His gibes against cumbrously-equipped English explorers, "of the portable-boarding-house school," aroused a certain amount of professional hostility among his fellow explorers. Stef couldn't understand why the helpless aristocrats on their overburdened safaris had to hire Eskimo and Indian porters to carry their bags and hunt for them. "I would as soon think of engaging a valet to play my golf," he quipped, "or of going to the theatre by proxy."

*Vilhjalmur Stefansson, Icelandic-Canadian anthropologist, was an exponent of the hospitable Far North and added 100,000 square miles of it to maps of Canada.* WIDE WORLD PHOTOS

His most lethal shafts were aimed at exaggerators who perpetuated the myth that the Arctic was a white hell of perpetual blizzards. He devoted one popular lecture to lampooning the children's book, *The Eskimo Twins*, in which little Menie and Monnie supposedly lived in the "Great White World where the snow never melts." But being a gentle mocker at heart, he gave up that particular spoofing when he found the author herself in the audience—and he had reduced her to tears.

Stephen Leacock, the celebrated Canadian humorist, accepted his chastisement much more charmingly. Stef once chided him for the grim Arctic depicted in Leacock's book, *Adventures of the Far North*. The humorist was gracefully contrite. His light-hearted apologia appeared as the introduction for one of Stef's books, *Unsolved Mysteries of the Arctic*.

Leacock wrote that his own book, composed from his armchair, "seemed to me pretty fine stuff and I must confess that in point of literary composition I am too fine an artist to worry about truth. But Stefansson is the other way. He has a weakness for fact. To him the Arctic is as full of life as Monte Carlo and has a social charm as high as that of Narragansett Beach. When I called it empty and lifeless he wrote to me in a tone of indignation which it grieves me to recall. His exact words, I do not remember; but the sense was that I might be a hell of a humorist but what I knew about the Arctic being lifeless would fill a book.

"And then he told me about the clouds of glorious mosquitoes on the barren lands and the bright flowers that carpet the Mackenzie delta. I wrote back meekly that I didn't mean *there*, that I meant farther north still: that the thing must stop *somewhere*. With which my soft answer turned away wrath and became the basis of a friendship which I have known and valued for twenty years."

Vilhjalmur (pronounced "Veel-yowl-mur") Stefansson always maintained that the high Arctic was balmier than the Canadian-United States prairies where he spent his boyhood. He was born on November 3, 1879, in the Canadian frontier hamlet of Arness, Manitoba, on the windswept west shore of Lake Winnipeg. His Icelandic immigrant parents christened him plain William Stephenson. But not too long after his family crossed the border by ox wagon to settle in the farm colony of Mountain, North Dakota, little Willie, with typical stubbornness, reverted to the original Icelandic name.

He later said he inherited his contrariness, as well as his love for learning and northern folklore, from his father, Johann, a bookish freethinker as well as a homesteader. The precocious boy spent the long

winter nights in their one-room cabin reciting the Norse *Eddas* folk poems and narrative sagas; before he was six he had read aloud to his mother, Ingibjorg, the entire Old Testament in the Icelandic tongue. She wanted him to become a Lutheran clergyman; he secretly yearned to be a poet and wrote reams of verse. Exuding boundless mental and physical energy, he worked his way through high school and college at a variety of jobs. Among other things, he was a ranch cowboy, newspaper reporter, schoolteacher and insurance salesman; in between he got expelled from the University of North Dakota because the heretic campus debater "undermined the morale of the university."

After breezily picking up a Bachelor of Arts degree from the University of Iowa in a one-year cram course, he entered Harvard University on a scholarship, almost unbearably erudite. There he plunged into a wholesale examination of the natural sciences, acquired a healthy irreverence for established precepts, and emerged as an assistant instructor in anthropology, that catch-all science that studies all mankind. Stef called it a new kind of poetry. "The explorer is the poet of action," he said, "and exploring is the poetry of deeds."

He itched to get involved in deeds about which he could write scientific poesy. He led a party of Harvard students on an exploratory archaeological field trip to Iceland, and prepared to join an anthropological expedition to Africa. Then he changed direction drastically. In 1906 he threw in his lot instead with an expedition sponsored by the universities of Harvard and Toronto: they wanted him to investigate native culture at the mouth of the Mackenzie River on the Arctic Ocean. Stef was to meet the shipborne party at Herschel Island, the rendezvous of the American whalers north of the Canadian Yukon. The twenty-six-year-old explorer elected to travel there by horseback, democrat wagon, raft, flat-bottomed scow, and Mackenzie River sternwheeler. The mosquitoes and scorching heat were awful, he wrote. "But I found the Eskimos even at civilization-ridden Herschel to be the happiest people I have ever met."

He was almost relieved when the expedition's ship got trapped by the ice off Alaska and never arrived at the rendezvous. Dressed in a light overcoat and blue serge suit, and equipped with notebooks, camera, Winchester rifle and two hundred rounds of ammunition, Stef zestfully prepared to face winter two hundred miles north of the Arctic Circle. He decided to stay on the Mackenzie Delta and live with the family of an Eskimo nicknamed Roxy "as combination guest, student and pauper." He spent eighteen months with them. He took pains to

pick up their native language (as opposed to the ersatz Eskimo trading patois). He jotted down their folklore; hunted and fished with them; and learned from them all the skills of polarcraft.

He kept an open mind about everything he observed, and described his adaptation to their customs with characteristic dry humor. At first Stef balked at eating raw, half-rotten fish, which had been stored frozen since summer and was then thawed to the consistency of ice cream. But then Stef reasoned that he had long been fond of strong cheese; surely cheese was nothing but "rotten" milk; so why shouldn't he enjoy the pungency of rotten meat as much as rotten milk? Soon he was nibbling stinking, half-decayed fish with as much gusto as if it had been corn on the cob. He learned to do without salt; he claimed he became "rather fond of hair in my food"; and even gave a testimonial to the gustatory delights of gnawing the lashings of his snowshoes.

"Fresh raw hide is good eating," Stef stoutly maintained. "It reminds one of pigsfeet if well boiled."

He went on to say that one of the advantages of skin clothing over woolens was that you could eat them in an emergency, or feed them to your dogs if your need was not quite as pressing as theirs. Stef was able to overcome, too, his preconceived notion that igloos were foul, blubber-smelling pigsties.

"Before going to live with the Eskimos I had heard much about the bad smell of their houses, and at first it seemed to me that they did smell bad," he said. "I soon came to realize, however, that this was only the smell of the food they ate, corresponding to the odor of coffee, bacon, or garlic in our own homes. If you are fond of bacon or coffee, you do not dislike the smell. Similarly, I found that, as I gradually became used to the Eskimo food and eventually fond of it, smells changed from odors to fragrances."

While Stef had a glorious time boarding with the "companionable" Mackenzie Eskimos, he was not quite satisfied. They had become too influenced by the encroachment of the white man's culture. They even used American chewing gum to plug up the keyholes of the utterly unsuitable, ugly winter shacks that the missionaries encouraged them to live in. He returned to New York with his curiosity whetted about a race of blue-eyed, fair-haired Stone Age Eskimos rumored to be living on Victoria Island in the central Canadian Arctic Archipelago. He was told that they had never before seen a white man. Could they possibly, Stef wondered, be descendants of his own Norse Viking ancestors who had explored Greenland and North America's Vinland almost a thousand years ago?

On May 13, 1910 (thanks to the sponsorship of the American Museum of Natural History and the Canadian Geological Survey), Stef sledged across the sea ice of Dolphin and Union Strait and stepped onto the icy shore of Victoria Island eager to seek the answer. With him were two noted Eskimo dog team drivers not quite as enthusiastic as himself. One was Natkusiak—"Nat" for short—an Alaskan Eskimo who was the most daring Stef had ever met. (Natkusiak Peninsula on north Victoria Island was later named in his honor.) Tannaumirk—or "Tan"— was a twenty-four-year-old Mackenzie Eskimo; usually a high-spirited and dauntless polar bear hunter, Tan was now trembling with fear. Both, in fact, were apprehensive at the prospect of facing this dreaded tribe who reputedly killed all strangers with caribou antlers. But they trusted "Stepahinna"—their pidgin English for Stefansson—for he was their respected *Ihumatak*: "He who does the thinking for the party."

Stepahinna thought that his encounter with this Stone Age tribe was as dramatic as the experience of Mark Twain's Connecticut Yankee, who went to sleep in the nineteenth century and woke up in King Arthur's time. The first man they met was poised over a seal breathing hole. The startled fellow whirled about and brandished a menacing long knife. He evidently thought the approaching strangers were evil spirits.

"I am a friend," Tan called out. "I am a man and not a spirit. I have no knife and I mean no harm. I come as a friend."

The seal hunter advanced cautiously. He felt Tan's clothing to make sure there were no concealed weapons—and to ascertain if he was indeed a flesh-and-blood man. Then he led them to his encampment of forty villagers.

Stef, who found he could understand their Eskimo dialect, was delighted by the warmth of their hospitality. They mended his footgear and fed him the best fat meat stewing in their stone pots. The women staged a dance festival for him, and the song which a fair-skinned maid sang for him so charmingly contained a rhythm which seemed to Stef to resemble that of the ancient Norse *scaldic* poems. The men graciously demonstrated their archery marksmanship with copper-tipped arrows, for which reason Stef called them the Copper Eskimos. In turn they were suitably impressed by the magic of his sulphur matches, his binoculars, and rifle "thunderstick."

What most impressed Stef was their nice sense of etiquette. They were too polite to ask where he had come from, although they were patently curious. "Their reticence and good breeding made me feel more

nearly ashamed of my calling than I had ever been before," Stef thought. "An ethnologist has to make constant and often impertinent inquiries. Our hosts answered me with the greatest good humor."

Had they ever heard of white men? Yes, they had heard of those wicked people of the east; they were said to be chinless wonders with only one eye set in the middle of their forehead.

Did they not consider his own blue eyes and light brown beard unusual? "We have no reason to believe you belong to a different people," one replied. "Your eyes and beard are much like those of some of our neighbors whom you must visit."

Stef spent a year visiting these amiable people. He noted that several were fair-skinned, had three-inch-long beards, and seemed to have Scandinavian features. He conjectured that they might indeed be descendants of Norse Vikings who had wandered inland. It was a theory to be hotly debated by his fellow scientists. They said that Stef was a publicity hound and his so-called "Blond Eskimos" were merely the offspring of whalers and fur traders who had intermarried with the natives.

Stef stuck by his guns. On returning from his expedition of 1908 to 1912, he added fuel to the fire of controversy by writing his iconoclastic *My Life with the Eskimos*. In it he poked fun at the missionaries for imposing an alien culture on the natives and he deplored how the Eskimos were being crushed under the juggernaut of invading civilization. One passage soared into poetic eloquence:

"They were men and women of the Stone Age truly, but they differed little from you or me or from the men and women who are our friends and families. The qualities which we call 'Christian virtues' (and which the Buddhists no doubt call 'Buddhist virtues') they had in all their essentials.

"They are not at all what a theorist might have supposed the people of the Stone Age to be: men with standards of honor, men with friends and families, men in love with their wives, gentle to their children, and considerate of the feelings and welfare of others. . . .

"I have lived with these so-called primitive people until 'savages' and all the kindred terms have lost the vivid meanings they had when I was younger and got all my ideas at second-hand. But the turning blank of this picturesque part of my vocabulary has been made up to me by a new realization of the fact that human nature is the same not only the world over, but also the ages through."

Stef's last expedition, from 1913 to 1918, was his biggest, his most

triumphant, and in some ways his most heartbreaking one. His sponsor was the Canadian government, which spent half a million dollars for six ships and the services of one hundred and fifty men. In return it got thirty thick volumes of valuable scientific data; a jumbo mapping of the Canadian archipelago northeast of the Beaufort Sea; and five new Arctic islands discovered by Stef.

Stef felt happily rewarded. The government much later named an island after him, located off the northeast corner of huge Victoria Island. More important, he got the chance to prove his most revolutionary theory yet: that it was possible not only to live off the fat of the Arctic land, but also off the meat of the frozen Polar Sea.

Still it was a tragic expedition. People simply would not listen to Stef's commonsense approach of meeting the Arctic on its own terms as the Eskimos do. As a consequence he was plagued by a series of semi-revolts and more than several good men under his command lost their lives.

His troubles began off Point Barrow, Alaska. Stef was scheduled to rendezvous at Herschel Island with his other ships which bore a "southern party" of scientists; they were to conduct geological, zoological, archaeological, and anthropological research on the Arctic mainland south of Victoria Island. Meanwhile, aboard the two-hundred-and-fifty-ton flagship, *Karluk*, Stef headed a "northern party"; this group was to explore the Arctic Ocean, take depth soundings, look for signs of marine and animal life and search for new land.

Stef's sailing master of the *Karluk* was Captain Bob Bartlett. He was the same lovable, profane, but wilfully stubborn Newfoundlander, who had skippered Peary's ship, the *Roosevelt*, on her Poleward voyage in the eastern Arctic.

Unfortunately Bob Bartlett was disinclined to accept Stef's advice that navigating in the western Arctic required different tactics. If you didn't want your ship trapped in the ice pack, warned Stef, you must steer her close to the shore water. Captain Bob breezily paid no heed. As a result the ice closed in and the *Karluk* was imprisoned by the floes ten miles from the north coast of Alaska.

In mid-September of 1913, Stef and a small group of men left the ship to hunt for needed caribou meat. They camped on the shore ice. Next day a violent gale blew up. The *Karluk*, with twenty-five aboard, vanished from Stef's sight forever. The brigantine drifted helplessly in the pack more than a thousand miles northwestward, until she was fatally crushed in the Arctic Ocean near Wrangel Island, off Siberia.

Clearly Captain Bob was not in accord with Stef's disdain for heroics. Before the gashed *Karluk* foundered, Bartlett gave the order: "All hands abandon ship." While the others camped on the ice, the sentimental skipper could not resist the grand gesture of staying with his brigantine until she sank. All night he sat in his captain's cabin—"like a Nero," as he phrased it—playing music on his phonograph. He ate oysters and read his copy of Omar Khayyam's *Rubaiyat* and after each of his one hundred and fifty records had played out its melody he would toss it into the roaring fire of the stove.

"Mary Garden was singing *Aida* for me when the ice that had been bolstering up the ship loosened and she began to settle fast," Captain Bob recalled. "I knew my concert had only a few minutes to go before the last curtain. So I put Chopin's *Funeral March* on the Victrola, wound it, and set it off. By then the water was splashing along the upper deck.

"As she tilted for the final plunge, I stood on the rail an instant. The Chopin dirge sounded above the moans of the dying *Karluk*."

He leaped onto the ice and raised his hat in farewell, and as the blue Canadian ensign at her main topmasthead was swallowed up by the icy black water, he whispered, "Goodbye, old girl."

Unfortunately Captain Bob and thirteen others were the sole survivors of the *Karluk* disaster. Eleven perished off the coast of Siberia through freezing, starvation, or scurvy.

Stef later contended there was no reason for their deaths if they had taken proper Arctic survival precautions. In the face of all opposition, he was resolved to demonstrate that a party of hunters could forage and survive for months off the meat to be found under and on top of the ice floes of the Arctic Ocean.

His bitterest opposition came from his second in command, Dr. Rudolph Martin Anderson, an American-born Ottawa geologist in charge of the expedition's southern contingent of scientists. Anderson staged a near-mutiny. He got his scientific staff to sign a declaration, deposing Stef as Commander. Stef was refused equipment or supplies. Anderson deemed him a madman seeking newspaper notoriety, and any aid offered for his suicidal project would be "a criminal misappropriation of government property."

Stef, with bemused tolerance, could understand their scientific conservatism. No white explorer ever before had attempted to maintain himself by forage on the allegedly lifeless frozen Beaufort Sea. Even Natkusiak, his daring Eskimo companion on his previous expedition, would not accompany Stepahinna on this seeming foolhardy mission.

Nat's Eskimo forefathers had never ventured far onto the sea ice to seek seal and bear, and what was good enough for his ancestors was good enough for him.

This philosophy might appeal to a landlubber or a predisposed scientist, Stef argued, but not to a fish. Where there were fish in the ocean, there must be seals to follow the fish and polar bears to follow the seals.

Stef was therefore compelled to hire locally two gambling men, whose minds had not been cluttered up by so-called science or prejudgment. And so, in March of 1914, with one sledge and six dogs, there set out from the Alaskan shore what the scientific staff scoffingly termed "one crazy and two deluded men going north over the sea ice to commit suicide."

Stef's two comrades seemingly bent on suicide were both Norwegians. They were former sailors who had fallen in love with the Arctic and had become Alaskan trappers. Storker (Storkie) Storkerson was a tall, blond, thirty-year-old romantic married to a pretty Eskimo woman; Stef called him a true poet of deeds ready to tackle any challenging venture for the pure hell of it. Ole Andreasen was a taciturn, pipe-smoking hermit, who positively relished the lonesomeness of his isolated trapping shack. For Ole civilization was creeping up altogether too fast in Alaska. With the wages offered by Stef—twenty-five cents per ice mile they traveled up to 71 degrees north latitude and tripled after that—Ole hoped to grubstake a trapping venture in the lonelier wilds of Siberia.

"Neither of them worries or whines and both are optimistic about the prospects," Stef was to characterize them in his diary. "Traveling with an empty sled and living off the country is no work for a pessimist."

Their two-hundred-pound sled was not quite empty. There was enough food to last the men thirty days: mainly pemmican, bacon, malted milk and chocolate. The dogs were to subsist on a forty-day store of dried fish and oatmeal. Besides scientific instruments, there was a blubber stove, two grizzly bear skins as bedding, and a Burberry tent in case Stef was left with inadequate snow for igloo building. There was also a sheet of tarpaulin which, with ski poles and rawhide lashings, Stef expected to use to convert the sledge into an ingenious sled boat for crossing water lanes. But the most important equipment, as Stef saw it, were two rifles and three hundred and thirty cartridges.

By May 13, Stef was confiding self-doubts to his journal. Perhaps the sceptics were right and he was wrong after all; perhaps the Beaufort Sea was indeed a marine Sahara. He was feeding the hungry dogs old

sealskin boots and the grizzly bear bedding. His companions were down to rations of three quarters of a pound of food per day and were eyeing the dogs wistfully. In vain he tried to cheer them up with one of his maxims: "Do not let worry over tomorrow's breakfast interfere with your appetite at dinner. The friendly Arctic will provide."

But the tumble of blue ice ridges, through which they were axing a trail for their sledge, did not seem very providential. The characteristic scars in the ice fields, caused by seals coming to the surface, were few and far between. His men were becoming discouraged. Stef attempted to arouse their spirits by reciting Kipling's barrack-room ballad, "Fuzzy Wuzzy." When that didn't work, he recited a comic verse he had composed when he was a college student living at a boarding house, each of the twenty stanzas ending with a chorus of "Hash! Hash! Hash!"

His recital may have been responsible for bringing forth an audience of a couple of curious seals. Stef promptly delivered a whispered lecture to his companions on the art of sneaking up on seals. He pointed out that seals, like humans, were afflicted with lice "cooties" and one must imitate their scratching gestures. They were to be shot at a distance of about twenty-five yards away; and then, before the wounded creatures slithered back into the water, one must briskly slide on the ice after them "like a player stealing a base in baseball." His instructions were sound; but unhappily both seals that Stef shot sank like weighted baseballs.

His men turned despondent once more. On May 15 their luck turned. Stef's bullet went through a seal's brain. "Storkerson was watching," wrote Stef, "and his repeated shouts of 'It floats!' would have delighted the hearts of the manufacturers of a certain kind of soap."

After that the seals were so plentiful, said Stef, that his comrades suffered a bellyache from overeating and couldn't travel for a day. Hundreds of beluga whales also leaped into sight, and Stef regretted he had not brought a harpoon.

As the weather grew warmer, gaps between the floes grew wider and on May 24 the troupe found further travel on their tarpaulin-wrapped sledboat precarious. They were marooned on a drifting island of ice about five miles square surrounded by miles of ice mush. There was a possibility that their Robinson Crusoe island might split in the night; but after building his igloo, Stef took the precaution of sleeping in the nude with his ear close to the ice listening. If he heard a threatening rumble, he could easily slip into his buckleless Eskimo-style clothes like a fireman answering an alarm. "This was a spice of prospective

danger," he wrote blithely, "which kept us from feeling the time monotonous."

Boredom was further averted by five polar bears that friskily invaded their igloo. Stef said they were more of a nuisance than anything else. "They simply have not the data to reason," he said, "for they never before have encountered any dangerous animal upon the ice." He could not resist adding a dig at his anthropological detractors: "The bears were not educated in the ways of men and may even have doubted that we existed, just as men who had never seen the Copper Eskimos doubted that they existed."

On June 3 Stef, usually the mildest-mannered of men, lost his temper. He had warned his comrades not to waste ammunition trying to shoot a bear in water, for the carcass would have been difficult to retrieve. "Yet there was Ole standing up, wastefully shooting from the shoulder like a cowboy firing at Indians in a movie," he wrote. Stef's anger quickly subsided. He apologised when Ole explained that the fusillade had been necessary in order to save the precious dogs who had been rushing at the half-submerged bruin.

Anyone flying over the Beaufort Sea today cannot help but marvel at Stef's courage and restraint. One is presented with the awesome spectacle of what appears to be enormous lumps of domino sugar, tumbling and grinding and squealing as they are being crushed together. Stef accepted the peril with wry equanimity. "We wished the poets and magazinists who write about 'The eternal silence of the Frozen North' might have been with us in the bedlam," he wrote of the fearsome racket. "But one gets used to danger and one gets tired of staying scared." He regarded their ice island drift as a pleasant picnic and kept his party busy doing scientific work. They collected meteorological data; opened fishes' bellies to see what kind of food was inside; and they carried a line of soundings through four degrees of latitude and nineteen of longitude, most of it unexplored. His trio had, in effect, determined the continental shelf off Alaska.

On the bright evening of June 25 Stef triumphantly stepped on land—little-known Banks Island on the western fringe of the Canadian archipelago. His theory was vindicated. Counting adverse ice drift, his audacious troupe had traveled about seven hundred miles across the Beaufort Sea in a relatively comfortable ninety-six days. They celebrated by feasting on the six caribou which Stef, the unerring marksman, shot with six cartridges. Stef felt a little sorry for Ole. The poor fellow insisted on eating the steaks of caribou tenderloin and said he yearned for salt and onions to flavor the insipid, stringy meat.

Stef theorized that the so-called Copper or "Blond" Eskimos were descendants of Norse Vikings.

Ole Andreasen (left) was one of the two Norwegian adventurers who accompanied Stef on his 1914 "suicidal" ice foray. Storker (Storkie) Storkerson (right) drifted 440 miles on Stef's scientific floating ice station in Beaufort Sea. BOTH:

NATIONAL MUSEUMS OF CANADA

"Caribou head is best," Stef mildly rebuked him, "and except for the marrow the most delicious fat is back of the eyes. . . . The nearer the bone the sweeter the meat."

Stef went on to lecture him, "Cooking increases the toughness and brings out the stringiness. I have never eaten any raw meat that was noticeably tough or stringy. Chewing half-frozen meat is like chewing hard ice cream, while eating unfrozen raw meat cut in small pieces is like eating raw oysters."

Stef and his two comrades had a wonderful time that summer exploring the western coastline of two-hundred-mile-long Banks Island. In the last century the British explorer, Robert McClure, had dismissed it as a barren wasteland. Stef thought it was a fertile summer resort of soft beauty. He went on for pages in his journal hymning praises of its loveliness.

It was sheeted gold and white with arnica and dandelions and cotton grass. Butterflies and bumblebees and bluebottle flies hovered over green prairies that seemed as homelike as North Dakota or Manitoba. Rivers and little lakes sparkled charmingly in the warm, butter-yellow sunshine. And the pastures were lush with grass fodder for the fat, docile muskoxen; Stef felt that these animals had been libelously named and insisted on calling the woolly pets the *ovibos* or "sheep-cow."

He came upon one west coast inlet, which he generously named Storkerson Bay, "in honor of the man who did more than any other member of the expedition towards the success of its geographic work." Farther south, on September 11, 1914, he noticed on a sandspit the footprint of a heeled boot. He was excited, for it meant white men were about. He climbed to the top of a hill overlooking a harbor. He peered through his binoculars and saw the tips of two masts.

"I could hardly believe my eyes," he recalled. "Somehow it seemed unnatural to find a ship in Banks Island where it ought to be."

He ran down to the beach of what has since become the Eskimo settlement of Sachs Harbour, named after the ship he found waiting there. She was the thirty-ton power schooner, *Mary Sachs*. Stef had been given up for dead these past five months, and his scientific staff had thought it would not be worthwhile sending out a ship to the rendezvous spot on Banks Island as he had ordered. However, a handful of loyal expedition members—among them his Eskimo sledge mate, Natkusiak—had made the voyage out of respect, expecting to bury their Commander's bones.

Stef thought it was the first time he had ever seen people's eyes literally "stick out of their heads" in astonishment. They were certain he was a portly ghost.

"Stefansson is alive!" cried one crew member, almost swooning away. "He's here!"

"Don't you think it," said another. "The fishes ate him long ago!"

Then came the exclamation: "By God, that *is* Stefansson. Don't a damn one of you move till I shake hands with him!"

Her skipper, Captain Peter Bernard, pumped his hand, and though astounded to see Stef looking fatter than ever before, was sure he must be famished for "good civilized grub." Stef claims that out of sheer politeness he accepted a mug of coffee and nibbled some bread and butter.

Though the *Sachs* was provisioned with tinned food, the ten people aboard her—including Storkerson's Eskimo wife and five-year-old daughter—obviously needed fresh meat if they were to avoid scurvy, Stef reckoned. So accompanied by Natkusiak, he immediately went out hunting and bagged twenty-three caribou with twenty-seven shots.

"It amused me," Stef wrote, "to think that I, the supposed dead man, was now in the position of having to support my rescuers."

In the next four years Stef was to become virtually a permanent fixture in the newspaper obituary columns back home. Accompanied by various traveling companions (notably Storkerson, Natkusiak, and a swift Eskimo sledge driver nicknamed Split-the-Wind because of his celerity), Stef cut a tremendous swath across the Canadian Arctic islands. He sledged well over five thousand miles. In one record hike alone he walked more than eighty miles in twenty-eight hours; and he maintained it was not his legs that wearied but his boots that gave out.

His farthest northing was an island he discovered at 80 degrees north latitude, immediately west of Otto Sverdrup's Axel Heiberg Island, in the far eastern Arctic. Stef named it Meighen Island, after a future Canadian Prime Minister; and its most northerly tip was appropriately christened Stefansson Point.

His greatest thrill was the discovery, on the north end of Prince Patrick Island, of a rock cairn. It had been built by the British explorer, Sir Leopold McClintock. Sixty-two years ago to the day, that famed sledging Irishman had deposited inside a papier maché cylinder a scribbled note. It indicated he had not found the lost Sir John Franklin expedition.

The Arctic is a wonderful preservative of history, and Stef marveled that the penciled and red-inked message was perfectly legible after so many years. To continue the tradition, he deposited inside a tea package his own message "for the next explorer who comes along;

*Stef, a crackshot hunter, referred to muskoxen as "ovibos" and experimented in domesticating these docile "sheep-cows." The champion of the friendly North died in 1962, a great visionary ahead of his time.*

surely it will remain in the cairn much less than sixty-two years." Surely enough it was picked up forty-six years later, in 1961, by a Canadian flying team of surveyors.

The greatest misery that Stef experienced on his safaris was caused by three deaths. Two were humans. Captain Peter Bernard and another white man (whose corpse was found wearing merely house slippers) died in a blizzard. Apparently they were trying to subsist on such "civilized grub" as sugar, syrup, flour and rice, despite Stef's orders to the contrary, and they perished either as a result of scurvy or getting lost in the snowstorm. Stef named an island in Bernard's honor, and lamented that the unfortunate sea captain had not been able to adapt to the Arctic's demands.

The other death was the loss of his favorite sledge dog, Dekoraluk. Stef felt so depressed in his grief that he even raged against his beloved north country. In his confidential diary—not reproduced in *The Friendly Arctic*—he sorrowed:

"Dekoraluk died this morning. He was the best dog I have ever known. It would do him little good to write him a memorial here; neither can I word my feelings any more than one can do so after the loss of his best friend. We have often worked hard together, he harder than I and often more cheerfully; we have often been hungry together, he oftener than I. . . . He was almost beyond nature honourable and magnanimous for a dog. When skin and bones from long hunger and hard work, he has refused to steal from a meat-cache. . . . He was the only dog I ever knew who would help a dog who was down. . . .

"It is the hardest thing about our life here to watch the death of dog after dog who has served you well and been a faultless friend through hardships and thankless toil. . . . His death has taken my courage away for the time being. I feel tonight like throwing work, responsibility and hope of success all to the wind and quitting this wretched, rewardless, bitter country."

It was, of course, a temporary anguish which he soon got over. Actually, his bitterest disappointment came toward the end of his five-year Canadian Government Expedition. He hoped to climax it with his boldest scheme yet: to camp on a floating ice island for a whole year, living mainly on seals and bears, and drift all the way up to Siberia.

But unhappily Stef was stricken with typhoid fever. He contracted the illness while he was organizing his project at the so-called civilized whalers' rendezvous at Herschel Island. The well-meaning Mounties there, he claimed, almost killed him with sulphur fumes and an

orthodox invalid's diet of tinned powdered milk. Indeed he was given up for dead. Since he was going to die anyway, the Mountie inspector reluctantly agreed to let him die as he wanted to.

So the famished invalid was dragged on a spring-bed sledge by three Indians the four hundred miles down south to the hospital at Fort Yukon. En route Stef joyously slept in snowhouses. He ate three square meals a day of frozen fish and raw caribou tongues. At the end of what the newspapers termed his "neck-and-neck race with Death," he trotted into the hospital having gained thirty pounds.

While Stef was chafing under enforced convalescence, his plan to camp on a cake of ice was being carried through by faithful Storker Storkerson and four other volunteers. For eight months in 1914 the campers had a pleasant time hunting and fishing on a seven-mile-wide ice island which drifted four hundred and forty miles north of Alaska in the frozen Polar Sea. They were forced to abandon the ice floe before it touched Siberia because Storkerson had a touch of asthma, but apart from that they had a marvelous trip.

"We experienced neither hunger nor thirst, danger nor hardships," Storkerson reported back laconically to his Commander. "We took every ordinary precaution and no extraordinary circumstances came up."

"It is a little hard to realize," Stef later wrote in appreciation, "that, apart from Storkerson's mental attitude toward them and his skill in meeting them, this journey had every terror of darkness and ice and storm that has taxed alike the strength, courage and descriptive powers of the explorers of the past."

Credit for conceiving this unique experiment was not immediately accorded to Stef. Sceptics laughed it off as another one of his publicity stunts. Not until the Russians in 1937 and the Americans in 1958 adopted his scheme of using floating ice floes as scientific stations was he given proper recognition.

But Stef became accustomed to being ahead of his time. In 1919, at the age of thirty-nine, he retired from active exploring. He intended to devote the rest of his life to "consolidating my knowledge of the North for the benefit of the human race."

He meant it. Altogether he produced twenty-four books and at least four hundred polemical articles dealing with every phase of the Arctic and its people. At Dartmouth College in Hanover, New Hampshire, where he eventually presided as curator of his amassed collection of more than twenty-five thousand bound volumes and some

forty-five thousand manuscripts of polar literature, he became a kind of one-man information factory of the North. Polar scholars came to visit him and he was an indefatigable letter-writer. To keep up with the latest developments in the Arctic, he corresponded briskly with many of its inhabitants, including some Eskimos who could neither read nor write; they enlisted the aid of the nearest Mountie or trader.

In his lectures around the world he was a tireless evangelist and visionary, constantly expounding the notion that the Arctic was a fruitful, vital, hospitable empire of the future. He predicted that submarines would one day submerge under the polar ice like narwhals and that scheduled air flights over the Polar Sea would be as commonplace as snow buntings. He envisioned oil pipelines; he forecast power plants where the rivers rush over falls; he anticipated coal, metal and gas exploration.

He urged modern pioneers from the south to colonize the new frontiers of the north. He advocated turning the vast northern meadows (not "barren lands," a term he detested) into grazing grounds for caribou and domesticated muskoxen in order to amplify the world's meat basket. He foresaw tourists reveling in the bracing air under the midnight sun, and sportsmen fishing in unpolluted Arctic streams, and towns and highways and weather stations springing up in the Mackenzie Valley and across Alaska.

He had the pleasure of living long enough in the twentieth century to see many of his prophecies come true. During the Second World War his *Arctic Manual* became the official survival handbook for American troops stationed in military bases spread from Greenland to Alaska. His incessant hectoring of the Canadian government that it was ignoring the people and untapped resources of the Canadian Northwest Territories and the Yukon was finally heeded on December 8, 1953. Prime Minister Louis St. Laurent introduced a bill in Parliament creating for the first time a Department of Northern Affairs.

The Prime Minister acknowledged, as Stef had so frequently pointed out, that Canadians in the southern "banana belt" had been overlooking the potential of the region which was 40 per cent of the total area of the Canadian nation. "It has been said that Great Britain acquired her Empire in a state of absence of mind," St. Laurent remarked. "Apparently we have administered these vast territories of the North in an almost continuing state of absence of mind."

When his friends congratulated him on being such a prophetic sage, so far ahead of his time, Stef, the mellowed, aging oracle, accepted

it with a characteristic touch of whimsical wit. "If you predict something six months ahead, you are a man of vision," he said. "But if you predict something twenty years ahead, you are a mad visionary."

Until the very end of his life, at the age of eighty-two, the un-mad visionary was holding forth on his favorite topic, the friendly Arctic and its friendly people. At his home on the Dartmouth campus he was giving a dinner party to celebrate two notable events. He had completed the first draft of his autobiography, felicitously entitled *Discovery*, for he had been a discoverer of new lands and fresh ideas for most of his long career. It was a joyful occasion, too, for he had invited the Dartmouth polar fraternity to help him welcome a fellow illustrious "Arctician and Eskimologist," Eske Brun, for many years chief of Denmark's Ministry for Greenland.

"The seemliness of Stef's death was that on his last night with us, his wits were sharp, and he was able to amuse, instruct, delight, and draw each of us out, making the evening a memorable one," his widow, Evelyn, was to remember. "During dinner Stef was in marvelous form, merry and witty, and, stimulated by Eske, a veteran of thirty Greenland years, he turned the conversation to medieval falconry (the best white falcons came from Greenland long before Columbus discovered America), to Greenland archaeology (Eske brought news of a churchyard discovery containing Leif Erikson's skeleton), and to the infinite variety of Iceland's literary forms. Flushed with good wine and delight in each other's company, we moved to the living room for coffee. . . . "

A few minutes later that evening Stef suffered from a massive stroke with its accompanying paralysis. He struggled in a deep coma and died on August 26, 1962. His Canadian friends later scoured the Arctic regions where he had sledged by dog team for an appropriate towering rock to be placed as an explorer's cairn on his grave at Hanover, New Hampshire.

He had, however, already carved out for himself a towering monument, not shaped out of stone, but from ideas. He had demolished forever the terrors of the allegedly unlivable Frigid Zones, and his enduring triumph was that he had first to succeed in destroying the myth in his own mind.

"There are two sorts of Arctic problems, the imaginary problems and the real ones," he once wrote in *The Arctic in Fact and Fable*. "Of the two, the imaginary are the more real, for man finds it easier to change the nature of things than to change his own ideas."

Stefansson deserves immense credit. The last great explorer from the days when it was man and dog versus hummock and floe had survived to banish the age-old fear of the Far North. He helped convert it from a perpetual Frozen North into a usable Friendly North. One hesitates, therefore, to challenge the ultimate conclusion of the open-minded scientist who was more often right than wrong. In *The Friendly Arctic* Stef maintained that the romance of the high north was as mythical as the false heroes who had glamorized and glorified their achievements in a mythic sporting arena.

Here the great debunker had surely gone too far in his debunking. Many explorers before him, dating back to his own Icelandic Viking ancestors, had given their lives hunting the horizons beyond the next iceberg. Unlike himself, some had blundered in their folly of ignorance and vanity. Some had been smothered by blizzards. Some had perished in the intense cold. Some had failed to learn from the Eskimos and had died of starvation or scurvy or had butchered one another like cannibals.

Yet many more had experienced strangeness and wonder, beauty and peril, and had survived to push back the mists of the unknown. They had been romantics, yes, but there had been a splendor about their romanticism that no amount of debunking can diminish. Each had a certain spark of man's unconquerable will, a craving to satisfy an unquenchable curiosity, and although Stef deplored the term, they were heroes endowed with courage that ennobles us all. Like Stef himself, the last of the heroic Arctic explorers, they were truly poets of action committing the poetry of deeds.

# Index

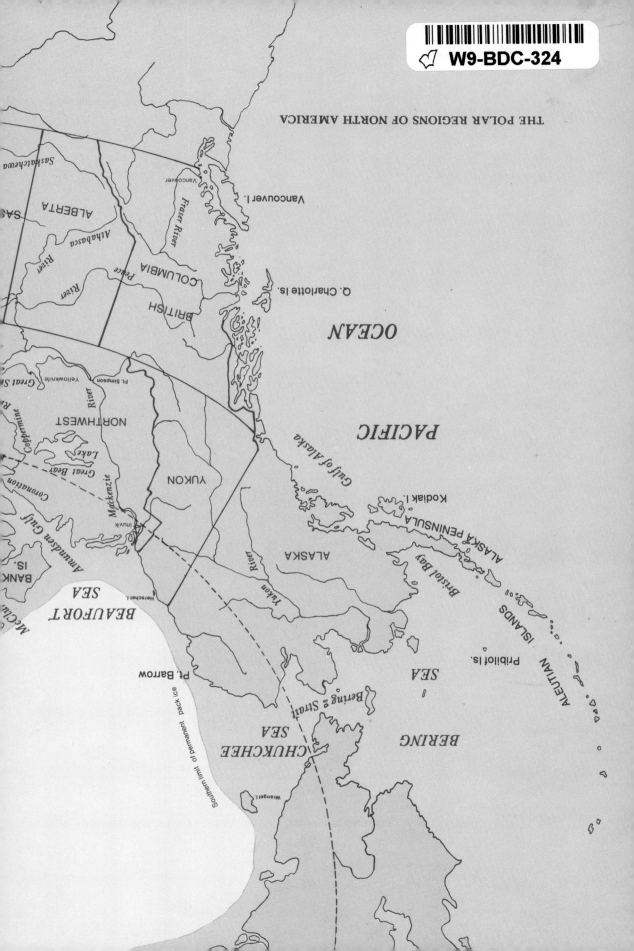

THE POLAR REGIONS OF NORTH AMERICA